D1713198

Go If You Think It Your Duty

Madison and Lizzie Bowler's wedding photograph,
November 30, 1862

Go If You
Think It Your Duty

A Minnesota Couple's Civil War Letters

ANDREA R. FOROUGHI

MINNESOTA HISTORICAL SOCIETY PRESS

www.mhspress.org

The Minnesota Historical Society Press is a member of the Association of American University Presses.

Manufactured in the United States of America

10 9 8 7 6 5 4 3 2 1

∞ The paper used in this publication meets the minimum requirements of the American National Standard for Information Sciences—Permanence for Printed Library Materials, ANSI Z39.48-1984.

International Standard Book Number
ISBN 13: 978-0-87351-600-6 (cloth)
ISBN 10: 0-87351-600-1 (cloth)

Library of Congress
Cataloging-in-Publication Data

Bowler, James Madison, 1838?-1916.
Go if you think it your duty: a Minnesota couple's Civil War letters / [edited by] Andrea R. Foroughi.
 p. cm.
Letters between James Madison Bowler and Elizabeth Caleff Bowler.
Includes bibliographical references and index.
ISBN-13: 978-0-87351-600-6 (cloth: alk. paper)
ISBN-10: 0-87351-600-1 (cloth: alk. paper)
 1. Bowler, James Madison, 1838?-1916—Correspondence.
 2. Bowler, Elizabeth Caleff, 1841?-1931—Correspondence.
 3. United States—History—Civil War, 1861-1865—Personal narratives.
 4. Minnesota—History—Civil War, 1861-1865—Personal narratives.
 5. United States. Army. Minnesota Infantry Regiment, 3rd (1861-1865)
 6. Nininger (Minn.)—Biography.
 7. Nininger (Minn.)—Social conditions—19th century.
 I. Bowler, Elizabeth Caleff, 1841?-1931.
 II. Foroughi, Andrea R., 1967-
 III. Minnesota Historical Society.
 IV. Title.
E601.B79 2008
973.7′8—dc22   2007032726

To Lizzie and Madison
And to their family

Contents

photographs follow page 196

Acknowledgments

When I was a first-term graduate student at the University of Minnesota, I requested Elizabeth and Madison's letters from an archivist at the Minnesota Historical Society, and ever since, their correspondence has been essential to my career. While completing my master's degree, I worked with these letters, which, for my doctorate, led me to investigate Nininger, Minnesota—Lizzie's home during the Civil War. For my dissertation, I analyzed how, in Nininger, gender shaped family migration, small-town boosterism, and financial hardship in the wake of an economic boom. When I first read these letters, I wanted to edit them and have them published, and with the generous assistance of many people and institutions, this hope finally has been realized.

At the Minnesota Historical Society Press, Sally Rubinstein and Michael Hanson shepherded this volume through the publication process, and I thank them for their patience and editorial expertise. I am grateful to the anonymous reviewers, whose productive comments provided additional narrative and analytical direction. I also appreciate the assistance I received from the archivists at the Minnesota Historical Society and the Arkansas Historical Society. Rebecca Snyder of the Dakota County Historical Society could not have been more generous in sharing her wealth of knowledge and resources with me over the years.

Grants from the Minnesota Historical Society and Union College—as well as a sabbatical from the latter—meant that I could devote the time needed to transcribe and annotate these letters. Summer research fellowships from Union also allowed students Christopher Hartnett and Gina Markowski to help with primary-source research. Their assistance has been invaluable. My colleagues in the Department of History and in the women's and gender studies programs at Union have been supportive both professionally and personally, especially Lori Marso, Teresa Meade, Joyce Madancy, and John Cramsie.

I must thank professors Sara Evans, who taught the research seminar that catalyzed my initial work with the Bowlers' letters; Lisa Norling, who challenged me to think critically about the letters; and Roderick Squires, who, with an encouraging smile, asked difficult questions about my analysis. A number of my contemporaries in the history graduate program at the University of Minnesota helped to create an intellectually challenging yet mutually supportive environment for discussing my research on the Bowlers, especially Wendel Cox, Anna Dronzek, and Katie Pierson. I am grateful for their friendship.

This volume would not have been possible without the generosity of Lizzie and Madison's descendents, who donated the couple's letters and other family items to the Minnesota Historical Society and thus made them publicly available. Bowler relatives even have sought me out, eager to share stories about their family's history. Clearly, Lizzie's heartfelt commitment to family has been passed down from generation to generation.

Finally, I thank my family for their support and love: my mother, Susan Andreini, and my father, Scott Matheny, who keep in touch, even when I don't; my sister, Samantha Kleven, and her husband, Bryce, who are my Minnesota family and gracious hosts; my daughters, Louisa and Juliet, who have had to share my time with the Bowlers; and my husband, Joe, who has always been there, even when I haven't.

Go If You Think It Your Duty

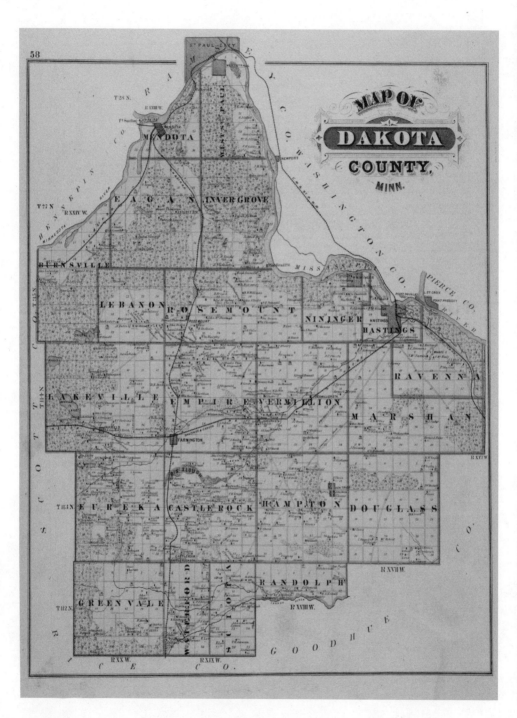

Map of Dakota County, A. T. Andreas,
Illustrated Historical Atlas of the State of Minnesota, *1874*

Introduction

During the American Civil War, James Madison Bowler and Elizabeth Caleff Bowler courted, married, became parents, and bought a farm. They attended dances and two circuses, shared political opinions and reading preferences, and confided their deepest fears and feelings for one another. They buried her sister, attended several funerals, and survived numerous maladies. They observed the cycle of seasons—fall's fair days; winter's cold, snow, and rain; spring's planting; and summer's sweltering heat. Because of the war, they experienced all of these relatively routine events separately, sharing them through nearly three hundred letters written between September 1861 and September 1865, while Madison served in the Third Minnesota Volunteer Regiment and in the 113th U.S. Colored Infantry and Lizzie remained in Nininger, Minnesota. During those four years, they had only two six-week furloughs when they were under one roof.

Although this collection of letters is between and about only two people, it also opens a window into the lives of those nearest to them. The couple kept each other apprised of their families' and friends' health, comings and goings, and war experiences. This exchange of information—or more often gossip and rumor—maintained connections between Lizzie and Madison not only as a couple but also as members of two distinct but overlapping communities: those of Nininger and its environs and of various military camps, including Union-occupied Little Rock, Arkansas.

When the war began in 1861, Madison Bowler was a twenty-three-year-old schoolteacher in Nininger City, Minnesota. Six years earlier, he had left his hometown of Lee, Maine. Apparently, his father, Edward Bowler, and his mother, Clara Augusta Smith Bowler, had separated, and there was a falling out between father and son, although Edward later admired Madison's "going away when only a boy and mak[ing] [his] own way in the world."[1] Madison's younger brother Joseph

---

1. Clara Bowler lived with her sister's children, Minerva and Martha True, in Patten, Maine, sometime between 1850 and 1862, according to the "Bowler-Caleff Family History

and sisters Sarah, Georgette, and Clara remained at home with their father, attending school and eventually teaching at various schools in Maine. Like many single, middle-class men at midcentury, Madison probably went west in search of new opportunities. Traveling through Wisconsin and Iowa, he eventually landed in St. Anthony, Minnesota, where his uncle and aunt Joseph and Lucy Smith resided. While there, he taught school and worked in a printer's office.

Madison Bowler and the Smiths joined the many white settlers who poured into Minnesota Territory in the 1850s after the Dakota ceded most of their land in 1852 and 1858. Even before the land cession, some whites moved into Minnesota Territory, including Elizabeth Caleff's uncles Peter and Henry Caleff from New Brunswick, Canada, who were among the first settlers at Bluff Landing (renamed Nininger in 1856). They ostensibly established a trading post but spent most of their time building a mill and waiting to register a land claim once the area was surveyed. Peter and Henry's father, Jedediah, and their sister Sarah also moved to Nininger, while another sister, Margaret Hawkins, and her family farmed nearby in Hampton Township. Sister-in-law Henrietta Caleff lived with her son Robert in Hastings. Latecomers Samuel and Susan Justason Caleff and their three daughters—Katherine, or Kate; Elizabeth, or Lizzie; and Dorothea, otherwise Dolly, Dollie, or Do—settled outside of Nininger at Rose Hill in 1856. The extended Caleff family, as well as their Bowler-Smith counterparts, were part of a wave of immigration into Minnesota Territory from eastern Canada, New England, and especially New York and Pennsylvania. Minnesota's white population soared from 6,077 in 1850 to 150,037 in 1857.[2]

Eager to direct as well as profit from the migration to the new territory, boosters promoted new towns that they promised would rival already established cities like St. Anthony and St. Paul and would provide newcomers with opportunities to establish prosperous businesses. Established in May 1856 twenty-five miles southeast of St. Paul on the Mississippi River, Nininger City was one of the 366 town sites recorded during a three-year land and population boom. Ignatius Donnelly, later the lieutenant governor and a representative to the U.S. Congress during the Civil War, was the town's consummate promoter. He promised that Nininger City would become a center for commerce, attracting farm produce from

and Genealogy," compiled by Anna Skovholt, Barbara Butler, and Elizabeth Morlock, 1976, box 3, Bowler Papers. Regarding tension within the Bowler family, see Georgette Bowler to James Madison Bowler, 18 June 1865, Bowler Papers.

2. For the Caleffs, Bowlers, and Smiths, see "Bowler-Caleff Family History and Genealogy," Bowler Papers. See also the appendix "Bowler–Caleff Family Tree" in this volume. For immigration, see Rice, "The Old-Stock Americans," 59–62. For population figures, see Wheelock, *Minnesota*, 125.

surrounding townships and counties and serving as a port to ship goods up and down the Mississippi River.[3] Within ten months of its inception, Nininger City boasted a population of over five hundred, with one hundred buildings erected and more under construction.[4]

But the flow of population changed dramatically in the fall of 1857 when a financial panic that spread from eastern banking centers to the newly developing, cash-strapped Midwest caused many businessmen and farmers who had speculated in land to fail.[5] Minnesota achieved statehood in 1858 even as its economy reeled from the effects of the panic and recent immigrants looked elsewhere for new opportunities. From the late 1850s through the early 1860s, many newcomers left Minnesota. Lizzie's letters describe this trend as it unfolded in the Nininger area, as when she notes families leaving to return to the East, to hunt for gold in the West, to profit from the war in the South, or to settle in new towns on the Minnesota frontier. From its population peak of 500 in 1858, Nininger's population fell to 297 by 1860. After the panic and well into the Civil War years, the town lost not only residents and businesses but also some of its homes and buildings. One of the most poignant examples of this comes from the Bowlers' correspondence. Lizzie notes that Mr. Hillhouse and his family left Nininger reluctantly in April 1860. By May 1863, after several people had rented the house, Lizzie reports that the Hillhouse home had been moved to Hastings, three miles down river. Lizzie wrote her letters from a town that was literally disappearing.[6]

Despite the town's losses, the board of education hired Madison Bowler in 1859, and Madison's 1860–1861 winter term schoolroom comprised over sixty students, ranging from five to twenty-nine years old.[7] Twenty-year-old Elizabeth Caleff was one of Madison's pupils, as were her two sisters. Lizzie Caleff was

---

3. See "To Western Emigrants," M138, roll 139, Donnelly Papers. For town sites, see Wheelock, *Minnesota*, 148. For the history of Nininger City and the township it was in, see Guelcher, *The History of Nininger.*

4. See *Emigrant Aid Journal,* 20 June 1857.

5. Although politicians optimistically estimated a total population of 275,000, the 1860 census revealed the number to be only 172,023, a disappointing rate of growth best explained by the financial panic. See Folwell, *A History of Minnesota,* 64.

6. Elizabeth Caleff Bowler (ECB) to James Madison Bowler (JMB), 30 April 1860 and 16 May 1863, Bowler Papers. See also *Hastings Independent,* 31 March 1864, for Hastings's benefiting from Nininger's buildings. For the process of moving buildings to Hastings, see Guelcher, *The History of Nininger,* 183. The 1860 figures are based on census returns; the 1858 estimate is based on newspaper accounts and is rough at best. Migration into Nininger was highest between the spring of 1857 and the summer of 1858. See Foroughi, "Ephemeral Town, Enduring Community," 212.

7. For the school list, see Biographical Sketches, P–W, folder 2, Case Papers.

surrounded by her extended family and friends, while Madison embedded himself in the local community by teaching school and boarding with Lizzie's Aunt
Sarah and Sarah's adopted son, Amon McMullen. Filling significant portions of
her letters during the first two years of their correspondence with gossip, Lizzie
supplied Madison with information about their mutual friends, their school acquaintances, and her family, revealing a vibrant community life in the eastern
portion of Dakota County.

In April 1860, a year before the Civil War erupted, Lizzie and Madison corresponded briefly while Madison visited friends and family in St. Anthony. Their
letters during this visit suggest they had just begun courting, particularly since
he asks permission to address her by her first name rather than as Miss Caleff.
One wonders how Samuel Caleff, a descendent of British Loyalists, felt about his
second daughter's receiving attention from the Maine schoolteacher. He might
have questioned their courtship initially, because his granddaughter later comments, "The marriage of Elizabeth Caleff to James Madison Bowler was the first
mixture of this family with Yankee blood." The correspondence suggests, however, that he helped the young couple, especially after their marriage.[8] In April
1861, one year later, Madison wrote to Lizzie again from St. Anthony, explaining that he would join the Union army to quell the rebellion in the South. He defended his decision, stating that "somebody must go; and who can go better than
young men like myself without business and with[out] family to demand my
attention." That letter inaugurated a four-year discussion about duty, family, and
gender roles.

James Madison Bowler and Elizabeth Caleff Bowler each understood duty
differently during the Civil War; it was a point of contention in both their correspondence and their relationship. At the war's outbreak Lizzie agreed that Madison
should enlist in the Union army, saying, "Go if you think it your duty." Eighteen
months later Madison confirmed his sense of duty: "Lizzie, you know that I love
you; but sinner as I am, I believe that next to my duty to God comes my duty to
my country and its sufferings." After their marriage, through her pregnancy, and
during the two years following, Lizzie came to question Madison's emphasis on
duty to his country over his responsibilities as a husband and a father. In September 1864 she wrote, "I want you to really think the matter over whether it is
your duty to spend all the best of your life away from those who love you best

8. See Victoria (Bowler) Law in "Bowler-Caleff Family History and Genealogy,"
Bowler Papers. For correspondence between single men and women and courting, see
Berry, *All That Makes a Man*, 89–91; Younker, "'I Was Some What Disappointed,'" 11; and
Lystra, *Searching the Heart*.

and sighs for your presence ever[y] moment of her life time, or to come home and get a good little home and live happy as we should while others who have had the comforts of home take their turn in the battlefield."[9] Throughout their correspondence the Bowlers wheedled and cajoled and argued over whose notion of duty would prevail.

The couple's conception of duty, ranging from personal responsibility within the family to obligation to the country, played out in different ways for both Madison and Lizzie. Through his duty to defend the U.S. government by serving as a volunteer citizen soldier, Madison could act on his ambition to achieve a higher status, earn a steady income, and receive recognition. For Lizzie this meant long-term military service claimed his time and attention, which interfered with his familial responsibilities. In other words, Madison saw duty to family and country as complementary while Lizzie saw duty to country as competing with obligation to family. Madison's ideas about duty and ambition remained essentially unchanged from the time he enlisted in the Third Minnesota and became a corporal in 1861 to his mustering out as a major at war's end and his position as a superintendent in the Freedmen's Bureau in postwar Arkansas. At first glance Lizzie seemed to be less consistent: she supported Madison when he joined the army but then steadily increased her insistence that he reevaluate his sense of obligation to the war effort and even criticized the country for requiring men to place its needs before those of their families. But Lizzie had not changed her ideas about duty at all; for her what had changed was Madison's relative obligations. He began the war as a single man, was married one year later, and within another year became a father. Lizzie thought his family should become his primary concern, especially when he signed up for a second three-year enlistment.

As well as offering an opportunity to reflect on duty and gender roles during the Civil War, the letters also provide glimpses into more typical Civil War topics such as battlefield experiences, military unit coherence, life in the army camps, and the Union army's occupation of areas of the South.[10] In the fall of 1861, Madison Bowler was mustered into the Third Minnesota Volunteer Infantry, Company F, as a corporal, which was a noncommissioned position. It is useful to

9. JMB to ECB, 27 April 1861 and 27 September 1862, Bowler Papers; ECB to JMB, 2 September 1864, Bowler Papers.

10. Civil War literature is expansive. In the past two decades many Civil War historians have focused their scholarly energies on the experiences of the common soldier or low-ranking officer in the war, moving away from studies of the generals and the political history of the era. The best summary of this literature and trend is Mitchell, "'Not the General but the Soldier.'" Notable from this vein of research is McPherson, *For Cause and Comrades*.

understand the structure of a typical Civil War regiment, in part because Madison refers to these positions regularly yet without much explanation. General Christopher C. Andrews, who was lieutenant colonel and then colonel of the Third Minnesota before his promotion to general, explained the regiment structure as follows: "An infantry regiment consisted of ten companies. Each company had three commissioned officers, a captain, first lieutenant and second lieutenant; also thirteen non-commissioned officers, namely a first or orderly sergeant, four other sergeants and eight corporals; likewise two musicians, a wagoner and at least sixty-four privates. . . . The aggregate strength of the regiment, including all officers and men, at the date of its organization, November 15th, was nine hundred and one."[11]

Late in November 1861, the Third Minnesota began its official duties at Camp Jenkins near Louisville, Kentucky, in the Army of the Ohio's Sixteenth Brigade. From December through March, the men spent their time drilling and guarding important railroad lines in Kentucky and Tennessee. Much of the regiment's spring and early summer was spent near Murfreesboro, Tennessee, where it anticipated moving into more active duty farther south. Instead, the Third Minnesota had a brief engagement with Confederate general Nathan Bedford Forrest's cavalry on July 13, 1862, at Murfreesboro. Much to the dismay of many noncommissioned officers and privates, most of the Third Minnesota's officers voted to surrender the regiment to Forrest, and so they became prisoners of war. Demoralized, the Third Minnesota awaited exchange at Benton Barracks, Missouri.

In early September the regiment returned to Minnesota to form part of the Indian Expedition, comprised of state forces organized to help quell Indian–white violence that had erupted along the Minnesota River late in the summer of 1862. The Third Minnesota was part of a force organized to capture Dakota Indians who had attacked settlers and towns in western Minnesota after an agent refused to distribute overdue treaty goods to starving Indian families until a late annuity payment arrived from the federal government.[12] Madison viewed fight-

---

11. Andrews, "Narrative of the Third Regiment," 147–48.
12. The evolving study of the U.S.-Dakota Conflict is undergoing a transformation from a narrative dominated by a white view of the events in the fall of 1862 to a more balanced history that presents the Dakota people's perspectives and experiences. For this literature, see Carley, *The Dakota War of 1862;* Anderson, *Kinsmen of Another Kind,* chap. 12; Anderson and Woolworth, *Through Dakota Eyes;* and Wilson, "Decolonizing the 1862 Death Marches." Although most of the literature has focused on the two warring groups and the local nature of the U.S.-Dakota conflict, it also is important to locate the conflict in the context of the Civil War. For this approach, see Josephy, *Civil War in the American West;* and Nichols, *Lincoln and the Indians,* chaps. 6–9.

ing the Indians in September 1863 as a way to redeem the regiment after its surrender at Murfreesboro in July and prepare it for future service in the South. In his negative attitude toward the Dakota, their way of fighting, and their treatment of white women, Madison expressed himself much like his contemporaries. He used these views to attempt to convince Lizzie that the work he was engaged in was best for her, the state, the regiment, and the war effort as a whole. After salvaging their military reputation somewhat at the battle of Wood Lake, the Third Minnesota enjoyed a much-needed furlough. While in Minnesota, the regiment was reorganized by replacing the officers who had surrendered with the regiment's noncommissioned officers, who were not implicated in the disgrace.

In January 1863 the regiment returned south, and by the spring they were part of a brigade in the Army of the Tennessee's Sixth Division, Sixteenth Corps, occupying Fort Heiman on the Mississippi River. Latecomers to the siege of Vicksburg—then being waged by General Ulysses S. Grant—the Third Minnesota was part of General Nathan Kimball's division of the Sixteenth Corps, which felled trees and dug rifle pits at Haines Bluff as a deterrent to Confederate general Joseph Johnston's attempting to interfere with Grant's siege. In the aftermath of the Union success at Vicksburg, the Third Minnesota participated in the Arkansas Expedition, an offensive to occupy Little Rock, as part of the Second Brigade in Kimball's division. After capturing the city on September 10, 1863, the Third Minnesota served with the Forty-third Illinois Infantry and Seventh Missouri Cavalry to guard Little Rock and then went through the process of reenlisting as their three-year terms of service expired. In the early months of 1864, the regiment was divided by rotating furloughs, detached duty in different locations, and some officers' leaving the regiment to take up positions in newly formed units of black soldiers. The regiment was discharged on September 16, 1865, with only 432 of its 1,417 members still on its rolls. Years later, General Andrews reflected on the Third Minnesota: "It had a checkered, striking, yet important experience."[13] Madison's name would not have remained on the rolls, because he had already left the regiment for other duties. By war's end he had been promoted from corporal to sergeant to second lieutenant to captain and, finally, to major in the 113th U.S. Colored Infantry.

Madison's letters to Lizzie cover a wide range of topics: his journey up the Mississippi to Fort Snelling for mustering in; his reasons for enlisting; his first battle; his experience of finding a dead Confederate soldier's letters home to his wife; his feelings about his regiment's surrender and parole; his confidence

13. This brief description of the Third Minnesota's military service is derived from Andrews, "Narrative of the Third Regiment," 147–77. His quote is from page 176.

returning from the South to fight the Dakota; his and his comrades' struggles with moral issues; his response to the deaths of fellow soldiers and officers; his participation in general courts-martial as both the accused and as a member of the court; and his concerns for the well-being of his wife and their child.

Beyond the more typical military topics that relate to men's war activities, the Bowlers' letters, especially Lizzie's, also convey the equally important but not as fully explored subject of Northern home front life for women in a rural community.[14] Lizzie Bowler wrote regularly about women's and families' responses to the war and the changes and continuities of home front life. She raised discussions about intimate topics in her letters to Madison after their marriage in November 1862, including keeping him abreast of the progress of her pregnancy and her sister's declining health. Well versed in middle-class values and women's responsibility to promote them, Lizzie reminded Madison of his duty to live a Christian life; to avoid unhealthy habits like swearing, drinking, smoking, and visiting prostitutes; and to return home and fulfill his role as the economic head of their family.[15] As thousands of men joined the army, leaving their families at home, many women performed unfamiliar tasks such as managing financial affairs and contributing to the war effort through volunteer activities, in addition to their more routine duties of child rearing, housekeeping, and inculcating morals.[16]

Lizzie's letters also shed light on her rural community's routines, which remained relatively untouched by the war—sleigh rides in the winter, strawberry picking, singing school, and trips to friends' homes and the post office. But she also observed indirect effects of the war and politics, including renting their farm as a poorhouse for war widows and reacting to the election-day murder of a

14. The connection between civilians and soldiers has garnered increased scholarly attention in the past fifteen years. See Clinton and Silber, *Divided Houses,* and, more recently, *Battle Scars.* More work has been done on Southern women's Civil War experiences than on Northern women's, as noted in Faust, "'Ours as Well as That of the Men.'" Scholars are now trying to remedy this disparity. See Cashin, *The War Was You and Me;* Cimbala and Miller, *Union Soldiers and the Northern Homefront;* and Silber, *Daughters of the Union.*

15. Nineteenth-century women's history was dominated by the ideology of "true womanhood" and separate spheres for almost twenty-five years after Barbara Welter's seminal article "The Cult of True Womanhood, 1820–1860." See also Hogeland, "'The Female Appendage.'" More and more studies are showing that women and men did not unquestioningly structure their lives around these prescriptive ideas. For two examples, see Jabour, "'The Language of Love'"; and Attie, "Warwork and the Crisis of Domesticity in the North."

16. See Cashin, "'Since the War Broke Out,'" for a Southern woman's running of a plantation with little male assistance. See also Attie, "Warwork and the Crisis of Domesticity in the North"; Leonard, *Yankee Women;* Attie, *Patriotic Toil;* and Rodgers, "Hoosier Women and the Civil War Home Front."

Union soldier by local Irish Democrats. What brought the war home to Lizzie most was her husband's absence, however, and that of many other young Nininger men. This was her connection to the fighting and the politics, which otherwise seemed relatively distant to her. The Bowlers' correspondence about national concerns, such as slavery, military organization, war strategies, and Abraham Lincoln's reelection and death, as well as local interests like what occurred in the community and how local "boys" adapted to military life, produced a compelling narrative of the Civil War in camp and at home.

The physical separation caused by military service challenged both couples' and communities' sense of a common cause, especially as the war lasted years rather than months. Early in the war, as Nininger women sewed a gigantic flag, local leaders gave speeches, and families sent care packages to soldiers, Lizzie willingly involved herself in all of these activities, and Madison applauded her efforts. With military stalemate in 1864 and war weariness increasing, however, communities often found it more difficult to support the war effort.[17] The distance and course of the war also had the potential to heighten tensions between husbands' and wives' senses of duty. Men often felt their obligation was to their country when they enlisted. As they spent more time with their fellow soldiers and officers, they created new friendships and ties of obligation. Over time, however, they sometimes decided their primary duty was to their wives and deserted the war effort. Women initially may have supported their husbands' choice to enlist but often complained about the "cruel barbarous war" and the absence of their husbands as time passed.[18] Under these circumstances women and men, separated by long distances and engaged in activities new to them, negotiated for authority over various aspects of their lives, including where their duties primarily lay.

In the Bowlers' case the fall of 1863 marked the beginning of a two-year debate over whether Lizzie would join Madison in Little Rock, Arkansas, where he was stationed, or whether he would desert—or at least not reenlist—and return to Nininger. They both wanted to be together, but they disagreed over where that would be. Their allegiance to their individual communities—his fellow soldiers and her female kin—recurred throughout their debate, he believing his duty was to stay with his comrades and she feeling his obligation was to provide solace to her ailing sister and mother. This argument figured prominently in their correspondence because it was an argument not just over where they would live together but fundamentally about who had the authority to make that decision. As their disagreement over his return home peaked, Lizzie asked Madison to consider

17. See Kemp, "Community and War."

18. For an innovative work on a Union wife's waning support for the war and her husband's service in it, see Smith, "The Reconstruction of 'Home,'" 157–77. See also Motz, *True Sisterhood*, 72; and Mitchell, *The Vacant Chair*, chap. 2.

whether his primary duty was to serve his country or fulfill his roles of father and husband. She viewed this as an *either/or* decision, whereas Madison thought that serving his country was a way to protect *and* provide for his family. For her part, Lizzie manipulated Madison's conflict between duty to country and duty to family so that she could gain leverage in their arguments. He struggled, however, with her authority as a wife and a mother and with her divided allegiance to her female family members and to him.[19]

Long separated from his family in Maine, Madison was comfortable in his role as a self-made, independent man and entered into courtship with Lizzie with an autonomous sense of self. When Lizzie began their relationship, she was a schoolgirl still living with her parents. After their marriage she discovered her ability to demand certain behaviors of Madison. As a mother she discovered the possibilities of wielding power, at least over child rearing. By the end of the correspondence, Lizzie had engaged in a long battle with her husband over an issue fundamental to their marriage—where they would live together—and questioned his assumptions about his obligations to home and country. Madison felt her challenge keenly. That Madison "won" in the end is of little importance; that Lizzie negotiated with him for at least three years is of great importance. Madison ultimately retained the right to decide if and when he would come home, but through their lengthy debate Lizzie gained a sense of herself independent of Madison, which she did not have in the beginning of their correspondence and relationship.[20]

The enduring value of the Bowlers' letters is that they preserve this couple's interactions at a variety of levels. Without the physical separation caused by the war and the correspondence meant to bridge the distance between husband and wife, little could be known about the Bowlers either as individuals or as a couple. Their poignant letters provided them with a space to voice their fear for and frustration with each other without meeting their spouse's response face to face. Interspersed with their frustration and loneliness, their love for one another and desire to be together bound them together when despair and longing threatened to drive them apart.

Most published Civil War correspondence focuses on soldiers' war experiences. Soldiers had more difficulty preserving letters from home, and families seem less likely to have saved them. In addition, the soldiers' letters answer military histo-

19. See Lebsock, *Free Women of Petersburg;* and Norling, "'How Frought with Sorrow and Heartpangs,'" 422–46.

20. See Rotundo, *American Manhood,* 130–40, on nineteenth-century marriages and their conflicts over authority.

rians' questions, who have generally written the history of the war. The Bowlers' correspondence offers different insights.[21]

The Bowlers wrote over 290 letters to each other over the course of the war; 231 of these are included in the James Madison Bowler and Family Papers in the Minnesota Historical Society's manuscript collections.[22] Many of these letters were written in haste or in a dim, candle-lit space, as both Lizzie and Madison mention in their letters. Researchers have transcribed some of Madison's letters in order to cite his accounts of the surrender at Murfreesboro and the conduct of the Dakota War. Madison relates his experiences confidently, describing his natural surroundings, military actions, and camp life in detail; he articulates his political beliefs eloquently and refers to history and literature on occasion. Even in his own handwriting, Madison's letters are relatively easy to read: his prose is clear, his grammar and punctuation standardized, and his thoughts orderly.

Nearly all of Lizzie's letters have remained untranscribed, perhaps because her letters seem mundane. The war is second to her concerns for Madison's safety, her Nininger acquaintances' actions, and whether battles would bring a speedy end to the war and to Madison's absence. In contrast to her husband's letters, hers are hard to read, because her prose is not as sophisticated and her spelling and punctuation are less consistent. She was aware of her lower level of education, which led her to be more self-conscious about her letters, calling them "scribbled concerns."[23] Also, her habit of writing perpendicularly across what she had previously written frequently obscured parts of her letters (see p. 24).

My task has been to transcribe these letters, supplying additional information where needed, and to provide historical context. Where possible, I have identified individuals using census data, local newspapers, and other manuscript sources from Nininger and Minnesota, as well as other published material for more famous or faraway people. Information obtained from the Minnesota Territorial Census of 1857, the Federal Census of 1860, or the Minnesota State Census of 1865 appears with a date reference to the specific census in the footnote and, if known, a location, an occupation, or an age. The *Annual Report of the*

21. For a letter collection between a Confederate husband, wife, and daughter, see Rozier, *The Granite Farm Letters*. Two recent collections of midwestern couples' Civil War letters have been published that also illustrate this home front–military camp connection. See Kiper, *Dear Catharine, Dear Taylor;* and Elder, *Love amid the Turmoil*. For an interpretation of the nature of women's Civil War writing, see Nelson, "Writing during Wartime," 43–68.

22. See the appendix "Madison's and Lizzie's Letter-writing Frequency" in this volume. As the chart illustrates, forty-one of the sixty-two missing letters are Lizzie's.

23. Again, for women's Civil War writing, see Nelson, "Writing during Wartime," 43–68.

Adjutant General of Minnesota and regimental muster lists from *Minnesota in the Civil and Indian Wars* have been consulted for similar information on Minnesota soldiers and officers. In addition, footnotes explain military, medical, political, social, religious, literary, and economic references made in the letters. For general information on the Civil War, I relied on James McPherson's *Battle Cry of Freedom* and *Ordeal by Fire,* except as otherwise noted.

All editors struggle with how much to alter historical documents, and my changes have been made in an effort to both clarify what was written and preserve historical accuracy.[24] For instance, most of Lizzie's and Madison's letters state whether they had recently received a letter and end with "give love to folks" or "give love to all" or "remember me to. . . ." In addition, the couple referred to many people in passing. I have dropped these repetitive phrases and allusions to people irrelevant to the central themes and people in the letters. To make reading the letters easier, I have added punctuation and paragraphs, especially in Lizzie's letters. Where possible, I have left the spelling unchanged, unless it obscured the meaning of a sentence. Some letters contain duplicate words, which I have deleted, or lack words that were intended as part of a sentence, which I have added and enclosed in brackets. Some of the letters have deteriorated over time, and so a footnote indicates where text is physically missing. If a sentence could not be reconstructed, ellipses were used to signify the missing words.

Finally, although modern readers know the outcome of the Civil War and know that the Bowlers lived for decades after the war's end, it is important to keep in mind that the couple did not have prophetic powers or our hindsight. They also had no idea their private letters would be read not only by each other but also by readers well into the future. I am reminded of a passage in A. S. Byatt's novel *Possession: A Romance,* which includes a couple's nineteenth-century correspondence: "Letters . . . are a form of narrative that envisages no outcome, no closure. . . . Letters tell no story, because they do not know, from line to line, where they are going. . . . Letters, finally . . . are written, if they are true letters, for *a* reader."[25] Fortunately, we have access to Lizzie and Madison's narrative and can be *their* readers.

24. A complete transcription of all of the letters with additional editorial background on people and events can be found in the James Madison Bowler and Family Papers, 1827–1976, archived at the Minnesota Historical Society in St. Paul, Minnesota.

25. Byatt, *Possession: A Romance,* 156.

Prologue

The following two letters deal with familiarity on two levels. First, Madison and Lizzie self-consciously recognized they were being "familiar" with one another by using their given names in their letters' greetings and by discussing their feelings for each other. These two letters signify their relationship's transition from teacher and student to mutual sweethearts and from face-to-face interactions to those on the written page.[1] Second, these letters also, if unintentionally, establish familiarity between the reader and the two correspondents by introducing the couple, their relationship, their feelings, their surroundings, and their community, as well as their respective writing styles. They acquaint us with the people closest to Lizzie, as well as with her community's persistent loss of population from 1859 through 1865. They also demonstrate Madison's ability to express himself and his concern that Lizzie develop a sense of the world beyond Nininger, as he describes images from his travels and sends her magazines and periodicals.

We do not know how long Madison was gone. Given the regularity of their Civil War correspondence, however, Madison's stay in St. Anthony probably was fairly short, as there are no further letters until the spring of 1861.[2]

*　　*　　*

St. Anthony, April 12, 1860

Dear Lizzie:

Perhaps you may think the above address rather too familiar in tone for me to use on so short acquaintance; but I believe it is one which custom allows to those

---

1. For the importance of correspondence in courtship, see Berry, *All That Makes a Man*.

2. Madison must have returned to Nininger by November 6, because Nininger school superintendent Levi Countryman examined Madison before he taught the winter term. See letter from Levi N. Countryman, 6 November 1860, box 1, Bowler Papers. Incidentally, Countryman visited Madison's school on January 18, 1861, and commented, "[Bowler] keeps an excellent common school." See Levi N. Countryman, diary, vol. 2, Countryman Papers.

who stand in our relation. Although I use it with its full force and meaning, yet I can but feel a little delicacy, since, with the exception of near relatives, you are the first and only lady whom I ever addressed in so familiar a manner. But, Lizzie, I believe we ought to write just as we feel toward each other, and I shall always try to do so as far as I am able, for I have not taken the step which I have, thoughtlessly or for the mere purpose of a flirtation, but in obedience to true affection and with none but honorable intentions. I assure you that it affords me much pleasure and is a great relief to have one whom I am at liberty to love above all others, and in whom I can confide, and at the same time feel the assurance that my love and confidence is reciprocated, especially one so worthy and kindhearted as yourself. Now let me ask that our correspondence and intercourse with each other be characterized by plainness and freedom, and that neither of us shall be backward in giving or asking such explanations as will often be necessary at many times, as misunderstandings will often occur to make true the old saying, viz., "The course of true love never did run smooth."

I wish you were here today, everything is so nice and pleasant as I stroll about and meet old acquaintances and review the old scenes, such as the Falls, Nicollet Island, &c. I partake in none of these pleasures with-[out] thinking how lonely you must be, and wishing Lizzie by my side to share them with me.[3]

I suppose you think that I am still loafing about Nininger as usual, as I bade you good-bye so many times without getting away; but I did get started at last, at about 1 o'clock of the night following the afternoon which I spent with you. Your good old mother was so very kind as to give up her bed for my comfort, as she feared I might take more cold if I slept on the Lounge, and I was thoughtless enough to run away in the night without saying so much as "thank you." Go where I may, I shall ever feel grateful to your kind parents and sisters for their many acts of kindness to myself as well as to every one with whom they meet. Your family is one of the few who may be ranked among the oases in the desert of human life. Think not that I exalt them far above all others, for there are others in Nininger, whom I shall ever hold in grateful remembrance.

I came to St. Paul on the "Time & Tide," thence to St. Anthony by Stage, and was landed at my destination just in time for dinner and to find all enjoying good health; also a lot of papers and letters waiting for me to read them. My correspondents seem to think St. Anthony the only place in Min., hence my letters

3. Madison traveled from Nininger to St. Anthony, a journey of approximately twenty-five miles by way of steamboat on the Mississippi River. St. Anthony would eventually be incorporated into Minneapolis. Madison presumably visited friends and relatives with whom he had stayed and worked before he moved to Nininger in 1859. See "Bowler-Caleff Family History and Genealogy," Bowler Papers.

come here. I sent you a paper the first day I was here, and shall continue to send some occasionally, for they will do much to cheer your lonely hours, even though they are not so good as they might be. Geo. reported the story that I was to be married, which, however I care nothing for, except on your account.[4] It certainly makes me think less than ever of him. Remember me to your Father, Mother, Sisters, and your Aunts Henrietta and Sarah, and Amon, i.e. unless you are unwilling that they should know that we correspond.[5]

> Yours very truly,
> J. Madison Bowler.

Nininger, April 30, 1860

My dearest friend,

I dont want you to indulge the thought for one moment that you are forgotten by me. I have looked anxiously for a letter every mail and have come away from the office disopointed a great many times, but last evening I had better luck then usual got two letters and ten or twelve papers. This the first mail from St Paul in two weeks. You may easily imagine how gratified I was coming home with both hands full of letters and papers from one whom I had waited so patiently to hear from.

Kate has been very ill for the last ten days. She is recovering slowly.

I was down home this afternoon. While I was there she had a very hard ague chill. I think she has taken a severe cold but hope she will get well soon.[6] It is very dull here now. Mary Bottomly leaves this afternoon for Waterford to attend

4. Madison probably refers to George B. Moulton. See Lizzie's March 9, 1862, letter: "It is something like the time George B. Moulton was going to put you through your facings last spring. I suppose you remember that." Farmer George B. Moulton was the oldest son of widow Mary Moulton. In 1860 George was twenty-three and living with his mother and two younger siblings in Denmark Township near Point Douglas in Washington County.

5. For a list of family members, see the appendix "Bowler–Caleff Family Tree." Here Madison refers to Samuel and Susan Caleff, Lizzie's parents; sisters Kate and Dorothy (in the letters "Dolly" or "Do"); Samuel Caleff's sister-in-law Henrietta Caleff; and Samuel Caleff's sister Sarah Caleff. Amon was Amon McMullen, her adopted son.

6. Kate Caleff, Lizzie's older sister, frequently suffered from ill health throughout the first half of the correspondence. An ague chill is a fever with chills, a common ailment among early pioneers. See "Nineteenth Century Diseases," www.rootsweb.com /~memigrat/diseases.html. At the time of this letter, Lizzie was staying in Hastings with her aunt Henrietta rather than on her father's farm in the Rose Hill area of Nininger Township.

to her school. Newton Poor left here this morning for St. Louis, also Mr. Dodge. Mr. Hillhouses family and children left a week since. It seemed hard work for him to leave this place. I presume the reason was he has so many friends here.[7] I had a call from Geo yesterday. He was very pleasant indeed, he did not say any thing about his afflictions. I think he is getting over his fit of anger. I am willing he should say anything about me he has a mind to if he only tells the truth. I am sorry George is so foolish. I should think he has lived in this world long enough to bear disopointments with patience, I expect when you come back you wont hardly know the city. It will be so changed, the grass is getting quite green, every-thing is beginning to look like spring, in wandering about among the bush I have found several very pretty bouquetts. It is so lonely I almost get the horrours sometimes.

Aunt Henrietta is very poorly yet. Sometimes I think she never will get entirely well. She has been sick so long. Our folks are all very poorly. Ma has a very bad cold, there is a great deal of sickness about here I think it must be caused by so many changes in the weather. My health is very good indeed. You speak of the Falls. How I should like to see them. You say you wish I was there. Nothing would aford me more pleasure then to take a stroll with you, but that cant be so I must be content. You speak of the step you have taken, had I not believed it was done with a sincear heart and pure motives you may depend I never would have done as I have, but ever since I became acquainted with you I have considered you worthy of any girls confidence. Our acquaintance has been but short but I presume it is all for the best and I hope as you have chosen me as a confident that I shall be to you all you antisapted. Well, [it] is getting so dark I can hardly see to make a letter so I must bring this to a close. Aunt H is out and since I seated myself to write I have had five callers. I cant write and talk at once so I think you will find a great many mistakes, so good by.

> from your ever loving friend
> Lizzie C . . .

P.S. I am very thankful to you for the papers you sent. Aunt Henrietta has just come. She says tell Mr Bowler I have got the blues, she wishes to be remembered to you.

---

7. These individuals are part of a larger pattern of population decline in Nininger City following the 1857 financial panic. St. Louis was a common destination. For a fuller account of out-migration from Nininger in the late 1850s and early 1860s, see Foroughi, "Ephemeral Town, Enduring Community," chap. 5.

Letter Facsimiles

Madison to Lizzie, April 12, 1860

Lizzie to Madison, April 30, 1860

An example of Lizzie's writing
perpendicularly across what she had previously written

St. Anthony, April 12, 1860.

Dear Lizzie:

Perhaps you may think the above address rather too familiar in tone for me to use on so short acquaintance; but I believe it is one which custom allows to those who stand in our relation. Although I use it with its full force and meaning, yet I can but feel a little delicacy, since, with the exception of near relatives, you are the first and only lady whom I ever addressed in so familiar a manner. But, Lizzie, I believe we ought to write just as we feel toward each other, and I shall always try to do so as far as I am able, for I have not taken the step which I have, thoughtlessly or for the mere purpose of a flirtation, but in obedience to true affection and with none but honorable intentions. I assure you thence to St. Anthony by Stage, and was landed at my destination just in time for dinner and to find all enjoying good health; also a lot of papers and letters waiting for me to read them. My correspondents seem to think St. Anthony the only place in Min., hence my letters come here. I sent you a paper the first day I was here, and shall continue to send some occasionally, for they will do much to cheer your lonely hours, even though they are not so good as they might be. Geo. reported the story that I was to be married, which, however, I care nothing for, except on your account. It certainly makes me think less than ever of him. Remember me to your Father, mother, Sisters, and your Aunts Henrietta and Sarah, and Amos, i.e. unless you are unwilling that they should know that we correspond. Yours very truly,

J. Madison Bowler.

Miss Lizzie Caleff.

Madison to Lizzie, April 12, 1860, page 4

Nininger, April 30,

My dearest friends

I dont want you
to indulge the thought for one moment
that you are forgotten by me. I have
looked anxiously for a letter every
mail and have come away from
the office disapointed a great many
times but last evening I had better
luck then usual got two letters and ten
or twelve papers, tis the first mail from
St Paul in two weeks you may easly ima
-gine how gratified I was coming home
with both hands full of letters and
papers from one whom I had waited
so patiently to hear from.
Kate has been very ill for the last
ten days she is recovering slowly

Lizzie to Madison, April 30, 1860, page 1

but ever since I became acquainted
with you I have considered you worthy
of any girls confidence our acquaintan
has been but short but I presume it
is all for the best and I hope as
you have chosen me as a confident
that I shale be to you ale you onless ap
-ted. Well is getting so dark I can hardly
see to make a letter so I must bring
this to a close. Aunt H is out and since
I seated my self to write I have had
five callers I cant write and talk at
once so I think you wile find a
great many mistakes, so good bye from
Write soon
Yours ever loving friend
Lizzie C

P.S. I am very thankful to you for the papers
You sent Aunt Henrietta has just come
she says tell Mr Bowler I have got
the blues, she wishes to be remembered to
you

Lizzie to Madison, April 30, 1860, page 4

letters from you since last wrote
dated the 5th & 8th. In both of them
you speak of not getting my
letters I cannot conceive the
reason for I have written every
Tuesday regularly for the last
four or five weeks It must
be that the mails have been
lost or miscarried you say you
think nothing but sickness
would hinder me from writing
you are right nor that would
not if I was able to hold
my hand up I am not sick
My health has not been
better in a long while

An example of Lizzie's writing perpendicularly across what she had previously written

My Dear...Yours Ever

APRIL 1861 TO MARCH 1862

One year after their first exchange of letters, Madison again penned a letter to Lizzie from St. Anthony. Although he saw old friends and visited his favorite spots, he was not in St. Anthony for pleasure. He wrote to tell Lizzie that he had enlisted in the St. Anthony Zouaves, one of Minnesota's eight volunteer militia companies before the war, which then collectively formed the Minnesota Regiment on April 30, 1861, in response to President Lincoln's request for three-month volunteers from each state.[1] Numbering among the first seventy-five thousand volunteers, they were only the beginning of an army that would enlist over one million soldiers in the next four years. In early May, Secretary of War Simon Cameron ordered regiments still in their home states to remuster and enlist for three years, rather than the three-month term they had agreed to in April.[2] On May 11, 1861, the *Minnesota State News* printed the names of soldiers joining the Minneapolis and St. Anthony companies, noting: "Our readers will all be interested to see who were the first to respond to the call of their country. Cut out the list and keep it for future reference."[3] Apparently, Madison decided not to enlist for the three-year term with the First Minnesota Volunteer Regiment. In September, however, he joined the Third Minnesota Volunteer Regiment, Company F, receiving the rank of corporal in December 1861.

Although Madison does not explain why he enlisted in September, he was likely influenced by organizing activities under way in the Hastings–Nininger

1. See *Minnesota State News* (St. Anthony and Minneapolis), 4 May 1861.
2. The "Minnesota Regiment" that first gathered in April 1861 was comprised of "two companies from St. Paul; one from Stillwater; one from Minneapolis; one from Red Wing; one from Faribault; one from St. Anthony; one from Anoka; one from Hastings and one from Lake City" (*Hastings Independent,* 2 May 1861). Madison did not join the Hastings company, which would have had men from Dakota County, but the St. Anthony company, with men he knew from his stay in St. Anthony in 1857 and 1858. For early organization of the Minnesota Regiment and then the First Minnesota Volunteer Regiment, see Folwell, *A History of Minnesota,* chaps. 3–4.
3. *Minnesota State News,* 11 May 1861.

area. Encouraging community members to enlist together was a common strategy, thus creating companies composed of neighbors, friends, and family.[4] By September 26, 1861, sixty men had been recruited in Hastings for a new regiment. On October 17 the *Hastings Independent* reported that "the Hastings Company now at Fort Snelling was not able to be Company A in the Third Regiment, a position it was most anxious to occupy," because A companies came first in drill and parade and showed the most patriotic devotion by being the first to enroll in a regiment. Instead, it became Company F and left for Kentucky, stopping in Hastings on November 15. The paper boasted, "Many of the best men of this city and vicinity, compose the gallant company that went from here."[5] Company F drew heavily from Dakota County. Approximately 70 percent of its 92 initial members hailed from the county; of those, 44 soldiers were from Hastings. Estimates from the end of the war suggest that Nininger sent 58 of its 240 men into Civil War units; 12 were in Company F alone, with Nininger men enlisting a few at a time in other companies and regiments.[6] Therefore, Lizzie knew many of Madison's companions, and so the couple's letters were filled with news about mutual acquaintances' activities and antics. For Madison everything seemed new and worthy of detailed description and explanation, as his letters between April 1861 and December 1861 reveal. For Lizzie there were no new surroundings, no new activities, only the regular pattern of small-town community life in which "nothing transpired lately worth writing."

Lizzie and Madison began the new year of 1862 separated by hundreds of miles but connected by letters about mutual acquaintances in both Nininger and the Third Minnesota and the conduct of the war more generally. Much of their correspondence from January through March 1862 is filled with news about who was "gallanting" or escorting whom and who was or was not adapting to army life. The couple felt that the gossip they shared could be damaging, and they worried that others might see what they wrote. From experience they knew that rumors about townspeople and soldiers spread rapidly, both at home and in the

4. See Mitchell, "The Northern Soldier and His Community," 82. See also Kemp, "Community and War," 4–5.

5. See *Hastings Independent*, 5 September, 26 September, 17 October, and 21 November, 1861.

6. These figures are based on the "Roster of Company F," in Board of Commissioners, *Minnesota in the Civil and Indian Wars*, 188–89, and are linked to the Minnesota Territorial Census of 1857, the Minnesota State Census of 1865, and the U.S. Census of 1860. These figures may be low because some of the men do not appear in census records but do appear in other manuscript or newspaper records or their residence cannot be confirmed.

military camp.[7] In addition to keeping track of local news, both Madison and Lizzie followed the course of the war avidly, but they responded to it differently. As news of battles reached Lizzie, she worried that Madison would be in the fray and wondered at his eagerness to put his life in danger. Madison, like many of his comrades, longed, however, for the excitement of battle.[8]

*   *   *

St. Anthony, April 27, 1861

My Dear Lizzie:

You must forgive me for not having written to you sooner than this, for I did not wish to write until you might know where to direct your letters to me. Though I promised you that I should try to keep from doing anything to make you feel bad, yet I have volunteered my services to my country as a private in the ranks of the Min. Volunteer Militia. So many of my friends are going and the cause is so just, that I cannot resist going with them and for the cause.[9]

I belong to company "A" of the 17th Regiment of Min. Vol. Mil. This company is known as the "St. Anthony Zouaves," and numbers about 90 men, rank and file. The whole Regiment consists of ten companies, or nearly a thousand men. In my company are four or five lawyers, as many doctors, several school teachers, a goodly number of merchants, and one editor (my friend W. A. Croffut) besides four printers and other respectable persons *ad infinitum*. We are armed with the long-range, sword-bayonet, ["]minnie rifle." The several companies composing the Regiment will rendevous at Fort Snelling the first of next week and go into quarters there until the 20th of May, when we shall be called into actual service if the war continues. Meantime I shall try to get off long enough to visit you, probably in two or three weeks from now.[10]

Lizzie, I shall not affect to believe that you do not feel bad to have me go away,

7. For the power of gossip between the home front and soldiers' camps, see Mitchell, *The Vacant Chair*, chap. 2.

8. For soldiers' eagerness to end their picket and guard duty in Tennessee and join the advance into Mississippi, see William D. Hale's—also of the Third Minnesota—letters from January through May 1862, Hale Papers.

9. For more on soldiers' motivations for enlisting, see McPherson, *For Cause and Comrades*.

10. For the organization of the initial Minnesota Regiment, see *Minnesota State News* (St. Anthony and Minneapolis), 4 May 1861. For the full list of both the Minneapolis and the St. Anthony companies, see *Minnesota State News*, 11 May 1861. For background on the St. Anthony Zouaves and their experiences at Fort Snelling in late April and early May 1861, see Moe, *The Last Full Measure*, chap. 1.

for I know you do. I feel bad myself. I deplore the condition of our country that calls upon us to fight for it. But *somebody* must go; and who can go better than young men like myself, without business and with family to demand my attention.

The heart which prompted the words, "Go, if you think it your duty," has increased claims to my confidence and my love. I have thought of those words a thousand times since you spoke them.

O, Lizzie, you don't know how often I think of you and how much I wish to be with you again. I did not leave for St. Anthony until the Sunday after leaving Nininger, and I was in Hastings on the Saturday preceding. You can have no adequate idea how I felt while so near you without ever going to see you. . . .

G. B. M. is as venomous as ever, I had [a] considerable talk with him. Look out for him, for his slanderous tongue is going in every direction, and nothing is too bad for him to say. Pardon me for not writing a better letter, and give my love to Aunt Sarah and your father, mother, and sisters. Write to me *immediately*, and direct to St. Paul, for I can get it there before any where else.

> Yours ever,
> Madison

Excuse mistakes, for I have not time to look this over. Mad.

Fort Snelling, May 2, 1861, 1½ o'clock, P.M.

[To Lizzie:]

Your kind letter of Apr. 24 was [received] this morning just after my being relieved from "Guard duty" which I had been engaged in for 24 hours. It is wholly unnecessary for me to tell you that it was a welcome message to me. I wrote to you last Saturday when I was in St. Anthony, and directed you to send your communications to St. Paul.

You say that you are very lonely. I do not doubt it, judging from my own experience. Although the greater part of my time is taken up in military matters, yet think not that I do not find time for serious thoughts. Your letter was seasoned with a sympathetic strain which brought the tears to my eyes, but not to remain there long for I had scarcely finished reading it when the order was given to "Fall into the ranks" and, though my having been on guard exempted me from drilling, yet I fell in and went through [the re]gular forenoon company drill.

This afternoon we are to have a Regimental drill, but as I am not obliged to go, I will look on at leisure. A regimental drill is a drill of the whole Regiment together (10 companies under our Colonel (Ex Gov. Gorman) and his Staff, assisted by Capt A. D. Nelson, U.S.A. You must pardon me for introducing so much of the military proceedings into my letters, for I have nothing else to write about. There are many interesting incidents connect[ed wi]th my few days of military experience, but I have not time to relate them all.

Last Monday morning our Company met at their Armory, and about 10 o'clock marched to Minneapolis under the escort of the Home guards and an immense throng of men, women, and children, many of whom were weeping as they were about parting, perhaps forever with sons, fathers, or brothers. The scene was quite affecting. At Minneapolis we were bid farewell in speech by the Mayor of St. Anthony, after which we marched a short distance to wagons waiting to take us to the Fort. We call[ed] at Minnehaha on our way, and arrived at the Fort at noon, and were mustered and sworn in after a dinner of beef, potatoes, bread, &c., in the presence of the Governor, Adjutant Gen., and a large concourse of people.[11]

After being "mustered in" we were allowed our freedom for [the] day, so I took a stroll about the Fort which seemed quite familiar to me, as I had often been there before. About 4 o'clock it was announced that the Stillwater Guards were opposite the Fort; and pretty soon the Ferryboat was seen bringing them over. As the Guards filed into the Fort, I watched them closely, expecting to recognize some old acquaintance. But I recognized none, though I thought one [wi]th a broad brimmed hat looked like Pray. He soon disappeared from my scrutiny, into the crowd. I took another close look and gave it up, when a few moments afterward as I was standing close by the rear of the Guards, chatting with a friend, who should extend his hand from the ranks and give me a shake, but R. N. Pray—the identical man I had been looking after. It gave me a thrill of joy which has not been at all decreased by frequent association with him ever since.[12]

5 o'clock P.M. I have just returned from witnessing the Regimental drill which occurred just outside the Fort. Pray and I watched it from the top of the Round Bastion—it was a splendid sight. When the companies marched out I went out too, and looked over the Stillwater Guards for Pray; but he was not there, so I went to their quarters which are outside the [fort], and there I found him—as good luck would have it—and we repaired to the top of the Bastion, as I said before. I have been with him ever since until, just now, when I left him at the gate that leads to his quarters. Just as I write he comes in again, and says that he will write to *Nininger* in a day or two. The Building in which I am quartered was once an Episcopalian Chapel for the Fort. It is inside near the main Gateway.

11. For descriptions of the presentation of flags, speeches, and the march to Minnehaha, see *Minnesota State News*, 11 May 1861.

12. In 1860 twenty-nine-year-old R. M. Pray lived in Afton Township, Washington County, and worked as a carpenter. For the Stillwater Guards and conditions at Fort Snelling, see Moe, *The Last Full Measure*, chap. 1.

Everything but the Pulpit has been removed; and I am now in that (the Pulpit) writing. It is covered with velvet and is a firstrate p[lace] to write. Pray wishes me to say, that they have left his company outside the Fort because they are so much more honest than the rest of us.

Oh, this is a beautiful place—the Mississippi on one side, and the Minnesota on the other, while the green prairie extends back for miles. Pray and I got a permit from the Colonel and visited Minnehaha, just two miles distant. It was Pray's first visit to that place.

W. A. Croffut, former Editor of the St Anthony News, has just come in from St. Anthony and has presented me with a good bundle of papers among which are four New York Ledgers. I shall send you one if I can find any way of "*doing up*" one.[13]

You wish to know if I have found any flowers. I have found a few very pretty ones; but there is one—always a flower to me—which I should prefer above all, but which I am not permitted to see now. But I have a *picture* of it—a great consolation to me. If you knew how my friends complement that picture, you would think yourself handsome. But I must close, for supper is ready. There [are] a thousand things which I want to say, but I can't think of them now. . . .

>   Truly yours till death.
>   J. Madison.

{written along the crease of the letter} You must forgive Mad for not making a more extended notice of your good letter. I acknowledge that I have been rather egotistical in this letter, but you will forgive me. . . .

{on top margin of the front page} Direct your next letter to J. M. Bowler, Private in the St. Anthony Zouave, Fort Snelling, Minn. Give my love to friends.

Nininger, May 11, 1861
Saturday evening

My Dearest Friend,

I recd your kind letter of the 2nd of May. Was so glad to hear you was well and seemed to be in good spirits. You dont know how much pleasure it gives me to

13. In 1858 Madison Bowler worked for W. A. Croffut, a partner in Croffut and Clark's printing business in St. Anthony; see Biographical Sketch, P1330, Bowler Papers. Both W. A. Croffut and Madison had worked for the *Minnesota State News,* and Madison was specifically acknowledged as having been "formerly a workman in the NEWS office." See *Minnesota State News,* 4 May 1861. Although reported as a clerk for the commissary department, William A. Croffut, like Madison, was one of the privates listed in the *Minnesota State News,* 11 May 1861.

know that you are happy. Sometimes when I think of the way you are living at night after drilling all day you must be tired enough to be on a good bed instead of lying on the floor. Perhaps I think more about it then you do for I have not much else to take up my mind. Sometimes when I think of being parted from you perhaps for ever it sends a thrill of sorrow through my heart that is not very easy subdued.

I will tell you what we have been doing this week. On Monday Percy got stuff to make a flag.[14] On Tuesday we got it cut and partly made. On Thursday we finished it. It looks very nice. Is 19 feet long and 11 wide. The staff is 90 feet long, they put it up today, about half way between Reeds and Aunt Sarahs. We had a real nice time. Had speeches by *Messrs* A.M. Hayes, Rich, Stebbins, Jones, and another gentleman whose name I do not know. There was about 100 persons in all.[15] I happened to look up. The first persons my eyes fell upon was Isah Mudgett and Johnson Truax. I spoke to Isah, but I did not get a chance to speak to Johnson. He told Amon that you was well and seemed to be enjoying yourself.[16] There is no news to write. Every thing is going on in the same old way. . . .

I want you to come down before you get away if it is a possible thing. I cant bear the idea of you going away without seeing you first. When you write I want you to tell whether you think this war will continue for this reason, you hear and know more about it then we do in Nininger. For anyone might almost as

14. David A. Piercy (or "Percy," as Lizzie sometimes wrote) lived in Nininger in 1861, although he does not appear in any Dakota County census. He was listed on the muster roll for the Andersen Guards of Nininger. See Copy of Muster Roll, John H. Case scrapbook, vol. 1, box 1, Case Papers. For the Nininger Guards, see *Hastings Independent*, 9 May 1861. Piercy remained a friend of the Bowlers long after the war. His calling card is in Miscellaneous Papers, und., 1858–1924 folder, box 3, Bowler Papers.

15. For the flag raising, see *Hastings Independent*, 9 and 16 May 1861. The newspaper reported speeches by A. M. Hayes, C. Stebbins, Wm. Jones, Mr. Haskell, and A. C. Poor. Archibald M. Hayes was a Hastings lawyer; Columbus Stebbins was the editor of the *Hastings Independent*; and William Jones was a constable in Hastings. Rich was probably J. D. Rich, a Methodist minister who lived in Hastings. See *Hastings Independent*, 25 September 1862. A. C. Poor was a farmer in Nininger Township in 1860. The newspaper commented, "The flag was the donation of the patriotic ladies of Nininger, who were alive to the occasion, as well as the circumstances which made it necessary, and many of them were present, and with their smiles encouraging the patriotic work." For women's home front efforts, see Attie, *Patriotic Toil;* and Silber, *Daughters of the Union.*

16. A seventeen-year-old laborer living in Nininger City in 1860, Robert Johnson Truax enlisted in Company H, First Minnesota, soon after Madison joined the St. Anthony Zouaves. He was discharged in June 1861. Later, both Truax and Isaiah Mudgett, a twenty-two-year-old farm laborer from Cottage Grove Township, Washington County, enlisted in Company F, Third Minnesota.

well be out of the world. . . . There is not hardly anyone moving around Nininger. In some days we dont hardly see a person. Most all the men are away
farming. . . .

> Good bye I remain yours as ever
> Lizzie

Fort Snelling, Sept, 30, 1861 Sunday morning 11 o'clock A.M.
My Dear Lizzie:

. . . We started from Hastings Thursday evening at 7 o'clock on the Frank Steele,
and arrived at St. Paul at 12 o'clock, where our Company had to unload the Boat
in consequence of her crew leaving on a strike for higher wages.[17]

As is usual on this River, the State Rooms "were all full," but as I knew how
easy Steamboat-Clerks could lie, I *took a look,* to satisfy myself, and found one
unlocked and unoccupied, so I just took quiet possession, and slept till about 10
o'clock, when I went into the Cabin much to the surprise of the boys who had all
been wandering . . . and sleeping on the floor and anywhere else. Upon my
return to my room I found [occu]pied by Knight, Pettibone, Woodruff, and
Pan[chot], who, of course, filled all the berths, so I took a mattress from one
Berth, locked the door, and slept on the floor until one of them gave up his place
to me. About 2 oclock Eugene Stone routed my bedfellow out and turned in with
me and slept until we were long on our way from St Paul to the Fort, where we
arrived at 7 o'clock on Friday morning. At 5 P.M. we were mustered in . . . and Eugene and I left for St. An[thony,] remained till last night. Eugene [and I slept] in
the same Berth.[18]

I am at present acting orderly Sergeant. No regular non-commissioned
officers can be appointed until the Company is full.[19] We are quartered within

17. This strike was not reported in any of the St. Paul or St. Anthony papers.

18. Madison refers to George Knight, Henry D. Pettibone, P. J. or D. Panchot, and
Eugene Stone, all in Company F. George Knight was a twenty-eight-year-old farmer in
1860 who left a wife and young son in Nininger when he enlisted. Pettibone's family
lived in Red Wing in Goodhue County in 1860, although he lived in Hastings. Seventeen-
year-old David Pinchot enlisted as a musician, and nineteen-year-old Peter Panchot was
a private. Both lived in Hastings. Twenty-two-year-old Walter Woodruff lived in Rosemount Township in 1860, though he does not appear in the *Annual Report of the Adjutant
General.* Nineteen years old in 1860, Eugene Stone lived in Nininger City with his wid-
owed mother, Sarah Stone.

19. Madison was formally enlisted on December 1, 1861, as a corporal, although the
regiment had already left Minnesota and established camp in Kentucky.

the Fort, while the 2nd Reg't and a part of the 4th are outside, the 2nd in tents and doing their own "*housework.*"[20]

I find many friends here whom I did not expect to meet. My friend Hunt is in the Minneapolis Company for our Reg't—the 3d.[21] Eugene and I had our pictures taken at St. Anthony. I will send you mine. It is not a good one, and you shall have a better one if I can get it. . . .

> You[rs ever]
> Ma[dison]

Nininger, Oct 2nd, 1861

My Dearest Friend,

I recd your letter yesterday and also your picture, for which receive my sincere thanks. I have been anxious to hear from you. I was afraid you would get a severe cold the day you left here walking in the rain, didn't think when you left as you should of taken *Fathers* big coat. You had been gone but a short time that day when a presbyterian minister, his wife, and two daughters were on their way from Lake City to St Paul. They were caught in the rain and [our] house being the nearest house they all came here and stayed until the next morning. I would not of cared if they had all been in Guinea. I didn't feel much like entertaining company after parting with the one whom I love above all other earthly beings perhaps for ever. If it wasnt for hope I think I should despair, but the hope that we shall some future day have a home where we can add to each others happiness makes me [feel] that I can bear it patiently.

Ma has gone to Hampton to attend Sally Hawkins' funeral. She died on Sunday morning, poor thing. I hope she is better off. Do is keeping house for Aunt Sarah and Kate has not returned from Mr. Basset's yet so you see *Father* and I are left to keep house. I dont know when they will get back again, for it is raining real hard, and every thing wears a gloomy aspect.[22]

---

20. William D. Hale, a new arrival serving in the quartermaster's department and in the Third Minnesota, wrote a fuller description of the crowded conditions for soldiers at Fort Snelling: "We are crowded in very close, making necessarily great discomfort & want of cleanliness and pure air. Quite a number are sick from this and other causes, something of course being due to change of life" (26 October 1861, Hale Papers).

21. Daniel H. Hunt was in Company A. Twenty-seven years old in 1860, Daniel Hunt lived in St. Anthony. Like Madison, he was born in Maine.

22. This was probably Lizzie's cousin Sarah Hawkins, who lived in Vermillion Township. See John H. Case, "The Caleff Family of Bluff Landing—Nininger," *Hastings Gazette,* 30 December 1921. John Bassett was one of the earliest landowners in Nininger

You spoke of meeting many old friends. I am glad to hear it. I hope you will enjoy yourself as you can. You spoke of your picture not being good. I think it is very good, indeed. When you write if there is any thing you need that I can make for you, I want you to let me know if I can get my plans to work. I am coming up to the Fort and will have a chance to take you any thing if you will let me know....

Did you get your snuffs? We sent it by Obet Russel to Hastings. Give my love to Eugene and all other friends.[23]

I remain your loving Lizzie

{in margin} Excuse all mistakes. Burn when rid.

Fort Snelling, Thursday, Oct. 10, 1861

My Dear Lizzie:

We arrived here at one o'clock last night. I found Piercy in my bed. There is some difficulty about the Cavalry being received. Ramsey telegraphs that he will not accept them until the 3d and 4th Regiments are full.[24] They in turn threaten to go to Wisconsin and join one of her Regiments....

We started on the Northern Belle from Hastings yesterday at 4 P.M. and arrived at St Paul at half past eight. The boys were in favor of going to the Fort on foot; but I went to the Clerk and obtained six state rooms which contained us all. We had just got asleep when some of the boys who had too much liquor took it into their heads to go to the Fort. They went to the Livery Stable procured a couple of carriages and teams, and routed out all the boys but Woodworth and me. Finally they found us and we concluded to go [with them as] we are....

Yours in haste.
JM Bowler

Township, selling his farm to Nininger City proprietors. Although Bassett did not live in Nininger in 1860, he is listed in the muster roll of the Andersen Guards of Nininger. See John H. Case Scrapbook, Case Papers. Bassett and his family had moved to Cottage Grove, Washington County, by 1860.

23. Madison apparently used snuff, finely ground tobacco inhaled through the nose. Lizzie refers to Obediah Russell. There were several Russells in the Nininger area. The Russell family included four brothers and a sister. See Biographical Sketches, P–W, folder 2, Case Papers.

24. Ramsey is Minnesota governor Alexander Ramsey. Governors headed efforts to raise and organize regiments early in the war. See Folwell, *A History of Minnesota*, 77–94.

Fort Snelling, Oct. 19, 1861

My Dear Lizzie:

... I came up Thursday night on the Frank Steele, and had the satisfaction of taking a couple of recruits with me. Our company has seventy eight men which is just five short of the required number.

Piercy has joined the Dutch Cavalry, and will probably be a Sergeant.[25]

There is so much confusion here that I cannot think of anything to write. Dakin has lost one of his gloves, and has been over to Capt Butler, who is in command of our Regiment, with his complaint. He is now telling the boys what to depend on if his glove is not forthcoming in five minutes. They are all making fun with him. Dr. Pride is stopping up the cracks in his Saxhorn with my Fir Balsam. Every now and then he toots up with a deafening sound. I am lying flat on my bed with my writing *consarns* before me. Hold on a minute. Cressy wants my tactics, and Dr. Pride is pulling my coattail for something.[26] Hunt and Bowler are going to St. Anthony today to *see the folks* and *get some peaches*.

You must excuse me for writing this with pencil for I am in a hurry. Please give my love to all and pardon me for not writing you a better letter. I will try to do better another time.

Yours ever, Madison.

Nininger, Minn, Oct. 29, 1861
Saturday evening

Dear Madison

I have just arrived at home after bidding you a *long* farewell and perhaps forever. Pray stayed until he got his tea and then he went to Hastings. You do not know how I do feel this night. It seems to me that I cannot bear to have you go away without seeing you again. I do wish you could come down. You spoke of going to see Donnelly. If I were you I would go immediately. If he can do anything to assist you I

25. David Piercy enlisted in Company A of Brackett's Battalion Cavalry as a sergeant on October 2, 1861.

26. "Dakin" probably refers to E. Deakin. Capt. Butler might have been Levi Butler from Minneapolis. Roger W. Cressey, John Pride, and Deakin were in Company F. J. C. Pride had lived in Hastings since at least 1857. Roger Cressey lived with his parents and younger siblings in Hastings in 1857, but by 1861, when the nineteen-year-old enrolled, he listed Medford in Steele County as his residence.

27. Lizzie must have worked out her plan to visit Madison at Fort Snelling, because she discusses their good-bye in her November 2, 1861, letter. Lizzie refers to Ignatius Donnelly, lieutenant governor and Nininger City cofounder and resident. This may be in reference to Madison's attempt to secure a position as a commissioned officer.

think he will do it.[27] If any one dont look out for themselvs no one will look out for them*self*. Is all they think of. I hope it will all come out right, and, all hard feelings will cease to be. I know it makes it unpleasant for you, and I persume for them too.

We got home about eight o'clock. Had a very pleasant drive. It wasnt near as cold as it was in the morning. I didnt enjoy it very much for I was thinking of him whom I had left behind whose countenance is impressed on my memory never to be forgotten. When thou art many miles distant I can think of thee and see thee as when I last saw thee. If it is the will of Providence that we shall ever meet again, may we strive to watch over our selves that while absent from each other we may be better fitted to begin a life of troubles together, with a better knowledge of what is our duty both to *God* and *Man*. If it is *that* we shall never meet again on this earth, I hope that we shall be of that happy number that will go where there is no more partings. . . . Excuse this writing for my pen is very bad. Burn it when you reads it. . . .

        Yours ever Lizzie S. C. . . .

    Dont get angry with me for writing you such a mess of stuff and dont play cards any more. . . .[28]

                                        Nininger, Nov 2nd, 1861
                                            Saturday Evening
Dearest loved one

I recd the letter you wrote me last Monday and was glad to hear from you. I think by the tenor of your letter that you are getting low spirited. I am sorry that I let my feeling overcome me so that day that I was at the Fort if it made you feel sad, but you never can imagine my feelings. I bade you rather a cool good bye. But the heart felt most when the lips moved not. At that moment when I looked on you, the one in whom all my happiness depends in this earth, and thought it might perhaps be the last time we should ever meet, my heart was sorrow stricken.

I am trying to make up my mind to submit to what ever may come and hope for the best. I suppose all these things are given us to bear to make us mindful that we should have a higher aim than the things of this wicked world.

You ask to be forgiven if you have ever done anything unkind. There is nothing to forgive. You have always been to me all and more then I expected, you have shown acts of kindness both to me and others that you shall be remembered for as long as earth gives me a home. I hope that some day I shall be able

28. The last paragraph is written in pencil and has faded significantly, so it is nearly indecipherable.

to return them by kind word and loving acts. When you go down river, I want, if it is not too much trouble, you to keep a journal so that when you come back if you ever should, while trotting your grandchildren on your knee, you can look over the time when you were a soldier. I don't want you to have the blues any more. If you do what you think is your duty both to *God* and man, you can do no more. When you write, tell me how your officers conduct themselves, if they are good with you. . . .

I will send you your clothes the first chance I can get if there is any one comes down from the Fort. I wish you would ask them to call here and get them. I have inquired but I can find no one going up there at present. Will send them as soon as I can. When you get them you open them and in the middle of the bundle you will find a sort of a needle book. I thought it would be handy for you to carry any little things such as buttons thread, etc.

. . . I believe you are not going as soon as you expected. I want you to write to me often. You do not know how anxious I will be all the time after you go down river. . . . Burn this when recd.

> Yours ever Lizzie
> Come down if you can any way . . .

> Nininger, Dec 6th, 1861
> Friday evening

My Dear Madison

While sitting here in Aunt Sarah's old kitchen my thoughts wonder away to my absent friend and loved one. I have just been thinking of the days that are past and gone when you used to sit where I am sitting now in this corner behind the stove and had many a socibal chat.

Shal you ever return to bless me with your smile is my thoughts by day and night. If you only knew my feelings when I get in some lone corner and sit down to think, and hear the wind whistle through the cracks, and the snow blow round the corners. *Minnie* says that at such times she thinks of the poor soldiers.[29] She is not the only one.

Kate recd a letter from you on Monday. In it you spoke of being treated with so much kindness. I am so glad you meet with friends away there among strangers.

29. "Minnie" probably refers to Jemima Russell, Charles Russell's sister. According to John H. Case, she married Lewis Govett, a carpenter and contractor in Nininger City. The Govetts left after the financial panic of 1857. Evidently, they separated, and she married another man later in the 1860s. See Biographical Sketches, P–W, folder 2, Case Papers. See also Foroughi, "Vine and Oak."

If you could only stay there, but very likely before this reaches you, you will be many miles from there.

Last evening there was a very large party at the hotel. I went down with Wilson and Emily Hanna and stayed nearly an hour. There was a very large company. . . .[30] I left them all and went back to Aunt Sarah's, where I have been staying for the last three days. Went to bed and had one good cry, for which I felt a good deal the better.

I see by a letter in the Press, written by one of your brother soldiers and signed "Hurbert" while going throug[h] Indiana, some of the ladies showed themselves very patriotic by kissing the soldiers. Was you one of the lucky ones? I want you to march and not be hunting up a little Italian girl for yourself down there.

I saw a letter that Piercy wrote to Mr Wm Valkenburg. By what he wrote about himself his Capt and the rest of the company, if he is not hooped soon I think he will burst. He thinks he will be appointed Sergant Major.[31]

Old Mrs Stone is very anxious to have Eugene write. She has not recd a word from him since he went away. . . .

Saturday Morning

I now resume my pen to finish this incomplete epistle.

We are having beautiful weather now. There has been two or three soft days. The snow has mostly all disappeared. How do you get your washing done? You mind or take care of yourself and if you get sick be sure and let me know.

School begins next week. The teacher is an old gentleman from Popular Grove by the name of Carpenter. So you need not be the least afraid of my going off with the school teacher as you used to say sometimes.

. . . Remember me to all acquaintances. I must close hoping this will find you well and enjoying yourself.

> I remain yours ever
> Lizzie S. Caleff . . .

Camp Dana, Dec. 18, 1861

My Dear Lizzie:

I received a letter from you a few days ago—the first letter I have received since I came to Kentucky. . . . I had almost begun to think that you had forgotten me;

---

30. According to the 1860 census, Wilson and Emma Hannah lived with their parents on their Nininger farm. Emma, eighteen, would have been escorted by her twenty-two-year-old brother.

31. William Van Valkenberg was on the muster roll for the Andersen Guards of Nininger. See John H. Case Scrapbook, Case Papers.

but your good letter dispelled the thought again, and I knew that Lizzie still remembered me.

You speak of being lonely and of the pleasant hours we have spent together. I know well how to sympathise with you, for I am lonely at times and often think of home, and the loved ones behind, especially of her who is seldom out of my thoughts. I can look back and see everything just as it was when I was there. Those old familiar haunts and scenes often float across my vision with all the distinctness of real life. It gives me a feeling of sadness when I think over the old times that have gone by never to return. I recollect that last Christmas when we were together on Rosehill we were speculating as to where we should be and what we should be doing by another Christmas. I little thought at that time that we should be so far separated, and that I should be a soldier, in arms for my country. But little can we tell what a year may bring forth.

. . . I think there will be no danger of your gallanting with that old Schoolmaster. I learn from some of those who know him that he is of little consequence any way. I hope you will go to school and learn all you can, though I am of the opinion that there is not much to be learned from him.

Our company marches tomorrow to Sheppardsville to relieve Co. K from guard duty at that place. We shall stay seven days and return to this place again. Day before yesterday 24 men three corporals one Sergeant and Lieut. of Co "F" were on picket duty at Bardstown Junction, three miles from here. A part of their duty was to guard a Rail Road Bridge and Water-Tank. In the night an attempt was made to burn it by three men who were discovered creeping up by Frank Colby and Page Howe. Frank attempted to fire, but his gun wouldn't go. The men ran and Howe fired after them but without effect. A little fellow by the name of Allen, some ways off, fired too. By this time Frank fired, dropped his gun, and he and Howe drew their Revolvers and rushed into the woods after them, but returned after firing three or four shots without any apparent effect. We have had several little skirmishes like the above but have had no serious result. We have taken some five or six prisoners on such occasions and sent them to Gen Buell in Louisville.[32]

32. William D. Hale noted, "We are in rather tight & uncomfortable fix. Just now too in guarding so extended and important points while we believe the country is full of sneaking *secesh* who long for a chance to assassinate us or burn a bridge. . . . Every rail and tie as well as bridge and tank is of utmost importance and in guarding a length of 15 or 20 mile we had less than one hundred serviceable cast iron guns! In a body we are not in the slightest danger, but only those detached picket." See letter, 18 December 1861, Hale Papers. For context, see Andrews, "Narrative of the Third Regiment," 148–49. Frank Colby and Page Howe were later discharged for disability in May 1862 and January 1863, respectively. See Lombard, *History of the Third Regiment.*

We are having very pleasant weather, and the sick are fast recovering, so that we have but nine or ten now in our company, who are unfit for duty.[33]

I am one of the Corporals of the Color Guard, a place for which Capt Preston recommended me to the Col. or I should never have accepted the office of Corporal.[34] Eugene Stone tells me that he has written to his mother several times, but received no answer. Eugene is one of the most daring soldiers in the Reg't, and is liked by all his comrades.

Several divisions of the Army of K'y are far in advance of our position and lively times are soon expected. We should have been with them but for the poor quality of our firearms. The[y] will soon be exchanged when we hope to face the enemy with the rest. . . .

You want to know how we get our washing done. Many of the soldiers do their own washing, but I have thus far hired mine done. There are plenty of women who are glad to do it for five cents apiece. You want to know if I got a kiss from any of those ladies. I did not, though I might have done so if I had stepped forward, but I kept back as I did not feel much like kissing any one I saw. The Press' correspondent is my friend Hunt.

I have not written a letter to any Newspaper since I left Minn. It is too much work for little pay. You need have no fears of my getting astray with the Italian or any other girls. Wenches are thick as fleas, but not to my taste.

Now, Lizzie, I want you to write to me often, whether you hear from me or not, for you have more time and better opportunities for writing letters than I have. I shall, perhaps, when I get time, write you a long lecture on the evils of going to Balls and flirting with young men in the absence of your poor soldier beau. . . .

> Yours ever,
> Madison . . .

[Camp] Lester, [Ky.] Dec. 22, 1861[35]

[To Lizzie:]

[We] marched from [Camp Dana] Wednesday and arrived at Sheppardsville where we pitched our tents in the afternoon of the same day, naming our Camp

33. Soldiers regularly commented on the mild winter weather in the South, especially as compared with Minnesota's winters. See letters, 18 December and 12 January 1861, Hale Papers.

34. Captain John B. Preston was from Hastings, although he does not appear in either the 1857 or the 1860 census.

35. The top left part of this letter is torn, and the salutation is missing, as well as some phrases throughout.

"Lester" in honor of our respected Colonel. As usual at every new place during the first night I was detailed Corporal of the Guard which, however, was no unpleasant duty as the night was very warm and pleasant, and the inner man was well supplied with hot coffee from our own pantry and apples from the root house of a neighboring secesh Doctor, feloniously abstracted by the light of the moon.

. . . We have a co[ok] . . . from Minn. [He makes] coffee . . . and meat, which is done in a very poor style. When he has more than he can do some of the soldiers are detailed to help him. Once in a while we get soft bread from Louisville, but most of the time we have hard bread. Just now we have no bread, except what we cook from flour, soda, grease, and water, by mixing it and baking it in frying pans held before the fire. Yesterday we had cold water flapjacks. Once or twice we have been without anything to eat except what we bought from the Sutler. Now and then we buy oysters, cheese, Sausage, pies, cake, &c, and have a good meal at our own expense. Besides the boys sometimes buy . . . poultry of some se[cesh.] . . . [A soldier] is supplied [with a pack in] which he carries . . . his rations [plate,] spoon, knife, and fork. When a meal is ready he produces these and "goes in" for his share, which when he has got it, he proceeds to demolish when, how and where he pleases,—in his tent, or on some stump, rock, or clean place upon the ground. When in heavy marching order a soldier is pretty well loaded, his load consisting of a full packed knapsack, haversack, canteen, gun, cartridge Box and Belt with the full amount of cartridges. We have small tents, each containing from three to five men. They are about eight feet square. The one I tent in is larger by several feet.[36]

To day is Sunday, and the rain is pouring down in earnest. . . . You [were asking about how the officers con]duct themselves . . . we have to be careful, as Gen Buell has turned off several colonels, Capts, and Lieutenants for bad behavior. They are kind to me though as I could desire. The small pox is in town, and the boys have been vaccinated this morning. The Minn 3d Reg't will be kept here until after payment, which will be between now and the 5th of Jan., and then sent to Green River. Co F will return to Camp Dana next Wednesday, and Co "G" will take our place here. I am Corporal of the Guard again to day, so is Knight. We have divided time. I serve until 12 o'clock to night; then Knight serves till 9 in the morning, so each will get some sleep. . . . I have allotted $10. per month which will be invested in Gov. Bonds when $50. has accumulated. . . . I have

36. For another description of camp life in the Third Minnesota, see letters, 24 November 1861 and 15 January 1862, Brookins Letters.

not made the acquaintance of our Chaplain. He prays at dress parade, but lacks energy and does no hurt or good that I can discover.

> Yours truly,
> Madison

{up margin} P.S. I have just been to my dinner of meat & beans, and have just taken possession of a deserted house in company with one or two others where we intend to stay until the rain is over. . . .

Nininger Minn Dec 23/1861

My Dear Madison

Why is it you do not write? I have just returned from the office where I expected to get a letter from you but came away very much disappointed. I hope sickness is not the reason of your not writing. The last letter I recd from you was dated the 3d of this month. Since then Albert Truax told me he had a letter from you and you was well.[37]

You do not know how lonely I feel this evening. It is drawing near Christmas. Every one seems to be trying to enjoy themselves. To-morrow evening they have one of the grandest balls of the season at Tremont [Hall]. . . . Do you remember one year ago where and how we spent our last Christmas eve? Then was the time you told me your intentions of being a soldier if you were ever needed. Those days were the anticipations of you what is now an awful reality to the whole nation. Then I listened to that in a thoughtless way as being a thing possible but not a tale likely. We can realize the present but who can fathom the future? I hope these are the darkest days of the once *United States.*

I have never asked you since you have been there what you think about the *ending* of this war. Is it the general opinion that it will last very long? I do wish that something would turn up, that peace might be made and this one peaceful Nation be again United. I suppose you often feel lonely but you have something exciting all the time. But you never can imagine how lonely I feel when I think of you being away down there exposed to every-thing. Even when the toils of the day is past, you have not a comfortable bed to sleep, in for I know that it cannot be other wise. Then wet and cold, if you are sick you have no one to care for you. When I think of all these things, then is the time I feel if it were possible I should be with you. I wonder if it is that I shall ever see you again. Shall I ever have a chance to imprint another kiss on that broad noble forehead that bespeaks prin-

---

37. Farm laborer Albert Truax was eighteen years old in 1861.

ciples too noble to be contaminated by the influences that is thrown across a soldiers pathway? In the silent watches of the night when all are asleep my thoughts wander away to my Madison away in a distant land. . . .

Give my love to Eugene and all the rest that I am acquainted with. How does little Myron Putnam get along?[38] Ma, Kate and Do all send their love to you and they wish you were here to eat your christmas dinner. I wish I could send you something good in this letter.

> I remain your ever
> Lizzie

Do write often

{up margin} Burn this when you read.

Camp Rough & Ready, Hardin Co, Ky, Jan 10, 1861 [1862]
My Dear Lizzie

I received yours of Dec. 30, yesterday, accompanied by a *"St. Paul Press,"* which were both welcome messages to me; but the *Pioneer* and the *Conserver* which you sent, as well as Kate's and Amon's letters I have not received.[39] Why I have not is more than I can guess, unless some mischievous individual has appropriated them to his own use and benefit, which has been done in several instances. The socks which your good old mother gave me and my towels have been stolen from me. . . . You refer to the fact that you were alone while writing to me, and wish I might have been with you. Nothing that I know of would have given me more pleasure than to have been with you, even though it were but an hour. I wrote to you about a week ago just before we came here where we now are. Our company is engaged in guarding two tressle work Bridges near Colesburg and one mile apart. The company is divided into two parts, the part in which I am being under command of Lieut. Tichenor at the farthest post.[40] The Bridge which we guard is ninety six feet high and five hundred feet long, with a small creek passing under it. We are encamped just at its feet within ten feet of it, so that we are often

38. In 1860 fifteen-year-old Myron Putnam lived in Afton Township, Washington County, with his parents and his younger sister.

39. Madison refers to the *St. Paul Daily Press,* a Republican paper; the *St. Paul Weekly Pioneer and Democrat;* and the *Minnesota Conserver,* published in Hastings, which began April 18, 1861, and became the *Hastings Conserver* in 1863. See Hage, *Newspapers on the Minnesota Frontier;* and Mitchell, *Dakota County,* 69–70.

40. Madison refers to First Lieutenant I. P. Tichnor, who was a thirty-three-year-old Hastings hotel keeper in 1860.

regaled by the music of the cars passing above our heads, both by night and by day. Not a day passes but that we receive the daily Louisville papers which passengers on the trains are kind enough to throw down to us. Some company will relieve us tomorrow when we shall go back to Belmont.

Yesterday I visited the tunnel one mile beyond here. It is just three quarters of a mile through it. The awful hills, or mountains rather, abound in plaster of paris which looks quite white and pretty. Just on the hill above us Gen Buckners Army was encamped for three months last summer, and afterwards the Union Brigade of the gallant Gen Rosseau. When Buckner was first driven away 800 men encamped and guarded where we do now. The Rebels destroyed the noble bridge over Rolling Fork, and tried, but failed, to destroy the one where the other half of our company is, and when they got here Gen. Rosseau was so close upon them that they had not time to attempt to destroy this Bridge.[41]

The 3d Regt have now got the famous Sibley Tent which holds from fifteen to twenty men. Co. F has six of them. Lieut Tichenor, Sergts Otto Dreher and Allison, corporal Esteabrook, privates Baker and Knowles, and my humble self occupy one of them for the present and I am now seated in it writing upon a pork barrelhead, while Dr. Pride is blowing the Bugle with a deepening sound.[42] Eugene Stone and Charley Russell are with the other part of the Company.[43] They were well and in good spirits when I saw them last. Eugene was here and stayed all night a few nights ago. . . .

I am just Twenty four years old today. Wish I was where you might make me a birthday present of a good kiss, then when your next birthday comes I could

41. Confederate general Simon Bolivar Buckner headed Kentucky's military forces until July 1861. In September he was named a brigadier general and placed in charge of Confederate forces in central Kentucky. On February 16, 1862, he surrendered to Union general Ulysses S. Grant at Fort Donelson. William D. Hale also comments on the Union's efforts to "repair damage" not only to bridges but also to telegraph wires and railroad tracks. See letter, 12 January 1862, Hale Papers. For information on General Lovel H. Rousseau, see Warner, *Generals in Blue*, 412–15.

42. Madison's April 24, 1862, letter describes a Sibley Tent. St. Paul resident twenty-six-year-old sergeant Otto Dreher of Company F was promoted to first lieutenant of Company A in December 1862 and later to captain of the same. Also in Company F were Sergeant William Allison from Hastings, Corporal Daniel Easterbrook from Empire City, and Private Eddington Knowles from Hastings. Private Baker could have been either George E. or Wyman Baker, both from Rosemount.

43. Charles Russell was the youngest of the four Russell brothers who lived in Nininger. His sister Minnie was Lizzie's best friend. See Biographical Sketches, P–W, folder 2, Case Papers.

pay you back with interest. I am glad to hear that you are attending school and hope you will make the best use of your time. . . .

      Yours ever

      Madison . . .

{up front page margin} This is the county in which President Lincoln was born. There are plenty of rails here but whether he split them or not I do not know.

Nininger, Minn, Jan 12th, 1862,

Sunday Morning

My Dear Madison

. . . It is too cold to go to sabbath school. I think I cannot employ my-self any better then to write to my absent friend. You may be glad you made your escape from Minn. You will shun this awful cold weather we are having. It is cold enough to day to freeze indians. I suppose it is time for we have had a beautiful winter thus far. Before I write any more I must ask you to excuse this sheet that I am writing on. I have no other kind at present. You want me to write you all the news, I will write you all I can think of that will not be much for there is no news. Our school is prospering very well. Have about sixty scholars, a great many small ones. Miss Rice, Annie Reed, the two Mabee girls, Jon Callahan, Ben Mabee, A Fish, Am, Lucy Reed, Viola, Do and I are all the large scholars. Miss Rice is the belle of the season. . . . She is gallanted by Mr. Albert Truax. Next is Annie. You know how she looks and what kind of a disposition she had (it is as bad as ever). She is gallanted by Mr. Manley Countryman, next is Lizzie Caleff gallanted by Mr. A McMullan.[44] You know how she looks. We all attend singing school. In the last letter I wrote you I gave you a description of our singing master. He is rather a good singer and seems to understand music very well. I am a going to learn to sing this winter so that you may have your anticipations or expectations gratified, I have not much music in my soul but I think I am as easily moved by sweet concord of musical sounds as most women, I dont know about men. . . .

    You wanted to know where all of your enemies are. I guess you have not any in Nininger. Now they have all turned friends since you went away. . . . I do wish this war was over so you could come home. . . . Mind and be a good little boy. If you are as good when you come back as you was when you went away (if you ever do come back), I shall have nothing to say.

44. The "large scholars" ranged from twelve to twenty-one years old. Lizzie was escorted by her adopted cousin, Amon McMullen. Nininger farm laborer Manly Country man was nineteen years old in 1860.

{on front page top margin near address} I thought you was going to give me a lecture on going to balls in the absence of my soldier beau. I have never seen any- thing of it yet. Excuse this poorly written letter.

{on front page margin} Ma says she wishes she could send you a pair of mittens. . . .

Good by
Lizzie

Camp Dana, Ky, Jan. 23, 1862

My Dear Lizzie

Yesterday as I returned from Bardstown Junction where we had been on guard, I was agreeably surprised to find three letters for me, one of which was from you. . . . I had a feast reading them, but felt somewhat homesick for a while when I learned what good times everybody was having. Your letter was very interest- ing, and I was very much gratified when I read it to learn that you were enjoy- ing yourself so well, going to school and to singing school. I am truly glad that you have determined to learn music. You will succeed if you adhere to your determination and study hard as you ought. . . . That Miss Lizzie Caleff and her young gallant must make a grand show when they appear in public. Eugene says it is queer that Am cannot go out of the family to get a flame. Ask him for me if his knees do not falter sometimes when he is so unfortunate as to meet some of the dignified people of Nininger while he has to support a young lady on his arm. It is an awful trial, and takes a man with beard and whiskers to go through the trying ordeal without trembling.

The company has gone out to Battalion drill and I can now write in peace. I got the Capt to excuse me from drill to day so that I might write some letters. Every time I receive a letter Lieut. Ingman wants to know if it is from Miss Caleff. He directed a letter to you for me one day, and ever since then he has to plague me every opportunity. Capt Preston hits me a dab too once in a while. Lieut. Ingman is a firstrate, kindhearted man, but not much of an officer. He says he is going to write to you and cut me out. He talks of resigning.[45]

I suppose that you have heard of the Union victory which was so lately achieved over Zollicaffer and his forces, and in which the 2nd Minn. was

45. Hastings men Second Lieutenant Samuel H. Ingman and Captain John B. Preston were both among the group of officers who were dismissed in December 1862 for their sur- render at Murfreesboro in July 1862. See Fitzharris, "'Our Disgraceful Surrender,'" 1–20.

engaged.[46] I was at Bardstown Junction at the time of the fight. Lieut Tichenor was in the Telegraph at the time, and the operator gave him the report as fast as it came. Pretty soon he came rushing into our quarters and asked me if I wanted to go to Belmont tonight. He then related the news amid the shouts of the boys who received it with great enthusiasm. It was the darkest night I ever experienced; but I arrived myself with a small dark lantern borrowed from a Union man and started for Head Quarters with a dispatch for Col. Lester and arrived just as tatoo was being beaten.[47] The Col. read the news to those who happened to be in at the time, and soon it was all over camp, as one could easily tell by the shouts which rent the air. The cannonading was heard at this place, but no one knew that a fight was going on as it is a common thing to hear them while engaged in artillery practice. It is a magnificent sight to see a Battery of six pieces manned by 156 men engaged in their drill. Every man rides, either on a horse or on some of the guns and carriages. They go at a full run making the ground shake and jar, when all at once they will stop on limber and bang away at a rapid rate, sometimes with shotted guns which makes the trees crash wherever they strike.[48]

At Camp Jenkins I have seen 15000 Infantry all drilling at once in every conceivable maneuver, besides several Batteries flying about in different sides of where I stood, and at the same time squadrons of cavalry were moving about some at a walk, some at an easy trot, while others were charging at full speed with sabres gleaming and flashing in the sun. But here we have to [be] engaged in real duties; there we saw only the preparatory, or play-day part of war.

To-morrow, rumor says, is payday for us. I hope so. It is also rumored that we are to have new guns in a *"few days."* We have been brigaded with the 9th Mich., 10th, 13th, and 15th, Kentucky regiments under Brig Gen. Ward. Col. Boone's 18th Ky Regt is also attached to our Brigade for the present. Ours is denominated the 16th Brigade.[49]

You say that you wish the war was over so that I might return to Minnesota. So do I; but, at the same time, I do not wish to return until it is over. I think,

---

46. The Second Minnesota participated in the Union victory against Confederate general Felix K. Zollicoffer's forces at Mill Springs, Kentucky, on January 19, 1862. See Carley, *Minnesota in the Civil War,* 52–53. For more on Zollicoffer and this battle, see Warner, *Generals in Gray,* 350.

47. Tattoo is a signal for soldiers to return to their quarters for the night.

48. Limbers carried artillery guns as well as ammunition chests. See Naisawald, *Grape and Canister,* app. 1. Shotted guns were cannons loaded with live ammunition.

49. For receiving guns and regular drilling, see Andrews, "Narrative of the Third Regiment," 149-50.

however, that the prospect is good for a speedy termination of the war, though no one can tell anything regarding the future with certainty, much less, to give anything definite in regard to the future progress of such a revolution as we are now in the midst of.

You desire me to be a "good little boy." I'll try, mother. Tell your mother that I am truly thankful to her for her kindness, in wishing to send me those mittens but that I do not need them enough for her to be to the trouble of sending them to me. The weather is not cold here, though most every body wears gloves or mittens. I have not worn any at all thus far, but shall be soon if I need them. I hear that it is very cold in Minn. just now. I am glad that I am where the cold can not reach me, though I would be willing to bear it to meet my friends. The weather here is very pleasant now. The ground is not frozen at all.

You refer to me as being so kind to you and doing so much for you, and hope that I may return so that you can repay me. I have done almost nothing for you compared to what you have already done for me. I know that I have never been so kind to you as I ought to have been. . . .

> Yours ever,
> Madison . . .

Nininger Min Jan. 27, 1862

My Dear Madison

. . . We are having a great snow storm to day. The snow is very deep. I think there has never been so much snow since the first winter we came here.

I am sitting at the window next [to] Nininger, if you could only see how lonely it looks. If you never never did have the blues I am sure you would [have] them. I do wish you were here. I think it is too bad for men to be taken down there and kept without doing any good for themselves or any one else. If I was among them I believe I would make a fuss if they kept me there much longer without anything to live for. . . .

I guess you will think I have not improved in writing very much by the looks of this letter. The ink has been frozen and my pen and paper are very poor. I have written this in great haste for I am going to coax papa to take this to the office with the hope of getting some body (you know who) [letter?] in return. . . . Our folks all send their love to you. Ma says she would send you some mittens and stocking if she knew of any way sending them.

> Good bye
> Lizzie

Nininger Minn Feb 1st 1862
Saturday evening

Dear Madison

. . . As singing school is the subject of conversation in Nininger I will tell you something about it. Four week[s] ago Mr St Clair came here and got up a singing class. The second night he came he was so much under the influence of liquor that he was unfit for anything. Then they all got disatisfied for the reason that he was not a very good teacher any way and when he was high he was worse then no one. Just when they were thinking what they were going to do, there was a young man by the name of Hartson offered to teach, I think likely you have seen him. Him and his brother used to carry about silk to sell (a Yankee occupation as Am says) but he seems to be a very nice young man, is an excelent teacher.[50] On the whole I think it was a good thing Mr St Clair got tipsy that time. We are going to meet three evenings in a week as he (the teacher) can only stay three weeks longer. You say you are glad that I am enjoying myself so well. I should enjoy myself if there was one thing as I wish it was, and until that is so I shall never enjoy myself very much. As long as you are down there engaged in the same business that you are now engaged in I shall feel the same unceasing anxiety that I now feel.

. . . All the large scolars from our school and the Spring Lake school are going to Point Douglas to a spelling school.[51] There has been three or four spelling schools here this winter. I have not attended any for you know I never liked to go. The folks all say I am getting "old maidish." I dont know what makes them think so.

We are enduring another Methodist quarterly meeting.[52] In consequence of the diptheria being in the place where it was appointed, they appointed it here. . . .

50. Mr. St. Clair might have been W. H. St. Clair, a Methodist minister living in Still-water, Washington County, in 1860. The only person listed as Hartshorn in 1857 or 1860 was Philander Hartshorn, a fifty-six-year-old justice of the peace in Hastings. Lizzie probably refers, however, to William Hartshorn, who used to trade with the Dakota Indians in the area and had a warehouse near the Mississippi River in Nininger. See John H. Case, "Pioneers in the Township of Nininger," *Hastings Gazette*, 2 April 1921. When Lizzie wrote worse than "no one," she probably meant worse than "any one."

51. Spring Lake is the western portion of Nininger Township. Point Douglass, in Washington County, is across the Mississippi from Hastings.

52. Dakota County regularly hosted religious meetings, including quarterly and camp meetings and love feasts, during the 1850s and 1860s. On February 2, 1862, Levi N. Countryman, a Nininger Township farmer, recorded in his diary that he attended the "Quarterly Meeting," which included a sermon by the Reverend Mr. Brooks. See diary, 2 February 1862, Countryman Papers. In 1860 there were more Methodists than followers

Pa has just come home from Hasting. The presiding elder Mr Brooks preached. Tomorrow morning at 9 oclock they have a love feast. I think if all the soldiers were Minn boys this war would not last long judging from the bravery of the Minn 1st and 2nd.[53] Dont you be running about in the dark alone. The boos will be catching you some of these nights. I will give you and Mr Ingman a good talking to when you come back. Why is he going to resign? Dont he like a soldiers life? ...

{up the margin, across the top and down} Please tell Eugene his folks are well, also Charley Russeles.

Do excuse this poorly written letter. The ink has been frozen so many times that I cant hardly write with it at all.

　　　Lizzie

I should like to get a letter from that young Lieut very well. Letters from the 3rd Regt are always acceptable. Mind and dont you tell him. Be sure and burn this when you read it. That is if you can read it. ...

Rolling Fork, [Ky.] Feb. 5, 1862

My Dear Lizzie:

... You say that you wish the war would end and that I would then come home. I wish so too, and would give much to be with you again; but at the same time, I do [not w]ant the war to end until the great object for [which] it commensed shall be accomplished, nor do I want to go home until then.

You think that those who have the power are not using it as they ought. To none does this seem more true than to the soldier, yet I am content to wait, trusting that all is for the best, and that something will soon be done toward crushing this monstrous rebellion.

I have just been looking at your picture—the one you gave me last spring—

---

of other denominations in Minnesota. See Wheelock, *Minnesota: Its Place among the States,* 140. For more on the Methodist church's structure in the first half of the nineteenth century, see Ahlstrom, *A Religious History of the American People,* 436–39. Although Lizzie regularly urged Madison to pray, she attended Sabbath school infrequently and did not seem to adhere to a particular church denomination. This was common in Nininger, where there was no permanent church until later in the century. See Guelcher, *The History of Nininger,* 103–4.

53. The First Minnesota had fought in the first battle of Bull Run in July 1861 and the battle of Ball's Bluff in October 1861; the Second Minnesota had fought at Mill Springs in January 1862. See Carley, *Minnesota in the Civil War,* 197.

and as I gaze on those sober but dignified features which indicate a true heart and noble character I feel a guilt for being so much behind you in every thing that is good and christianlike. That pale, sad face is a silent, potent monitor to me that reproaches me for every evil thought or deed. O, if I could once more place my cheek, rough and tanned as it may be, against that face as I have done before, it would be a happy moment to me. When will that be? . . .

Tell Mr. Russell that Charley is getting along finely. He is a steady boy and one of the toughest soldiers in the Regiment. G. H. Knight is spleeny, playing sick most of the time. I am not so well as he yet I am serving in his place at this very moment. Eugene has been appointed Corporal for the time being and will in all probability be permanently appointed. He deserves it too. Do not forget those pictures. Mr. Donnelly sends me papers now and then. Remember me to him and to Mrs. Donnelly when you see them.[54] I am sorry to hear that your singing school proves a failure—very sorry. . . .

> Yours ever,
> Madison.

Nininger, Feb. 9th, 1862
Sunday Morning

Dearest Loved One

I recd yours of the 30. When I read it, it gave me a feeling of joy and sorrow. I was glad to hear from you but was sorry to hear of you being sick. I hope you have entirely recovered. Hope you will not get sick again while you are down there. Did not you wish you were with some one (when you were sick) beside rough soldiers? I bet you did. I have the blues. . . .

The elite of the town were all down to old Mr Truaxes to a ball night before last. There was over fifty couple there. I guess by the nodding of heads in school the next day they had a high time. Aunt Margaret is here.[55] Our folks keep such a talking that I cant think of anything to write.

---

54. George W. Knight was a twenty-six-year-old corporal in Company F. He deserted January 10, 1863. See Board of Commissioners, *Minnesota in the Civil and Indian Wars*, 188. Ignatius and Katherine Donnelly lived in Nininger City, although Ignatius spent much of his time in St. Paul as the lieutenant governor. See Ridge, *Ignatius Donnelly*.

55. Gersham Truax was seventy-three in 1860, and he lived with his son Daniel B. Truax in Nininger. Either of these men may have seemed old to twenty-one-year-old Lizzie. Aunt Margaret Hawkins, Lizzie's father's sister, lived in nearby Vermillion Township.

I think that brother of yours must be a pretty good yankee. I will get a picture taken for you and one for your sister if I can get a good one.[56] I have not been to Hastings since the day you left Minnesota. I am going befor long....

If nothing happens [to] you when the war is over you ought to go home and see your folks, if you should you ask that little sister to come to Minnesota and live with you.[57] I have just been looking at her picture for you and I think you look so much alike. You ought to live together. I do wish they would put an end to this war. What will you all do if you have to stay there through the warm weather? I wish you had never gone.... If you were here now I would try and sing with you. Uncle Peter was up here yesterday. He is perfectly crazy about singing school. We had the greatest days singing I ever had....[58]

You mind and take care of yourself. Dont expose yourself any more then you cant help. You speak of someone reading the Tribune that I disliked so much. If you were here you would not think I dispised so much. I read [the] Tribune and all other kind of war papers. I think I am as much interested in the war as you used to be when I used to make fun of you....

>   Yours ever
>   Lizzie

{along margin and top} . . . I gave Old Mrs. Stone her letter. LCS

Camp Dana, [Ky.], Feb. 13, 1862

My Dear Lizzie:

... I was glad to hear that you were all enjoying your time so pleasantly this winter, and especially so to hear that you are so well—this being the first time you have been well since the first winter I spent in Nininger. I presume it is because I am not near to plague the life out of you.

While you are quietly enjoying your time in going to school, etc., all here is excitement and flurry so rapidly does one startling event follow another. (Lieut

56. Madison's brother was Joseph Bowler. Madison also had three sisters, Clara, Georgette, and Sarah. See "Bowler-Caleff Family History and Genealogy," Bowler Papers.

57. Madison's father lived in Lee, Maine; his mother, Clara, lived with her sister's children while the couple was separated between 1850 and 1862. Thirteen-year-old Clara Augusta, named after her mother, was the youngest Bowler sister. See "Bowler-Caleff Family History and Genealogy," Bowler Papers.

58. Uncle Peter was Lizzie's father's brother; he married Elizabeth Truax in 1853. See John H. Case, "Another Reminiscence of Dakota County Pioneers—'The Caleff Family of Bluff Landing—Nininger,'" *Hastings Gazette*, 30 December 1921.

Tichenor has just poked his head into my tent and informed me that we get our pay to-morrow.) Good! Never did our cause look brighter than now, and never has there been a more cheering prospect of a speedy termination of the war.[59] The success of Gen Thomas at Somerset, of our forces at Forts Henry and Donaldson on the Tennessee and Cumberland and of Burnsides expedition at Roanoke Island, as well as the rush our Ky Army is making toward Bowlinggreen are indeed important events which point unmistakeably to an early conquest of the rebels in arms against the Union. But greater than all is the event of the stars and stripes being hailed with such joy by those who we expected were our enemies. I refer to the citizens of Tennessee and Alabama. Besides, our admirable policy toward them, which has been adopted by the administration is working wonders wherever the misguided people of the south get a chance to understand it.[60]

I may be mistaken, but I think the beginning of the end is at hand.

There are rapid movements of troops going on in this state at present which we are not at liberty to disclose at present. I have never seen any thing like it before. There is a continued scream of the whistle and rattling of cars as the heavily laden trains rush along night and day with their burthen of troops and all the requisites of war, besides the immense quantities of ties and rails which go forward to lay the track, torn up by Buckner, as our troops [go] forward for Bowlinggreen and Nashville.[61]

I was at the Depot several days ago and saw seventy six of the prisoners, taken at the battle of Somerset. They were on their way to Louisville. There was one Lieut. Col. and a Capt among them. They were clothed in Ky Jeans of various colors from faded blue to a reddish brown and very dirty and ragged at that. They had no overcoats, and their caps were about like such as one would expect to find among the poorer class of Nininger schoolboys. They were generally a sorry looking set of fellows, but I could see mingled hate and scorn in the countenances. They spoke in high terms of the Minn. 2nd. Most of those who saw them treated them kindly and civilly, some giving them stockings, mittens, &c., but now and then some ignoramus would reproach them with having been whipped and by calling them rebels and traitors. For my own part I could but regard them as misguided beings whom I pitied more than hated, and they in

59. For another positive reaction to news about the paymaster and hopeful prospects for military action and a positive outcome to the war by someone in the Third Minnesota, see letter, 22 February 1862, Hale Papers. See also 20 February 1862, Brookins Letters.

60. Ash, *When the Yankees Came*, 29.

61. See Andrews, "Narrative of the Third Regiment," 149.

turn seemed grateful to those who treated them with courtesy. Galusha was the most impudent to them of all I saw.[62]

Our Regt is getting ready to go somewhere, as certain unmistakable evidences indicate, unless the fates are against us. We have been provided with several four horse ambulances.

I had the pleasure of reading a letter which Eugene Stone received from Anna Reed yesterday. It was the richest thing I have seen. Among other things she wanted to know "where is Bowler and the rest of the boys"! She said that Lizzie wore a "suspicious looking ring" which was "surely a new one."

To-day is very bright, warm, and beautiful; and everybody looks cheerful and happy at the prospect of pay and the progress of our armies. There is a funeral this afternoon the deceased being of some other regiment, who was brought here yesterday with some sixty others of various regiments, this place being a General hospital for the sick of our whole K'y army. Poor fellow! he did not live long after his arrival here to lie upon a little straw spread upon the rough board bunks which have been built for the accommodation (!) of the sick. The quarters are not near so good as those you saw at the Fort. I believe if I were a girl I should offer my services to nurse the sick soldiers of our army. It is a pitiful sight to see a poor helpless soldier away from home and friends, sick and alone, with no eye to pity or hand to save.[63]

We have been at skirmish drill all the forenoon (I have got to go to Battalion drill—the bugle is calling).

(After drill) I have just returned from drill. We have had a good drill. It would have done you good to see old Co: "F" as it marched down the front of the line, up the rear, and wheeled into its place on the right center. The Col. was watching us and we never marched better, breaking into platoons and forming into company again as we marched. The Col gives us the name of being the best drilled Co. in the Regiment. Our Co. is encamped in Sibley Tents—five to a company, with one Sibley and one wall tent for the officers. Each tent contains about seventeen men and is put in charge of a Sergeant. I have command of the tent next to the Captains so we have to conduct ourselves pretty straight.

... It affords me much pleasure to hear that you were fortunate enough to secure a good singing teacher at last. I wish I could step in some night and hear your school sing. While I write the 2nd Minn. is at Lebanon Junction only four

62. For an overview of the battle of Somerset, see Board of Commissioners, *Minnesota in the Civil and Indian Wars*, 86. F. B. Galusha from St. Paul enlisted in Company B, Third Minnesota, but was discharged for disabilities.

63. William D. Hale also complained about conditions for soldiers in the hospitals and lack of adequate medical care. See letter, 4 March 1862, Hale Papers.

miles from here, they having come up from Somerset to go down on the Nashville Road for Bowlinggreen. They are heroes wherever they go.

You say you wish I would come home. I should like to be with you once more, so I could see how you look since you are fleshed up and have blooming cheeks. I think, however, that we shall not stay another winter in the army.

>Yours, etc.
>Madison...

{on the top back page} I think you must have gay times this winter. Anna writes that the Caleff girls—except Lizzie—are gallanted by the Hanna boys So you see I am posted; and if you do not walk straight I shall hear of it. Look out, Miss. Mad [64]

{side front page} I should think the girls would give the cold shoulder to those timid, unpatriotic, young men who cowardly stay at home when their country calls them, and go to singing school alone until we return, then we will make up for lost time. Mad

{across top, front page} Just as I close the fifes are playing "Scots who hae oer Wallace bled," with muffled drums, for a funeral march while the poor soldier of whom I spoke is being carried to the grave. A comrade remarks that that poor fellow has got his discharge, and there is no knowing how soon we may get ours. Very true.

>Nininger, Feb. 16, 1862
>Sunday evening

My Dear Madison

... It has snowed for the last two weeks about every other day. Is snowing now as hard as it can snow. We have never had so unpleasant a winter since we came to *Minn.* as we have had this winter. ...

I was weighed a few days since, weighed 126 lbs, ten pounds more then when I was weighed before.

Our singing school is ended. Had ten lessons in all. We are going to continue our meetings once a week. Isaiah Mudgett is our corrister. I *wish you* were here to go. Mrs Rice (Miss Rice's mother) is to be head lady singer. She understands music well, has a splendid voice.

---

64. In 1860 there were four Hanna boys in Nininger: William, Walter, Wilson, and Jerome.

Some of the boys saw two soldiers the other day in Hastings from the 2nd Minn Reg. They had several things they took from the rebels at the time of the battle.

... School is to last but two weeks longer. I am sorry for we are having a very good school. I don't know what we shall do then. It will be so lonely. I was reading a piece in the *Tribune* saying they anticipated the termination of this war by May. I hope it is so. It seems to me if this war was ended and you was once more back to Minnesota I should be happy....

Aunt Sarah is well and getting along in the same old way. Am is going to school. Pa is well. Ma is better than when I last wrote but not well. The lump on Kate's neck remains the same....

... I cant get my ideas together enough to write a letter. My mind is here and there and you know where. Give my love to Eugene. Tell him his folks are all well.

    Lizzie S. Caleff...

Camp Lester, Shepherdville, Feb. 21, 1862[65]

My Dearest Lizzie:

... I should have sent you ten dollars by Express, but owing to the uncertainty of sending by mail I shall send but five dollars this time, reserving the rest until I learn whether this arrives in safety. I do not feel in quite so good trim for writing as I did at Belmont as it is so rainy muddy and gloomy. Besides, I have nothing but steel pens to write with. The pen which I had when I left Minn. I broke at Camp Jenkins, borrowed one of a comrade, lost it and paid $3.25 for it, then bought another in Louisville for $2.25, broke it one day last week, and Sergt Morgan broke the holder for me, which left me without a pen altogether.[66] Yesterday I borrowed Eugene's Gold Pen to write to you with, lost that too last night, and paid him $3.00 for it this morning. Besides these little lapses I have had shirts, stockings, and other articles, stolen from me *ad infinitum*.

Misfortunes never come singly. Last Monday while in command of the Guard I lent my gun to one of the Guard who returned it to me with a load in it in the morning. After [I was] relieved I went to the Quarter[master. After] breakfast [we had] drill for some [time] so I had no time to discharge my gun during the proper hours (We are not allowed to shoot after 11 o'clock A.M.) So in the afternoon I went to battalion drill with a loaded gun. During the drill and while the regiment

65. This letter had many holes in it.
66. David L. Morgan gave his residence as Ilioce, New York. In Minnesota he lived in Rosemount. He was twenty-three years old in September 1861 when he mustered into the Third Minnesota, Company F, as first sergeant.

was drawn up in line just in front and facing the tents of Co. F., we were ordered to go through the motions of loading, aiming, and firing. I was very dull and sleepy, and forgot all about my gun being loaded. After aiming in the different directions, and while at the left oblique aim my gun being pointed just to the left of Col. Lester who was a few rods in front, the order *fire!* was given, and I pulled with the rest, not thinking of the load in my gun. The cap burst, but the powder was wet and did not burn. Col. Lester hearing the cap burst, inquired with perfect coolness, who had a loaded gun on battalion drill. I stepped forward and told him that I had at the same time explaining to him. "Such work as this will not do;" "we cannot afford to die here in this way," said he in a pleasant tone. Had any other man been in place of Col Lester, so grave an [error would have been] punish[ed].

. . . We came to this place, seven miles from Belmont, last Wednesday through one of the most drenching rains I ever saw. Arriving here we pitched our tents, and wet and hungry went to work to make things comfortable for the night. I levied upon a pile of brick and a few joints of stove pipe with which my squad built a real comfortable stove in our tent. We have been in the service just long enough to know how [to] take advantage of circumstances in camping and marching. Had we not been late we should have rode up as usual on the cars. Our Reg't has been paid off and many of them make dirty beasts of themselves with liquor and other wise. . . .[67]

This little trifle of money which I send you is *intended for you to use for your-self.* . . . There is a rumor [here] that orders have arrived at Belmont for our Reg't to march to Tennessee. *Hope so.* Capt. Rice has just come up here and informs us that the report is true. Good!

Write to [me] immediately if you received this so that I may not remain in uncertainty. Give my love to all. I am glad that you take so much interest in the war and that you read the papers so assiduously.

> Yours ever.
> Madison.

> Nininger Minn. March 2nd, 1862
> Sunday afternoon

My Dearest Madison:

I have just returned from meeting. Am now at Aunt Sarah's, where I listened to an excelent sermon preached by a gentleman from Prescott. His text was "I know

67. The companies of the Third Minnesota rotated guard duty at the railroad bridges and drill at the headquarters in Belmont. Madison's story about the gun going off during drill was while in Belmont. Two days later his company left for Camp Lester near Shepherdsville's railroad bridge. See Andrews, "Narrative of the Third Regiment," 149.

that my Redeemer liveth." I wish you could have been there and heard it. Or have you since you became a soldier lost your taste for going to meeting and things pertaining thereto and given yourself wholly up to serve your country? Have you forgoten your old resolution? *I hope not.* Remember now is the time above all others when dangers soround you on every side that you should remember your Redeemer liveth. Dont think that I have set down to lecture you for I have not intened[ed] it for a lecture. If you knew how often I think of your being there sorounded by wickedness on every side.

I hope it will not be long before you are released from your present duty, and I shall once more have the priviledge of enjoying that long sighed for company of him that is absent. How shall it be if before that day arrives my hopes are blasted? I dare not think of it. I received two letters from you last evening one containing a five dollar note, for which accept my sincere thanks. Whatever money you send I will keep for you until your return. I shall not use any of it for I do not need it. I expected to have got those pictures before this but have not. Will get them as soon as I can. . . .

Those verses you sent me are very pretty. I think you are getting very tasty fixing up your clothes and blacking up your shoes. I expect by the time you get back to Minn you will be a real dandy. You must mind and not flourish that gun about so much or I shall begin to think you either make a practice of setting up with some of the gals down there or taking you[r] bitters pretty freely. . . . You seem to be so anxious to be in a battle. I hope you never will. It is snowing as hard as it can snow, has been snow all night and all day. Am has got well of the measles. Aunt Sarah & him send their love to you. Do come home.

> I remain your ever loving
> Lizzie

P.S. Our school ends Tuesday. . . . I shall be glad when summer comes so we can have some ink that has not been frozen.

> March 9th, 1862
> Sunday evening

My Dearest Madison:

I wrote to you last Sabbath did not get a chance to mail my letter until Wednesday so I suppose you have not rec'd it yet. I rec'd two letters this evening before from you which I mentioned in my last letter, the last I have heard from any member of the 3rd regiment I hope to get a letter from you when Papa comes from sunday school. It is raining quite hard to-day, the first rain we have had this winter. The going is perfectly horrible. The slush is mostly three feet deep. . . .

I was at Hastings this week and had those pictures taken. They are not good. I tried to get a good [one] but could not. I sat five times. The daguerrean is a young Lady from Louisville K.Y. She generally takes nice pictures but when I went she had just been mixing new chemicals. She could not get them to work well.

Kate is quite sick. She was down to the Dr again. She has the neuralgia very badly and her neck is very painful. I am afraid her neck will turn to something very bad yet but am in hopes when the weather gets pleasant she will get better. . . .

I received a draft . . . of 31 dollars and 40 cents. I got Pa to take it to Hastings to the bank. They would give gold for it at two per cent on dollar for dollar, giving one third in gold, the other two third in treasury notes, saying the treasury notes are just as good as gold. I thought if they were as good as the gold it was no use paying two per cent so I got two thirds in treasury notes, the other third in gold, which will be safe until you return.[68] I hope that will not be many months. You have no idea how lonely it is, Kate being sick all the time and everything so dreary and dull. O! if ever it does come spring again I shall be so glad. I never was so tired of winter. It has stormed about every other day for the last month. . . .

O! Do, do come home, you dont know how impatient I am getting to have you come. Give my respects to Eugene and all others who wish to hear from me. . . . Excuse this poor apology for a letter for I do not feel in a writing mind to day.

> Yours ever Lizzie

(Monday morning)

. . . Was glad to hear of you still enjoying good health. You seem to be anxious to leave the place where you now are and move forward where you will be more likely to be in a battle. I should think you would rather stay where you are. You cant look on a battle field with the same feeling of horror that I do or you wouldnt want to be a partaker in it.

> Good morning
> LSC

{front page on the top} It has cleared off to be a beautiful day after the rain storm. The chickens are singing and every thing seems to say spring has come. . . . I dont believe you can read this it is so mixed up.

68. The transaction Lizzie describes was common because there was not a fixed national currency until greenbacks were issued later in the war. Depending upon the bank a draft came from, its amount could be discounted in value. See Paludan, *"A People's Contest,"* 222–26.

In camp, near Louisville, Ky, March 13, 1862

[To Lizzie:]

... I am sorry to hear that you have been unwell; and I believe that you have been sicker than you represent. You must always let me know the *whole* truth. ... You seem to be impatient for the war to close. I think the prospect is good for a speedy termination. I feel as great a desire to be with you again as you do with me, and hope the day is not far distant when we shall meet again.

You ask whether I have "forgotten my old resolution." No, I have not, though I ought to be ashamed that I do not make greater efforts to accomplish it. I am far, very far, from being what I ought to be. The opportunities here are very limited for moral cultivation. Our chaplain is *Methodist all over,* and knows or cares but little about anybody else.[69]

I sent that money for *you to use for yourself,* and if you do not do it I guess I will keep it here and spend it for some useless thing or other, so you had better do as I disired you to.

... As to my sitting up late at night you are partly right and partly wrong. I have to sit up all night now and then, but not with the "gals." I do not have to go on duty quite so often as I used to.

I have to take Nick O'Brien and another man tomorrow morning and go to Louisville to hunt up a deserter.[70]

Our Regt. struck tents last Monday and marched toward Louisville through Shepherdsville one mile—making nine miles in three hours, the mud being almost knee deep. Pretty good marching. We pitched our tents and stayed all night. In the evening Corporal Jameson[71] and myself took a stroll from camp and brought up before a beautiful country farm house, knocked at the door, when "come in" was sounded by some voice who seemed to speak as though some member of that family was at the door, fooling. Pretty soon, when the [inhabitants] found that we did not go in, they began to rush and hustle about, each whispering to the other to "go to the door" and presently the door opened and we were invited in, when we asked for milk and eggs. A saucy looking wench belched out in double intensified Sarah Hickman style that "ye'll get no yegs here, but

69. "The Northern Methodist church alone provid[ed] nearly five hundred chaplains" to the Union army (Ahlstrom, *A Religious History of the American People,* 675). For Methodist theology, see ibid., 438–39.

70. Twenty-five-year-old Nicholas O'Brien, a Nininger resident, enlisted in Company F.

71. For another description of the march and the camp near Louisville, see letter, 16 March 1862, Hale Papers. George L. Jameson was, like Madison, a twenty-seven-year-old corporal in Company F.

wee's got heaps so milk." Pretty soon the lady of the house succeeded in hushing up Dinah and we took a seat by a comfortable fireplace. They filled three canteens with milk, gave us a dozen (all they had) of eggs, and made us stay until they baked about a half a bushel of very nice biscuit, for all of which they would not take a cent of pay. The young lady said that her mother had a son in the Union Army, and she did by us as she hoped others might do to him. They were nice, kind, well educated folks. They informed us that they passed one summer in Wisconsin.[72]

The next morning we took up our March, and after marching eighteen miles halted where we now are—within five miles of Louisville. Next Sunday we start for Nashville via Louisville, stopping perhaps a few days at West Point, on the Ohio, just below Louisville.

The boys are all in the finest spirits, and hope to be in a fight soon. Our Regt is the praise of all. Everybody speaks in the highest terms of us. It would do you good to see us drill or at dress parade. The Col. is highly pleased with his Regt. Strickland, the orderly Sergt of Co H, was reduced to the ranks to-day. Perry D. Martin, orderly of Co. G. was reduced some time ago. Both cases were for drunkenness. I acted as orderly in the absence of our orderly at Battalion drill to-day.[73]

I intended to send a Rebel canteen to Albert Truax by Roger Cressey, but his application for a discharge was refused by the Surgeon General, so I cannot do so at present.[74] I sent you my "picture" over a week ago. Did you get it? You can send those pictures to Louisville, and they will be forwarded to us wherever we are. All communications should be sent to Louisville until otherwise directed. The Bugle sounds for Roll Call, so I must go. . . .

   Yours ever
   Madison

72. For early interactions between Union soldiers and Southern civilians, see Ash, *When the Yankees Came*, 29–30.

73. Being reduced to the ranks was a form of discipline used for low-ranking officers that stripped them of their noncommissioned officer rank. For problems of discipline and officers, see Shannon, *The Organization and Administration of the Union Army*, 174–76, 186–89.

74. Roger Cressey was discharged on March 29, 1862, for disability. Madison wrote the following letter to Albert Truax on March 16, 1862: "I have a canteen which Lieut Tichenor picked up just beyond the battlefield at Munfordsville a day or two after the skirmish took place. I intended to send it to you by Roger W. Cressey who expected to receive his discharge and go home to Minnesota; but the Surgeon General refused his application for discharge, and of course you will have to wait until another opportunity occurs before you will be able to rejoice in the possession of that relic of rebeldom. It is the only relic I have now, and I will send it to you as soon as I get a chance to do so. I had an opportunity to look about Louisville day before yesterday, having been sent into town

Nininger Minn March 16, 1862
Sunday evening

My Dear Madison

I now seat myself to answer your good letter which I received a few days since and to thank you for that good picture which you sent. When I gaze upon it, it brings back those familiar features, which I am waiting so patiently to gaze upon in reality. You don't know how much I wish to see you.

(Monday evening)

... For the last half hour I have been sitting by the window looking out upon one of the most beautiful evenings that ever cast its shadows o'er Minn. fair plains. My thoughts have been wondering back to the days that have long since sank into the vast, ages of eternity that have gone, gone never to return. It casts a feeling of joy and sorrow over me when I think over the few last years of my life. As far as my intercourse with you has been it has been mingled with unspeakable joy and sorrow. It was joy to know there was one whom I could trust and confide in, one whom I knew would not betray that is as far as any knowledge goes, and I believe even will he find sorrow to know that that one for whom I have found so great an atachment should be placed as it were in the very face of death. Mr Bowler don't think that this is the feeling of a few moments or an hour, tis the feeling of weeks and months.

We are having beautiful weather now. I think the ice will soon be out of the river. I shall be so glad when the boats begin to run.

I saw Anna while at singing school a few evenings ago. She asked me to show her your picture, she had heard some way that I had [it]. I happened to have it in my pocket [and] of course, showed it to her. She said she was going to keep it to remember you by. She said she wanted you to write to her. She said, 'I do wish Mr Bowler would write to me.' I told her she ought to write to you first. She wouldn't do that but wanted me to tell you to write, but she knew I would not for I wouldn't dare to. I dont know what she ment by that. She said she would write

---

in charge of a squad of men to arrest a deserter from Co. 'F.' It was Knowles who used to work for Danl W. Truax. I found him in the Military Prison, he having been picked up by the Provost Guard, and confined in the same building with a hundred and twenty rebel prisoners, some of whom were taken at Mill Spring, and others at Fort Donelson. Louisville is a very dull place at present, though it contains a large population. Military bustle is the only item to be witnessed there at present, though whisky and bad women are about as plenty as soldiers" (copied from original by E. B. B.—probably Edna Beatrice Bowler, Madison's daughter—in 1930, box 1, Bowler Papers).

you a letter as long as her arm and tell you all the news. I guess I would write to her, then it would be [a] *triumph*....

Our folks are all well accepting Kate. I think the swelling on her neck is not quite as large as it was. Her health has been very poor all winter. I am very well acepting a large boil on my shoulder which causes me a great deal of pain, tis the tenth one I have had on my neck and shoulders this winter.... I will send the picture I had taken for your sister in this letter. Will keep the one I had taken for you until I can get a better one, which will be before long. I will send you a braid of hair with this.

... Dont mention a word that I have written and distroy all the letters I send you so no one shall see them. I saw a letter that Gus rec'd from you a short time a go.[75]

Lizzie S. Caleff

75. This was probably twenty-one-year-old James Augustus Case, who lived in Nininger City in 1860.

2

I Wish You Could Be Here To-day with Me

MARCH 1862 TO AUGUST 1862

Madison joined the Union army assuming he would fight in battles that would ultimately lead to a Union victory. By the spring and summer of 1862, however, he became discouraged that inaction, poor leadership, and "this baby way of fighting" would deprive him of contributing significantly to the Union cause through battle. In the meantime Madison, the Third Minnesota, and the rest of the Twenty-third Brigade resumed their task of guarding railroads and towns, this time near Murfreesboro, Tennessee, an assignment that brought them little more than skirmishing with Confederate cavalry. Their presence was part of a plan by General Halleck to maintain railroads and effectively occupy captured Confederate territory while General Buell moved slowly toward Chattanooga, Tennessee, with the Army of the Ohio, via Stevenson, Alabama.

Although Madison was eager for battle and assuredly disappointed by his assignment, his guard duties did provide him leadership opportunities and new experiences. He took the lead in organizing his men on picket guard to respond to the Confederate cavalry advances. He also dealt with escaped slaves who conveyed military information to the Union army—as well as various officers' reactions to these informants—and with slave owners seeking escaped slaves. Madison also continued to update Lizzie about the health and performance of Dakota County soldiers and assure her that he had plenty to eat because of the abundant wild berries and well-stocked Confederate farms.

Lizzie's two main concerns during this period were her sister Kate's declining health and various rumors about the fate of the Third Minnesota. In late April she heard that the Third Minnesota had been taken prisoner, which at that time was only a rumor. In mid-July she would have heard the same news, but we do not know her reaction to the truth because some of her letters are missing from April through August 1862. Instead, we have Madison's account of his first battle, his regiment's surrender, and his feelings about being a prisoner of war.

Early in the morning of July 13, 1862, Confederate cavalry commander Nathan Bedford Forrest attacked the Ninth Michigan on the eastern side of Murfreesboro.

By daybreak the Third Minnesota was in battle position, but they did not move against Forrest's cavalry. Around 8:00 A.M. a regiment from Georgia attempted a charge against the Third Minnesota, and there was brief fighting, which Madison describes. The Confederate infantry was repulsed, and the soldiers of the Third Minnesota felt sure that they had won a victory. But Forrest concentrated his cavalry forces against the Third Minnesota's camp, one-half mile behind the regiment, and after intense fighting against the cook, wagon drivers, and convalescing soldiers, the Confederates took the camp. By afternoon Colonel Lester, the temporary commanding officer of the Third Minnesota, summoned his officers to discuss surrendering to the Confederates. Two votes were taken: In the first vote a majority of officers voted against surrender. The second vote, taken after some officers who had voted against surrender returned to their companies, reversed the earlier decision, however, and at 3:30 P.M. Colonel Lester surrendered the stunned soldiers of the Third Minnesota. At McMinnville the noncommissioned officers and privates were paroled and eventually transferred to Benton Barracks, Missouri, near St. Louis.[1] As he waited to be released, Madison wrote letters filled with frustration and disappointment, describing the high rate of desertion in his regiment and calling the officers who voted to surrender cowards, even intimating that some were drunk. Bitter and lonely, Madison waited for his next assignment, hoping that it would bring him home to Minnesota and, more important, to Lizzie.

*   *   *

Steamer Denmark, March 20, 1862

My Dear Lizzie:

Last Thursday, the date of my last letter to you, I was at camp near Louisville, expecting to be on my way to Nashville the following Sunday, but the Regt had to wait for transportation from day to day, expecting to start each moment. Yesterday, however, a messenger came into camp at full speed with despatches to Col. Lester ordering the Minn. 3d to start immediately for Lousville, where we immediately went on board Boats which were waiting for us. The right wing, comprising Co's B, H, F, K, and E, are on the Denmark (the same old Denmark which runs to St Paul in the summer season.) and the left wing Co's A, G, I, C, and

1. For information on the Third Minnesota at Murfreesboro, see Andrews, "Narrative of the Third Regiment," 151–58; Fitzharris, "'Our Disgraceful Surrender'"; Trenerry, "Lester's Surrender at Murfreesboro"; and William D. Hale, "A Statement of Facts Concerning the Surrender of the Third Regiment of Minnesota Volunteers at Murfreesboro, Tenn., July 13, 1862," Hale Papers.

D, on the Undine. It took the whole Regt. from 2½ till 8 P.M. to get all our traps on board; so you can imagine what a load we have.[2]

I am in the cabin, sitting by one of the tables, while some 15 or 20 others are doing likewise writing to their friends. We have a serenade band, which is also in the cabin, playing. They have five "fiddles," two cliaronets, and one Guitar, all of which were purchased by subscription among the different companies.

(Dave Morgan has just come along and made a pencil mark on my sheet, which he says, stands for Maine). All these little incidents together with the motion of the Boat, make this rather a poor place for writing letters. The mail leaves the Boat at Evansville about fifteen minutes ahead, so I shall have to hurry.

We supposed when we started that we were going to Nashville, but it is now doubtful whether we go to Nashville or down the Mississippi to Island No. 10. If we go to Island No. 10 we shall have to participate in the fight going on at that place. The report that it [was] already taken proves untrue.[3] We may possibly never be in an action, but it is not very probable. On the other hand we may be in an action in less than forty eight hours.

These thoughts create solemn feelings. With us all is at present gayiety and happiness as we glide along the beautiful Ohio, writing to friends, &c.; but who can tell but that this may be the last time that many of us will ever write? Who can tell how soon the scene will be changed?

The Jacob Strader, Grey Eagle, and three other Boats are with us, all loaded with soldiers—the other Regts of our Brigade. We have been brigaded anew. We now belong to the 23d Brigade, composed of the 9th Mich., 3d Minn., 8th and 23d Ky. It is commanded by Col. W. W. Duffield of the 9th Mich. The country along the Ohio is truly magnificent. I saw an orchard this morning of over 100 acres. There are none of those disagreeable bluffs that you see in Minnesota. Beautiful fields of sp[r]outing grain skirt the banks, and the weather is warm as summer. Co. F slept on deck last night without any inconvenience from cold.

---

2. William D. Hale explained the ride on the steamer *Denmark:* "The boats were badly crowded carrying as they did a very large amount of rations, forage, ammunition & ordnance stores.... The passage down the Ohio was without especial incident. The Weather was unpleasant windy and some of the time raining and rough nights were very dark compelling the boat to lay till morning" (letter, 26 March 1862, Hale Papers).

3. George Brookins of Company I wrote in two letters on March 20 and March 23 about leaving Louisville for "I suppose Nashville"; see Brookins Letters. According to the "Narrative of the Third Regiment," "The general forward movement consequent took our regiment to Nashville, where, March 24, 1862, it went into camp ... two miles out of the city, near the Murfreesboro pike" (Andrews, "Narrative of the Third Regiment," 180). Island No. 10's garrison and guns were captured on April 7, 1862.

Last Sunday night about twenty of us got together and passed the evening singing old, familiar tunes. Oh, you cannot imagine how it made my heart swell and the tears rush to my eyes as I thought of other times that [I had] heard those same tunes, of the times when I used to listen for your voice as it arose among others at the old hall in Nininger. Oh, what wouldn't I give to be there again as in times gone by, even but a few hours? I have not received any letter from you since writing my last to you. . . .

You ought to have seen our Regt march through Louisville yesterday. I felt proud that I belonged to the Minn 3d. We made a far different appearance led by Col. Lester after three months severe drill, than we did led by Lieut Col Smith three months ago. Shouts of praise went up from every beholder. . . .[4]

I was all over Louisville last night, and had a good time. Found a friend who took us to the Commercial House where he boards, and gave me a good supper. . . . Please excuse this ill written letter, and I will try to do better next time.

> Ever your affectionate
> Madison.

> Camp Minnesota, near Nashville, Tennessee
> March 26, 1862

My Dear Lizzie:

Two weeks ago to-day I wrote to you from camp near Louisville, since which time I have not heard a word from you. I wrote to you again one week ago to-day while "floating down the Ohio" on my way to *Dixie*. We arrived at Nashville last Sunday, where we remained on the boats until Monday morning when we marched to this place, two miles from the Levee, though hardly out of the city limits. Coming up the Cumberland River we passed Fort Donelson and other fortifications at Smithland and Clarksville, and Fort Zollicoffer, three miles below this city. These sights were quite interesting to me, though I did not have the privilege of a nearer view than could be obtained from the boats.[5]

The left wing of our Regt., on board the Undine, landed at the Fort and buried young Raymond, of Co. A, who died suddenly while coming up the River.

---

4. For the appearance and discipline of the Third Minnesota at this point, see Andrews, "Narrative of the Third Regiment," 150.

5. George Brookins also comments on seeing Fort Donelson and other former Confederate positions on the way to Nashville; see letter, 23 March 1862, Brookins Letters. See also letter, 26 March 1862, Hale Papers. Fort Donelson had fallen into Union hands the month before.

They had the privilege of examining the scene of the dreadful conflict which raged there for four days and nights. . . . [6]

It is very warm here to-day, and, was it not for the strong breeze which comes up from the South, it would be suffocating. The trees are leaving out beautifully, the grass and grain is as green as can be, and orchards of every species of fruit raised in this climate, are in full bloom. Many kinds of flowers, too, are in bloom.

Secession rule has ruined almost everything here. *Everything,* almost, has been consumed or destroyed by the ruthless villains of the rebel army. Such has been the terror raised by exaggerated stories about the Union Armies, that many have left their beautiful houses and followed the Southern Army. Beautiful residences, once the houses of happy families, are now either deserted or occupied by the poorer people who could not or would not go away. Their rich fields and lands lie idle for want of cultivation, and since only as commons for cattle and hogs, or for camping grounds for the Union Armies. The people are as vividly *secesh* as the most ardent could desire. They avoid, as far as possible, all communication with Union men. There are few, *very few,* Union men. Some are very saucy and impudent, as can be seen by the scornful looks of the men and the disdainful faces and pouting lips of some of the ladies even; but the greater portion are sullen and obstinate.[7] The only real Union ladies I have heard of are the seven daughters of Gen. Zollicoffer, who are very kind and attentive to the wants of the sick soldiers in the Hospitals at Nashville. They took pains to see the 9th Ohio and 2nd Minn.— the Regts. which conquered their fathers army and laid him low in death—while at dress parade during their stay here.

There are innumerable regiments here now. Our Brigade is encamped here. Col. Duffield, our Brigade commander gives us the praise of being the best drilled regiment he has ever seen. When at dress parade we draw the crowd from all other regiments, all of whom give the Minn. 3d great praise. We have better dress than any other.

---

6. William D. Hale also commented on this burial: "We are sorry enough that we could not land [at Fort Donelson]. The 'Undine' now several hours behind, did so, to perform the sad duty of burying a man who had died on the trip suddenly. They stayed two hours and had a fine opportunity of moving about, picking up mementos &c &c" (letter, 26 March 1862, Hale Papers). S. J. Raymond of Company F "died en route from Louisville to Nashville March 31, 1862," according to the muster rolls, although both Madison and Hale date his death earlier (John H. Case Scrapbook, Case Papers).

7. William D. Hale also noted deserted homes and that "Sesesh is open and universal—not a waving handkerchief or smile or adieu greeted us—but plenty of frowns and angry countenances" (letter, 26 March 1862, Hale Papers).

There are not less than thirty and perhaps forty thousand soldiers encamped within the space of three miles square here. We now have a Battery of Artillery and three companies of cavalry in our Brigade, which has been assigned to Gen. Mitchell's division. It is quite probable that we shall move within four days, though we may stay longer. The 2nd Regt. is far away from here—probably a part of one of the armies which will attack Memphis.[8]

I wish you could be here to-day with me to see what a pretty place we have here. I can see the State-house from my tent. It is one of the finest buildings in the United states, and no doubt you have often seen it praised and described in print. I have....

> Truly, yours ever.
> Madison.

Camp Minnesota, Nashville, Tenn., April 4, 1862

My Dear Lizzie:

... [I] received your picture and the braid of hair, both of which were gladly received. Your picture looks quite natural indeed, though it is a little dim. The braid is very nice....

You did just right in cashing that draft. We were paid off to-day up to the 1st of March, but for some reason, unknown to me, no attention was paid to the allotment and we received the full amount of each month's pay. I want you to use any money I send to you when you want it. If Mr. Caleff or any other member of your family are ever in need of money it is my desire that you let them have it if there is any more than you want. You have all been very kind to me, and the satisfaction of having the money when I return would be nothing compared to the pleasure it would give me to do anything to help any member of your family when help would do them any good.

You seem to be very lonely and quite tired of winter. I wish you could be here for a while—everything is *so lovely.* I have never seen anything to equal the beauty of the country here. The beautiful peach orchards with their bright red blossoms contrasting with the snowy blossoms of plum and cherry trees which are intermingled among the peach orchards and the fresh green carpet of grass beneath, and green majestic woods for a background, form a lovely picture. The weather

---

8. The Second Minnesota was in Nashville in early March. By the end of March, however, they faced crossing the flooded Duck River near Columbia, Tennessee, trying to get to Savannah near the Tennessee River. See Board of Commissioners, *Minnesota in the Civil and Indian Wars,* 86–87.

is very warm—sometimes too warm—and pleasant, being almost free from clouds and rain.

The excitements of the Camp and the new scenes which recur to us while moving in a strange country tend to divert ones mind from loneliness, yet there are times—and frequent too—when I am lonely. At such times my mind becomes wholly absorbed in thoughts of old times and the loved ones behind. It was but the other day when I got to thinking over the time of our first acquaintance and the events which have followed. I have no reason to regret my action then. It is a little singular that at the same time I was indulging those thoughts I should receive your letter referring to the same subject.

Lizzie, I am sorry you are so lonely without me, and wish I could be with you once more; but cannot, of course. I do not wish, however, to leave the army while I am of any service to the country in such a fearful struggle as the present. I am more than ever impressed with a sense of the duty which every able bodied young man owes to his country at this *critical* period. You seem to wonder that I should wish to be in a battle. I do not wish to be in a battle just for the sake of killing anybody, and would rather, to-day, that no necessity ever had, or ever would, exist for a battle to be fought; but so long as the actual necessity does exist and in view of the facts that we enlisted to conquer the enemies of the Union, and that we have a regiment able to do its duty on the field, I feel as though this is where we ought to be, even though it is much easier and less dangerous for us to stay where we are.

Two regiments and a battery of our brigade have left here and gone to hold Gen Negley's position while he goes forward with his division. One—the 23 Ky— is engaged in the delectable business of guarding railroads. The 3d Minn. is body-guard to Gen. Dumont who is in command at Nashville during the absence of Gen. Buell, who started last Sunday morning with Mitchells, McCook, Nelson, and Thomas' divisions on an expedition against Corinth, Mississippi, where the rebels are concentrating their forces.[9]

There is no doubt but that a fierce and bloody struggle will ensue near there, perhaps before this reaches you. One Co. at a time from our Regt. goes to Nashville every day to guard Gen Dumont's Head Quarters. Co. F went down last Monday and returned Tuesday. We were quartered in an Episcopal Church, and had to

9. General Don Carlos Buell had joined General Grant near Pittsburg Landing, Tennessee, planning to capture Corinth, Mississippi. Instead, Grant's and, later, Buell's forces fought at the battle of Shiloh on April 6 and 7, 1862. George Brookins wrote in his April 3, 1862, letter that his lieutenant mentioned that General Buell "ordered the very best Regt. to be left at N[ashville] to Guard." For information on the Union generals Madison listed, see Warner, *Generals in Blue*, 132, 327, 296, 343, 501, respectively.

send sixteen men under charge of a Sergt. every two hours, to stand guard about the Gen's Head Quarters. Everybody is pleased with the looks and conduct of our Regt. Gov. Gen. Andy Johnson says, so the Adjutant told me to-day,—that ours is the best regiment he has seen, and you must recollect he has seen the Potomac regiments, he having been U.S. Senator.[10]

While we were in Nashville I visited the residence and tomb of President Polk and the State house.[11] Unless "something turns up" we shall have to go home without any hard won laurels. Our position is easy and honorable at present, but who can say how soon we may be called upon to guard Rail-roads again. . . .

Co. A was in Nashville last night, and I stayed with Hunt who was left behind, being sick. Joe Murtz, of Afton, and Frank Redland of Minneapolis came in the evening with Guitar and Violin and played "Bonnie Eloise" and other tunes which set Hunt and me to thinking over old times which we chatted about [sweethearts] until late in the night. . . . If there is anything truly good it is woman when blessed with a womanly disposition. It is that which I prize so much in you. You have one of the best dispositions I ever yet discovered. I ought never to be unhappy so long as I can claim so large and kind a heart as beats in your bosom. My only regret is that I am not able to requite all the kind actions which flow from it. . . .

I will send you some peach blossoms in this letter. I gathered them last Sunday, while walking with Hunt. Many of the brigades have left here for "way down in dixie." Hereafter you can direct your letters to Nashville, Tenn. . . .

> Yours affectionately.
> Madison.

Camp Minnesota, Nashville, Tenn., Apr. 10, 1862

Dear Lizzie:

. . . I sent you a Nashville paper with some cotton in it. You must not take offense, as I do not mean to insinuate that you have any need to use cotton as the girls sometimes do.[12] Before going any farther you must make up your mind to put up with a desultory letter this time, though I do not know as any of my scribbling is entitled to any better name. What hinders me from writing much to-night, is

10. For Andrew Johnson reviewing the regiment, see also Andrews, "Narrative of the Third Regiment," 150.

11. On April 17, George Brookins also mentioned visiting the statehouse and former president Polk's residence.

12. Madison's insinuation here is not clear. He might have meant that women used cotton to accentuate their figures.

this. "Deakin" has got sole possession of an accordeon, or Flatina, as he calls it, which has drawn a crowd to my tent to hear him and Eugene play; and between the playing and jabbering I am forced to write without thinking what I am writing about. I have a box of pilot-bread for a writing stand and mother earth cushions ... for a seat.

I presume that you being to-day or will by to-morrow to hear the news of the awful battle which has just been fought at Pittsburg, near Corinth. My first intimation of how it resulted was received at Gen. Buell's Head Quarters yesterday morning, happening to be there when the Gen. telegraphed the result to his adjutant Capt. Greene. It has been a terrible battle[,] one which we have been expecting everyday for the past week. The advance of our brigade is at Murfreesboro, under Col. Duffield. Once during the battle when everything seemed to be lost to us, Col. Duffield became uneasy, fearing an attack from a body of rebel troops who were reported to be near Murfreesboro in the rear of our main army, and sent here to Gen. Dumont, requesting him to send the 3d Minn. to reenforce him. We were ordered to hold ourselves in readiness to march at a moments warning should the necessity become urgent. As it was we should have been sent forward immediately but for the necessity of our presence here—the 51st Ohio being the only regiment besides ours to keep the numerous *secesh* of this vicinity from rising—all the other regiments having gone forward sometime prior to the battle. Our sick were all hurried of[f] to Nashville and everything got in readiness to move on short notice; meantime we all stood waiting with intense anxiety, expecting every moment to get the desired order to march, but the tide taking a favorable turn doomed us to stay here for a while at least.

What effect this great victory will have upon the rebellion cannot be accurately foretold; but it appears that it must be its death. How, since appearances indicate that the South staked their all upon that one battle—every available man and every resource being concentrated there under their best Generals, one of whom is killed and the other wounded.[13] The flower of their army is cut to pieces, innumerable resources taken from them, and boasted superiority upon the

13. Madison refers to the Union victory at Pittsburg Landing (Shiloh). Confederate general Albert Sidney Johnston died during the battle. It's unclear who the wounded general is that Madison mentions; the other Confederate generals at Shiloh were Hardee, Polk, Bragg, Breckinridge, and Beauregard. Lucius Polk was wounded in the face but was a colonel. General Leonidas Polk was also at Shiloh and reported wounded. See Warner, *Generals in Gray,* 243-44. Madison's opinion about the win at Shiloh virtually ending the Confederacy was common early in the war, although James McPherson points out that Shiloh disabused some soldiers—at least those who fought in the battle—of their conviction that it would be a short war.

battlefield shown to be a humbug. According to my ideas the great contest is decided, the ordeal has passed, and our country stands to-day among the proudest and strongest of the earth. We shall soon be home again, when we will unite our voices in singing *"Home Again"* in reality.

...I should [have] thought you would have gone to hear Mrs. Swishelm lecture.[14] I have heard her lecture and can join with your Uncle Peter in praising her....

While in Nashville day before yesterday [?] another [?] among the "sights" among which I [saw was the] tomb of James K. Polk. Mrs. Polk happened to be in [her gar]den, superintending the setting out of some shrubs and flowers. She bowed and bid me good morning (Here it is all morning before noon, and evening afternoon) as I stepped over the stile, and conversed quite freely with me. She is a tall, sharp-featured, blackeyed woman, and not what one would naturally term good-looking. She is, I believe, a sister of Gen. Pillow.[15] I intended to pick some flowers from the tomb, but, as she was present, I only picked some leaves from the boxwood and rose bush. I send them to you in this letter. I wish you could be here and see the State Library and curiosities in the Capitol. It contains everything from Egyptian mummies down to Cannon balls from the battleground of New Orleans.

I have had another miniature taken, which I shall send to you soon. Cousin Helen wants my picture taken with full uniform, so I shall have to get one more taken.

When we got ready to return from town yesterday Charley Russell, Willis Countryman, and six or seven others were missing, and I was sent with a guard after them. Where do you suppose I found them? It was in a —— house on smoky-row noted for such houses which abound plentifully in this city. They were surrounded by some dozen hags, with whom they were quarreling about change in return for a treasury note which one had paid her. They wanted me to make the hags give up the money, but I kept them at a safe distance from me while I marched the boys off up street to quarters. This is the first time Charley has been in such a place. Do not say a word. I only write this *to you*, just between ourselves.[16]

14. Jane Grey Swisshelm, who edited a newspaper in St. Cloud, Minnesota, espoused antislavery views and supported women's rights. By the end of 1862, however, she was villifying those Dakotas involved in the Dakota War. See Hoffert, *Jane Grey Swisshelm.*

15. For information on Sarah Polk and the occupation of Nashville, see Nelson and Nelson, *Memorials of Sarah Childress Polk,* chap. 11. Confederate general Gideon J. Pillow was not a relative but a friend and political ally of James K. Polk.

16. Willis Countryman was sixteen years old in 1860, living in Nininger. Reid Mitchell notes, "An Ohio private recalled of Nashville's district, Smokey Row, 'there was

... It is now past taps and I am violating orders by keeping a light burning after that time, so I will stop here.

> Ever yours affectionately
> Madison.

I send you some Southern money, as a curiosity only, as it is worth nothing to me.[17]

Camp Minn., Tenn., Apr. 13, 1862

Dear Lizzie:

... I am sorry you had to go home disappointed from the P.O.; but, at the same time, I should think disappointment in not having to read my weekly ebullitions of trash would be more a pleasure than otherwise. I should think you would tire of reading them, as they are the same thing over and over again, and poor at the beginning. In one of your letters you refer to a story that I had been promoted to 1st Lieut., and add that you think me rather sly abut it. I have received no such promotion; and what is more, do not expect or desire it. All promotions *now* are made by favor, and without any regard to the wishes of the privates. When Sergt. Bissell was discharged Capt. Preston had to recommend some one to the Col. to be appointed in Bissells place, but as there were three of us whom he regarded with equal favor, not knowing which to choose, he permitted an election, and I happened to be the lucky one. My [rivals] were Jameson and Estabrooks, 1st and 2nd Corporals, I being 3d. As they were both very good men and above me in rank I did not expect it; but to my surprise received more votes than both of them on the 1st ballot.[18]

The non commissioned officers have to carry a steady hand or down they go into the ranks. The Col. has reduced three orderlies, several Sergts, our 1st Sergt Major, and corpls *ad infinitum*. He has a book containing all our names opposite to many of which are divers signs and marks. The last time I heard from it my

an old saying that no man could be a soldier unless he had gone through Smokey Row.... The street was about three fourths of a mile long and every house or shanty on both sides was a house of ill fame. Women had no thought of dress or decency. They said Smokey Row killed more soldiers than the war" (Mitchell, *The Vacant Chair*, 90). See also Clinton, "'Public Women' and Sexual Politics."

17. The Confederate government printed Confederate currency at far faster rates than it collected money through taxes or raised it through loans. The currency depreciated over time, losing value following military defeats in the spring of 1862.

18. Francis M. Bissell was discharged January 20, 1862, for disability. For the officers' election, see Mitchell, *The Vacant Chair*, 46; and Linderman, *Embattled Courage*, 40, 70.

name was one of the few opposite which was written "all right." Col. Lester is a man of great discernment, cultivated tastes, and untarnished honor, possessing great perseverance and coolness. His eagle eye is everywhere, searching out evil doers, who receive deserts meet for their actions. One of our Sergts. is going to be court-martialed for striking a man. . . .[19]

Things remain *in status quo* as when I wrote last, with the exception of a little more excitement. Last night we were ordered to be on the alert and ready to march on shortest notice, as the Gen. feared an uprising in Nashville. The fiends there do not credit the news of our success; but still persist that Beauregard will yet occupy this city, and assert that the south conquered at Pittsburg. About ten o'clock last night two companies were sent for, and Co's I and D went into town in a hurry, returning this morning. The devils were taken by surprise when they heard the quick, steady tread of our men as they marched up High street with their bayonets glistening in the bright moonlight, and no further demonstrations were made. Co. F goes to town to-night to "make assurance doubly sure." If any trouble is kicked up by these fiendish creatures I shall fight them with a will which could not be exceeded if I were on the battlefield, for I hate them more and more every day.

Of southern soldiers we know just what to expect; but from these wretches who can now enjoy the blessings of life and protection of the government entirely free from fear of any thing, we have a right to expect something better than efforts to kill our Genl, murder and insult our soldiers, and burn and destroy our property. I have just heard that Beauregard is a prisoner, but do not give the story much credit.[20]

Three of our men were discharged lately—Cressey among them—making five from Co. F now. Co. F has not lost [any] by death yet. Almost every other Co has lost from one to three.[21]

I send you some flowers from the cemetery, not because they are pretty, but because you have none yet, and the associations connected with them may be of some interest to you.

Hereafter you may direct to Nashville. If you have not got your picture taken for me yet, I wish you would have it taken on glass instead of on iron plate; I think glass takes the better pictures. I wish I could do as you ask and go home to

19. For discipline in the Union army, see McPherson, *For Cause and Comrades*, 54–59; Mitchell, *The Vacant Chair*, 43–50; and Linderman, *Embattled Courage*, chap. 3.

20. For partisan activity in Kentucky and Tennessee, see Cooling, "A People's War."

21. Roger Cressey, Cyrus Fuller, Corbin Hill, Page Howe, and Edward Kellogg were all discharged from Company F by this date.

see you all. I could not think of staying at home though so long as the war lasts, and I am needed here. . . .

> Affectionately yours,
> Madison

Nininger April 15, 1862
Wednesday morning

My Dear Madison

. . . You may be assured [yours of April 4th] was a welcome letter. The letter you wrote shortly after you arrived at Nashville saying you expected to leave there shortly confirmed the report that the 3rd Minn Regt was in the awful battle at Corinth. You may have some idea of my feelings when I heard of the different accounts of the misery and the suffering at the same time thinking perhaps you were a sharer in it all. Then you may imagine my joy to know you are so comfortably situated in old Tenn. It must be beautiful there. I do wish I could be with you for a little while to admire the many beauties you speak of. We are organizing a "soldiers aid society" as we meet this afternoon.[22] I am hurrying this letter so that I dont know as you can read it. The officers are to be elected to day. Mrs Donnelly will be president I suppose. I was at Hastings yesterday with the committee to buy things that was needed. Mr Newman gave a dollar. While there I had my tooth taken out so I think I will not be troubled with the toothache any more. It is very backward here this spring. There has been no wheet sowed yet that I know of. It's cold and cloudy most of the time. There has not been any boats through the Lake yet. There is no news to write. Times here are very very dull. Tell Eugene his mother has got quite over her ill turn. The rest of his folks are well. . . .

. . . You dont know how highly I prize those flowers you sent me. They are the first of the kind I ever saw. If you find the seed of any pretty kind of flower save them. . . .

> Yours ever Lizzie . . .

Guard Qtrs. Nashville, Tenn., April 17, 1862
Just after midnight.

Dear Lizzie:

. . . You seem to think something has happened since you do not receive my letters. I am happy to be able to assure you that I never enjoyed better health in my

---

22. For women organizing volunteer societies to aid soldiers, see Attie, "Warwork and the Crisis of Domesticity in the North." See also Gordon, *Bazaars and Fair Ladies*, 58-60.

life than I have since we left Minn. Almost every spring I have been more or less unwell, though not exactly sick; but this spring I am as tough and hearty as a bear. I do not intend to boast about it, however, for there is no knowing how soon I may be sick; and now when we do get sick we are sent to the General Hospital which is about a sure a road to the grave as one can travel. It was only last Monday that one of our hardiest men, who had not been sick at all before, was stricken down by disease, and it is doubtful about his ever recovering. Eugene and O'Brien are tough and hardy, but Knight, Briggs, and Johnson Truax are unwell—the two former being unfit for duty most all the time. . . .[23]

. . . There is any quantity of excitement in town nowadays. Over two hundred arrests were made by the Provost Guards last night. Several men have been shot lately. Eugene and I have just come in from the street having been into every nook and corner of the town just to see what was going on. No one could trouble us, as we have the countersign, but persons without the countersign cannot walk the streets after 9 o'clock at night.[24] The streets ar[e] constantly patroled by the Provost Guard which consists of the 51st Ohio and the 7th Penn. Cavalry. We have nothing to do but guard Head Quarters.

It is now after midnight, and I have not slept a wink, nor cannot to-night as I have to take command of the Guard after two o'clock. Eugene is my corporal to night. . . .

I have had some photographs taken; but the artist almost ruined them by getting black spots on them through carelessness. If I had time I would get more taken to see if I could not get better ones. I will send you one of them now, and perhaps another one by and by. Do what you please with it; if you think it too outrageous throw it away.

Lizzie, I hope you will be more fortunate hereafter in receiving my letters, not because there is anything very interesting in them, but to keep you from being disappointed when you expect one from me. I receive a great many letters in all, but none which afford me so much pleasure as yours, though as good perhaps and twice as lengthy. You have no idea how eagerly I watch the mail when it comes near the time when I may expect a letter from you; and I, too, am sometimes disappointed as well as yourself. While Eugene and I were eating supper in a saloon tonight all at once he spoke up, saying that he would give almost anything to be at Aunt Susan's eating supper to night, though he did not recollect

23. Hastings resident Alonzo Briggs, twenty-six years old, deserted on August 1, 1862. "Johnson" was Robert J. Truax's nickname.

24. Curfews were often part of martial law imposed by occupying armies. A countersign probably exempted the person carrying it from the curfew. See Ash, *When the Yankees Came*, 56–57, 59.

having eat there but once in his life. He said he never knew the time when he would rather see those girls than to night. He was wonderfully pleased with your and Dollies letters. The town-clock strikes and I must go, so, Dear Lizzie, Good-night! . . .

> Yours ever.
> Madison.

Camp Minnesota, Nashville, Tenn., April 24, 1862

My Dear Lizzie:

. . . Yesterday I wrote a letter to the *Conserver*, and to day I wrote another immediately after we had received orders to March to Pittsburg's Landing; but had hardly closed it when a dispatch came from Gen. Buell countermanding the first orders.[25] When Gov. Johnson heard that we were ordered away from Nashville he immediately telegraphed to Gen. Buell requesting him to permit the Minn. 3d to remain here for a short time longer at least, if we were not absolutely needed at Pittsburg. Gen Buell granted his request, and so we have to stay here, losing an opportunity of being in a great battle which will be fought soon. The Gov. visited our camp and made us a speech. He thinks a great deal of us, and will, I think, if he cannot keep us here, get us sent to the eastern part of the State to free the people of his own home, many of whom have always been loyal in spite of rebel bayonets.[26]

We have been relieved from all duty here and all of the companies have returned to camp. We had a splendid battalion drill this afternoon, performing most of the evolutions in double quick time. In the absence of the orderly I acted in his place to-day.

While I am writing a fearful thunderstorm is raging through the sky; the rain comes down in torrents, nor does it stop when it strikes the tent, but comes through upon us poor mortals, some of whom are trying to sleep while others are trying to write.

In your letter you refer to the lonely time you are having when everything is so dreary and the wind whistling around the corners. Lizzie, would it make any

25. Unfortunately, Madison's letter to the *Hastings Conserver* cannot be located, because collections of the *Conserver* date from January 1, 1863, at the Dakota County Historical Society and the Minnesota Historical Society.

26. Andrew Johnson had been a U.S. senator from Tennessee who remained loyal after Tennessee seceded in June 1861. Eastern Tennessee had the largest number of Union supporters but was occupied by Confederate troops early in the war. President Lincoln appointed Johnson military governor of Tennessee in February 1862 after Union successes at forts Henry and Donelson. See Donald et al., *The Civil War and Reconstruction*, 164–65.

difference if I could happen in on such an occasion? I believe it would. I know that nothing on earth would give me more pleasure than to be with you even but a little while, especially when I am lonely. Your kind expression of willingness to suffer every privation to be with me if such a thing were possible gives me additional assurance that my regard for you is fully returned. Your letters to me are always freighted with evidences of your regard for me; they are the outpourings of a generous heart, always breathing love and friendship. You do not know how I prize them and with what gratification I read them. Perhaps in my hurried and meager letters I do not write as one writing to a loved one; but, Lizzie, I know that you are well aware that I do not regard you with indifference, that I love you sincerely, and that there is no one whose presence can fill the void of my heart when you are absent, though I must acknowledge that your kindness to me is deserving of better usage than you have ever received from this rough being. Oh Lizzie! You do not know how much more I feel than my unpolished manners could ever express. How often have I thought of the many kind actions which used to spring spontaneously from your hand every day and hour when we were together last summer. I may never see you again on earth; but so long as I live those little acts of kindness will never be forgotten. I hope as you do, Lizzie, that if we do not meet again on earth we may meet above. Yes, I *do hope* so. . . .

    I wish you could see us to night as we appear in our Sibley Tent. It covers about as much ground as your porch, and runs up about twelve feet coming to a peak at the top—just the shape of a round cone. In the center is a pole which supports it and around which we stack our arms and hang our equipments. We lie with our heads toward the outside, and feet all pointing to the center towards each other, when they get mixed up so that it is difficult to pick out the right ones in the dark. There are from fifteen to twenty men in a tent; and when all lie down it is difficult to find an unoccupied spot large enough to put your foot down. In my tent is—Bowler, Knight, Richmond 1st, and 2nd, Pickett, Briggs, Deakin, Nemier, Haman, Fowler, Johnson, Pettie, Ritchey, Mills, Ridgeway, Porter, Neill, Howe, and Bush. 19.[27] We have a way of making our tents more comfortable during this warm weather by raising them and sewing a breadth of cloth around the bottom which can be raised and lowered at pleasure whenever it is too warm.

    . . . Eugene is well as usual, and does more duty than any other corporal in our company. Most of the Nininger boys are well, though Knight and Truax are not able to do duty much of the time, and Briggs has done no duty in over two months. We left him in the Hospital at Belmont, but he joined the regiment about two weeks ago. He will probably be discharged. Frank Colby is quite sick in the

---

27. All the men but Neill appear on the roster of Company F.

hospital at Nashville. Charles Russell is the only one in our company who has not been to the doctors or missed at least one days duty. He has never missed one minutes duty, and you would be surprised to see how he has fleshed up.

If we march from here I think I shall send some of my surplus clothing home, as we do not need it [in] this warm weather and shall probably be discharged befor cold weather comes again. I have an ambrotype which I shall send you if I send my clothing. . . .[28] Briggs has just come from the doctors with a bottle of whiskey, which the doctor has prescribed for him—one ounce three times a day before eating. I have to make the sick call every morning for our company—i.e muster the sick and take them to the Surgeon who examines and prescribes for them. Want of room compels me to bring this garbled sheet to a close.

> Ever your
> Madison.

Camp near Murfreesboro, Tenn., April 28, 1862.

Dear Lizzie:

Perhaps you may think when you compare dates, that I am in a hurry about writing this time, as I wrote to you only last Thursday; but as we are on the march and shall have limited opportunities for writing, it stands us in hand to write when we can. When I wrote last Thursday I little thought that we should be so soon on the march; but Saturday we received orders and on Sunday we were on our way at 5 A.M. We marched fifteen miles and then halted at 11 A.M. in a beautiful grove of red cedar when we encamped for the remainder of the day and for the night, sleeping out of doors for the first time since we enlisted. There was no restraint and everybody selected his own spot for camping. Knight and I selected a place beneath the branches of a large cedar, having [to] push aside and prop up the wide spreading limbs before we could get beneath them. At dark we lay down with cedar boughs beneath and blankets over us and slept sweetly and soundly until the sound of the bugle awoke us at three this morning. It was a pretty sight to see the various modes resorted to for camping during the night.[29] Some went

28. For a description of an ambrotype, see Robert Leggatt, "The Ambrotype Process," www.rleggatt.com/photohistory/history/ambrotyp.htm.

29. Colonel Andrews describes the march to Murfreesboro and the area in similar terms: "We marched for Murfreesboro, a town in the heart of Tennessee, whence radiate eleven highways, some of which were good macadamized pikes. It contained a depot of supplies; also, was a place requiring much picket duty. The first camp was about a mile below the town, on open land, watered by a clear stream, and in the vicinity were some fir or cypress thickets. The country around Murfreesboro is a natural park; the surface is

at it as naturally as you would to cook a pan of biscuit, while others labored for hours in building temporary habitations and yet did not get any better shelter than I did in ten minutes time. Knight is sick and just able to keep along by having his load hauled and me to do all the fixin.

Yesterday afternoon several slaveowners visited our camp in search of "contrabands" but had to turn them away empty handed although we had as many as fifteen or twenty with us. Several joined us yesterday from near Nashville.[30]

This morning we were on our way by four o'clock and after going sixteen miles halted here at 10 A.M. where we shall encamp for the rest of to-day and tonight. We are in a beautiful wood through which passes a crystal creek [?] with rising and extending away on each side. The trees are tall and sparse and one can see all over our camp. The weather is delightful, and the country with its rich plantations and unrivaled scenery, is still more delightful; but oh! the blasting hand of war is every where visible—homes destroyed and deserted, fields laid waste, fences burned, and helpless women and children left in poverty to shift for themselves. The roads are strewn with the decaying carcasses of horses, cattle, and hogs, killed by the rebels during their flight before the advancing columns of Gen. Mitchell.[31]

This morning as we passed along I noticed a woman standing in the door with two bright looking children by her side and a little one in her arms. I thought she looked very sad, and watched her, when pretty soon she began to cry. Others noticed it and asked the cause of her trouble. She replied with sobs and tears stifled as well as she could, that her husband was pressed in the southern army and she feared that he was killed at the battle of Pittsburg. Poor woman!

Most of the inhabitants—who, by the way, appear to be mostly female, the males having joined the army—view us in dogged silence as we pass them, the younger ones occasionally hurrahing for the southern confederacy and looking

---

undulating, well watered, with here and there groves and open forests of hardwood" ("Narrative of the Third Regiment," 150).

30. On August 6, 1861, Congress passed an act to seize Confederate property, including slaves that were used for military purposes. On March 13, 1862, Congress passed another measure, this one prohibiting Union officers from returning slaves to their masters. A more far-reaching act on July 17, 1862, "authorized the seizure of the property of persons in rebellion against the United States and specified that all of their slaves who came within Union lines 'shall be deemed captives of war and shall be forever free.'" See McPherson, *Ordeal by Fire*, 290, 293.

31. "General Mitchell" likely refers to Ormsby MacKnight Mitchel, a brigadier general in General Buell's Army of the Cumberland. Mitchel had been instrumental in sending raiding expeditions out along the Memphis and Charleston Railroad, but Buell thought that Mitchel's command lacked discipline. See Warner, *Generals in Gray*, 327.

daggers at us. Since leaving Nashville we have seen but one avowed Union family. The old man stood by the roadside swinging his hat and speaking words of encouragement, while his noble looking wife waved a white handkerchief, the little children, full of animation, hurrahing for the Union, and one little girl stood by with an apron full of bouquets throwing them beneath our feet. We pass rebel taunts without notice, but Union demonstrations bring out loud cheers. Just imagine our whole regiment swinging hats and sending up loud cheers as we passed that one little, devoted, Union family.[32]

There has been one occurrance lately which has brought a sad feeling to my heart. Night before last an order was read on dress parade reducing Barney McKenna to the ranks. When it was read he stood beside me in his file-closers line, little expecting such an order, though I knew it was coming. Poor Barney has his faults—serious ones—and according to military discipline, was deserving of the punishment, but there were features connected with it which made it peculiarly painful. He generally tried to do his duty, but was not very competent for the position. Those lazy, black-leg, mock aristocratic Allisons have labored for this very result notwithstanding he was a fellow townsman and has a young wife who will be pained to hear the sad news of her husbands disgrace,—just because he was a poor, hardworking, Irishman dray driver instead of a gambler and hotel keeper like themselves. Poor Serg. as Barney was he was worth two of Bill Allison, who will soon have to go into the ranks, too, if I can guess straight.[33] Corpl. Jameson—a first rate fellow—was made Sergt. and Nick OBrien was made Corporal, so Nininger now has one Sergt. and four Corporals besides Corpl. Pettibone who may fairly be reckoned as from Nininger.[34]

I shall not close this letter until we get to Murfreesboro sometime to-morrow, as I cannot mail it here. . . .

32. For Southern women's varied responses to Union soldiers, see Faust, *Mothers of Invention,* 196–207; and Ash, *When the Yankees Came,* chap. 2. For a discussion of Unionists, see Fisher, "Definitions of Victory."

33. Massachusetts-born Bernard McKenna was listed as a Hastings farmer in the 1857 census with his wife, Bridget, who was born in Ireland. William E. Allison, a hotel keeper, and Morrison Allison, a clerk, lived in Hastings in 1860. Both men were nearly ten years older than McKenna. For a discussion of class in the Union army, see Mitchell, *The Vacant Chair,* 42–43. For attitudes about the Irish, see Paludan, *"A People's Contest,"* 282–84.

34. Herman Pettibone was in Company F, Third Minnesota, although the records do not indicate that he was a corporal in that company. He transferred to a colored regiment in August 1863 but then returned to the Third Minnesota as a lieutenant in Company B.

(Tuesday, April 29th)

After a delightful nights sleep the bugle awoke us at 3 o'clock this morning, and at 4 we were on our way again, arriving here at 9 A.M., where we were welcomed by Col Mundy and the band of the 23d Ky. The 9th Mich., 8th Ky, and our cavalry and artillery are encamped about ¼ of a mile from here on the opposite side of the stream from which we get water.[35]

Before leaving Nashville I sent a box of clothing to the care of Mr. Caleff. In my overcoat pocket is my miniature for you, my pretty little needlecase, your miniature, which I shall not want when I get another from you, and two pocket handkerchiefs which are of no use to me here. You will find our coats rolled up as we have them to lash on our knapsacks during a march. The clothes are dirty, but I was in such a hurry that I had no time to get them washed. I sent back your letters which I want you to keep for me.

We do not know yet when our brigade will march. To-morrow we have general inspection. We are encamped ¾ of a mile from the pretty town of Murfreesboro. Eugene has got angry at the orderly and moved into my tent to-day. The weather is delightful and the scenery unrivaled by any I have ever seen....

      Yours as ever,
      Madison.

Wednesday Morning, April 30 [1862]

[To Madison:]

The news has just come that they have taken *New Orleans* whether it is true or not I don't know but hope so for every little [move] healps to bring this war to a speedy termination.[36] When the day does arrive that peace is proclaimed it will be a day of rejoicing long to be remembered.

I suppose you have an opportunity of getting your washing done with[out] any trouble while you are so near the city. I dreamed last night that you came home, that you had changed so in your looks that I did not know you. You can just imagine how disopointed I was when I awoke and found it all a dream. Oh! how I wish you would come home. I forgot to say I rec'd the Tenn money you sent me. Kate is about the same as when I wrote before, not able to sit up all the time.

35. Andrews notes, "With Kentucky regiments and the Ninth Michigan we also practiced brigade drill under Colonel Duffield" ("Narrative of the Third Regiment," 150).

36. Navy commander David Farragut and Union general Benjamin Butler forced the surrender of New Orleans on April 29, 1862.

Wednesday noon

Since I wrote the above Pray has come from Afton where he says 'tis reported the 3rd Regiment has been taken prisoners but says he does not believe it. I hope not. He has been quite sick, is quite smart now. Sends his love to you. . . . I have been working in the garden till my hands are so stiff I can't hardly make a letter.

Good bye yours ever
Lizzie

As the office was not open I could not mail this until after the Aid society met. They have desided to send the box that they now have ready to the 3rd Regt so perhaps you will get some of the pretty things there is in the box. L. S. C.

Camp near Murfreesboro, Tenn., Monday, May 5, 1862

My Dear Lizzie:

To-day it is raining as hard as one could possibly desire, which gives me leisure to write, a thing which I have not enjoyed since the first day of our arrival here. . . .

The Minn. 3d and Ky 23d were drawn up as brigade head-quarters when the mail came in yesterday, ready to be sent out against the enemy. Everybody was full of animation. Gen. Duffield was out with the 9th Mich. and 8th Ky after the rebels who had captured four companies of the 8th Ky., which were at Shelbyville, twenty five miles below here; Col Lester was in command at Head-quarters, receiving despatches from the various detachments already out after bodies of rebel Cavalry, when the mail came in after being anxiously looked for in vain for three days. Here again we had more exciting news. As the train was coming in from Nashville it came [to] a place where the rebel cavalry had torn up the track, laid the rails upon a pile of burning cotton, and then retreated toward Nashville as the train came up, to get into its rear, tear up the track, and thus capture the train. The train immediately backed up for Nashville, but soon came in sight of the rebels tearing up the track in its rear, when the train started again for Murfreesboro which they succeeded in reaching by taking the hot rails from the fire laying them upon the ties, enabling them to pass along just as the rebel cavalry came in sight several hundred yards behind them. When the mail was distributed and the orderlies were passing along the lines with letters for everybody but me I felt as though I had been forgotten.

Woolford's cavalry five thousand strong immediately put out after the rebels, and Co's A and B of our regt. were taken out on the cars which have not been heard from since. Several companies of the 23d Ky and Co's C, I, and D of our regt. were ordered out in different directions to reconnoiter, returning late last night. About 5 P.M. the rest of us were ordered back to our quarters.[37]

We have pickets extending about two miles from camp in every direction. It takes 200 men, 4 corpls, 4 Sergts., 2 Lieuts., 1 capt., and one field officer of the day. I was out on the Salem Pike two and one half miles in command of a part of the picket day before yesterday, and as luck would have it was the first one to get information of the approach of the enemy which was not supposed to be nearer than twenty five miles of here any way. Just after dark, the day having passed quietly, I drew my advanced picket in some four hundred yards, posting it by a bridge across a stream which circles around Murfreesboro some two [and] three fourths miles south of it. I had one mounted picket from our cavalry, whom I posted near them to bring information back to the main picket, which I had posted about three hundred yards in the rear in a different position from that occupied during the daytime, a precaution which all pickets are enjoined to observe. We lay hid in the bushes till 10 o'clock in the evening when the cavalry man brought back two negroes—slaves—who had come to give us notice of the enemy. From them I learned that about 25 of Morgan's Cavalry were at Salem, three miles from us. Some of the boys doubted, but from their story, and knowing circumstances which the rest did not, I *knew* they had told the truth; so I ordered the mounted picket to take the negroes to Col. Lester, Duffield being absent. I then moved all but one up to the bridge, took one man with me, and advanced down the pike and secreted ourselves within two ½ miles of Salem, expecting every moment to hear the rebels coming, knowing if there were but twenty five their object must be to capture pickets. In about an hour and a half, having seen nothing of the enemy, I returned to the bridge just in time to meet the returning picket who had gone with the darkies to the Provost Marshal at Murfreesboro instead of to Col. Lester. The marshal sent off an orderly to Head Quarters, but instead of going there he went to the major of the 23d who told them not to believe too much of niggers talk and went to sleep again. About 1 o'clock I heard some noise on a fence up the stream, and crept cautiously up stream when pretty soon I heard some one cough, inquired "who comes there," and was answered "a friend." I ordered a negro who had come around through

37. Colonel Frank Wolford commanded the First Kentucky Cavalry. In April 1862 the First Kentucky Cavalry was assigned to General Dumont's command and on May 5 defended Lebanon, Tennessee, against Confederate cavalry commander John Hunt Morgan. Wolford was wounded and taken prisoner. See "The First Kentucky Cavalry," www.unionregimentsofkentucky.com/thomasspeed/cavalry/1kycav.html; and Duke, *Morgan's Cavalry,* 95-96.

the woods from Land Jarrett, two miles beyond Salem "to inform de union men dat Morgan wid four hundred cavalry" was there. He also informed me that he heard Morgan order out a detachment to Salem for pickets, which readily accounted for the twenty five of whom I had already heard. I then felt safe, as I knew these twenty five were only out to protect the rest from surprise. As I was about to send him to Head Quarters, he informed me that he had a friend a few rods behind. We got him and sent them both, but the thick skulled messenger did no better than at first; so when he returned I gave him a jawing and sent him to Lieut. Tichenor who was in command of a picket some two miles on my left up stream, and he sent a note to Col. Lester, which did not reach him until morning. Lieut. Tichenor came up to my post just as it was getting light, with two of Capt. Troyman's mounted scouts. He was on horseback, and at my request with the two scouts and my mounted pickets and went within sight of Morgan's pickets, six of whom chased them back a piece. By sunrise no less than six squads of our cavalry, about 20 or 30 men each came to me at different times for information and then started down the pike, but it was too late, for Morgan had gone off around to the west of Murfreesboro to get at the railroad between Murfreesboro and Nashville. One scout went to Salem and to Land Jarrett and found that every word the negroes had told was true.[38]

From reliable information we learn that there are three bands near here consisting of from five hundred to eight hundred each. At 4 oclock yesterday I was relieved, and returned to camp to find that the whole regt had gone to headquarters preparatory to being sent away after secesh. Tired, hungry and sleepy as I was I got ready and joined them, when we were at 5 o'clock ordered to quarters as I told you before. Gen. Duffield returned last night with sixty horses, one prisoner, and a numerous quantity of bacon, which he captured.

Since commencing this letter Co's A and B have come to camp. They captured six horses. I feel so tired and stupid that I cannot write so I will quit....

Yours ever
Madison.

38. For fugitive slaves bearing military information and the various reactions to them by Union officers, see Berlin et al., *Slaves No More,* 34-36, 93. "Morgan" refers to John Hunt Morgan, a Kentucky cavalry commander. Cavalry led by Morgan and Nathan Bedford Forrest conducted highly successful raids throughout Tennessee and Kentucky during the summer of 1862. For more on Morgan, see Duke, *Morgan's Cavalry.* Captain Troyman is unidentified.

Nininger May 6th 1862
(At twilight)

My Dearest Madison:

I rec'd a letter from you yesterday. . . . But was sorry you were ordered to march. I was in hopes you would be kept at Nashville until after the battle of Corinth. I think it will be one of the worst battles of the campaign. We heard they were fighting there when I wrote my last letter, but I suppose it was as many of the reports false. I presume before this reaches you the battle will be fought and all those who are destined to fall at that time will meet their horrible death, for horrible it must be. I have pictured it out in every imaginable shape. [I] can imagine it no other way but perfectly awful. I do hope that you will be one of the lucky ones that shall be spared for some good purpose to return to your old home again. Some poet says (Tupper I believe) that "hope deferred maketh the heart sick." It may in some cases but not in all, for I have hoped sincerely for your return. Have not tired but [will] hope on with as good courage as ever.[39]

. . . I have been sitting on the floor writing on your trunk part of the time and the other I have occupied in looking over the letters I've rec'd from you. Among the rest I come across the first one you sent me after you enlisted last spring a little more than a year ago. It carried my thoughts back to the evening we stood at Aunt Henrietta's door and I bade you "good bye." 'Twas the first time I ever knew what real sorrow was at bidding "Good bye." I have parted with intimate friends relatives and those whom I thought much of but have never parted with any one who was bound to me by the sacred ties of love so strongly as you are. But that was but a beginning. Where is the end?

Kate is a little better then when I last wrote. She has changed her physician. Dr Finch has been dotoring her all winter. Has not helped her any. She is now being Doctored by a lady who came to Hastings last fall from St. Louis. She says her heart is very much diseased. 'Tis that which causes the swelling on her neck that she has the conjestion of the brain. She thinks she can help her in a short time.[40]

. . . I am sorry I sent that picture it was so poor I guess you will begin to think I am not going to send you. If that woman Dont come to Nininger soon I will go to Hastings and get one taken.

[Lizzie]

39. The phrase is part of Proverbs 13:12, which ends, "but when the desire cometh, it is a tree of life." Lizzie wrote "with hope on with"—the first "with" should have been "will."
40. "Dr. Finch" refers to Jeremiah Finch, listed as a physician in Hastings in 1860. Kate's female doctor is unidentified; she was not listed in the Hastings newspapers or census.

Camp of 23d Brigade, Murfreesboro, Tenn.
Thursday, May 8th, 1862

Dearest Lizzie:

... Lizzie, you can hardly imagine my feelings. I have not heard from you since we left Nashville. I *know* that something is wrong; and the first cause for your not writing, which occurs to my mind, is sickness. Can it be that any other cause has arisen? No, Lizzie, you would, *surely,* not fail to write to me if you were not sick and unable to write. But if you are sick I should think Kate might write for you, at least enough to let me know. I shall not feel easy again until I hear from you.

In my other letter I gave you an account of my being out on picket and of the proximity of the rebel cavalry to our lines. Since then our cavalry has had a fight with them, a partial account of which you will find in the *Nashville Union,* which I sent you this morning. ... I feared Eugene had been captured, but he has returned to camp after being on picket two days and two nights in succession, the last night and day without rations, except a pig, which the boys killed.

We went to Shelbyville last Monday night, returning on Tuesday. When only six miles from here the cars were fired into by some rebel miscreants hid among the rocks and cedars. The cars were stopped, and we hunted the woods high and low, but found nobody, though a woman, living near, informed us that six rebel cavalry passed a few minutes before.

On Tuesday the country was full of rumors in regard to a large force of rebels who were said to be near for the purpose of attacking us that night.[41] At 10 o'clock Tuesday night we were cautioned to get ready to fall in on a seconds notice. About half past eleven we were called out and formed in silence and marched over to Headquarters, which are just outside the town. We were ordered to take a position in front of the camp of the 9th Mich., our line facing the road leading to town. Our position was about ten rods from the road and considerably elevated above it. One section of Hewitt's battery was placed on our right and one on our left to crossfire in front, as it was expected that the enemy would attack us at that point.[42] The rest of the artillery was in position to command another road some distance to our left. The 23d Ky. was formed to the left of us and the 9th Mich. in the rear of both. Had we been attacked it was the intention for the

41. On May 6, Colonel Morgan arrived in Sparta, Tennessee, with his cavalry to resupply and regroup after his defeat at Lebanon. They remained there until May 9 when 150 cavalrymen set out for southern Kentucky. The rumors Madison mentions may have been related to Morgan's movements. See Duke, *Morgan's Cavalry,* 99.

42. Encamped near the Third Minnesota, Hewitt's Battery was the First Kentucky Battery, which was part of the Twenty-third Brigade. See Andrews, "Narrative of the Third Regiment," 152; and "A Statement of Facts," Hale Papers.

artillery, after firing a few rounds, to retire to another position and shell the town, as it was expected that the citizens intended to cooperate with the enemy.

After a while it was discovered by Col. Lester that the right of our regt., Co's B, H, and F, were in exact range of the artillery on our left, so the right of our line was swung backward up the hill to get out of range. As soon as we were in position the cavalry was sent out to make a feint upon the enemy should he advance. There we stood in line of battle from 12 till sunrise when we were ordered back to camp. This is the first time the *whole* regt. has been called out at night, and I hope it is the last time we are to be called out *for nothing*. Morgan is fairly whipped out now, and we shall not be molested here again. This trouble has kept us from going forward as we expected to, but we shall not remain here much longer.

. . . I forgot to refer to your new society for the relief of sick soldiers. It gives me pleasure to hear of the patriotic efforts which the ladies of the north are every where putting forth to alleviate the afflictions of those who have become prostrated by sickness while so far from home and friends, fighting for the Union. You could not, to my mind, engage in a better cause. This Government has a great sin to answer for in having so shamefully neglected to *properly* take care of her sick soldiers. Was it not for what charity has gleaned from the friends and their humanity their conditions would be a disgrace to even the savage tribes.[43]

The woods and fields look very beautifully now—the one full of tall waving grain, the other shady and alive with beautiful shrubs and flowers. I never saw *anything* in the shape of flower gardens at the north which can *begin* to compare with these here. There are hundreds of kinds which I do not know the name of. Peaches are now about as large as walnuts. Strawberries have been ripe for two weeks. While marching from Nashville I pressed two or three flowers which the boys called honeysuckle. I do not know whether they are or not, and they are not very pretty, only as you find them in the woods, winding up trees and along from bush to bush. I will send them to you. You desired me to preserve the seed of some of the prettiest flowers, and send them to you. I will do so if I can. . . .

(Friday morning)

. . . We have lost our Col. Last night it was announced that he would take immediate command of the 23 brigade. Duffield has been ordered back to Ky. to take command of all the troops left in that state. Col. Lester will probably be promoted to Brigadier General before a great while.

43. For the U.S. Sanitary Commission's efforts on behalf of soldiers, see Attie, *Patriotic Toil*, 114–16; Silber, *Daughters of the Union*, chap. 5; and Maxwell, *Lincoln's Fifth Wheel*.

I have some pine leaves which I shall send you sometime, either in a letter or paper.

Now, Lizzie, I hope that you are not sick, and that I may soon hear from you again. Letters from you I prize above all others, and feel the keenest disappointment when I do not receive them regularly. I have tried to write often to you, though my letters contain very little interesting matter. Perhaps I write more about war than you wish to hear, but you must recollect that I have little else to write about. . . .

> Yours with true affection,
> Madison.

Nininger May 13, 1862
Tuesday evening

Dear Madison

. . . We received the box you sent before leaving Nashville all safe and sound. I was pleased when it was open and to get hold of that good picture but would have felt a great deal better satisfied if I could have seen the original come poping out of those long pockets. I prize those pictures very highly. . . . The last one you sent was very good indeed, though it wears a sorrowful expression on the countenance. Are you getting to look care worn and sorrowful? Or was that the indication of your feelings for a few moments? If so cheer up, for I think there is a better chance for a speedy termination of this war then has been since it began.

The 5th Regt or at least seven companies went down river this morning. Among them was Dan Sheldon and John King. . . .[44]

(Wednesday morning, 14)

Since I wrote the above I heard the 5th Regt is going to the same place the 3rd is. Tomorrow there is a going to be a great time at Nininger at Tremont hall with a speech by Gov. Don[nelly] and music singing by Mrs Gov. D. and several others with refreshments of ice cream and cake. The proceeds is to go to our Soldiers aid society. I am going to freeze one can of ice cream, if you were here you should have all you could eat.

> {across the front page perpendicular} I suppose before this time you are at Pitsburg Landing. We have just got the news of the Merrimac being blown

---

44. Daniel Sheldon and John King enlisted in Company G, Fifth Minnesota, on the same day, the latter as a sargeant. In 1860 twenty-three-year-old King was a laborer. Daniel Sheldon was nineteen years old in 1857, working as a sawyer in Nininger.

up by the southerners. 'Tis a pity they hadn't have had Jef Davis along to share the same fate.[45]

  Yours ever Lizzie

Murfreesboro, Tenn., May 15, 1862.

My Dear Lizzie:

Though dull and sleepy after being on picket last night, yet I will try to write something in the shape of a letter since it is my regular day for writing to you.

  Your . . . letters were gladly rec'd., as I had begun to think you had ceased to write to me. It makes me feel very sad to hear of Kate's continued ill health, for I had hoped to hear of her entire recovery ere now. I hope that her disease will not prove serious, but I must confess that I feel more than ever concerned about her, from the account which you give. I can not bear to contemplate the idea of her health being broken so soon in life, much less can I endure the thought of her being taken from us. But, Lizzie, I have fears, serious ones.

  In regard to that Truax yarn, it is not worth talking about. I have no fears of being hurt by Johnson, for soldiers in time of war, have enough to do without fighting each other. If those gabbling simpletons knew how little I care for their vain attempts at mischief, I think they would save their breath for other purposes.[46] I think that some of them would look better fighting for their country than they do lying and tattling. . . .

  I have given up all hopes of the 3d Reg. ever being in a battle of any magnitude. We may by chance come in contact with some of the bands of cavalry, which rove about in this section. We should go to Pitsburg at once, but for the fact that we cannot possibly be spared here. News has reached us of the destruction of the Merrimac and the splendid success of McClellan's Army.[47] Things are fast coming to a crisis. Less than twenty days will decide whether the war will end before July or be prolonged until cold weather will again permit our army to finish the

---

45. The Confederates had captured the ironclad *Merrimac* at the beginning of the war. On March 9, 1862, the *Merrimac* and the Union's ironclad *Monitor* fought near Hampton Roads, North Carolina, ending in a draw. In May the Union captured Norfolk, the Confederate's shipyard, and the Confederates scuttled the *Merrimac*.

46. This statement is almost prophetic, considering Madison faced a court-martial instigated by local Dakota County men in the summer of 1863.

47. Union general George B. McClellan had embarked on a complex campaign to capture the Confederate capital of Richmond in the spring of 1862. One perceived Union victory was Confederate general Joseph E. Johnston's evacuation of Yorktown, May 3 to 4, 1862.

work so nobly begun. My own opinion is that the war *cannot* last much longer. Corinth and Richmond will soon speak, and then we shall know.

You refer to old times, when we first became acquainted and to the different times we have parted, and ask when it shall end. I can tell you. If we both live to see peace restored to our country, then you may rest assured that I shall return to you again, *to stay* with you, if you are willing to suffer my presence after having left you so many times. You speak of the sorrow it would give you to hear of my being sick while so far away from home, mother, and sisters, and ask if it would be any consolation for me to have Lizzie by to smooth my aching head. From what little experience I have had at sickness in the army I think I can fully appreciate the blessing and comfort which such timely aid as you speak of would afford. I know of nothing which I could desire more than your presence if I were to be sick.

The Saturday night that I was on picket near Morgan I took a severe cold, and have not been very well since, having a hard cough, sore mouth, and dysentery. I paid $1.00 for a pint of whisky to make cherry bitters. What do you think of that for a price? . . .[48]

> Ever your
> Madison.

Nininger, May 20, 1862

Dearest Madison

. . . [Y]ou speak of not getting my letters. I cannot conceive the reason for I have written every Tuesday regularly for the last four or five weeks. It must be that the mails have been lost or miscarried. You say you think nothing but sickness would hinder me from writing. You are right, nor that would not if I was able to hold my hand up. I am not sick. My health has not been better in a long while. Even if I should be sick I would have everything done for me that a kind mother and sisters could do. I hope before this, you have got my letters, for I know how any one feels when they are expecting letters and do not get them.

Kate's health is very poor, though a little better then it has been. She is staying in Hastings this week with that Doctoress that I told you was doctoring her. She is an electrician. She thought if she would stay there so she could give her a

---

48. During the mid-nineteenth century, people used alcohol mixed with bitters medicinally; bitters took a variety of flavors, including cherry. See Digger Odell, "Bitters Bottles History," www.bottlebooks.com/bitterin.htm. Frank Colby was discharged for disability on May 26, 1862.

bath or shock or what ever it might be called that she could help her much sooner. I do hope she may for no one knows how she has suffered this winter.[49]

I told you we were going to have an ice cream entertainment. We did have it and had what some of them call a "real good time." Mr Donnelly delivered the same lecture that Mrs McMullen listened to. It was very interesting, the most so of any thing I heard or seen during the evening. There was singing, promenading, talking, and several other kinds of amusement. But as I enjoy such amusements but little, Mary, Gus, and I enjoyed our selves by having a social chat in one corner, when we were not needed to help wait on the company.[50] Gus wished me to tell you he wished you to write to him. You don't know how lonely it makes me feel to go to any place like that. There is one whom my thoughts are continually upon (I guess you can think who that is).

. . . I think I shall do as you wished me to and take a school this summer. I have one partially engaged between here and Pine Bend. Am not sure of it yet. . . .[51]

. . . I think you came pretty near being in a battle and missed it after all. I hope you will never be needed so that you will have to be in a battle. You don't know how much I wish this war was ended so that you could come back. I want to see you so much sometimes. It seems to me that cannot wait for the war to end that I may see you again. Take care of your health as well as you can, for health is

49. This "doctoress" practiced galvanism, or the use of electric current to stimulate muscles and nerves. Incidentally, when William Hale returned to Cottage Grove, Minnesota, just north of Hastings, in September 1862 on sick furlough, he commented on electric therapy: "I find the new quackery in full vogue & so submit myself to *general & local* treatment . . . with the best graces, half inclined to think it a grand thing" (11 September 1862, Hale Papers).

50. The *Hastings Independent* on May 15, 1862, carried this announcement: "The ladies of Nininger have had in operation some two or three weeks past a 'Soldier's Aid Society.' They have already filled one large box with hospital goods for the use of the Company from this County in the 3d Regiment. They propose to hold on Thursday evening of this week a 'Sociable,' at Tremont Hall, in Nininger, the proceeds to be applied to the same praiseworthy purposes. The programme will include singing, short speeches and refreshments. As the price of admission is but ten cents, and the object most laudable, we trust that Hastings will be largely represented." Mary Bottomly, twenty-two years old in 1860, lived in Nininger City. She and James Augustus Case married, but the date is unknown. See "Articles on Grey Cloud Island, Nininger, and Early Minnesota History, 1854–1856," folder, Case Papers.

51. Pine Bend was at the southeastern corner of Inver Grove Township, approximately six miles from Lizzie's home.

everything, more especially down there where you have such hard duty to perform. Dont the warm weather make you feel badly? I suppose it is very warm by this time. Is it very much warmer then Minn.? Mrs Russell wanted me to ask you to coax Charley to get his picture taken and send to them. I will send mine shortly as that Lady is coming next week. I will get it taken over again. Do says she is going to write to *brother Mad* so I must close.

> *{across top of the front page perpendicular}* If you dont get letters when you expect them dont think that I have forgotten to write, for that will never be the case. Your letters are always very, very welcome and gladdens my heart to hear from you. You dont know what joy it gives me to hear from you often. Your letters are always very interesting, much more so then my poor apologies that I send. I like to hear war news or anything that you feel the most inclined to write. Do excuse this poorly written thing, 'tis so dark can hardly see to make a letter. Hoping to see you before many months. I remain yours ever

> [Lizzie]

> *{across top of the front page perpendicular}* I have just been washing your blanket. I think by the number of stars and stripes that you have worked on one side that you intend to let the seceding states go for what they will fetch....

> Lizzie

Murfreesboro, Tenn., May 22, 1862.

Dearest Lizzie:

Last Saturday morning at 3 o'clock we took the cars for Columbia, via Nashville, arriving at our destination at noon, marched through town and bivouacked in a pasture adjoing town. The cavalry which we expected to meet, instead of coming to Columbia, passed to the south of the town and went toward East Tennessee.[52]

As soon as we broke ranks most of the boys, being tired, lay down in the shade and went to sleep. I got into the shade of a cedar and went to sleep with a couple of flat stones for a pillow, and about 4 o'clock awoke with a severe headache. In the evening Knight and myself took up quarters beneath a shady elm, and went to sleep for the night with our heads resting on a root. The 2nd night I took my cartridge box for a pillow, and the next day went down town and confiscated my haversack full of cotton, which made a very good pillow.

Tuesday we moved into the tents of the 11th Mich. regt. which had gone to

---

52. See Andrews, "Narrative of the Third Regiment," 150.

escort a wagon train to Pulaski. Yesterday at noon we took the cars again and arrived at our old camp again before dark. The Union sentiment is fast increasing here. During our trip we were often cheered, and yesterday a crowd of ladies showered the cars with bouquets as we passed Franklin, the home of Dr. Cliffe, who stopped over night once with Co. F when he had charge of the bodies of Gen Zellicoffer and Bailie Peyton, at Lebanon Junction, Ky. He has resigned his position as Surgeon in the rebel army, and now lives at home, a good Union man.[53]

While at Columbia I felt quite homesick, not being very well. One night I felt very lonely and sat down and wrote a little memorandum which I will copy off verbatim though you may think it foolish. Here it is:—Columbia, Sunday evening, May 18th.—It is sunset; the twilight is deepening into shade; I am on my primitive bed beneath the ample foliage of a large elm; around me is seated a solemn group of soldiers who have come to spend an hour in song and prayer; we are in a rocky pasture with a majestic wood in the background, an occasional oak, elm, cedar, and locust scattered over it, and the lovely village of Columbia spread out before us with its pretty houses, shady streets, and rich gardens chocked with flowers and fruit; strains of music come streaming over the hill from the band of a Wisconsin regt.; and all around may be heard the busy hum of real life. This is all very pleasant to those who feel like enjoying it.

But Oh! Lizzie, there is one now who does not enjoy it. If there ever was a time when your presence would cheer me, it is now. O, if I could only be near you and recline my aching, throbbing head upon your lap and have your hand once more to press my temples, I should feel happy. I have not been very well since taking such a cold on picket some two weeks ago, and to-night I feel worse than ever. It is now past 8 o'clock and I am writing by the light of a burning stump. Good night!—That is all of it, and no doubt you will think it silly enough. I am better now, but do not feel quite well yet.

. . . I am going to send my dress coat home in a box. . . . I shall return some of my letters for safe keeping and want you to take them. I do not send the coat because I consider it worth anything, but as we do not use them now since it has become so warm, I may as well send it home as to throw it away, and should

---

53. Bailie Peyton was a lieutenant killed near General Zollicoffer during the battle of Mill Spring in January 1862. For some accounts of and the controversy over these deaths, see "Death of Gen. Felix K. Zollicoffer," compiled by Geoffrey R. Walden, www.geocities .com/Pentagon/Quarters/1864/zolldeath2.htm. Dr. Cliffe was an Ohio-born surgeon in the Twentieth Tennessee Infantry. For more information on Cliffe and his role after Zollicoffer's death, see "Twentieth Tennessee Infantry Regiment," www.tennessee-scv.org/ Camp854/shy.html.

I ever return, it will serve as a relic to remind me of the time when I was a soger. The Box will probably reach Hastings by the time you get this letter.[54]

While I write a regt of cavalry is passing our camp. They look pretty. What would you think to see 1100 men, all mounted, passing along in one body? You would probably think them as many as 5000 as they look to be more numerous than they are, especially to those who have not been used to seeing them.

It seems good to be back to camp once more, where we can get plenty of soft bread from our regimental bakery, after sleeping outdoors and eating hard bread and salt pork for several days. We have a real pretty camp, and the whole ground which it occupies is kept as clean as a house floor. The trees are so leafy and large that hardly a ray of sun can reach us.

... I am very glad you planted those melon seeds, for I feel sure that we shall be at home to help you eat them, or rather, the fruit which springs from them. ...

> Ever yours truly.
> Madison.

                                        Murfreesboro, Tenn., May 29, 1862.

My Dear Lizzie

... [Your letter] found me on the sick list where my name has been but once before since I enlisted. I have been sick more or less during the last three or four weeks, but did not give up duty till last Sunday. I am better now, and reported for duty this morning. All the infantry but our regt. have been sent of[f] to different places. The only troops here at present besides our regt., are the two regts of Ky. Cavalry, and two sections of Capt. Hewitts battery. We have to furnish all the guard-picket, provost, and camp. It takes twelve sergts a day, which brings us on almost every other day. ...

The ambrotype which I sent you is, I think, as good a one as I can get, and if it were not for the homely "soger duds," would do. If I ever get on a decent suit of citizens cloth again, I will get one more taken, and then you may throw all the others away. I shall look anxiously for yours till I get it. You seem to think that there is a good prospect of a speedy termination of the war. I *did* think so, but recent events have changed my mind. Halleck cowardly lies idle before Corinth, Banks has been driven back across the Potomac, and the Government calling for more troops. O, it does aggravate me to think what imbecile fools we have at the helm. They dont know what war is, but try to overawe the rebels with superior

---

54. For a description of the Third Minnesota's uniform, see Andrews, "Narrative of the Third Regiment," 150. "Soger" is a colloquial form of "soldier."

force, and complain of the rebels because they *will fight* and because they kill our
men. If killing had as little terror for some of our pet generals and old woman-
ish officials as it has for the gallant soldiers [who] are impatient to fight, the war
would soon be done. If old Halleck had staid at St. Louis a short time longer,
Grant, Buell, and Mitchell would have had the campaign of the west wound up,
and the Mississippi free to the ocean.[55]

But things cannot go on this way much longer. I am by no means sick of being
a soldier, but I am sick of this baby way of fighting. Our soldiers are dying off in
the Hospitals faster than they are on the battle field, and soon we shall have a dis-
organized, demoralized army unless something more is accomplished, or at least
attempted. Besides an awful debt is accumulating which will soon begin to hang
down heavier than we anticipate, and will be more to be feared than hostile
enemies.[56]

I guess you had a hard job, washing that old blanket. I ought to have thrown
those dirty rags away instead of sending them home for you to wash. Tell "sister
Dollie" that I am waiting patiently for that letter she was going to write to
"brother Mad." If she will call in some fine day I will go tame cherrying with her
in some old *secesh's* garden. Did you ever see a Mulberry tree? There are thousands here, all covered with ripe mulberries, too. I wish I could have "happened
in" just as you were having your ice cream party. I would have added one to the
little circle that chatted in the corner while the others made merry. . . .

I recd a letter a day or two ago from Piercy. He was at Paducah, Ky., just
recovering from his sickness, which has lasted over six weeks. He says: "Oh!
Bowler, it is a hard thing to be sick while in the army, but we must put up with
it while we are soldiers. I am nothing but skin and bones." Poor fellow! I can
appreciate his condition. When a soldier is sick he cares little for the army, and
only wishes to be out of sight of it altogether. The army is no place for a sick man.

55. Union general Nathaniel P. Banks lost in the Shenandoah Valley against Confederate general Thomas "Stonewall" Jackson. Madison's gloominess about military leaders
predates a more general critique of General George B. McClellan after he failed to take
Richmond during the Battle of the Seven Days. Madison also anticipates Lincoln's arrangements with Northern governors to recruit new troops in July 1862.

56. William D. Hale also voiced his frustration with inactivity: "We are lying here
useless and doing writing, save camp guarding & Picket duty. The warm weather is
affecting us by its natural consequences of lassitude & sickness. We are fairly rusting out.
I regret that we should be so situated. We came for a more noble & glorious purpose" (16
May 1862, Hale Papers). The Legal Tender Law was signed on February 25, 1862. Before
then the Treasury Department operated only with specie. With the law, greenbacks
became the common currency, and the government was better able to secure loans and
sell bonds to raise money.

I am very glad to hear that you are trying to get a school and hope you will succeed. It will, however, be rather lonely business for you during the long summer days but you can improve the spare hours in reading useful matter and studying some useful branch of education. I will try to have a letter at the P.O. for you at the end of each week as you return from your weeks labor.

How long our regt. is to remain here is more than I can tell. There is a prospect of our being sent to East Tenn. Gen Mitchell, to whose division we belong, came up day before yesterday and went to Nashville with Col. Lester. I should not be surprised if he with Andy Johnson are going to get up an expedition in command of Col. Lester to go to east Tenn. Gov. Johnson was here the other day, and hinted as much to our regt. in a speech to us.

. . . I recd a nice Havelock from the Hastings Scholars. . . . It came with some 90 others sent to our company. . . .[57]

Lieut. Col. Smith and Major Hadley have resigned. The Regt. is under command of Capt. Griggs, of Co. B, Col. Lester being in command of the brigade. Griggs will be Lieut. Col., and Capt Mattson will be major. Then Gurnee, senior Capt., with his Co. E will be on the right and ours, Capt Preston being second Capt., will be on the left of the regt.[58]

I haven't much confidence in Kate's new Dr., though I hope she will help her. I wish Kate would write to me, but I suppose she does not feel like it while she is sick. . . .

> Yours ever.
> Madison.

Nininger, June 3, 1862
Tuesday evening

My Dear Madison

As this is my regular day for writing I will endeavor to keep my promise, but . . . I do not feel in a writing humor as I have been washing mostly all day and feel tired. . . .

When Kate was at Hastings yesterday she heard the 3rd Regg had marched for Alabama, when she told it, it gave me the blues. I thought that didn't sound much like being back again to spend the 4th with your old friends in Minn. But

---

57. A havelock was a soldier's cap with cloth attached to cover the nape of the neck in the hope that it would protect soldiers from the Southern sun.

58. For these changes, see "Roster of Field and Staff Officers," in Board of Commissioners, *Minnesota in the Civil and Indian Wars*, 178.

I suppose we shall have to submit to whatever comes while this war lasts, which I hope will not be a great while longer, though judging from present appearances I am afraid we have not seen the worst of it yet. There is a rumor to-day that they have had an engagement at Richmond. We can't tell whether it is so or not. There is so many things reported that prove to be false.[59]

Minnie stays with us part of the time until her father gets his house put up. It seems like old times to have her back again. She is a good girl. . . .

Kate is getting better very slowly. She continues to be doctored by that lady of whom I spoke in one of my former letters. She is very poorly yet. I told you I thought of teaching. I had two schools partly engaged so I would be sure of one. The one that I was most sure of getting, when they had the school house almost finished they quarreled and concluded they would have no school. I believe they are not going to have any in the other place for some reason. I do not know what. So I am not sure whether I shall get a school or not.

We have one large box from our society ready to send to your Regt when they are stationed at some place long enough for it to reach you. Remember me to Eugene. . . .

{up the side} . . . When you write be sure and tell me whether you have got well. If not, do spare no pains nor any thing else in trying to doctor up. . . .

Yours ever

Lizzie . . .

Murfreesboro, Tenn., Thursday, June 5, 1862.

Dear Lizzie:

I rec'd a letter from you yesterday, brought to me while I was on picket duty, from which I have just returned. Col. Lester has got his back up on account of the pickets "drawing pigs, chickens, &c, &c.,["] and will not allow corporals to command pickets, but puts it all upon the sergeants whom he holds to a strict accountability for all depredations committed by their respective commands. This new rule brings the sergts. on duty at least as often as once in four days and frequently as often as once in two days, which, with being up with the regt. as often as two or three nights a week, in line of battle to repel some rumored

59. Lizzie probably refers to the battle of Seven Pines, which took place five miles from Richmond on May 31 and June 1, 1862. The Union suffered fewer casualties than the Confederacy; the most significant outcome of the battle was, however, replacing the wounded Confederate general Joseph E. Johnston with General Robert E. Lee.

attack, makes it rather burthensome for me. I have, however, got over my little sick spell and do not mind it much now.[60]

You must allow me to change the subject a little. "A dog that isn't a dog," a great favorite of Co. F with whom she has been for the last two months, is playing under the table with her five little mischievous additions, while Capt. Preston's little coon with his feet and nose daubed with milk and dirt, has climbed all the way up to my shoulder where he sits rooting down the back of my neck. Sergt. Otto Dreher sits at the same table, writing a Dutch letter and laughing at my situation. Isn't this enough to bother one trying to write?—

It gave me a feeling of joy and relief to hear that Kate is getting better. I do hope she may continue to recover until she is once more in good health. I was also glad to hear the unexpected news of your friend Minnie's return to Nininger, for now you can have somebody to be happy with. I believe you think more of her than of any other being on earth.... (O dear! that plague of a coon, assisted by Eugene, is at me again.)... He has upset the ink and is making tracks all over the table. I will send you one.

More troops came in here yesterday and to-day to help us in case we are attacked by some 4,000 rebels hovering around to the east of us, with their scouts coming almost daily within five miles of us. Collisions frequently occur between them and our scouts. We have several prisoners. (Beans are ready and I must go to dinner.)

After dinner, Coon asleep on Capt's bed, 1862.

The 7th Ohio Regt. is just marching past our camp, going to encamp near us for awhile. I should not be surprised if we should have a fight here before the war closes, though we keep everything so ready to meet them that it may deter them. If they could surprise us—which is almost impossible—I have no doubt but that they would attack us in less than 48 hours. If they ever do you may set it down that the city of Murfreesboro, whom they rely upon for help, will be burned to ashes. All our sick have been removed from town, and every night Capt. Hewitt places two of his howitzers and a Parrott Rifle Cannon in position to shell the town upon the first demonstration of hostility by the secesh living in it....

You desire me to take care of myself and keep from duty when I am not well. You need have no fear, for you may rest assured that I shall take care of myself at all times. I had no business to let you know that I was not well for you are bound to let it worry you. My sickness is never anything more than a temporary affair,

60. Madison was elected sergeant in April after Francis Bissell was discharged in January 1862.

which gives me the blues for the time. I am quite well again now with the exception of diarrhea which is a prevailing trouble in this climate. Briggs has not done a days duty since last February. I presume he will have to be discharged. I believe he is more homesick than anything else. After a soldier gets thoroughly homesick he is seldom good for anything afterward. They will conjure up some disease and imagine themselves sick any how. Some men are more *babies* than *men*.

. . . Your opinion upon the conduct of the war is much like my own. I think more, *much more*, might be done. This fighting the devil with tufts of grass is not to my mind the most approved method of conquering him. It is not so much on my own account that I care. If I thought it necessary and the Government able to stand it, I would cheerfully serve three years, or even longer. . . .

> Yours with much love.
> Madison.

> Nininger June 17, 1862

Dear Madison

I wrote to you last sabbath one week [ago]. Should have written last Sunday but my time was taken up all day with Sunday school and meeting so that I did not get time. And yesterday being washing day, I felt so tired that I thought I would not til to-day.

I rec'd a letter from you last Saturday. Was *very very* glad to get it, to hear you were getting well again. I hope you will continue to have good health while you remain south. I rec'd a few lines from Eugene in your letter. Please tell him I will endeavor to write to him this week if I can conjure up anything to write. I also rec'd the coon's paw, or rather mark of his paw which you sent. . . .

We are having very pleasant weather now though very cool for June. Kate is some better than when I wrote last. I feel quite in hope she will get better now. Her and Minnie is teasing me so that I hardly know what I am writing. . . .

I have just been out picking a boal of strawberries.[61] I wish you were here to help us eat them; they are not so plenty as they were last year. We heard that sixty of the 3rd Regt has been taken prisoners and several killed. I think it must be false as I have heard nothing about it lately. We recd the coat you sent in good order. . . .

> Good bye
> Lizzie S. C.

Our folks all join me in love to you

61. "Boal" probably is "bowl."

Murfreesboro, Tenn., Sunday, June 22, 1862.

Dear Lizzie:

Yesterday I wrote you a short note thinking I should not feel like writing much of a letter, for several days, but this morning I felt some better, my boils not giving me so much pain as they did yesterday. This forenoon I hobbled out to enjoy a little ease, seated in a chair beneath the branches of a shady tree in front of the Captain's tent.

The bugle sounded the church call, so long unheard and unheeded by us, and I wanted to go, but felt as though I could not remain at ease long enough to hear a sermon. Presently I heard the voices of those assembled, as they sang the first hymn, and I got up and walked to within hearing of the chaplain's voice, where I listened to a short, but one of the most impressive, sermons I ever listened to. It was preached by Dr. Crary, our new chaplain.[62] Since leaving Minn. we have heard very little preaching of any kind, and none before like this. While surrounded by the stirring scenes of an active military campaign the soldier's mind has little chance to think of anything else than what is passing before it, and when a little temporary rest does occur, during which his ears are saluted by words from such a soul stirring speaker as Mr. Crary, is it any wonder that emotions, hard to be repressed, should arise in his breast? In spite of all I could do I had to cry.

Monday, 23, 1862.

Everybody kept such a blabbing and my nerves were so easily disturbed that I had to give up writing yesterday. I do not feel in the writing mood to-day, but will try to write something. I wish I could be with you for a while, then there would be no need of writing, for we could talk.

You ask if I distrust Kate's doctress because she is a woman. By no means. It is her method that I fail to confide in. I think it will take something besides Galvanism to cure Kate, though I know of no harm in that. I do hope that she may soon get relief from some source, poor girl! If she ever needs money do not fail to let her have it so long as I have any in your hands.

I heard by way of Gus Case that Nininger has had another Ice-Cream party, and that a certain trio had another old fashioned chat again. Be careful, "Sasy Lib," or you will cut "Maym" out, high and dry; besides you do not know how soon I may get jealous, but I presume as I am in the army, I cannot help myself.

62. The Third Minnesota's first chaplain was Chauncey Hobart, who resigned April 13, 1862. B. F. Crary from Red Wing, Goodhue County, served as chaplain until June 2, 1863, when he too resigned.

There are so many movements going on now in Tenn. that it is almost useless for me to attempt to give you a history of any of them. About three weeks ago 60 of our cavalry were captured some 12 miles from here. They passed me on picket while coming in after having been paroled. Others have been captured at different times. On Wednesday the 11th, 5000 troops including our regt., which led the advance, started for McMinnville, 40 miles from here, on a forced march. Arriving at that place, our regt and some cavalry and artillery were ordered to Pikeville over the mountains, into the valley of the Sequatchie, a branch of the Tennessee River. It is in the edge of East Tenn. We caught a lot of rebels and captured considerable property. Our march over the mountains was tedious indeed, and the weather awfully hot.[63] Huge rattlesnakes defied us at every step, scorpions darted along the ground and up the trees, and lizzards crawled about in sickening profusion. Bugs, worms, beetles, spiders, &c., &c.... House flies, too, are more numerous than you can imagine. The inhabitants of that rough country are most wretchedly poor, and I cannot, for my life, see how they keep soul and body together.[64]

About 12 hours after we left McMinnville, the rest of the division followed us, Gen. Dumont expecting our regt. to meet with heavy opposition, but the cowards retreated before us as fast as they could.[65] When the division got within 10 miles of us it was turned about and orders sent for us to return, which we did, starting Sunday night, the 15th. We left McMinnville Tuesday, 5 A.M., leaving the stars and stripes waving over them with an injunction from Gen Dumont not to take them down, at the expense of having their town burnt.

63. Regarding this movement, Andrews writes, "June 11th the regiment moved with the expedition (column of 3,000 with about eight hundred cavalry), under General Dumont, to Pikeville, Colonel Lester having immediate command of the troops. Marched the first forty miles to McMinnville in twenty-four hours. Pikeville was reached the 14th of June, and the column got back to Murfreesboro the 18th. The Cumberland Mountains were thus twice rapidly crossed amid intense heat and dust" ("Narrative of the Third Regiment," 151).

64. William D. Hale also remarked on this march and the poverty of the mountain people in an undated letter, which describes the scenery and purpose in many of the same terms as Madison. See undated letter, Hale Papers. For soldiers' attitudes toward Southern civilians, see Ash, *When the Yankees Came,* 35.

65. William D. Hale remarks on riding on a bumpy, dusty road for many hours to find "Nary butternuts tho a few had been in the Town that day. They heard of our coming of course by a [?] courier whose Father was one of them and they took to the mountains double quick." Hale assessed the march in much harsher terms than Madison: "The whole expedition was futile, save to give the people an impression of our power.... I am glad I went. Twas very hard & useless, yet the fatique is no more to be remembered for we have some what to talk about" (undated letter, Hale Papers).

On Friday morning we got back to Murfreesboro once more. The whole distance from here to Pikeville is 78 miles. How soon we may have to go again on some other expedition is more than I know, but soon I think. Gen. Mitchell sent to Col. Lester this morning to know how much force he could spare, saying he wished to concentrate at Stevenson in the N.E. corner of Ala. Whether it will be ours or some other regt. to go, is not yet known.

Since our return we have again moved our camp. It now occupies the grounds in front of an Academy, the building itself being used as Col. Lester's Brigade Head Quarters.[66] We have plenty of new potatoes, apples, onions, and any quantity of blackberries which grow in every nook and corner. It seems like "down east" to walk into the orchard and help one's self to fruit.

I recd another letter from Piercy lately. He speaks of having recd a letter from you, which he is going to answer, and tells me not to get jealous. Eugene has been a little unwell, but is all right now. Nick Obrien, while out foraging some two weeks ago, fell from a wagon and hurt one of his legs seriously. He is able to limp around a little now, and will, I hope, soon be well. You asked me sometime ago if I had opportunities for getting my washing done. I have never found any difficulty yet.

Now, Lizzie, you must excuse this mixed up mess of a letter, and I will try to do better when I feel better. If I ever get tough and hearty I shall not brag again, for I am sure to be sick when I do.

> Ever yours truly.
> Madison

> Murfreesboro, Tenn., June 26, 1862.

Dear Lizzie:

... I should indeed be glad to be *where* I could help you eat that bowl of strawberries which you spoke of, but not so much for the fruit as to be with you. Fruit of almost every kind, is very plenty here.

You refer to the report that sixty of our regt. were taken prisoners and several killed, but from my last letter to you and from Jno. P. Owens letter in the Press you have no doubt ere this learned the truth in regard to the report. You may bet your bottom dollar that when you hear, in truth, that we have been in a fight, the missing will not exceed the killed and wounded.[67]

---

66. See also Andrews, "Narrative of the Third Regiment," 151.

67. John P. Owens probably was a private in Company I, Third Minnesota, from West Albany in Fillmore County. He enlisted in 1864. His letter was published, however, June 19, 1862, in the *St. Paul Press*.

I never saw a cooler set of men—how different from the raw mass when first congregated at the Fort! I shall never forget how perfectly cool [and] quietly the regt. behaved on our second trip when at one time we thought we were surely in for a fight at last. The cavalry scouts discovered the enemy about a mile ahead, getting ready to attack us as they supposed, but in reality to run away. The column was halted, the 3d Minn. ordered by Co. forward into line of battle, extending out on each side of the road and supported by the other regts in parallel lines in our rear; the artillery was brought up and placed in position on the center, right, and left of our regt., and 800 cavalry sent forward to bring on the engagement, when lo! it was found that the enemy had fled, leaving only a few traps behind. The cavalry pursued them, capturing fifty prisoners, three drums, and some other articles, including a lot of ammunition.

It is rumored that two com'd and four non-com'd officers will soon be sent to Minn. to recruit for our regt. I should like to be one of them, but shall not as there are so many eager ones to go. This, if it be true, does not look like our being discharged very soon. Well, if we are to stay a year longer, I hope the government will be forced to allow her troops to fight instead of sending them out on a courting tour to woo back those malignant devils, known as rebels, who fight us by all the means in their power, in accordance with civilized, and even barbarous, warfare. . . .

> Ever your
> Madison.

Murfreesboro, Tenn., July 2, 1862.

My Dear Lizzie

To-morrow is my regular day for writing to you, but as there is a rumor that we are to march and it is my turn to go on picket if we do not march, I will write to-day. It seems as though it had been a month since I last wrote to you, perhaps it is because I have not recd. any letter from you since then.

It is very clear here to-day, just cool enough for comfort—such a day as I would like to take to step across the threshold and seat myself by your side, while the man of the house is out at work, Aunt Susan gone visiting, Kate up to Mrs. Russells, and Dollie gone strawberrying. How would that suit you? Wouldn't we have a good time at least for one afternoon. But it is of no use for one to be fancying pictures like that in these times.

A year ago I was in the habit of sitting near you and reading about the movements of our army—not then near so far south as this—and thinking what it must be suffering from the heat. Excepting when we have been on the march—which has been but little of the time—we have not suffered at all from the heat. The nights are cool enough for comfort. Our camp is in the shade and by cool springs and a good stream for bathing, and, as we do not drill at all now, there is no occasion for leaving the shade except when we go to or return from picket posts. I presume the warm weather must come from now to the last of August, or not at all, bringing with it fevers and cholorea morbus. We already have some cases, but not *near* so many as one would expect even in Minnesota.[68]

I feel, I think, as well as ever I did in my life, and can eat almost anything in quantities ranging from a "pile" upwards. Upon examination I find in my nice, new haversack a loaf of baker's bread, some dried beef, herring, lemons, crushed sugar, and some fried lamb—the latter "hooked" only last night by some of the boys from an old "secesh planter." Pigs, beef, mutton, potatoes, onions, chickens, fruit, etc, etc. find their way to our cookhouses—owing to the fact that the "soger" boys have got their hand in; so you see we do not mean to starve. The "secesh" give us a wide berth, and when we want anything all we have to do is to take it. Union men's property is sacredly respected by us, though they must hold out the sure sign of a little red, white, and blue waving over the premises.

The Nininger boys are all well and doing duty. Charley Russell was sick for the first time and staid behind when we went to Pikesville.

I heard, Miss, that you are not content with going to Ice Cream parties, but have recently attended a sort of private party where the elite partook of straw-berries, etc.[69] One who was there sent me word by the grapevine telegraph. I was not aware before this that you had got to be one of the *upper crust*. If you get too high you will discard your "soger" boy altogether for one of the *upper tens*. . . .

Last Friday Eugene and I took a stroll into the country and ate as many plums and blackberries as we could hold. Go where you will here, you find blackberry bushes, and this year they are as full as can be of large, sweet berries. Bushels come into camp daily. . . .

> Ever yours truly.—
> Madison.

68. Cholera morbus occurs in the summer and autumn and affects the digestive system.

69. Madison might refer to one of two strawberry and ice cream festivals in Hastings organized by the women of the Baptist and Presbyterian churches for June 21 and 23, 1862, respectively. See *Hastings Independent*, 26 June 1862.

Nashville, Tenn., July 19, 1862

My Dear Lizzie:

Presuming that you are a little anxious to hear from me, I will just drop you a line to assure you of my safety. Last Sunday morning we were awakened by the report of guns in the Camp of the 9th Mich. We were soon formed in lines and marched into an open field where we got into line of battle just in time to resist a charge from the rebel Cavalry, driving them with considerable loss on their side. We held our position till three o'clock P.M., repulsing them at every attempt they made upon us, when at last *our officers* surrendered us amid the tears and curses of the men. The Cavalry and 9th Mich had been overpowered and surrendered three hours before.[70]

We were taken to McMinnville and paroled, and got to this city last night. The enemy consisted of the 1st, 2nd, and 3d Georgia, Texas Rangers and parts of a Ky. and a Tenn. regt.—all Cavalry well armed with good double barreled shot guns and two good revolvers apiece. We were well treated. The most of the regt saw but little fighting, but companies E and F deployed as skirmishers and fought for several hours.

Co. F is all right but Nick Obrien slightly wounded. Eugene and I were side by side, the enemy's bullets flying at us and the shot and shell from the artillery screaming over our heads at the rebels, knocking down bark and limbs from the trees. One ball passed through my coat and one hit Eugene's ankle cutting away his stocking and bruising the flesh a little. He fought like a hero. Gen Nelson is at this moment fighting at Murfreesboro.[71]

Good Bye
Madison.

70. Madison described the Third Minnesota's involvement in its first major engagement, the battle of Murfreesboro. For additional accounts see 20 July 1862, Brookins Letters; 22 July 1862, Hale Papers; and the July 21, 1862, letter by George H. Peasley in *Annual Re-Union of the Third Regiment Minnesota Veteran Volunteers*, 7. See also Andrews, "Narrative of the Third Regiment," 151–58; Fitzharris, "'Our Disgraceful Surrender'"; and Trenerry, "Lester's Surrender at Murfreesboro," 68–70.

71. General William Nelson was part of General Buell's Army of the Ohio, which was to advance on Chattanooga. Little is said about his activities at Murfreesboro, but he was promoted to major general on July 19, 1862, days after the battle. See Warner, *Generals in Blue*, 344.

Benton Barracks, St. Louis, Mo., July 31, 1862

My Dear Lizzie:

. . . I wrote you a short letter just after I arrived at Nashville from McMinnville—
a paroled prisoner of war.[72] Since then I might have written all I wished to write,
but I feel very little inclination to write about events which are painful to me
to think of. It makes me feel down-hearted when I think of my military career
thus far.

I enlisted last fall through patriotic motives, with very little regard to my personal conveniences or to position, and because I considered it my duty and privilege to do something for my country at an hour when my humble services were
of some avail. I did so, to, with a full knowledge of what I should have to endure,
and have never allowed myself to look back over my shoulder or murmur at
what lay before me. Our regt. won a reputation of which I felt proud. I longed for
the time to come when we should have the opportunity of trying our mettle on
the field of battle, not that I felt particularly brave, but because that was what we
enlisted for—*to fight*. That time came. We met the enemy and put him to flight in
every encounter, when all at once our glorious [advance] was turned into a shameful surrender by the unaccountable conduct of our officers. "Thereby hangs a
tale," a fearful development is yet to be made, but I will not make it; I will only
tell *you*. I[t] is contained in one word—*whisky*![73] I cannot now tell you all, but
when I see you again you shall know all. There were many little incidents in the
week that we were first conquerors then captives, then paroled pilgrims from
rebeldom to the land of our friends again.

It was our first battle, and all was new to me—the shouts of charging squadrons,
the sublime tumult of a foe in confusion, plunging horses, falling with dead and
living riders and all trying to escape from the jaws of death hurled from our
Minnie rifles, the terrific roar of artillery and volleys of infantry firing, and the
horrifying sight of the mangled, ghastly dead and dying.

The first wounded man I saw was just after the first charge. I had seen him
fall from his horse, and I went to see what I could do for him. My heart melted in
pity at the sight. He belonged to the 2nd Ga. cavalry. He begged for water, which
I gave him and then placed his hat over his face to keep the sun from it. I asked

72. Lizzie's letters from early June through early August 1862 are not in the correspondence. They may have been lost when Madison sent a package of letters home, or Madison may not have been allowed to take them as a prisoner of war after the surrender.

73. For more on this accusation about alcohol, see Trenerry, "Lester's Surrender
at Murfreesboro," 196. William D. Hale labels them "whisky guzzling officers" two
months after the battle but did not mention whiskey in his initial letter after the surrender (11 September 1862, Hale Papers).

him how he felt, to which he calmly replied that he could bear it. I took his gun and saber and hid them. I have the gun now—a double barreled shot gun. The poor fellow died in a few hours.

I saw many others during the day. At one time I stopped during our skirmish in front of the regt to look at a dead man. He was a large, good looking man—an orderly Sergt—lying on his back, a pool of blood which had issued from the fearful looking wound through his head from ear to ear, showed that the work had been done. He looked calm and natural, except the glazed eye. Pretty soon one of our men came up and pulled a package of letters from his pocket, one of which he gave to me. It was from his wife, F. E. Preston, and dated "Social Circle, Ga." She has sent him some pies, cakes, and peas, and is going to do everything for him. She does not want him to get his miniature taken until she sees him again. Poor woman! She will never see him again on this earth. I could not help thinking how badly she would feel when she recd. the sad news.[74]

It would have done you good to see how our boys behaved. I had command of the right of our line of skirmishers and had all I could do to keep the boys from going far in advance of where we were ordered. Eugene and I were together on the right, by far the most exposed position, all the time. I saw him bring down two of them. I fired some 25 rounds but cannot say that I hit anybody, for I did not stop to look but stepped at once behind a tree and loaded again and again, till recalled upon the battalion.

The most magnificent part of all was the humming, screaming and hissing of shot and shell over our heads, once a charge of cannister struck too low and threw the bark and dirt all around us, but fortunately we had got on the opposite side of the trees, expecting it from the way a previous charge was directed lower than usual.[75] Once Eugene and I ventured too far to the right and were fired at by some of our own men 500 yards in the rear, they mistaking us for rebels. I stopped them by waving my hand and hallooing to them, but not until two more shots came very near striking me.

After we had fallen back to our last position Capt Preston entrusted me with the command of a section of skirmishers which Lieut. Col. Griggs ordered him to throw out on the left. After the surrender was agreed upon an order was sent for me to bring them in, and when I told the boys of it they broke and threw away

74. The dead orderly was probably Frances Preston, a sergeant in Company D of the Second Georgia Cavalry. See "Civil War Soldiers and Sailors System," www.itd.nps.gov/cwss/soldiers.htm; and Poole, *Cracker Cavaliers*, 22. For attitudes toward enemy soldiers, see Linderman, *Embattled Courage*, 66–69.

75. A type of case shot used for short range fighting, canister shot sprayed numerous small bullets into advancing armies.

many of the guns and all their cartridges, some of them fairly crying and others cursing at the thought of surrendering to an enemy we had beaten and whom we could not see.

The officers who voted to surrender tried to avoid their men who openly accused them of shameful cowardice, and by the time we got to McMinnville a meaner sneaking looking set of beings could not be found. Lieut. Col. Griggs, Capts Andrews, Hoit and Foster, and Lieuts. Taylor of our regt. and Ellisworth of the battery were cheered and praised wherever they were met by their men, and they held their heads up like men even at the hour of parting with their men at McMinnville.[76] Poor Col. Lester! Sunk in one day from the enjoyment of the highest confidence of brave men to the deepest shame and disgrace.

We left Nashville on the 25 and Louisville on the 26th on board the Forest Queen arriving at Jefferson Barracks last Monday, thence here day before yesterday. Jefferson Barracks are ten miles below St. Louis and only 2½ miles below Casoudelet. Benton Barracks are two miles N.W. of St. Louis. The street cars run out to her.[77]

E. S. Kellogg, of Faribault, is the boy who told stories about our officers. . . .[78]

> Ever your
> Madison.

{top back page margin} It is a singular coincidence that the same day and hour you were writing your last letter I was fighting on Sunday, too. J. M. B. . . .

{top margin on the second to last page} What made you dream of me three times in the week previous to my being taken prisoner? Did not you think something was going to happen to me? J. M.

Benton Barracks, St. Louis, Mo., Aug. 8, 1862

My Dear Lizzie:

I feel lonely to-day and wholly unfit for writing letters, but as it has been a little more than one week since I wrote to you I feel bound to write something.

---

76. These are the officers Andrews identifies in his "Narrative of the Third Regiment," except for Ellisworth, who was part of not the Third Minnesota but Hewitt's Artillery. See Andrews, 155.

77. For a narrative of the movement from Murfreesboro to Nashville, see 22 July 1862, Hale Papers. For more on Benton Barracks, see 20 July 1862, Brookins Letters; and Carley, *Minnesota in the Civil War,* 72–73.

78. Edward S. Kellogg, listed as thirteen years old in 1860, lived in Faribault Township of Rice County; he gave his age as eighteen when he enlisted in Company F in October 1862.

Several days ago we drew new clothing, and day before yesterday we were paid off up to the 1st of July. Ever since payment almost a continual stream of desertion has continued. Half of Co. K has already gone and nearly as many from some of the other companies. Johnson Truax went yesterday. I presume he will go to Nininger unless caught before he can get there.[79] There is considerable sickness in camp here—the climate being far more disagreeable and unhealthy than in middle Tennessee. I am suffering from the effects of a severe cold and diarrhea at present, which is one of my reasons for not having written when my regular day came round.

...I have seen several of my acquaintance since we came here ... [and] several of the Minn 1st who were captured at Bull Run. The other day I ran across the name of Wm Govett while looking over the City Directory. It appeared twice—once as Wm Govett, architect, boards such a place—next as Wm Govett architect residence such a place. I have forgotten which regt. you said he was in. I should be glad to meet him.[80]

In one of your letters you ask what I think of this war, &c., &c. Well, I think a great deal—much more than I say. There has been too much *said* and too little *done* already, so I am content to say little and do all I can, trusting that all will yet be right. The war has been in many respects badly conducted, and I knew it as well eight months ago as I do to-day, but it is coming round all right as I knew it would. The worst is yet to come. Terrible have been the sins of the south and terrible must be their retribution—thousands of lives yet to be taken, homes and property laid waste, and slaves to be freed.[81]

79. On desertion, see letter, "Sunday 17th," Washburn Papers. Historian Joseph Fitzharris determined that seven men had deserted the regiment before the battle of Murfreesboro on July 13, 1862. Another nine deserted between mid-July and late August 1862. While at Benton Barracks, many men were absent without leave, often returning the next day. On August 8, 61 men were not at roll call, and as many as 141 were absent on August 24. See Fitzharris, "'Our Disgraceful Surrender,'" 9–10.

80. William Govett was Lewis Govett's brother and Minnie Russell Govett's brother-in-law and lived in Nininger City until at least 1860. See Ignatius Donnelly to George H. Burns, 1 January 1859, roll 151, Donnelly Papers. The captured First Minnesota volunteers is an unclear statement. In his history of the First Minnesota, Richard Moe accounts for the regiment's killed, wounded, and missing after the first battle of Bull Run in July 1861 without mentioning any captured soldiers. The second battle of Bull Run would not take place until August 28 to 30, 1862. Some of the First Minnesota were taken prisoner after an engagement at Savage Station, Virginia, on June 29, 1862, but they were sent to Libby Prison and Belle Island. Some wounded were sent home from the prison and might have stopped at Benton Barracks on the way to Minnesota. See Moe, *The Last Full Measure*, 152–56, 166–71; and Carley, *Minnesota in the Civil War*, 73.

81. For vengeance and freeing slaves as a motivation to fight, see McPherson, *For Cause and Comrades*, 120, 154.

The President has at last been forced to cut loose from the clutches of the border state half-way traitors and heed the enlightened sentiment of New England and some others of the Northern States. The glorious confiscation act—the edict of freedom to the slave—has at lest been passed. Good! The proper steps for raising a competent army are being taken namely, drafting. Better!! The signs of the times fully indicate that the war is at last to be carried on as it ought to have been from the beginning. "Governing by love" is played out. If so I will add—*Best!!!*[82]

But all is not to be roses and honey as many foolishly [say]. Public opinion will hereafter, as it has before, bestow extravagant praise upon some Gen. or some particular act or measure to-day and without a shadow of reason, condemn to-morrow. Reason in such times as these, seems to run mad. But enough. Gods hand is in this work, and I feel confident of the result.[83]

A General exchange of prisoners has been agreed upon and several thousand already exchanged. When this regt will be exchanged is more than we know, but before long I expect. Meantime I wish the government would grant us furloughs to visit our homes since we are doing no good here, but as it will not we must do the best we can and remain where we are. I hear since I commenced this letter, that some of the deserters have been caught. It will go hard with them if they are caught.[84]

Give my love to all and write as soon as you can.

Very truly yours.
Madison.

Nininger City, Minn. Aug 10, 1862
Sunday

My Dear Madison

I again seat my-self to write you a few lines. It is not because I have anything interesting to write about. It is because I think of you more then anyone else that

82. Abolition sentiment in the Republican Party was strongest in New England. The second Confiscation Act, passed July 17, 1862, freed slaves who reached Union lines. A quasi draft was put into place in August 1862 to encourage enlistment in the Union army after the Militia Act was passed in July 1862.
83. Madison describes the common shift in public opinion that followed both victories and defeats on the battlefield. See Paludan, *"A People's Contest,"* chap. 12.
84. Prisoners of war were kept in parole camps, like Benton Barracks, until they were exchanged, according to rank, between the Union and Confederacy. See Donald et al., *The Civil War and Reconstruction,* 242–43. See also Carley, *Minnesota in the Civil War,* 72. For desertion, see Linderman, *Embattled Courage,* 174, 176–77.

is absent from me and this is the only (unsatisfactory) way I have of letting you know how often I do think of you. And you dont know how much I want to see you.

Am received a letter from Eugene yesterday saying if you were not exchanged soon he with several others were coming home, that they would run away. If I were Eugene I would not do that. Whatever I did do I would do honorably. Dont mention that for any thing to Eugene.

Such a time as there is round here at the present about drafting you never heard. Am is going to join the army in two or three days. There will not be any more volunteering after the 15th of the month in this state. I am glad they are going to draft. Think if they had have resorted to that long ago the war would be ended now. . . .

I think judge from your last letter (written the 31 of last month) that you have the blues. I think you have enough to make you feel badly and almost give up in despair but you must hope on. If it was not for hope the heart would break. When troubles press heavily there is one on whom you can depend. It seems to me that there never was a time when people in general needed a time of comfort more then at the present. Mr Bowler, when you feel homesick and lonely and when you think of the loved ones at home and their afflictions, you can think of them, I believe, with a clear conscience and know that you have never done anything to make their sorrow any more. And ever rest assured that I am with you in all your troubles. Not one hour passes in the week that during it I dont think of you and wonder if you are passing it in joy or sorrow. Do come home if you can. . . .

      Yours ever Lizzie

. . . Poor old Mrs Truax is very uneasy about Johnson. Has not heard from him since the battle.[85]

{top margin} Do burn this when read.

                   Benton Barracks, St. Louis, Mo., Aug. 13, 1862.

My Dear Lizzie:

. . . You speak of looking for me home, and how much you wish you might not look in vain. The Government grants no more furloughs at present, very properly,

---

85. Mrs. Truax was Sally Truax, who operated a boardinghouse in Nininger City in 1860. Robert Johnson Truax was her oldest son, seventeen years old in 1860 (although listed as twenty-two in the muster rolls).

too. None could be more desirous of visiting their friends than I am, but as it cannot be done honorably, I try to content myself as best I can, trusting that the time will come when I can do so without deserting. I have thus far remained at my post and performed my duty as well as my limited abilities would permit, and now when I can [do] no more good, at least do no hurt. It would be a very easy matter to get away from here and go to Minnesota or any where else, but no true soldier would do it. There is a prospect of our soon being exchanged and sent to Minn. to recruit, in which event I hope to meet you once more.

I cannot but feel deeply concerned for poor Kate when I think of her condition. I do hope that Dr. Thorne will be the means of helping her. As far as I have observed the Scrafula is almost incurable. Mother's family have always suffered from it.[86]

It gives me pleasure to hear that my plum tree was leaved out. When I heard that it was dead I fancied it as emblematic of the result of my labors in Nininger.

You ask how I felt in battle, whether afraid or cool. It is useless for me to say much about it. If I had been base enough to act cowardly, I should also be mean enough to deny it now, so I will leave it to my comrades to say whether I acted like one afraid or not. My feelings during the battle were different from what I expected. I always thought that I should feel some hesitancy when engaged in the business of shooting my fellow beings, but I did not. My only desire was to kill, and nothing gave me so much pleasure as to see them drop and tumble from their horses. The only bad feeling I experienced was when implored by the wounded to render aid or to kill them, but it did not last long, for the business before me soon made me forget them after they were out of my sight, and after a while I would pass them without even looking at them any more than just to take one glance, loosing all care for them.[87]

Shortly after the surrender, being in advance of the rest, I fell in with Major Whaley, of the 2nd Ga. He ordered his servant to give me a horse and together we rode and conversed until we arrived at Readyville where we were to encamp for the night. After a short parley with Gen. Forrest about the camping ground, he ordered some eatables from the hotel where we found the Gen., and gave me as much as I could eat of such as he could get. It was him who led the charge on our regt. Several of us noticed him as he emerged from the woods, brandishing his sword and cheering on his men. He was one of the few who passed through

86. Dr. William Thorne lived in Hastings in 1860. Scrofula is tuberculosis of the neck or cervical tuberculosis.

87. For courage, ferocity during battle, and attitudes toward enemies, see Linderman, *Embattled Courage,* chap. 4.

between Co.F and the battery, coming within twenty feet of our Co. and firing his revolver and swinging his sword as he went. He was a large, swarthy man and rode a fine white horse. Eugene and two or three near him tried to shoot him, knowing that he must be an officer, but he escaped unharmed.[88]

I wish I could go with Pray after a claim. Tell him to select one for me by all means. Give my respects to him.[89]

I am very glad to hear that Mr. Donnelly has secured the nomination for Representative in Congress. He will surely be elected, and will make the best representative Minn. could possibly find inside her borders....[90]

I went to St. Louis Monday, thence with Frank Cobb to Belleville, Ill. where we staid all night and returned yesterday. St Louis is quite a city. I have been all over it....

Yours ever.
Madison...

88. Madison refers to Major Caleb Arthur Whaley of Company H (Magruder Dragoons), Second Regiment Georgia Cavalry. See gacsa.cobbslegion.com/units/2nd_reg_cavalry.htm. For General Forrest at Murfreesboro, see Andrews, "Narrative of the Third Regiment," 153; and Wyeth, *Life of General Nathan Bedford Forrest*, 85–90.

89. Lizzie's letters of July 26 and August 5 are not in the correspondence. Pray might have been seeking a homestead claim after the Thirty-second Congress passed the Homestead Act on May 20, 1862. For the importance of the Homestead Act in Minnesota, see Jarchow, *The Earth Brought Forth*, 12, 65.

90. For Donnelly's campaign for the House of Representatives, see Ridge, *Ignatius Donnelly*, chap. 5.

3

Anxious to Hear from You . . .
More Anxious to See You

Madison returned to Minnesota in early September 1862, not on a recruiting mission but on a new military campaign. Since August 18, western Minnesota had been in turmoil. The Dakota Indians living on a reservation along the Minnesota River had been waiting for the federal government's annuity payment of $71,000 in gold coins, which would allow them to purchase food from traders on the reservation. It was six weeks late. Families at the Lower Agency had retained much of their traditional cultural practices. Families at the Upper Agency, often known as farmer Indians, who had adopted agriculture and, to some extent, Christianity, had received some food, but both groups were growing hungry and were desperate for the government supplies. Tensions ran high at the Lower Agency, especially after traders denied the Dakota access to the food in their warehouses on August 4, one going so far as to say, "If they are hungry, let them eat grass or their own dung." Although some food was distributed to ameliorate their condition, it was not enough and only temporary.

Within two weeks young warriors and frustrated chiefs unleashed their anger on white settlers along the Minnesota River. Dakota warriors used the same methods of warfare they had practiced against the Ojibwe, attacking isolated farmhouses and small settlements. They killed men, women, and children, raided and burned households and farms, and took white captives. The Dakota were defeated at New Ulm and Fort Ridgely, both of which had time to prepare defenses.

From the beginning, the Dakota had been divided about attacking the whites, with many Indians at the Upper Agency advocating peace, thus earning the label "friendly" Indians. By the time the Third Minnesota arrived on September 13 at Fort Ridgely, where ex-governor General Henry Hastings Sibley awaited them, the "hostiles" had abandoned the Lower Agency and tried unsuccessfully to convince the friendlies to join the uprising. The Third Minnesota set out for the

Upper Agency, at the confluence of the Yellow Medicine and Minnesota Rivers, and on September 22 set up camp near the agency. Early in the morning the next day, some men from the Third Minnesota went in search of potatoes at nearby Wood Lake. They encountered Indians hiding in ambush, and a battle ensued as the rest of the Third Minnesota, under a new commander, Major Abraham Welch, joined the fray. After two hours, the 740 Dakota retreated to their camp near the Upper Agency, and then some of the hostiles fled farther along the river to Big Stone Lake, leaving most of the white captives with the friendly Indians. Seven were killed and thirty-four were wounded from among the Minnesota regiments engaged at Wood Lake. Sibley delayed three days before he moved his troops to a new camp, Camp Release, where his soldiers received the white captives from the friendly Indians and then required those same Indians to surrender.

For several weeks following the release of the captives, Sibley's men scouted for additional Dakota who were willing to surrender and buried the many dead, some having remained in the late summer sun for almost two months. A military commission was formed to try nearly 400 Dakota men; 307 were sentenced to death. Minnesota citizens demanded vengeance and hoped to see the convicted hang for their crimes. President Lincoln requested the commission's files, however, and after review sentenced thirty-eight Dakota to death for murder and rape. The largest public execution in American history took place on December 26, 1862, in Mankato. The remaining prisoners were sent to a prison in Davenport, Iowa, while the Dakota men, women, and children who had put themselves in government custody at Camp Release endured a forced march in November to Pike Island, below Fort Snelling, where they spent the winter in an internment camp guarded by Minnesota troops. Over 130 died of exposure and disease. In spring 1863 they and the Ho-Chunk (Winnebago) Indians, who had not been part of the uprising, were forced to leave Minnesota and live at Crow Creek, a remote and drought-stricken site in Dakota Territory, where hundreds more died from disease and malnutrition. Although the Dakota uprising was over in Minnesota, the federal government continued to support military campaigns in the Great Plains to track down the fugitive hostiles and subdue the western Dakota bands, which inaugurated the quarter-century war between the Plains Indians and the U.S. military.[1]

The men of the Third Minnesota, including Madison, used their victory at

1. For the U.S.-Dakota Conflict, see Carley, *The Dakota War of 1862;* Anderson and Woolworth, *Through Dakota Eyes;* Anderson, *Kinsmen of Another Kind,* chap. 12; Folwell, *A History of Minnesota,* chaps. 5–7; Andrews, "Narrative of the Third Regiment," 158–62; and Josephy, *The Civil War in the American West,* chaps. 4, 5.

Wood Lake to buoy sagging confidence after the surrender at Murfreesboro and subsequent detention at Benton Barracks. Over the course of the campaign against the Dakota, more soldiers from the Third Minnesota returned to duty, thus restoring the ranks from the 270 men who began the campaign to nearly 350 by mid-October. Madison considered himself a loyal and dutiful soldier who eschewed desertion, even temporarily to see Lizzie as the Third Minnesota passed by Hastings and Nininger on its way to Fort Snelling in early September. She did not view it in this light and, by November, issued a mock threat that if she did not see him within two weeks, she probably would not see him again.

* * *

St. Clara Nine [steamer], Minnesota River,
Sept. 5, 1862

My Dear Lizzie:

We have just pushed off from the Levee at old Fort Snelling, amid the cheers and blessings of our soldier and citizen friends, assembled to see the Minn. 3d off to fight the Indians. How peculiar have been my feelings since my return to Minn. Everywhere we have been enthusiastically cheered and welcomed by Minnesotians. It makes the tears come to my eyes, and yet it makes my heart swell with pride and gratitude to feel we have not yet lost the confidence of the people whom we were sent to represent on the battlefield. It seems to give these frightened people a feeling of relief to have the Minn. 3d between them and the Indians.[2]

I wanted very much—Oh, you do not know how much—to see you before leaving the Fort; but duty calls, and I must go. The other Sergeants of our company have all sneaked off, and I am left alone in command of Co. F—the honorable portion of it—about 35 in number—who prefer to fight for their homes and friends rather than seek our own comfort and pleasure. I little expect to see the indians; but, if we do, I know there will be no dodging by the boys who have stuck by so long. I was disappointed at not meeting you at either Hastings or Nininger—It made me feel sad, for I longed to see you so much.[3]

I was up to St Anthony last night, and returned this morning. Eugene had

2. For a similar assessment of the Third Minnesota's reception, see 11 September 1862, Hale Papers. Clearly, the expectations were for the Third Minnesota to redeem itself under new leadership: "that the valient men of the Third may have an opportunity of showing what they can do, when they have men to lead them who have the ability to plan and the bravery to execute" (*Hastings Independent*, 18 August 1862). See also *Hastings Independent*, 4 September 1862; and Andrews, "Narrative of the Third Regiment," 158.

3. On men not reporting to duty for the campaign against the Dakota, see Fitzharris, "'Our Disgraceful Surrender,'" 9.

not arrived at the Fort when we left, although he promised to be up last night without fail.

I hope we shall meet Capt. Kennedy's company before we return, for I want to see John Moulton and Amon. I was gratified to see Aunt Sarah and Peter once more, though I did not have a chance to say much to them. . . .[4]

Good-Bye!

> Ever your
> Madison.

Forest City, [Minn.,] Sept. 10, 1862.

My Dear Lizzie:

Having a few leisure moments I will scratch you a few lines, first to let you know that the Indians have not devoured me yet. It has been five days since we left Fort Snelling, during the whole of which time we have been on the tramp. We left Carver at 1 o'clock last Friday night, arriving at Glencoe on Saturday afternoon, where we found the town entirely deserted by everybody but fighting men and one heroic woman, though not an Indian had been seen there. Sunday, we reached Hutchinson, at which place the indians have committed murders, burned 11 buildings, including an academy, Grist and saw-mill, and several fine dwellings, and driven off hundreds of cattle and horses. Not one woman and but one man had left the town but stood up bravely to defend their homes.[5] At Hutchinson I found several of my acquaintances, who were there in the capacity of independent soldiers. Sanborn who used to work in Eaton's Mill, was among them. Monday we marched out to a grist mill, about 10 miles, to protect it while flour is ground to keep the people from starving. Yesterday we started for this place coming some 10 miles out of our way to intercept a body of indians, which we failed to do, as they are sure to keep out of our way. We passed over the ground where Capt. Strougt's company were attacked. We buried three of his men whom we found fearfully mutilated. Two were scalped, and had their heads cut off. One's

4. John Kennedy (the register of deeds in Hastings in 1860), Amon McMullen, and John A. Moulton joined the Seventh Minnesota Volunteer Regiment, Company F. John Moulton, twenty-four years old, gave his residence as Lakeland, Washington County. The governor called for a new regiment, the Seventh Minnesota, in response to the Militia Act and the hostilities between the Dakota and the Minnesota civilians and militias in the late summer of 1862. See Folwell, *A History of Minnesota*, 103–5.

5. See Andrews, "Narrative of the Third Regiment," 158. See also Carley, *The Dakota War of 1862*, 45, 48. For the Dakota response to this and other attacks made by Little Crow's band and the formation of the peace party, see Anderson and Woolworth, *Through Dakota Eyes*, chap. 8.

breast was cut open, and his heart torn out. One had his skull broken in and abdomen cut open; while all had their clothes stripped off and pieces of flesh cut out of their bodies.[6] The sight had but little effect on our men, for they were used to such scenes, and nothing could increase their determination to exterminate the devils. The companies of raw recruits with us seemed horrified at the sight. To-day we return to Hutchinson to get provisions, and start on their trail.

Lizzie, I forgot to mention in my other letter that I rec'd your miniature just before leaving St. Louis. It is a good one, and I prize it highly, all the more because I did not see the original before coming up here. O, Lizzie, you don't know how I felt, to come off here without seeing you. Our marches are long and hard but we bear up and do our best hoping to do at least some good. . . .

> Ever yours.
> Madison.

Fort Ridgeley, [Minn.,] Monday, Sept. 15th, 1862.

My Dear Lizzie:

. . . Our regiment arrived here on Saturday morning, since which time I have had a good time among old friends in the different regiments, some from St. Anthony, some from Minneapolis, and some from Nininger.

We marched at the rate of 25 miles a day for seven or eight days, found four dead men all cut to pieces by the indians, and had a pretty good time generally notwithstanding our hard march. I have only just time to write you a line or two. I am well and hearty. . . .

> Ever yours,
> Madison.

Camp near Yellow Medicine, [Minn.,] Tuesday, Sept. 23, 1862
5 o'clock P.M.

My Dear Lizzie

I have not heard from you since I saw your friends at Hastings and Nininger, when I came up from St. Louis. I feel very anxious to hear from you, and still more anxious to see you. . . .

6. Sanborn is unidentified. Miller Samuel S. Eaton lived in Nininger City in 1860. Captain Richard Strout commanded the Tenth Minnesota Volunteer Regiment. His fifty-five men were routed by Little Crow and White Spider's band, suffering six soldiers killed and twenty-three wounded. See Carley, *The Dakota War of 1862,* 45. For an explanation of mutilating bodies, see Anderson, *Kinsmen of Another Kind,* 267-68. For the regiment's movements, see Andrews, "Narrative of the Third Regiment," 158-59.

We left Fort Ridgely six days ago, followed by three pieces of artillery and the 6th and 7th Regts., arriving here yesterday, within three or four miles of Yellow Medicine. On our way we saw Indians in squads of 10 or 20, retreating and burning bridges before us. About 7 o'clock this morning 30 or 40 of our regt. with teams, started off to dig potatoes, and when about a mile from camp were attacked by the Indians.[7] Our boys began to harness up for a free fight, when Major Welch told me that my co. might fall in and go out to the aid of the others, but the firing having considerably increased the whole of our regt.—270—were ordered to fall in; so Co F took its old place on the left flank, and forward we went till within gunshot of the Indians, when Major Welch ordered the left wing to deploy as skirmishers. The indians retreated before us until we were upwards of a mile and a half from camp; then we commenced firing on the red scamps, when all at once they rose up on our right and left flanks and in front, and at the same time a lot on ponies just round in our rear. Then commenced the fun—indian yells enough to split the ears, and bullets falling thick and fast around us. Just then an aid of Col. Sibley came up with an order for us to come back, as Major Welch had gone out without orders. Slowly and steadily we retreated, dealing death to the red skins as they pressed upon us, until we were within 100 rods of camp, where we made a final stand. The indians got into a wide ravine on two sides of our camp and within about 80 or 100 yards from us. Here we exchanged shots for awhile, the artillery assisting us. Pretty soon the gallant 7th—Am, Wheeler, and Wells among them—charged on the right of the ravine, and our regt on the left of it, completely routing them and peppering them well as they retreated up the bluff on the other side. After they had got away a lot of their dead, which they are always particular to carry off if they can, we picked up and buried 14 of them.[8]

During our retreat 2 of our regt. were killed and 31 wounded. Corpl. Pettibone and privates Heath, Griffin, and Eastman were wounded. Major Welch behaved like a hero, and was severely wounded in the leg.[9] Poor, brave Pettibone

7. Yellow Medicine is another name for the Upper Agency, a portion of the Dakota Reservation created after the 1851 treaty in which the Dakota ceded twenty-four million acres of land to the U.S. government. See Anderson, *Kinsmen of Another Kind*, 184–87. For digging potatoes, see 27 September 1862, Brookins Letters; and Andrews, "Narrative of the Third Regiment," 159.

8. For a description of the battle, see Anderson and Woolworth, *Through Dakota Eyes*, chap. 9; Josephy, *The Civil War in the American West*, 134–36; Folwell, *A History of Minnesota*, 179–82; and Andrews, "Narrative of the Third Regiment," 159–60.

9. Madison refers to Herman Pettibone (sometimes Heman in his letters) and Howard Griffin of Hastings and Isaac P. Heath and Adoniran Eastman of Medford, Steele County. Major A. E. Welch, who had served in the First Minnesota as a lieutenant, took command of the Third Minnesota when it arrived in Minnesota in early September 1862. He was shot

fell wounded in the head while dragging Griffin off the field. Rising, he called out—Bowler, I am wounded in the head. I told him to go to camp as fast as he could while others helped Griffin; but no;—seizing his gun, he fought by my side until just before the charge when I made him go to the surgeon. We brought off all our wounded, but left the dead, and when we reconquered the ground found them scalped and cut to pieces. One of them I used to know at Hale's Corners, Wisconsin. If Sibley had sent men out to our support or got the artillery into action sooner, we should not have had so many wounded bad he said—The 3d Regt have [only started] on the fight, now southern fights [ahead].[10]

While writing this I am out in command of a hundred men constructing a long rifle-pit. I can see squads of indians some two miles off. The indians sent in two flags of truce, asking Sibley to make a treaty. Our friendly indians fought like tigers. Other Day got three scalps and three ponies. He shot his own nephew, and wouldn't scalp him. Our boys bayonetted all the wounded, but the 7th took one prisoner, who gave us some information. He told us that we were fighting 1000 under Little Crow and that the Upper indians had gone off refusing to fight us.[11] All the Nininger boys are safe....

> Ever your
> Madison

P.S. If the Indians do not get the messenger, you will get this. I have your good miniature to look at.—Mad

Red Iron, Minn., Sept. 27th, 1862.

My Dear Lizzie:

Yesterday we heard from the world for the first time since we left Fort Ridgely. The train which carried our wounded to the Fort, returned yesterday, late in the afternoon, bringing yours of the 14th. It was handed to me by the Sergt. Major,

---

in the leg during the battle of Wood Lake. For Major Welch and the casualties and deaths resulting from the battle, see Andrews, "Narrative of the Third Regiment," 158, 160.

10. The preceding line has faded and is nearly indecipherable.

11. Madison refers to John Other Day. According to Schultz, Other Day killed two Indians and captured two horses. See Schultz, *Over the Earth I Come*, 233. For divisions within the Dakota, those in favor of fighting the whites and those who wanted to pursue peace or were friendly with whites, the latter tending to come from the Upper Agency, see Anderson and Woolworth, *Through Dakota Eyes*, chap. 8. Approximately 740 warriors were present for the battle of Wood Lake, although only 300 had actively engaged in the battle. See Anderson, *Kinsmen of Another Kind*, 274.

just as I was roasting an ear of corn on an Indian muskrat spear to keep old hunger down; for, be it known, we have had no bread and pork since day before yesterday—our only living now consisting of coffee, salt and potatoes, with occasionally a little beef. If provision does not arrive soon we shall have hard scratching to live.[12]

Day before yesterday we marched to within fifteen miles of this place, intending to come on in the night and attack Little Crow and his band by daylight in the morning; but a flag of truce came into camp, announcing that the hostile Indians had taken the young women and all who were able to drive team, and fled to Big Stone Lake, leaving the older women and the children in the hands of a lot of friendly Indians who refused to go with them. So our night march was postponed, and we came up here yesterday forenoon, and encamped alongside the Indian camp which numbers some 200 tepees. We found wagons, buggies, cattle, ponies, &c., *ad infinitum.*[13]

In the afternoon two companies of the 6th Regt. went over to the Indian camp with music and flying colors, and escorted the captives into our camp amid the cheers of the gallant blue-jackets who came so far to rescue them. And Oh! such cheers—they came from the hearts of the men, and were followed by tears from many a manly eye. The women looked hard as they marched along with infants in their arms and little ones toddling by their sides. The women—many of them—have been treated awfully. To-day we are having a court martial to try these *friendly* Indians many of whom have been foremost in the work of murder and theft, and will no doubt be either shot or hanged.[14]

You don't know how glad I was to hear from you once more after so long a suspense. Lizzie, you must not "scold" or think that, because I did not get to see you "I did not care to"; for you can have little idea how much self sacrifice it cost me to pass by my friends at such a time, and come off here where nothing but danger and hardship are my reward. Lizzie, you *know* that I love you; but, sinner as I am, I believe that next to my duty to God comes my duty to my country and its suffering, unfortunate people who have become victims to the enemies

12. The sergeant major was probably William D. Hale.

13. For the friendly Dakota turning most of the white captives over to the soldiers, see Anderson and Woolworth, *Through Dakota Eyes*, 219–21; and Schultz, *Over the Earth I Come*, 235–36.

14. A military commission tried 392 men, sentencing 307 to death and 16 to jail terms. Lincoln approved death sentences for only 39 of the eventual 303 condemned men, a move that angered the white settlers. One of the 39 was given a last-minute reprieve because the only testimony against him came from two young boys. On December 26, 1862, 38 Indians were hanged in Mankato. See Carley, *The Dakota War*, chap. 14.

of God and humanity. At best I know that I fall far, very far, short of the performance of these duties. If you were in distress or danger my first efforts would be to seek your safety. Did you ever contemplate how horrible it is that young, respectable females, like yourself and your friends, are in the hands of savages who have *not the least restraint, either moral or physical, upon their conduct toward their victims?* To the horrors of death and captivity they add every possible torture and outrage. I believe I could yield my life willingly to see these savage devils exterminated.[15]

I am really glad to hear that Gus and Mary are married at last. I hope that happiness and prosperity may attend them through life. Give them my best wishes.

I am sorry that Eugene should be so short minded. He promised faithfully to meet me at Fort Snelling within twenty-four hours after landing at Nininger, and his failing to bring the money greatly disappointed me. But it is too late now— money is useless here.

It seems hard that poor Kate should be sick so long and suffer so much. I do wish that she could get relief. Give my love to her, and tell her that her misfortunes, though hard to bear, are light compared with that of these poor indian captives. The train which takes this letter to Fort Ridgely, will carry the white captives whom we got yesterday. I hope that those enjoying the comforts of peaceful homes, will not be backward in rendering them substantial aid. . . .

You must not think that I could not have remained behind as well as others of my regt, for I could. Most of them are absent without leave, and no true soldier would have stayed behind at such a time, even with leave. As commander of Co. F I have to report, daily, four Sergts., four Corpls., and twenty-seven privates absent without leave.[16] I had the honor of leading twenty-eight good, true boys into the fight at Woods-Lake the other day, and am ready to go into another

15. Although there were many incendiary reports of white women being raped and then killed or taken captive, "only two cases showed credible evidence of rape" (Anderson, *Kinsmen of Another Kind,* 277). When determining if a prisoner was to be hanged, Lincoln took into account whether he had been accused of "violating women." See Folwell, *A History of Minnesota,* 209. For Lincoln's decisions about sentencing, see Nichols, *Lincoln and the Indians,* chap. 8. Madison's attitudes about the Dakota were typical for the period, especially in Minnesota during and following the U.S.–Dakota Conflict. See Folwell, *A History of Minnesota,* chaps. 7, 8. See also Hoffert, "Gender and Vigilantism on the Minnesota Frontier," 353–54, 357–58.

16. Fitzharris notes, "The [commissioned] officers of the 3rd were mostly prisoners of war, enroute to a camp in Georgia. At Benton Barracks the first sergeants took command of the companies. . . . Sergeant James Bowler, who was in command of the company during the Indian campaign, was commissioned" ("'Our Disgraceful Surrender,'" 10).

on the first opportunity. I hope I may be able to do it well. Well, Lizzie, . . . wait patiently till I return. . . .

> Ever yours,
> Madison.

> Nininger, Minn. Oct. 5th, 1862

Dearest Madison

I rec'd a letter from you written immediately after the battle. Was glad indeed to hear of your safety. I wrote you a letter last Sunday. Suppose you have not rec'd it yet. It takes letters a long time to go too or come from Fort Ridgely. Your last letter was on the way nine days. . . .

I will tell you that you need not expect much of a letter as mama is reading Col. Sibley's report of the battle at all intervals. There is so much talking that I can not tell one moment what I have written the one before so I beg you to excuse any mistakes. Eugene is about here yet. Says he is going to join the Regt soon, though I dont know whether he will [go], for I think there is not much dependance to be put in him. . . .

I am going a grapeing to-morrow. I do wish you were here to go too. I think you ought to come down, If it were but a few days. It is so lonely. I don't think you would want to stay long. . . .

Well I have scribbled everything I can [think] of at present. How do you like the looks of the country of up there? Do you think you would like to live there?

> Well I must say good bye. I remain yours ever
> Lizzie

> Camp Release, Red Iron, Minn., Oct. 9, 1862.[17]

My Dear Lizzie:

. . . Last night 85 of our regt came up all mounted, Johnson Truax and Dave Morgan among the number. Horses and equipments are on the way for mounting the rest of us. I surely expected to meet Eugene when I saw our boys coming in, but was disappointed. Eugene is acting very differently from what I had reason to expect, for he has always before been ready to perform his duty. I hear that he is

---

17. Camp Release was the name of the camp Sibley's troops established after securing the captives from the friendly Dakota. See Andrews, "Narrative of the Third Regiment," 160.

greatly smitten with the charms of Rose Colby—if so, I am more than ever surprised at him.

I have just been reading the late papers, brought up by yesterday's mail. I have read with great pleasure the Presidents' late Emancipation Proclamation. I now feel that we are upon the right road at last. I think we have nothing to fear.[18]

During the long months that I have been a soldier I have felt sure that things would come around right in time, and so I believe they have. In previous letters I have foreborne to refer to our recent disasters. They were not at all unexpected to me, and I felt glad when I heard of them—not glad because of the distress and loss of life attending them, but glad because I felt that we had got to be turned back by adversity before we should be willing to take the right road and pursue it properly. The disasters in Buell's department, though enormous, are even less than expected and predicted since I became aware of the condition of matters there about the time of our surrender at Murfreesboro. The end of our disasters there will not come until Buell is removed from command there; at least, so thinks your humble servt.[19]

I cannot account for all the fuss Gen Pope is making in Minn—needless expense. I believe the Indian outbreak to be fairly quelled, and that little or no more fighting will be done. We might as well be at home as doing nothing here. Little Crow's Band is all broken up. Many of them have returned and given themselves up to Col. Sibley. More are coming. The farmer Indians have been sent below to their farms at Yellow Medicine and Lower Agency. Capt Kennedys company have gone down to guard them from the hostile indians. It is probable that a part of our force will soon make a trip to Big Stone Lake before the Expedition returns to Fort Ridgely.[20]

When we left Fort Snelling I expected to be back and with you before this time, and if we had a proper commander it would have been so; but Sibley is so

18. President Lincoln issued a preliminary Emancipation Proclamation on September 22, 1862. The proclamation declared that slaves in areas not held by the Union would be forever free as of January 1, 1863, unless the states that had seceded would end the war. It also allowed blacks to enlist in the Union army as soldiers.

19. The disasters Madison refers to actually were strategic victories for the Union, but very bloody battles, including the battle of Antietam on September 17, the battle of Corinth from October 3 to 4, and the battle of Perryville on October 8, 1862. As before, all through the fall, General Buell had moved very slowly and was castigated by leaders in Washington.

20. Little Crow had fled capture after the battle of Wood Lake and went to Big Stone Lake in Dakota Territory. See Anderson, *Kinsmen of Another Kind*, 278. For Union general John Pope's involvement in the U.S.–Dakota Conflict, see Josephy, *The Civil War in the American West*, 138–42.

slow and cautious that our return may be delayed until the fall fires cuts off our supply of prairie grass, then we shall be obliged to return.[21]

I am not discontented or homesick, but I do think of home and long to be there—more perhaps because I expect to be there soon. It seems to me that I never thought of you so much before. I can see you all and imagine everything that transpires as plainly as though I were there. I long so much to be with you once more that I sometimes think some accident will intervene to hinder the realization of my desires; for what we want most is often kept from us....

> Yours, Dear Lizzie, with much love.
> Madison.

Camp Release, Red Iron Reserve, Minn., Oct. 14, 1862.[22]

My Dear Lizzie:

...I had begun to despair of ever hearing from you again.... I expected at the time we came off up here, to be back to Fort Snelling in less than two weeks. Col. Sibley thinks he can do nothing [without the aid] of the Third Regt.; so we have [to remain] here when we ought to have been [staying] at our homes.

We are at last [finished and] will, probably, be sent to Fort Snelling [before] many days, to reorganize; and then I shall make one grand effort to get a furlough to visit my friends. I wish, indeed, that I could be in Nininger to go graping with you. O how I do want to see you once more! It seems to me that I never thought of you so often before, or longed to see you so much as I now do; and not only to see you, but to meet all the members of your family who have been so kind to me....

I am sorry that Eugene should conduct himself in such a manner since his return to Minn. He was always honorable and ever on hand for duty while south. This girl business must have turned his head, or else the air of Minn. has *discomfuddled* his brain. I presume there will be another marriage by the time I return, since marriages are the order of the day....

...We have all the hostile warriors here in a temporary jail. Capt. Kennedy, I learn, has been complained of and will probably have to stand a court martial for having made too free with Mrs. Adams, one of the white captives. *She* did not complain, but Capt. Whitney, formerly a clergyman in Minneapolis, reported the

---

21. Madison refers to Henry Hastings Sibley, who was the initial commander of the expedition to quell the U.S.-Dakota Conflict. Sibley was often criticized for moving slowly during the campaign. For comments on Sibley's slow pace, see Josephy, *The Civil War in the American West*, 123.

22. This letter has several holes in it.

case to Gen. Sibley.[23] I cannot tell you how Amon is at present, as I have not seen him lately. I guess he likes soldiering fully as well as he anticipated, but he wants a furlough very much, and wants to go South instead of staying in this "frigid country."

One piece of artillery and 300 men including 100 of the 3d regt., started for Big Stone Lake at twelve o'clock last night, to be gone six days. I was called upon to detail six of my best men, but was not allowed to go myself though I wanted to very much.[24] Eighty-five of the Third, mounted, came up here a short time ago. More men, and horses to mount us, are on the [way] here....[25] Crary—our good, noble chaplain—[?] there is something in his preaching which [deeply] touches me, and to listen, as I did last Sabbath, to one of his practical sermons, in such a place as this, away up in our own Minn. wilds, the home of the savage and the beast,—affected me more than ever....

Your letters are very acceptible to me; but it seemed when I read them, as though I did not want to reach the end of them so soon, though they were as lengthy as usual. I like the country here very much in some respects; but it is not so good here as in some other portions through which we have passed since leaving Carver. From Glencoe to Forest City the country is rich and beautiful. Here it is all prairie except a narrow strip along the Minn. River and its tributaries. I should hardly be content to live this side of Fort Ridgely; but at Hutchinson, Glencoe, or Forest City I could live contentedly, if properly situated. Now, what are your ideas about living out of sight of the Mississippi? "Indians!" I hear you

23. Mrs. Harriet Adams lived with her husband, John, in Lee, McLeod County, in 1860. At that time she was eighteen years old. She was captured near Hutchinson on August 20, and her infant was killed. Her husband escaped. Mrs. Adams was at Camp Release in late September after the battle of Wood Lake. Satterlee calls her "Minnie" on one page but "Hattie" in the list of prisoners. See Satterlee, *Outbreak and Massacre*, 57, 91. Mrs. Adams's conduct elicited unfavorable comments from two other white female captives. See Wakefield, *Six Weeks in the Sioux Tepees*, 300, 302; Schmidt, "The Story of Mary Schwandt," 472–73. Captain Whitney, captain of Company D, Sixth Minnesota, was a Presbyterian minister living in Minneapolis. See Anderson and Woolworth, *Through Dakota Eyes*, 265n. If there was a court-martial, Captain Kennedy did not lose his rank, because he was discharged with his regiment as a captain in 1865.

24. George Brookins of Company I was one of the fifty men selected to mount as cavalry and go on a scouting expedition. See 27 October 1862, Brookins Letters. For a discussion of the mounted expeditions to capture additional Dakota, see Andrews, "Narrative of the Third Regiment," 160–61.

25. Around a large hole are the words: "Dave Morgan and Johnson Truax [?...]. Dave has not been permitted to ta[ke?...] Co. F yet. He hates me for coindent[?...]" Of later interest, both of these men were involved in the court-martial against Madison in May 1863.

say. Well, I had almost rather beg for a living, rather than have you live within the remotest danger from Indians. I never want any of my friends to fall into their hands. . . .

Wednesday, 15th

. . . This morning a big black wolf came up to within forty rods of Co. F's tents, and the boys shot at him, but without effect, except to scare him. Well, I guess by the time you read this mess of trash, you will want to rest; so I will close. . . .

> Ever yours,
> Madison.

Camp Release, Red Iron, Minn., Oct. 22, 1862.

Dearest Lizzie:

I wrote to you about a week ago, since which time I have heard nothing from you. Our scouting parties are all in, and we start below to-morrow morning, to go as far as Red-Wood where we expect to remain awhile, and then go to Fort Ridgely. The expedition which started out for Big Stone Lake over a week ago, returned yesterday. They went beyond Big Sioux River, over 100 miles from here, and captured forty warriors, a lot of squaws and papooses, and some plunder.[26]

Yesterday we had the heaviest wind I ever witnessed. All day long the air was full of sand and cinders from the burnt prairie. Tents were blown down, and everything below medium specific gravity, went off in a hurry. No fires could be kept up, so we had to fast for one day. One thing peculiar, we have had no rain to speak of since we left Fort Ridgely, over a month ago. I presume that you have had plenty of it along the Mississippi.

Last Monday I received a letter from sister Sarah, giving me the only news from home since last July. It was directed to Louisville. Sarah wants to know whether I am still a prisoner, and says, she heard that my regt had gone to fight the Indians; but hopes that is not true, for brother Joseph has been drafted and

26. For additional information about the expedition and Camp Release, see 22 October 1862, Hale Papers. According to Andrews, the Third Minnesota left Camp Release soon after October 21 and went to Fort Ridgely near the Lower Agency, where it stayed about a week. After additional marching, it returned to Fort Snelling on November 14. The men were on furlough until December 3. See Andrews, "Narrative of the Third Regiment," 161.

27. Joseph Bowler enlisted in the Twenty-second Maine Regiment, Company E, in October 1862 for nine months' service under the Militia Act. See www.state.me.us/sos/arc/archives/military/civilwar/reghis.htm.

gone away, and now she feels as though she had no brother at all.[27] She intended to go to Bangor to school, but father is in very poor health, and she considers it her duty to stay with him now that brother has gone. If Father's health should permit, she and Georgette will teach school this winter. Poor girl! She feels very lonely now. I wish I could be with them awhile.

I have long wished that brother would enlist, and think he would have done so, but for the necessity of his remaining at home; but I do not feel right since he has been drafted—it seems like disgrace. It is a sad hour when one enlists and bids his friends adieu, but it must be a sadder hour when *forced* from motherless sisters and a sick father. I know just how poor Joe must have felt, and it makes me feel bad to think of it. Poor boy! If he should lose his life, how I should feel—a thousand times worse than though he had gone of his own accord. But, willing or unwilling though he may be, I know that he will never turn his back to the foe so long as there is any hope of winning. I know him to be brave and true to the last, if I do say it. "O," says Sarah, "Is not war a sad calamity? and such a war as this, too?"[28]

It has been six years since I left my home, then happy and pleasant, at least to what it is now. Fortune has not made me rich or great. I have met with many unpleasant incidents during that time, like many others; but I have never allowed them to mar my happiness beyond the momentary pains of the time being. I look upon them as incident to life, just what might be expected in this world, and I feel just as happy—yes, happier—today than I did six years ago, when I started out full of boyish hopes and confident with youthful expectations; but I cannot feel otherwise than sad when I look back to my once happy home, and think over the misfortunes which have befallen it and which now leave the fireside lonely and still. . . . O, how I wish I could be with them. But perhaps it is out of place in me to intrude this catalogue of troubles upon your attention. If so, you must pardon me—it comes uppermost in my mind.

The fall campaign against the Indians is now ended, and we shall probably return to Fort Ridgely before the end of the present month, in which event I hope to have the privilege of seeing you before next Thanksgiving. I want to get where I can get a piece of good bread with butter on it, a good cup of tea in a clean cup and saucer on a clean table-cloth, with kind friends and pleasant faces to meet my gaze, and then when that is done, pick up some book or paper and read awhile. I can yield to military restraint as well as any one, but I want to be free once more for a little while, just to see how it would seem. I don't think I could sit in a chair with ease, and in a room larger than a tent I should feel lost, and to

28. For attitudes about draftees, see McPherson, *For Cause and Comrades*, 8–9, 116.

shake hands with, or to speak to, one of the feminine gender, would be very much like an elephant walking on eggs. If I should start for church with the usual number of girls, the first thing would be "right shoulder shift arms"— "deploy as skirmishers," if any one appeared in the distance—and "on the right by file into line" when we come [to] go up all those old schoolhouse stairs. If during the sermon, the minister should quote scripture, I might forget myself, and dispute his tactics, telling him Caseys were the latest, and so on.[29] How ashamed you would be of my actions. But enough of this. Good-night!

> Ever your loving
> Madison.

Nininger, Oct. 31, 1862.

[To Madison:]

... George Truax was down from the Fort yesterd[ay] he says the 3rd and 7th Regts have been ordered to Fort Snelling I do hope it is so for I want to see you so badly I hardly know how to wait *any longer.* I will direct this to Fort Snelling.[30]

Oh dear! It is comming on winter again; how shall we ever get through it? It is so lonely and dreary. I thought it was as bad as it would be last winter but I think it will be a great deal more this winter.

Sunday afternoon Nov 2nd

I rec'd a letter from Piercy at the same time I rec'd yours. He is well. ... Seems to think it hard that part of the young men have to fight for the [whole] country while the other part stay home to marry. ...

... There was a dance at Archer's and a great time generally.[31] There is meet-

29. "Casey's" is a book of military tactics by Brigadier Silas Casey titled *Infantry Tactics for the Instruction, Exercise and Manoeuvres of the Soldier, a Company, Line of Skirmishers, Battalion, Brigade, or Corps d'Armée.* He revised the third volume of Winfield Scott's *Infantry Tactics, or Rules for the Exercise and Manoeuvres of the US Infantry.* See Griffith, *Battle Tactics of the Civil War,* 102-3. For distinctions between military discipline and home life, see Hess, *The Union Soldier in Battle,* 122-25.

30. George Truax was seventeen in 1860, living in Nininger City. Based on their ages, he might have been the twin brother of Robert Johnson Truax, Company F.

31. A Union fair took place in Hampton in Dakota County. It was an agricultural fair to attract farmers from nearby counties. See *Hastings Independent,* 25 September 1862 and 9 October 1862. Archer's Hotel in Hampton regularly hosted "gay and festive" occasions. See *Hastings Independent,* 19 June 1862.

32. This might have been a prelude to the Methodists' quarterly meeting, which took place the following week. See *Hastings Independent,* 6 November 1862.

ing at Nininger to night. Our folks are all going.[32] How I wish you were here to stay with me. I bet we would have one good talk about "matters and things." I am going to wait two weeks longer with patience for you to come home. If you dont come in that time I will give up all hopes of ever seeing you again. . . .

. . . I was at Hastings yesterday. [Whi]le there I thought of the time about a year ago when I gave you a parting hand and watched you as you pushed off from the shore and looked at you as I thought for the last time. How thankful we ought to be when we think how kind providence has been to us while thousands have laid and died on the battle field, yet you are among those that have been brought through as many dangers and privations as many that rest beneath the sod.

Well I must stop scribbling, for I can call it nothing else. Hopeing you will excuse this poor apology for a letter. I remain yours in love

Lizzie S. Caleff . . .

4

My Dear Wife . . . Dearest Hubby

DECEMBER 1862 TO AUGUST 1863

After fulfilling its duties in the Dakota War in the fall, the Third Minnesota returned to Fort Snelling on November 14 and received furlough until December 3, 1862, marking the end of its first year of service in the Union army. That year had meant a long separation for Lizzie and Madison, and so in the precious few weeks that Madison was on furlough, the couple were reunited and settled "matters and things," as Lizzie said, by marrying on November 30, 1862.[1] Their letters did not indicate any preparation for a wedding ceremony. Their wedding picture survives, however, as a testament to their marital union: a young man dressed in an army uniform and a small woman with her arm linked through his, perhaps keeping him near her until the duties his uniform represented required that he leave her again.

Madison not only assumed the new role of husband but also received a new rank when he was commissioned as captain of Company F in December 1862. Most of the commissioned officers who had surrendered at Murfreesboro in July had been dismissed, so the regiment underwent a significant reorganization in the last month of 1862 as it prepared to return to service in the South. With new officers the regiment—and the public—anticipated better results when it met the enemy. On January 15, 1863, the *Hastings Independent* commented, "The Third Minnesota have received orders to march south. They start to-day. We have no doubt that this is glorious news for the boys, for we know that with competent officers, that glory will wreath their brows." Madison relished his new position as captain, which gave him official authority he had lacked while leading Company F during the fall campaign in Minnesota. Not all was going smoothly for him within the Third Minnesota, however. While stationed in Cairo, Illinois, and Fort Heiman,

---

1. The Third Minnesota received a fifteen-day furlough, according to the *Hastings Independent*, 20 November 1862. Notice of their marriage appeared in the *Hastings Independent*, 4 December 1862: "MARRIED.—On the 30th ult., by Rev. T. F. Thickstun, at the residence of the bride's father, Lieut. James M. Bolar, of the Third Regiment Minnesota Volunteers, and Miss Lizzie Caleff, eldest daughter of Mr. Samuel Caleff of Nininger."

Kentucky, Madison faced a court martial, beginning in early May 1863, though he anticipated and received a full acquittal. As he began to move up the military hierarchy, Madison also distanced himself from some of the men he knew from Dakota County, even ordering one put in the guard house for disobeying orders. Commanding respect and disciplining friends from home were common problems for officers in the highly localized citizen army of the Civil War.[2]

Madison also relished his new position as a husband, greeting Lizzie as "My Dear Wife" and promising her money to help support her now that it was his duty to do so. Unfortunately, the regiment faced delays in receiving their pay, and Madison's letters indicate that payment, like mail from home, was always looked for but frequently delayed in coming.[3] Lizzie reassured her "Dearest Hubby" that she did not need the money, because she was still living with her family, even sharing a bed with her sister Kate, whose health was declining steadily. Although married, Lizzie had not left home, and her day-to-day household duties had not changed substantially. As a married woman, she did not attend school, and so this was the first winter that she was not one of the "large scholars" in Nininger. Even more significant, Lizzie became pregnant before Madison went south in mid-January, and over the next few months she hinted at her condition and joked about "little Mad" and "little Jeems," assuming the baby would be a boy. The couple kept her pregnancy a secret from all but her immediate family, although by the end of May concealing it was getting harder. Once pregnant, Lizzie's greatest desire was that Madison return in the fall for the birth of their first child. Madison was reluctant, however, to promise that he would return, and by early June 1863 it looked less likely as the Third Minnesota was sent to Vicksburg, Mississippi, where a siege was under way.

Although Madison assured his wife that he would like nothing more than to be with her, his summer was a busy one, and furloughs were hard to come by. As the end of June approached, the Third Minnesota felled trees to build barricades for the Union forces engaged in the siege of Vicksburg. Madison's brief but more frequent notes read like a diary during the siege, when he wrote daily but waited to post a letter. By early July, Madison expected the Confederate surrender to be imminent and described the elation of Union troops on July 4 when they at last held the city. In the immediate aftermath of the victory, the Third Minnesota was

2. See McPherson, *For Cause and Comrades,* chap. 4; and Linderman, *Embattled Courage,* 48–53. For professionalism in a volunteer army, see Hess, *Liberty, Virtue, and Progress,* 61–64.

3. For example, see *Hastings Independent,* 1 January 1863. William D. Hale explained the payroll problems in his December 4, 1862, letter (Hale Papers).

sent on a new campaign to push Confederate general Joseph E. Johnston out of Jackson, Mississippi. With that accomplished, Madison waited expectantly for the Arkansas Expedition in August, which would occupy Little Rock and set up a reconstruction force there. While Madison gained new experiences and saw new places, Lizzie's world narrowed during the last half of her pregnancy. She went to town less, saw fewer people, and relied on others to post her letters and collect those Madison sent to her. She continued to pass along information and gossip to Madison, but she was more concerned with his moral and physical well-being and her vain expectation that he would be home in the fall for their first child's birth.

* * *

American House, St. Paul, Dec. 17, 1862.

Dearest Lizzie:

I ought to have written to you yesterday, and you would have received my letter to-day. Contrary to my expectation when I left you, I shall remain here probably until the first of next week, for it is the request of Col. Griggs and Lieut. Col Andrews that I remain here until Ingmans case is decided. Gov. Ramsey telegraphed to Washington yesterday to know whether dismissed officers can be commissioned again in case he should desire to do it in any case. An answer is expected every day. If favorable, Lieut Ingman will probably be Captain. All the dismissed officers are here, and most of them trying to get back into their former positions, but it is an uphill game.[4]

. . . By the way, it is settled that we are to go South as soon as those companies are paid off and have their furlough. . . .

Ever your
Madison.

4. On December 1, 1862, President Lincoln dismissed the Third Minnesota's officers who had voted for surrender at Murfreesboro. Second Lieutenant Ingman was dismissed along with the other officers and not given a new commission. The records show that Madison was commissioned as captain on December 1, 1862, along with Colonel Chauncey Griggs, formerly captain of Company B. According to William D. Hale, when the surrendering officers were exchanged and returned to Fort Snelling, "we were glad enough to meet most of them, but Col. Lester and the three Capts who sustained him in the surrender met a terribly cool & insulting reception—pointedly and persistently forced upon them by officers and men" (4 December 1862, Hale Papers). For the reorganization of the regiment, see Andrews, "Narrative of the Third Regiment," 162.

Nininger Jan. 21, 1863
Wednesday evening

Dearest Hubbie

What would I give to-night if my hubbie was here. It is so lonely. But that is not
and will not be the case, so I must do the next best and write you a few lines. Aunt
Henrietta died the evening after you left in the morning. She was buried yesterday.
Rob sent after me the next morning, so you see that I have been away from home
most of the time since you've been gone. Poor Rob really feels very badly. . . .[5] You
dont know what a dreary lonely day I put in the day you went away.[6] It does seem
really too hard for you to have to go. . . . I did not see Dr. Tho, for he was not in
town. But think the conclusion we came to is as right, but you shall know when
I find out. . . .

> Now dear hubbie good night
> Lizzie

> Mind and be a good hubbie. Dont say naughty words. I hope you will write
> when you get to Winona.

Winona, Minn., Jan. 22, 1863.

My Dear Wife:

We arrived here yesterday, all safe and well. Our trip was quite pleasant considering that a part of the time was stormy.

At Red Wing we were treated to as good a supper and breakfast as an epicure
could desire—roast Turkey and chicken, ham, pork and beans, bread and butter,
cake, pie, apples, coffee, and pretty lasses and women to serve it up for us. Long
live Red Wing and its patriotic whole-souled inhabitants.[7]

The boys were well treated at Hastings, too. Lake City did nothing for us, but
Wabashaw and Minneiska reminded us that we were yet among our friends, by
trying to fill up the inner man and make us otherwise comfortable.

---

5. Henrietta Caleff died on January 19 of consumption. See *Hastings Independent,* 22
January 1863.

6. Madison predicted in his letter of January 14 that he would pass through Hastings
on Saturday, January 17. Lizzie would have seen him there on his way south on the Mississippi River.

7. Andrews comments that they had a fine dinner in Winona rather than Red Wing.
See Andrews, "Narrative of the Third Regiment," 162. Companies H and I of the Third
Minnesota wrote to the *Hastings Independent* to express thanks for the hospitality they
received in Hastings. See 22 January 1863.

To-morrow morning we leave for La Crosse where we shall take the cars Saturday morning for Cairo, [Illinois]. . . .

>Ever yours,
>Madison.

>Nininger Minn., Jan 26, 1863
>Monday evening

Dearest Hubby

I have not rec'd any letters from you since you left but think I shall by to-morrow or next day. You don't know how patiently I am waiting to hear from you, to know where your place of destination is, and how you got along with your tedious march. I do sincerely hope you will not have to go to Vicksburg, for I think there will be another battle there before long.[8]

. . . There is quite a time about town to day making ready for the donation party that is to take place on Thursday evening. I dont know whether I shall attend or not. Mr Burnham gave a large party on Thursday evening last. Mary had to change her dress two or three times during the evening according to Mr Burnhams wishes for he was afraid she would spoil the one he gave a dollar a yard for.[9]

. . . I want you to make up your mind to come home next fall whether the war ends or not. If you get sick you must be sure and come before. Everyone about here says George Knight has left this country.[10] We have been having quite a snow storm. The weather is a good deal colder then when you left. I guess you will see by this letter that the ink has had one good freezing.

Lieut Huddlestein had been home just one week when his wife died. He has resigned.[11] Well, I have been washing all day and feel tired. I will leave this til morning. I believe I have dreamed of you every night since you left.

8. Union general Ulysses S. Grant attempted to attack Vicksburg, Mississippi, in November and December 1862. Additional offensives were delayed until spring 1863 due to waterlogged roads and swampy terrain.

9. A donation party to raise funds for the Reverend Shaw was held at Kemps Hall in Nininger on January 29. See *Hastings Independent,* 22 January 1863. Hiram Burnam was a twenty-eight-year-old Nininger farm laborer in 1860.

10. Corporal George Knight from Nininger deserted January 10, 1863, from Company F, Third Minnesota. He might have left the area so that he wouldn't be disciplined or returned to his regiment.

11. Lieutenant Thomas R. Huddleston resigned January 7, 1863, from Company F, Seventh Minnesota. See *Adjutant General,* 343; and *Hastings Independent,* 15 January 1863. Twenty-eight-year-old Julia Huddleston died on January 23 in Hastings. See *Hastings Independent,* 29 January 1863.

Tuesday evening

I did not send this to day. Thought I would wait till I heard from you. I did not have to wait long for there was a letter waiting for me at Nininger this morning when I went down there.

I was glad indeed to hear that you had a pleasent journey from here to Winona but felt rather disapointed at not finding out where you were to be sent. I had a nice little sleigh ride to night. Uncle Peter brought me home from his house up here. It is splendid sleighing. . . .

Do excuse this poor apology for a letter. My head aches so badly I can hardly see. Be sure and write as often as you can. I will write my name at the end of this to let you see how it looks written.

    Lizzie S. Bowler

Cairo, Ill., Jan. 29, 1863.

My Dear Wife:

I wrote to you yesterday, a short, unsatisfactory letter. A few hours later I rec'd one from you, quite unexpectedly; for I did not think you would write so soon. Then poor Mrs. Caleff is gone at last, and I hope to a happier home than this world has been to her. You must not permit yourself to be lonely because I am gone; but if you will write me so good, kind letters every time you are tired and lonely as you did this time, I will not object to your being a little lonely now and then.

I am glad to hear that Kate is a little better and hope she may be much better when you write again. I stated her case to my good friend Surgeon Greely, who listened with much interest, and promised me a prescription for her.[12]

You think, then, that we came to a correct conclusion about that small affair. I hope so. I wish, however, that you would consult a doctor. Has anybody noticed it yet? You must be very sure to take good care of yourself. Do not work hard or lift anything heavy. *Now be sure.* If you hurt yourself I shall [not] forgive you very easily. I am glad that you [ha]ve got that Certificate at last.[13]

I have got fairly to housekeeping. Otto, Jameson, and myself together, with a man to cook for us.[14] We have a common room furnished with a coal stove, table,

12. From Hennepin County, thirty-nine-year-old Moses R. Greeley mustered in September 5, 1862, as an assistant surgeon.

13. Lizzie's letter of January 21 and this letter hint at Lizzie's first pregnancy. The certificate mentioned probably was their wedding certificate or perhaps a certificate related to Madison's commission as captain.

14. Madison refers to Otto Dreher and George Jameson, promoted to first lieutenant and second lieutenant, respectively, on December 1, 1862. See *Adjutant General,* 120.

and two Bunks for sleeping. A smaller room adjoins it, for washing and cooking purposes. Yesterday I bought my first dishes and cooking utensils—4 pink boals, 4 heavy earthen plates, 4 knives and forks, a good copper bottom coffee-pot, frying pan, and skillet for baking. We get excellent soft bread, plenty of pork, beans, coffee, beef, and the very best of brown sugar, almost white, besides other things too numerous to mention. If you were only here to cook it, I could ask no more.

Otto and Pettibone are writing at the same table with me—Otto to his Marry. Eugene—Sergt. now—sits near reading the Army Regulations. The Regt. is now in the finest of spirits and good health.[15]

Cairo is the muddiest place I have ever seen. It is about like the flat around Reed's Shop, in situation, and a hundred times muddier. The eye cannot discover one rise of ground in any direction—all one vast flat. The Levee is raised about ten feet to keep the waters of the Ohio and Mississippi from submerging the town. The Levee is lined with huge Gov't transports and floating Navy depots, and out in the river two Gun[boa]ts lie at anchor—the Cincinnati and Lafaye[tte]. There is also a captured rebel gunboat a[t the] Levee, undergoing a change into [a] U.S. Transport. It was captured at Memphis. There is a Fort here mounted with heavy guns. We have to garrison it for the present. We have a few rebel prisoners here.[16]

About one month ago the 128 Ill. from Williamson county, came here, 1000 strong, and now they have only 100 men in all, and only 37 of them fit for duty, the rest of the Regt. having died and deserted. I can but be proud of the old Third when I contrast it with such regiments as the above. The 109th Ill., in Grants army, has been disarmed and put under arrest for disloyalty to the government. Both the above regts are from Egypt—the *democratic* portion of Illinois.[17]

15. Madison later notes in this letter that Captain W. W. Webster of Company A, who had formerly been dismissed following the Murfreesboro surrender, was reinstated. According to a letter written by E. D. Townsend, assistant adjutant general, on November 20, 1862, "Company A is entirely satisfied to continue under the command of Capt. W. W. Webster" (Hale Papers).

16. For Anthony Reed's business, see Guelcher, *More Than Just a Dream*, 89–90. William D. Hale remarked on the mud and the levee, but with less restraint than Madison, asserting that the levee made "the most perfect reservoir of filth mud and *rats* possible. . . . Suffice it to say then that to a man we desire above all things to get away—anywhere—from Cairo" (29 January 1863, Hale Papers).

17. For the Third Minnesota's experiences in Cairo, see Fitzharris, "'Our Disgraceful Surrender,'" 16. The 128th Illinois "disbanded April 1, 1863, by order of Gen. Grant, having lost in 5 months over 700 men, principally by desertion, and the Officers having proved themselves utterly incompetent, were mustered out of service. The few remaining men were consolidated into a Detachment and consolidated with 9th Illinois Infantry April 1, 1863" (Dyer, *A Compendium of the War of Rebellion*, www.rootsweb.com

I am going to the Theatre to-night, having, in common with the rest of the captains and the field officers of our Regt, received a Complimentary ticket.[18]

Friday Jan. 30.

I will now try to finish [this] crazy letter. . . . Lizzie, do not allow yourself to be lonely because I am away; but content yourself with the thought that I shall be back before many months, and then we can enjoy each others society the more for having been separated so long.

If I do not get that prescription for Kate in time to send it now, I will send it in my next. He tells me in the first place, that the very best thing she could do would be to marry and, if possible, get with child. But I told him that I presumed that to be out of the question. Now perhaps you had better not tell her of this; for she might think that I had no business to speak of that matter. The prescription is for starting her monthly flow of the menses. Dr. G. says that she should soak her feet often, and always keep them warm, and keep her head cool. . . .[19]

I have just got that prescription from Surgeon Greely. The one on the small slip is for monthly spells. It means, in English, four ounces syrup Idodide of Iron, to be taken in doses of one teaspoonful night and morning. The other is for a restorative. Its ingredients are to be put into a *pint* bottle with one-half pint of syrup, and the bottle then filled up with rain water. Dose: teaspoonful three times

/~ilcivilw/dyers/128inf.htm). The 109th Illinois disbanded April 10, 1863, and was transferred to the Eleventh Illinois Infantry. The Adjutant General's report said that, by April 1863, the regiment had been "greatly reduced in numbers." See www.rootsweb.com/~ilcivilw/history/109.htm. For an interpretation of why these regiments had problems in 1863, see Hicken, *Illinois in the Civil War,* 124-25, 128-30, 139-40. Williamson County is in southern Illinois and is sometimes called Little Egypt. In the fall 1862 elections, Illinois Democrats gained seats in the House of Representatives and control of the state legislature. The Democrats were opposed to Lincoln's Emancipation Proclamation and, by the spring of 1863, his war policies.

18. Madison saw *The Barrack Room* by Thomas Haynes Bayly, probably written in 1860. Several of Bayly's plays, including *The Barrack Room,* were advertised by Samuel French as part of the Collection of Plays from Dicks' Standard Plays series. Bayly is better known for his poems and songs. See www.xrefer.com/entry/368105. Madison also saw *Grimshaw, Bagshaw & Bradshaw,* a comic farce written by John M. Morton in 1859. See "The Adelphi Theater, 1806-1900," www.emich.edu/public/english/adelphi_calendar/auth.htm. He noted that the performance was "quite good for this latitude."

19. It was common for doctors to assume that women's medical problems derived from their uterus. Some doctors stressed that female patients should embrace motherhood and childbearing to solve their medical problems. See Wood, "'The Fashionable Diseases,'" 223-27.

a day. Take hip bath every night when there is pain in the head; also foot bath, and use cold to the head in form of wet cloths for the headache. Use but little salt food; but live chiefly on Beef-tea, Broth, Steak, and Vegetables.[20]

If there is any impropriety in what I have done in this matter, you can keep it all to yourself; but if you think any good will result from it, you can acquaint Kate of the whole or a part of the prescription, and, if you see fit, not let her know where you got it. She might blame you if she knew you told me about her affairs. Give my love to poor sister Katie, to sister Dollie, to father and mother.

> Ever your own true
> Madison.

Columbus, Ky., Feb. 6, 1863.

Dearest Lizzie:

. . . I have felt considerably disappointed by not hearing from you, for I felt sure that this morning's mail would bring me a letter from you. O, Lizzie, you can hardly realize how often I think of you during these long, lonely days. I never felt your absence so keenly before. In other days I have felt unhappy without you, but now, somehow I feel as though I ought to be with you—as though I *could not* stay away from you so long again. I want to sit beside you, to look at your face, full of kindness toward me, and to give you an earnest kiss as I have often done before. But it is of no use for me to want, for I am determined to keep on the path I have chosen, hard though it be.

I am in my tent, sitting upon a pile of blankets, and writing on my mess-chest. My only source of warmth is from a few shovelfuls of coals deposited in a hole dug in the ground. Without is the frozen ground covered with about six inches of snow; all around the chilly wind is making those ugly sounds which you so much dislike to hear. But this is unusual in this latitude, and will not last long.

We came here from Cairo last Tuesday. An attack was feared here, as the rebels were pitching in at Island No 10, only twenty-five miles below here. This is, by far, the most important point we have ever helped to guard. These heavy fortifications, once in the possession of the enemy, and the whole of Grants army would be cut off and lost. The position is very strong, and the fortifications extensive.

---

20. Scholars on H-Science, Medicine, and Technology suggest that syrup of iodide of iron (or ferrous iodide) was prescribed for central nervous system ailments, as well as scrofula, based on the *United States Dispensatory* and *United States Pharmacopoeia* from the 1860s and 1870s. Later in this letter, Madison gives further instructions for the hip bath and predicts that if Kate was under the army doctor's care, she would be cured.

I cannot tell how many guns there are in all, but just about our camp are upwards of twenty, ranging from 32 to 100 pounders. Within twenty feet of my tent is a 64 pounder, used as signal gun. It is fired at sundown and daybreak, and I can assure you that it does not "go off" unheeded by me, for it fairly lifts my fragile domicile from the ground.[21]

At Cairo I was on board the Ram Lafayette. It is very formidable, covered with two-inch iron plates under which is a plating of rubber one inch in thickness. Under both are two feet of solid oak. Projecting beyond her bow, and running wholly under water is a huge iron headpiece running out to an edge in front. For the bow port-holes are two 184 pounders. At the sides are four 100 pounders—rifled—and at the stem two 84 pounders. She is not quite finished yet. This ram belongs to a breed of sheep little raised in Minnesota. It lives on water chiefly.

Feb. 7

... I wrote to Aunt Sarah from La-Crosse to send me $10.00 if she had it to spare. I do not want it unless she can spare it as well as not.

We made out our pay rolls while at Cairo, but we shall not get any pay until after the first of March, and then, probably, we shall receive four months pay. Greenbacks are getting to be considerably below par. Gold is worth sixty per cent premium now in New York.

The indications are now that no great victories will be won in this department for sometime to come, for I think no attack will be made on Vicksburg until spring. A good rousing victory would bring government credit up to a living rate....[22]

> Yours ever.
> Madison.

---

21. Confederate cavalry commander Nathan Bedford Forrest, along with General Wheeler, attempted to recapture Fort Donelson and was active in western Tennessee. See Wyeth, *Life of General Nathan Bedford Forrest*, 146–53. See Kennedy, *The Civil War Battlefield Guide*, 303, for cannon size and weight. Madison probably refers to various sizes of Parrott rifle, which were used at fortifications.

22. McPherson calls the period from December 1862 through May 1863 the "Winter of Northern Discontent." The Union army's military campaigns had been either defeated or halted and some Northerners experienced "a crisis of confidence." See McPherson, *Ordeal by Fire*, chap. 18.

Nininger Minn. Feb. 7th 1863
Saturday night

My Dear Hubbie

. . . It is three weeks ago to-night or rather tomorrow morning since you left. You may depend it has been three anxious lonely weeks to me. You don't know how much I would give to see you if it were but a few hours.[23] I am glad you all seem to be in so good spirits. How much I should like to take a peep in and see you in your new home. I think it must be an interesting looking place. How do you keep your floors clean where there is so much mud? You ought to have me there to mop for you. You know Ma says I am so good a hand.

I read that part of your letter to Kate that was concerning herself. She was very thankful to you for your kindness. She is no better than when you left and I think she is no worse. It is very sickly here now. There has been a funeral in Hastings every day this week. The people in Nininger don't think much about dying or any thing else but dancing. They had a ball in the Tremont Hall last night. I think they said there was over 60 couple[s].[24]

. . . Minnie is here. If I get some of her nonsense in this letter you must not think [it] strange. Well, Minnie has got to cutting up so I shall have to stop for the present.

Feb. 8—

Minnie has gone to Sabbath School. I will now try to finish this poorly written letter. I did not go to Sunday school. The weather is too cold for any one to hardly dare to show their nose out doors. It is nice sleighing now. . . . Now if I wasn't an old married woman or any way if it hadn't been for you, I might slide down hill with the rest of them. I believe I will, as it is what you would say if I should and you know.

We heard last Thursday that the 3rd Regt has gone to Columbus K.Y. I found it on the map and find it is but a very short distance from Cairo. The perscription that you got from that physician amounts to about the same as Dr. Thorne's. The Iron that he mentions is a little different in name but I suppose about the same in affect. The treatment is the same as Dr. Thorne gave her last fall but all to no purpose.

I saw a short piece taken from the Chicago Times giving some of the 3rd Regt

23. The sentence ended with "sometimes" crossed out.

24. A cotillion was held in Nininger City on Thursday, February 5. Tickets for the supper and dance were $1.50. See *Hastings Independent,* 29 January 1863.

boys rather a bad name for some of their performances while there. . . .[25] And you have got to going to Theathres. I think that is pretty well for an old married man like you. Rose Stone is going to school. She stays with old Mrs. Stone. I heard that her father was very angry with her for her private marriage. . . .[26]

> Now dear Madison Good Bye
> Lizzie

{side margin} Do you know any thing about Knight? I think those photographs were real good. Did you get yours?

Nininger Feb. 14th 1863
Saturday Evening

Dearest Husband

I feel very much disapointed to-night. I have waited for a chance to send to Hastings for the last four days and have not got any yet. Consequently have not heard from you for two weeks. You may feel assured that I feel anxious to hear from you. I shall wait patiently till Monday. If I dont get a chance to send to the office by that time I shall be tempted to walk my self. . . .

I heard someone saying that the 3rd Regt has been ordered to Vicksburg. I sincerely [hope] it is not so but am afraid it is for I have always expected you would have to go there.

. . . You said you were afraid to ask questions for fear some of our foulks would see your letters. Don't mind that, for I will tell them not to open them and after I once get my hands on them I assure you no one will see them. No one knows any thing about matters and things excepting our folks. I could not keep it from them. I have had the sick head ache most ever since you have been gone. You know I told you if something was so I would be sick.[27]

I want you to make up your mind to come home by the middle of Sept, not to make a visit but to stay. If the war is not ended by that time it doesn't make any difference whether you stay or not. If you are sent to Vicksburg I want you to write

25. Some soldiers from the Third Minnesota "spent their two-hour layover destroying a hotel bar room" (Fitzharris, "'Our Disgraceful Surrender,'" 16).

26. Eugene Stone and Rose Colby must have married around the same time that Lizzie and Madison married, in November 1862, because it is not mentioned during Lizzie and Madison's correspondence in September and October 1862. See Biographical Sketches, P–W, Case Papers. Rose Colby Stone's flirtatious behavior in the winter and spring of 1863 stimulated both comment and censure, according to Lizzie. See the full annotated transcription of the letters in the Bowler Papers for details about this couple.

27. In this paragraph Lizzie confirms her pregnancy.

often for I shall not take one minutes peace. If you get sick I want you to be sure and come home. *Now mind* and *do it will you?*

... It has been storming all day, to night the wind whistles and every thing is as dreary as possible. Do excuse [this] horrible looking letter for I have written it in about five minutes. . . .

> *{right margin and along the top first page} Be sure and destroy this as soon as you read it. Mind and tell me if you are sick. . . . Did you rec'd the money that you sent to Aunt Sarahs for?*

> Lizzie

Fort Halleck, Columbus, Ky., Feb. 17, 1863.

My Dearest Lizzie:

Yours of last month, containing $10.00, was received the next day after I wrote my last letter to you, and another of Feb. 7th came to hand yesterday. . . .

You wonder how we managed to keep our floors clean while in the muddy land of Cairo. That was a very easy matter, for we had a good shovel, you know. But, dirt or no dirt, it would have been very agreeable to me if you had been there. I wish you could be with me here. . . .

Tell Minnie that, if she don't let you live in peace, there will be a day of reckoning when the "Third Regt." returns from the "wars." You must not allow yourself to envy [those sleighing], nor scratch out your eyes to spite your face by sliding down hill and—"you know." Just think of it! Don't you feel ashamed of yourself for such talk? Maybe it *isn't so* after all; and if it is, you had as much to do in making such a state of affairs, as I did.

Condemnation from the *Chicago Secesh Times* is the best kind of *praise*; but why should the St Paul papers copy blame from the *Times,* and yet say nothing about the compliments which the *Tribune* and the *Journal* showered upon our Regt? Three or four of the boys demolished some whisky decanters, but Col. Griggs paid from his own pocket ten dollars, all that was asked for them. . . .[28]

In one of your letters you write that I must go home next Fall whether the war ends or not. You must not set your heart on anything of that kind. I don't want to go home until the war is over; then I can have good company to go home with—the soldiers who have fought for the Union. If I should go home now, I could

28. The editor of the *Chicago Times,* Wilbur F. Storey, was highly seditious. The *Times* was also called "Old Storey's Copperhead Times." The *Chicago Tribune* had, however, an editor that fully supported Abraham Lincoln and the Republican Party. See Waugh, *Re-electing Lincoln,* 142.

not feel at home among the unpatriotic stay-at-homes. Besides, I might be taken for one of that class, which would be rather galling. Why should your mother say that "she would rather you would have ten young Madisons than go south?" What does she know about "Young Madisons?"

I have just this moment received a letter from Piercy. He sends his regards to my wife. His letter is full of brag about the recent battle at Fort Donelson in which his company was engaged. He says that 700 of our men fought and whipped 6000 rebels, but forgets to mention the fact that a fleet of our Gun-boats arrived just in time to save our forces from being captured. He has, as usual, "received" my *"welcomb leter."* Mrs. Rose Stone's education must be sadly lacking, when she has to go to school now. You must beat her in *one thing,* or I shall lose an oyster supper on a bet. Will you?

Our arms have just arrived from St Louis. They are of the first class, being Enfield Rifles—*English* manufacture. . . . To-morrow we are to have battalion drill in the presence of Gen. Asboth and other officers. The only competitors worthy of our steel, is a company of the 15th Regulars, and we can beat them, I know, unless they do better than I have seen them do yet. The 34 Wisconsin is here. It is a drafted regt. numbering about 350, all that is left out of 4700 drafted from Wis., the rest having run away. Yesterday the enemy's cavalry came within a few miles of here, and nobody could have made me believe, had I not seen it, that men could be so frightened at almost nothing, as some of these drafted germans were.[29]

All the cannon we could spare have been taken to our army before Vicksburg. It looks as though something is going to be done.

Last Friday I was Captain of the Picquet Guard, and had a good time riding around all day through the mud, accompanied by a Cavalry escort to keep the bushwhackers from gobbling me. You need not be afraid of our going to Vicksburg; for Gen Asboth will not allow us to leave here, if he can help it. I will finish this to-morrow. I must go now and study my lesson in tactics or get a scolding to-night from Col Griggs, at recitation. I find no trouble in keeping up with the class.[30]

29. General Asboth was in command at Columbus, Kentucky. For lack of guns until February 17, see Andrews, "Narrative of the Third Regiment," 163. Madison also had a new sword, which he bought after leaving his sword and sash with Lieutenant Tichenor in Minnesota. For attitudes about German American regiments, see McPherson, *Ordeal by Fire,* 346–47.

30. Bushwhackers engaged in guerilla warfare and were not officially part of an organized army. See Cooling, "A People's War," 130. On learning tactics, Andrews comments, "At Columbus the officers assembled evenings at the colonel's quarters in the school of the regiment" ("Narrative of the Third Regiment," 163).

Feb. 18

. . . It is quite foggy to-day, and almost raining, so I guess that battalion drill will be put off until to-morrow.

In one of your letters you refer to your having just got through with your washing, and say that you feel tired. Now, Lizzie, I must earnestly *protest* against your doing hard work and getting tired. There is no need of your doing it. If your breast is suffering now from the effects of hard work, what may you not expect as you grow older? Unless you are very careful the result will be very serious when it is too late to get remedy. If you knew just ho[w] solicitous I feel about the preservation of your health, you would, I know, be more careful.

I am sorry that there is no good promise for Kate's recovery. I thought that Dr. Greely's [prescriptions] might, perhaps, do her some good. But it seems not. . . .

Dan Hunt sends his regards to you. Pettibone wishes to be remembered, too. Eugene is as steady as a clock. He neither drinks nor chews, and seems to think all the world of his wife and to have a very good idea of the responsibility resting upon him in his new relation. As soon as we receive our pay, if we ever do at all, I will send you some money, which I know you must need. . . .

> Ever your loving
> Madison.

Nininger Minn. February 21st 1863

My Dear Madison

. . . To-day is a beautiful day. The sun has melted the snow so that the water is running in all directions. The ground is mostly bare. Do has gone to Nininger and Kate has gone in to Mrs. Poor's.[31] Mama and I are left alone. You say we must mind what we write. I think if people will meddle themselves with what don't concern them, let them find out what they can. If I knew who it was I would give them something to read about themselves. Ma says if you ever come back again she will give you one lecturing about telling her such a wrong story.

I saw Rose two or three days ago. She was just coming out of Hickmans with her hands full of letters. I heard her telling the girls that was the 15th letter she had sent to Eugene since he has been gone. They have got it all around here that Eugene is a hundred dollars in debt to the Government for clothing that he got while he was down South before. Is it so? . . .

31. Mrs. Poor was probably Caroline Poor, who was twenty-one years old and lived in Nininger in 1860.

Mrs. Faiver saw the 3rd Regt while at LaCrosse. She said she looked round for you but did [not] notice you. Said she thought you had a very hard time crossing the river at LaCrosse. No one knows anything about Knight. He has not been heard tell of here since you left.[32]

... I have felt a great deal better this week then I have since you have been gone. That pain that I used to have so much in my chest I have not felt for three weeks. I guess you must have cured it some way.

You ask me if I am not lonely sleeping alone. You may be assured that I am lonely enough nights, though I don't sleep alone. Kate and I sleep together. There are many nights that but few hours find me asleep, and while awake you may easily inquire what the subject of my thoughts are. Does my hubbie ever pray for his Lizzie while lying awake nights? I do for you. You never say naughty words. Now if you do I won't let you have anything to do with *little Mad* when he comes to town. Now if any one gets this letter they will find out everything they want to know.

... Mr. Carpenter's school closes next Tuesday. I believe his successor is to be Miss Lucy Reed. Am has not come home yet. The last Aunt Sarah heard from him he was in the hospital sick with a cold. ... Give my respects to Mr. Hunt and all other friends in the Regt. ...

    Lizzie

{on the back} ... You dont know how much I want to see you. Do get done fighting as soon as you can so you can come home. LSB

                                  Fort Halleck, Columbus, Ky., Feb. 26, 1863.

My Dear Wife:

... I am sorry that you have to suffer so much on account of what we surmised and which seems now to be a fixed fact. I hope that things will take a favorable turn in the course of a few weeks, and that you will be better. I hope, Lizzie, that you will not insist upon my coming home by September, especially that you will not insist upon my staying there unless the war should be over. Your wishes in that respect are not as they were when we were single—wishes of one individual in regard to another, to be complied with or not at pleasure; but they are calls which I feel bound to obey not merely to gratify one I love but to honorably fulfill the obligations enjoined by the conditions [of] our new relation. I know that you are a considerate and unselfish woman and would ask nothing in earnest which would be in the least unreasonable, and for that reason I should feel still more

---

32. Mary Faiver was Ignatius Donnelly's sister-in-law and the wife of Louis Faiver, Nininger's postmaster.

bound to comply with your requests. Time and ever changing circumstances may change your wishes and the necessities which would require my presence at home. And so we will let the subject rest until the time for action draws near.[33]

An escort has gone to Memphis to guard the Paymaster on his way to Columbus to pay the troops here; so I am in hopes to have some money to send you before many weeks. When you get money enough again, you must have a dozen or more photographs—*good ones*—taken. Let it cost what it may. You can—*you must*—go to St Anthony, and there you can easily go to Whitney's, in St. Paul, or Beats, in St. Anthony, and have them taken, and taken right if you have to sit a hundred times. Do you hear?

There is less prospect than there was a week ago of our going to Vicksburg, and if we do go the agony will be over by the time we get there, for the work has commenced already. You think that if the war is not ended by September there will be no use in my staying longer. Now, do not, I beg you, permit yourself to think, or at least, *talk* that way. There are doubting Thomases enough without your becoming one. I want my Lizzie to be a patriot and of firm faith in the ultimate triumph of a just cause. When things look dark and weak-backed individuals tremble and speak out their distrust, then is just the time to find out the true metal. Fire separates the dross from the gold; so trial will show who are *men* and *women*.

. . . One of our boys the other day recognized in a pretended citizen one of Forest's Cavalry whom he met at Murfreesboro last July, and had him arrested. Subsequent events showed the correctness of his suspicions, for it was one of Forest's men in the guise of a citizen, and acting as a spy.

Feb. 27th.

. . . You say I may ask any questions I please, but I will not this time. You must tell me *all* without asking.

We are having beautiful weather now. I wish you were here to enjoy it. . . .

> Ever your affectionate "Hubbie,"
> Madison

Fort Halleck, Columbus, Ky., March 3, 1863.

My Dear Lizzie:

Yours of Feb. 21st came to hand yesterday, just as we were marching out to battalion drill, and I had to wait until we took a rest before I could get a chance to

---

33. For competing duties to home and country, see McPherson, *For Cause and Comrades,* 134.

read it. Several others were in a similar predicament. Capt Webster tried to read his while marching, and the wind blew it away, causing him an undignified race.

O, I am so glad to hear that the state of your health is so much improved. I hope that it will continue. I would give almost anything if you could always be free from that pain in your chest. But you must not be too smart while you are well, for you may bring your trouble back again.

You wish to know whether I ever pray for my Lizzie while absent, or think of her while lying awake nights. You may rest assured I do—my first and last thoughts are of you, when I wake in the morning and go to sleep at night. Then if I say naughty words you intend to monopolize "Young Mad." Indeed! There is, you must remember, many a slip between the cup and lip; and your "Young Mad" may not "come to town" after all. Mustn't count the chickens before they are hatched.

It seems very strange that any one should start so fiendish a story about Eugene's indebtedness to the Government. His clothing account was settled up to the 31st of October; so up to that time he owes nothing. Since then, according to the company records, he has drawn clothing to the amount of $22.18, and has enough now to last him a year from the 31st of last October, at the end of which he is entitled should he [have] drawn no more, to the balance between $22.18 and $42., the yearly allowance for clothing. If anybody feels particularly concerned I will make an affadavit to the above statement, or give them permission to examine the Books of Co. F.

I cannot write much at this time, for we shall be on the march in an hour or two, just as soon as three days rations can be cooked. There is a report that 20000 rebels are marching upon this place, and our regiment is to form a part of the force sent out to flank them. Troops were on the move all last night, and lines of them may still be seen moving off to various points to intercept the enemy. Everything indicates action, and should we meet the enemy lively times may be expected.[34]

We did, as Mrs. Faiver said, have a hard time crossing the river at Lacrosse, but we do not mind hard times so much as we did a year ago. To any but tried soldiers our trip from Fort Snelling to Cairo would have been heart sickening and discouraging, but we got along with, *to us,* very little trouble. . . .

> Ever your loving
> Madison.

34. On March 3, 1863, William D. Hale wrote of an expected Confederate attack on Cairo and orders to "be in readiness at a moments notice to march." Like Madison, he viewed Cairo as an important location for both armies.

Nininger March 7th 1863
Saturday evening

Dearest Hubbie

. . . You say you hope I will not insist on your coming home next fall. You know that I always told you I would never be the one that would hinder you from doing what you thought was your duty. I never really tried to hinder you from joining the army when we were not so closely bound together as we now are. You may be sure that I would not try to take the advantage of you in any way any more now then when you were an entire stranger. If you can I would like to have you come home in the fall. What I said in that letter I wrote to you I said partly in fun, for I know that as long as this war lasts you will never be easy any where else only in the midst of it. All that I hope is that you may be spared to return home in good health after this war is over, if you are determined not to come before. Why dont you write to Gus Case? He thinks [it] very strange that you haven't written to him before this.

I feel a great deal better then I did when I wrote to you before. No one mistrusts that there is anything more than common [in] the matter excepting our folks. And they won't know as long as I can help it. When they do find out you will catch it. There is one request that I am going to make of you and I want you to take into serious consideration, that is that you will become a christian, that you will care less for the things of this wicked world and pay more attention to Heaven and Heavenly things. I find that there is not much dependance to be put in anything here. Though our paths may appear to be strewn with pleasures, yet there will [be] something come to disappoint us. I want you to pray for me and I will pray for you though we are separated by many miles, yet we can pray for each other, which is a great priviledge. . . .

You said if I really requested it that you would burn up my letters. I do not care what you do with them if you keep them where no one will ever put eyes on them excepting yourself. . . .

Sunday Morning

. . . Would you be allowed to receive newspapers if they were sent to you?

You seem to think that I did wrong in saying if the war didn't come to an end soon it would be no use to try. You know that it is no use for any one to try to make themselves believe any [thing] that they dont believe. It is not because I am not patriotic enough. It is because I cant help it and I wonder as things look now that you are not of the same belief. . . .

Good Bye from your loving Lizzie

Cairo, Ill., March 12, 1863.

Dear Libby:

Well we are off at last. This fine afternoon finds our Regiment on board the Steamer Bostona, bound up the Tennessee. One company of the 16 Regulars, an Indiana Battery, and Gen Asboth and staff are with us. The Steamer J. D. Perry has the 111 Ill. and 25 Wisconsin, all going with us. We are going to retake Fort Hindman, which is within a mile or two of Fort Henry and 13 miles from Fort Donelson. The federal troops evacuated Fort Henry on account of high water, and Fort Hindman in order to concentrate at Fort Donelson, and save at least one from the rebels who were advancing from 14,000 to 20,000 strong. Several gunboats are going with us. We have just arrived at Cairo, and I thought I would just drop you a line before we leave for the battle. I expect to see Piercy. We may go up the Cumberland to Fort Donelson, and from there by land to Fort Hindman.[35]

Ever your loving
Madison.

Nininger Minn., March 14, 1863

Dear Madison

. . . I am very anxious to hear from you again, as you said when you wrote that you expected to meet the enemy soon. O! Such a life as it is to have any one in the army that you love. It is nothing but anxiety all the time. No one knows how glad I shall be when this awful war is ended.

Little Charlotte Bottomly was buried to-day. She died with a disease called the spotted fever. There has been several cases of it in Hastings this winter. The first ever known in this state.[36] To day is a lovely day. The water is running in little rivers every way you can look with the sun melting the snow. Is looks more like spring then it has before.[37] You don't know how glad I shall be when sum-

35. On February 5, 1863, cavalry commander Nathan Bedford Forrest attacked Fort Donelson but was repulsed. *Harper's Weekly* reported that Union colonel Lowe, stationed at Fort Henry, pursued the Confederate cavalry. See *Harper's Weekly*, 21 February 1863, 115. See also Wyeth, *Life of General Nathan Bedford Forrest*, chap. 7. Madison means Fort Heiman, rather than "Hindman." Andrews writes, "March 12th the regiment embarked on a steamer, and, with other forces, proceeded on an expedition under Gen. Asboth to reoccupy Fort Heiman, on the west bank of the Tennessee" ("Narrative of the Third Regiment," 163).

36. Five-year-old Charlotte Bottomly lived in Nininger City in 1860; her sister was Mary Bottomly Case. "Spotted fever" was another name for typhus.

37. Lizzie meant "it" rather than "is" in this sentence.

mer comes. I feel real well now. My appetite is real good. Do you have plenty of apples down there? We can't hard[ly] get any here for love nor money.

I heard a day or two ago that Case was going to buy this place across the road. I wish you could find out where the man that owns it lives, for I want you to get it for a home if it is possible. Kate is much the same as when you left, growing a little weaker all the time. Sometimes I wonder that she lives so long while so many other well persons have been taken away. . . .

> From your affectionate wife
> Lizzie S. Bowler

Nininger Minn. March 22, 1863

My Dear Hubbie

. . . I feel very anxious to hear from you again to know that you are safe. I think you could not have had the battle you expected or we should have heard some thing about it before this. To-day is Sunday. Every thing is so lonely and dismal that I can hardly find any thing to keep me from going to sleep. It has been raining all night and this morning. The first thunder shower we have had this spring. . . .

Gus Case told me that he recd a letter from you. I was glad you wrote to him for he thought [it] very strange [that] you had not written before. Him and Mary have both been sick for this last week. They all feel very badly about Charlotte's death. . . .

O!! dear hubbie, you dont know how much I want to see you. If you were only here to-day I would be happy. When I read the papers and see how many discourageing things there is constantly happening I almost give up in dispair and think this awful war will never end. If this war lasts next winter, you must try and get a furlough some time during the summer and come home.

. . . O. T. Hayes is Major of the Mounted Rangers. Rob Caleff has gone with him. He has chosen F. M. Crosby as his guardian. I think it is the best place for him. Kate remains pretty much the same as when you left here. Aunt Sarah got a letter from Am since he went back. He has had the mumps but is better now. When he was home he went to see Dr. Thorn. He told him that he had no more business in the army then a woman, which pulled his courage down considerable on the army question. . . .[38]

> From your loving Wife
> Lizzie

38. Orrin T. Hayes had been in the First Minnesota but resigned July 29, 1861. He became major of the First Regiment Mounted Rangers on March 10, 1863. Twenty-year-old

{along the inside pages at the top upside down} Do you have good health since you went down there? Are you troubled with the dyriah any?[39]

Fort Heiman, Ky., March 31, 1863.

My Dear Lizzie:

. . . I am really rejoiced to hear from you once more, and learn that you are well. . . . Last week I was over to Fort Donelson, and made Piercy a three days visit. He came back here with me, and stayed two days. He is now quite well, and getting along finely. I think he has a notion after a certain miss of strong *union* (In more than one sense) proclivities, living up near Hopkinsville. He has considerable to say about getting married; but thinks that he shall wait until the war is over. . . .

I knew you would not insist on my going home this fall. When the war is over I will go home to stay, if spared until then. I judge that you have not much hope left for the Union Ca[u]se. I never feel more confident of success than I do now. You are too impatient, like many others. You ought to read the history of the Peninsular war, and draw a parallel between that war and this. The English at first were as enthusiastic to crush Napoleon and drive him from Spain as we were to crush this rebellion; but two or three years of apparent disaster dampened their arder, and caused them to almost despair, and came very near bringing the war to a stop and Lord Welington and the British ministry into disgrace; but the Government and the Iron Duke persevered, and the British arms were, after many years, crowned with complete success. But you no doubt have read it, and I will leave you to reflect, and take new hope.[40] I will not try to prevent you from *thinking* what you please; but I would not like to have my little wife *say* things which might discourage the patriotic, or associate her in the least degree with the peace traitors of the north.

Robert Caleff does not appear in the military records for the regiment. Robert was orphaned when his mother died in January. His father had been a sea captain, and according to John H. Case, Rob Caleff inherited a sizable estate of forty thousand dollars, and he "squandered it in a reckless manner." See Case, "The Caleff Family of Bluff Landing," *Hastings Gazette*, 30 December 1921. Francis M. Crosby was a twenty-nine-year-old Hastings lawyer in 1860.

39. "Dyriah" is, of course, diarrhea, a common and potentially deadly illness for many soldiers during the war. James David Hacker calculates that diarrhea and dysentery, which were often reported synonymously, resulted in 56,498 deaths in the Union army. See Hacker, "The Human Cost of War," 18.

40. The Peninsular War took place from 1808 to 1814. Madison might be referring to Robert Southey's *History of the Peninsular War*, published in London, 1823–1832.

The boat is going soon, and I must close. Your particular request is a good one, and one with which I should be proud to comply. I am anything but a christian, but hope that we may both live in the ways of God. The army is a poor place for the cultivation of christians, but I do believe that one can be a christian, even in the army. I shall not cease to try. My prayers shall be for you, and I know that Lizzie will pray for me. . . .

> Ever your loving
> Madison

Nininger April 5th 1863

My Dear Madison

I have not heard from you since I last wrote. Have almost come to the conclusion that Mad has forgotten his Lizzie or else you must be sick. . . .

To-day there is quarterly meeting at Spring Lake. Minnie and Ma have gone. The rest of our folks are all at Nininger, excepting Do. She is quite sick with the mumps yet. Kate is down making Uncle Peter's folks a visit. She has been quite smart for her for the last few days. Aunt Sarah is real sick with the mumps. I expect nothing but I shall have them. To-day is a beautiful day. Every thing is beginning to look like summer. You don't know how glad I am that the winter is past, for you may depend it has been a dreary winter to me. There has not been two weeks at a time since you went away that there has not been two or three of us sick. I am in hopes that it will be more healthy now since the snow has gone and the ground dried up.

. . . Do write often. Tell me all about how you are getting along. Are you as fleshy as you were when you left Minn.? My health is pretty good. Remember me to all friends in the Regt. Tell Eugene [h]is mother is well. I hope to get a letter from you next mail which comes Tuesday. If I don't I shall surely think there is something the matter.

> Yours ever
> Lizzie

Fort Heiman, Ky., April 7, 1863.[41]

My Dear Libby

. . . I want to hear from you ag[ain very] much, for it is so lonely here that I almost get the blues, and a letter from you would be like a visit from a friend.

41. This letter contains several holes.

1

2 GO IF YOU THINK IT YOUR DUTY

We are very busy now, fortifying this place. An attack is daily expected. Detachments are out pressing negroes and teams to work on the fortifications, and foraging for supplies.[42]

You wish to know whether we are allowed to receive newspapers. We are. The daily papers from St Louis, Chicago, Cincinnati, and Louisville reach us every mail. Minnesota papers are seldom seen in camp.

It is quite warm here now, yet those accustomed to this climate, call it a late spring. The fields and gardens have been alive with flowers for several weeks. The forests are beginning to put on their green robes.

It is very pleasant to-day. I am "Field officer of the Day" to-day. It is my business to command the picket guard for the next twenty-four hours. I have a beautiful white horse to ride, and if you were here I would get another from the quarter master, and we would ride around and inspect the pickets together. It would make you feel proud to receive the honors from the pickets. Those on duty at their posts, present arms as the "officer of the Day" passes, and the reserves fall into ranks and do the same at his approach.

Barney McKenna has been [tra]nsferred to Co. F again, and W [?], one of my [men r]eported the other day, which makes my company one of the largest in the regiment, it now being third in size. I have three men at Fort Snelling yet. . . .

Ever your affectionate
Madison.

Fort Heiman, Ky., April 15th, 1863.
Wednesday evening.

Dear Libby:

I have just been looking at your miniature, and wishing that I could have the pleasure of looking at the original instead. It seems to me that I never thought of you so constantly as I do lately. I cannot help thinking that you are sick most of the time—much more so than you let me know of. I wish [this w]ar would end soon so that I could be with you again to stay.

In yours of March 30th, you ask me if I can get my washing done conveniently. I can, now. There are several colored women in camp, who do washing for the officers, and do it quite well.[43] I am sorry to learn that Ammon is still sick.

42. Blacks were regularly used as laborers in the Union army. See Berlin et al., *Slaves No More*, 120–21.
43. For black women working in Union army camps, see Jones, *Labor of Love, Labor of Sorrow*, 50–51; Berlin et al., *Slaves No More*, 118; and Forbes, *African American Women during the Civil War*, 53–55.

If he cannot endure a soldiers life I hope that he will be discharged. It must make Aunt Sarah feel badly, to have him sick while away from her. Gus Case has been sick, too, you say. It seems that everybody in Nininger is getting sick this spring. There will be another sick man when Gov. Donnelly gets into his enormity of loneliness down among those desolate grubs, or I am mistaken. I have [not] written to, nor received letters from, Mr. Donnelly since I left Minn. this last time. I think of writing to him soon. I have forgotten all about "Special Order, No. 1," referred to by Minnie. What was it?

As to "keeping house," I get along pretty well considering that I have to do without the company and help of Libby. Willis Countryman is cooking for me now but he is not one of the best of cooks. I am going to have a "contraband" as [I can] get a *good* one. I can get colored *women* enough, who know how to cook; but I do not relish the idea of having one about to furnish material for stories to go home to you.[44] Lieut. Jameson and myself live in a good log house, 12 by 16 feet, with a good board floor. We sleep in separate bunks made of cypress boards, with a few rushes for feathers. We have a good table, and wooden benches in lieu of chairs. Our food consists of Fresh beef, Fresh and Salt Pork, Ham, eggs, beans, potatoes, biscuit, pancakes, doughnuts, pies, tea, coffee, sugar, apples, rice, hominy, and mixed vegetables, besides butter, chickens, &c., which we occasionally get from the country, which is not rich enough to furnish a regular supply. Most of the inhabitants are awfully poor, and as ignorant as they are poor. Last week I rode out to the "shoemakers"—the only one known of about here—and found the shop, hencoop, and pig-pen in the same room with the family, which consisted of a father, mother, two boys, and three girls, besides a baby (sex unknown), not one of whom could either read or write. The work corresponded very well with the rest, for the second days wearing found my boots minus the soles I had paid $1.40 for.

. . . Minnie writes to Charley that she heard of his being drunk in Hastings. He says that she heard the truth; but that he does not intend to get drunk again. Eugene has not drank a drop of liquor but once since we were furloughed last fall, and that was a drink of brandy for medicine. There is a very marked improvement in his whole conduct.[45] He does not even drink beer. He has a great deal of writing to do since he has been acting quarter master Sergt. of the Regiment.

You refer to Mr. Williams and the good meetings which have been held by

44. For soldiers "keeping house," see Mitchell, *The Vacant Chair,* 82. For worry about gossip between home front and camp, see Mitchell, "The Northern Soldier and His Community," 84–87.

45. For drinking, see Mitchell, *The Vacant Chair,* 6–7, 35–36.

him. I am glad to hear it. I hope that he will remain with you. Mr. Crary, our chaplain, preaches every sabbath, and holds prayer meetings twice a week. He talks
of resigning.[46]

Three or four thousand troops came to Fort Henry to-day on their way up this
river. Ten transports are expected up to-night. Two gunboats went up the river
yesterday, to reconnoiter. Those men are here, waiting for the transports. It begins to look as though Rosecrans intends to make [some?] movement on the
rebels preparatory to striking them in front. If I mistake not, you will hear of a
general engagement of Rosecrans army soon unless the rebels retreat. This would
be considered contraband news if it were likely to get into the hands of the rebels;
but I guess you will not tell them about it. . . .[47]

> Ever yours truly.
> Madison.

*{back page side and top margins} Do write to me often, Libby—good long
letters—for I am so lonely now. . . .*

*{front page side margin} We have not been paid off yet. If you are need of
money—and I presume that you are by this time—I will try and borrow some.
Let me know truly. Madison*

Nininger Minn. April 19, 1863

My Dear Madison

. . . I have been very sick for three days with the mumps. Feeling much better this
afternoon and this being my regular day for writing, I thought I must write you. . . .
. . . I wish you could have been here when they had their town election.
Daniel B. Truax was elected chairman of the board of supervisors which was
rather against old Mr. Reed's notion, and Donnelly gave him a regular low lived
black guard dressing. The old man felt so bad he talked of selling out and going
away. . . .[48]

---

46. Lizzie's letter regarding Mr. Williams is not in the correspondence. B. F. Crary
resigned June 2, 1863. See Board of Commissioners, *Minnesota in the Civil and Indian
Wars*, 178.

47. Union general William S. Rosecrans had won a bloody and inconclusive victory
at Stones River on January 2, 1863. Although he did little between January and May, he
did authorize some military activity in central Tennessee.

48. Daniel B. Truax was a forty-two-year-old farmer in Nininger in 1860. Mr. Reed
was probably Anthony Reed, mentioned previously. For the Nininger Town Board, see
Guelcher, *More Than Just a Dream*, 133.

I have been making [a] garden for the last week till I got so sick I could not work any more. Uncle Peter is going to give me some goose berry bushes "to begin with" as he says. When you come home I want you to bring some pretty flower slips with you such as roses and Peony, or Piny as they are pronounced. . . . I dont feel like going away from home to visit among strangers [in St. Anthony]. I will wait till you come home again but when will that be? I wish I could have as much faith about this war as you have.

Amon is in the hospitle yet. Leander Wells has taken his departure and gone to Canada. Mrs Wells is at Sam Truaxes yet. She is going to where he is soon. . . .[49]

You say you wish I could be there. I wish I could but what is the use of wishing? Remember me to all friends in the Regt.

When do you expect to get your pay? I don't know how you get along with so little money. I think you must be a poverty stricken Regt by this time. . . .

LSB . . .

Nininger April 23, 1863
Thursday evening

My Dear Hubbie

. . . As I read [your last letter] I could not help a tear droping often, for I know well how you felt when you wrote it. If you knew how many hours I past in feeling as you describe, for you have explained my feelings better then I can. I sleep now in the bed we occupied and there is seldom a night but that I feel the fact very sensibly that the darkness helps one to think. But the different situation of the subject of ones thoughts makes a great change in feeling. When you think of me you can think of me as occupying some vacant spot in some place that you are familiar with.

But when I think of my hubbie my imagination first leads me to wonder whether he is yet in the land of the living. If so, his whereabouts and this imagination runs on with no resting place till I at last am lost in the arms of Morpheus. . . .

(Sunday Morning)

I will again commence this and will try and finish it before I leave it. Gus says give my love to big Jeams and tell him that I am expecting a letter from him. Mary says when you get tired enough of this war to wish it was ended she will give you three cheers.

49. Mary Wells's husband, Leander, deserted from Company F, Seventh Minnesota, on March 15, 1863. Samuel Truax was a twenty-four-year-old Nininger farmer in 1860. His connection to Mary Wells is unclear; both were originally from New York.

Have you forgotten this soon what special order No 1 means when you went away? Minnie said if Charley was not a good boy she wanted you to punish him and the punish[ment] was to make him write home, and you said you would issue special order No 1 as soon as you get south.

I heard that they have sent all the Indian prisinors down the river. Some say they are going to put them in states prison and others say they are going to take them to Rock Island. The Indians have been quite troublesome about thirty miles above Mankato, killed three persons and stole three horses. Mrs. Truax wants me to ask where Johnson is. They have not heard from him since he went away, excepting a note he sent two or three days after he left. They are very anxious about him.

My health is pretty good now. I have got quite over the mumps. It was nothing. That Uncle Peter knew as any thing, he could tell any other way than by my looking differently in the face. You know old rogues are sore judges and all he knows yet is what he imagines for he could not tell by any marked changes. It is time for me to stop writing and get ready for sabbath school.

... I am quite willing as far as I am concerned to trust you with a colored woman for a cook. If any one is bad enough to have anything to do with a black woman, I think likely they have opportunities enough without having them employed.[50] Is Eugene's pay much more now then it was before. If you can borrow four or five dollars conveniently you may. But if you cannot without putting yourself to trouble don't you do it, and dont send more then that for as likely as not it will never reach me, and that will be as much as I will need at present.

I forgot to tell you that your plumb tree has died. Pa has set out a lot more. If they live we may expect to have some plumbs sometime. This has been the earliest spring we have had since the first spring we came here. The prairies are quite green. What would I give if I was only near where I could go and make you a visit to-day? But what is the use of talking about something that is almost impossible.

Piercy wrote to Gus that he was acquainted with a young lady, one at Hopkinsville. That she is very much accomplished, plays on several kinds of musical instruments, and is a perfect lady in every sense. Is he like he used to be or has he changed since he went south?

I cannot think of any news so I shall have to bid my absent hubbie good Bye.

From your Lizzie ...

---

50. African American women were often assumed to be promiscuous by whites both in the army and at home. See Forbes, *African American Women during the Civil War*, 218, 222–24. Soldiers on both sides raped black women. See Lowry, *The Story the Soldiers Wouldn't Tell*, 37, 84, and chap. 12.

Columbus, Ky., April 30, 1863.

My Dear Libby:

It seems almost an age since I heard from you, though in reality it has been a little more than a week. It is now eight o'clock in the evening, and I am alone in my room—a nice large room on the second floor, overlooking the main street leading out of the business portion of this city. It is pleasant indeed; and if you were only here, my happiness would be complete. Libby would hug up so close to Mad, nestle her head on his arm, give him a dozen good kisses, and then tell him all about everything that has happened since you last saw him. Wouldn't you?

Libby, ever since I wrote you an account of my little trouble, I have been thinking that it was wrong for me to do so, because it might worry you, as you cannot fully understand all the circumstances, and may perhaps attach more importance to it than it deserves. But I could do no less than let you know the truth. If I had kept it from you I should not have felt right. It is my desire ever to be frank with you. Should I be otherwise I should feel that I had forfeited my claim to your love and respect; and I would rather meet death than do that. Did I do right in telling you? Let me assure you that no harm will come of my trial. I know that I shall come out all right.[51]

My case will come up next week, after which I shall go to Fort Heiman; so you need not direct any more letters here. While I think of it I will give you the most approved form of directing soldiers letters. For instance, Capt. A. B., Co. "F," Minn. Infy.; or, Lieut. J. S., Co. "B," 5th Iowa Cav'y.

I wrote to you twice last week, and sent you ten dollars in one of the letters. I wish I could send you more, but cannot until we are paid. That little may do you some good. I heard some time ago that Wm Govett was not in the army, but was keeping a bad house in Memphis. Whether there is any truth in the report I know not.

---

51. Madison's "little trouble" was a charge of "Conduct prejudicial to good order and military discipline," which resulted in a trial before a court-martial on May 5 and 6, 1863, in Columbus. Madison was accused of "knowingly and intentionally" carrying $50.00 of "worthless Bank Currency of various amounts and denominations . . . with the intention of fraudulently using and disposing of the same for their pretended or some other value." Although the charge was submitted by Major Hans Mattson and proceeded up the chain of command to be referred to the court-martial, it was instigated by Sergeant David Morgan and Sergeant William Allison in Company F, both of whom Madison had referred to unfavorably in earlier letters. The transcript of James M. Bowler's court-martial file (LL-600) can be found at the National Archives and Records Administration, Washington, D.C.

There is a young widow, real good looking, looks like Maggie Callahan,—at "our house."[52] She is just from St. Louis. If you do not hear from me again you can guess "what is the matter." But unfortunately I was simple enough, when asked if I were married, to acknowledge the fact. Perhaps though that will make no difference. What do you say! Well, I have written nonsense enough. . . .

> Ever yours.
> Madison.

Columbus, Ky., May 7, 1863.

My Dear Libby:

. . . It gave me great relief to hear that you were well; for during the last week or two I have felt sure that you were sick. As you say nothing about having the mumps, I presume that the crisis is past, and that you will not have them at all. I am rejoiced to learn that you are so well, and hope that you will continue so. You did not mention how Dollie got along with the mumps.

I have not made friends with Morgan and Allison, and have had no talk with them except so far as official duties were concerned, and even then, though courteous toward them, I have never permitted the least familiarity. I have no fears of any misconduct on the part of Eugene. You have no idea of the great change in his conduct. So far as Johnson Truax is concerned he has done quite well, and has done nothing against me. During my trial I could find not the least fault with his testimony, and he testified very highly as to my character as a man of integrity and as an officer. Lieut. Col. Andrews testified in my defense, giving me the reputation of having raised my company from almost the lowest to the highest state of discipline, and of having, while but a Sergt., led it gallantly and bravely in the battle of Wood-Lake. My trial was closed day before yesterday. There was no material evidence against me. What the finding of the court was, cannot be known until Gen. Asboth reviews the case and publishes it in an order. Meantime, I expect to return to my regiment, and await his order before I take command of my company. I have every reason to believe that I have been honorably acquitted, but of course cannot be assured of it.[53]

52. Nineteen-year-old Margarett Callahan lived in Nininger City in 1860.

53. Johnson R. Truax, Joseph Barker, and Peter Panschott [Panchot], all from Hastings or nearby and men in Madison's company, were the witnesses, as was Colonel Andrews. As Madison notes, none of the illegal currency was produced, and the men presented the interactions over fraudulent money as a practical joke between themselves. When Madison questioned Johnson Truax, it was revealed that sergeants Morgan and

You say that you wish the war were over and we were once more together in some little place of our own. You already know my wishes in that respect. Nothing would afford me more happiness.

We have interesting news from the Potomac. Hooker has not only surprised Gen. Lee, but he has, as you might say, surprised the world by the suddenness, daring, and brilliancy of his recent movements. So far he has been successful, and we have much [to] confirm us in the belief that he will win a great victory. The prayers of the loyal everywhere are with him. Should Hunter, Rosecrans, and Grant follow the example of Hooker and Banks at once, and with success, we could then hope for a speedy solution of our troubles. Time will tell.[54]

The weather here has been very fine until yesterday when it turned in rainy and very chilly. To-day is not much better. I presume you have it very pleasant in Minn now. Four of my deserters have just been returned to the company—Deakin among them. Knight has not been heard from yet. I am very anxious to hear from brother Joseph, as Banks army has been fighting lately. . . .

> Yours ever.
> Madison.

Allison "both say that they thought they had not been used right by Capt Bowler, thot he didn't use them right in getting promoted over them, and that they intended to have revenge on him. They also said that they didn't think he used them right in having other Sergeants promoted over them to be Lieutenants." Truax reported that he overheard the two men discussing with others in the company their unfair treatment by Bowler, saying, "They could afford to be reduced to the ranks if they could only get Capt Bowler dismissed." Following Truax's testimony Colonel Andrews testified much as Madison described in his letter. Madison's defense focused on his good character and reputation, an essential line of defense in a court-martial trial. See DeHart, *Observations on Military Law*, 344–59. Madison would not receive the order, or verdict, from his court-martial until July 30, 1863.

54. Madison refers to the battle of Chancellorsville. At the end of April, Union general Joseph Hooker divided his troops, and some "captured the surprised Confederate pickets, and moved eastward to close in on the Rebel rear." Initially, the Union command thought they had surprised Confederate general Robert E. Lee. He knew, however, what was happening, divided his army, and engaged Hooker's troops from May 2 to 6. It was a Confederate victory ultimately, although Madison would not have known this by May 7. General Nathaniel Banks would successfully besiege Port Hudson on the Mississippi River before the end of May, which coincided with General Grant's stepped-up action at Vicksburg. General Rosecrans hoped to take central Tennessee. General David Hunter had been serving on courts-martial in the winter of 1862–1863. See Warner, *Generals in Blue*, 244.

Nininger May 16, 1863
Saturday evening

My Darling Hubbie

... Nothing gives me so much pleasure as to hear from you, to know that you are getting along well, and enjoying yourself, if there is any enjoyment to be had in the army. I wrote to you two or three days ago but as I feel lonely to-night I will scribble you a few lines more, if they are not very interesting. I will now try and answer your questions.

The money you sent me is sufficient for all my wants at present. I do not wish you to worry about that. My health at present is very good indeed. You say I do not write a word about what you want to know. I know what it is and will write you something about it. You ask if I go to church or elsewhere. I can go any where as far as that is concerned for I do not show it but very little, and any one that is not very smart at finding out such a state of affairs would never think of such a thing.[55] If you had been in my place since you left here I guess you would not doubt such being the case. You ask what I am going to do in a few months from now. I do not know what I shall do. If you could come home at that time, you know better then I can tell you what pleasure it would be to me. But if you cannot come without too great a sacrifice I cannot think of urging you. Time tells all things and we will wait four months and see then.

I do not know what Ma thinks of things, but think if I were over the danger of being sick that she would be pleased. She has never said anything about your coming at that time and I do not know what she would say. Kate often tell[s] what she is going to call little M, but poor Kate. I am afraid she will never live to see that time.... Now I will say good night and go to bed to think of my M.

> Now Good Bye
> Lizzie

{top margin front page} I think you and that young widow is getting along pretty well. I wish I could poke in some time when you are setting in that nice room having such nice times. Is she a war widow? They have moved Hillhouse['s] old house to Hastings. You dont know how strange it makes Aunt Sarahs place look.[56] Lizzie ...

55. Lizzie refers to cultural norms about pregnancy, including a woman's not appearing in public once her pregnancy begins to show. See Wertz and Wertz, *Lying-In*, 78–81.

56. Several Nininger City houses and buildings were moved down river on logs to Hastings in the 1860s. See *Hastings Independent*, 31 March 1864.

Fort Heiman, Ky., May 20th, 1863.

Dear Lizzie:

I am at last able to send you something more substantial than promises. Enclosed please find Two hundred dollars ($200). I was paid to-day, the Paymaster having returned to this place to pay the 111th Illinois, and I taking advantage of his presence to get a little pay for myself.

I promised your father enough to pay his indebtedness to Mr. Russell. Please let him have it if their is more than you need for your own use. Also remember to pay Aunt Sarah with all the interest she desires and my thanks into the bargain.

Now you must go to St. Anthony on a visit, and to St Paul to *have your photograph* (a dozen good ones) taken. Do you hear? *I shall not take "no" for an answer.* Love to all.

Ever yours, Madison.

Fort Heiman, Ky., May 24, 1863.

Dear Libby:

Yours of May 14th was received this morning. Eugene laid it upon my face this morning before I was awake, the mail having come in during the night. It makes me feel so badly to know that you worry so much about me, just as I expected you would. Libby, you must not permit yourself to worry about me unless you want to make me miserable.

I can assure you that my case is all right, though the result has not been made public yet. I am in command of my company and everything goes along pleasantly. We had a grand review to-day before Maj. Gen. Hurlburt's Asst. Adjt. Genl. He pronounced us the best Regt. he had seen in the Department, the 40th Iowa being next best. We belong to the 16th Army Corps, commanded by Maj. Gen. S. R. Hurlburt whose Head qrs. are at Memphis. Our more immediate commander is Brig. Gen. Asboth, commanding a division of the 16th Corps.[57] The reviewing officer has ordered a set of colors for us. You know we have had none since our surrender at Murfreesboro.

I am glad to hear that you got so safely through with the mumps, and hope you will not be sick again. You must not entertain fears that you are to be sick because others are. It must be very hard indeed for Mr. Dicken now that his wife

57. For more on generals Stephen A. Hurlbut and Alexander Asboth, see Warner, *Generals in Blue*, 245 and 11, respectively.

is dead, a little one left helpless, and he away in the army.[58] It seems to me that in such an event I should court death by the first bullet from the enemy. . . .

In one of your letters you refer to the idea of absent benedicts *associating* with colored females, as something horrible and not to be tolerated among respectable people. Now you do not mean all you say, surely. You know we are away from home, and *you* are not selfish enough to wish to see anyone suffer by being denied what few little privileges he is able to secure. Let me know whether you were really in earnest; and do not write upon too hasty conclusions, for you cannot fully realize the pressure of our circumstances at the first thought. You must first imagine yourself in our situation, and then you will be able to judge more fairly. . . .[59]

>Ever yours.
>Madison.

{top margin back page} The 111th Ill had a funeral to-day, the 3[?]th they have had since we came to Ft. Heiman. Not [one] death has occurred in our Regt since we came south this time. . . .

Nininger, May 28, 1863.

My Dear Madison

I rec'd a letter from you this morning saying that you had expressed $200.00 to Hastings. If I can get a chance I will go to-morrow. If you had to borrow it why did you borrow so much? You dont know but I may get on a spree some of these days and spend it all. You say you have written so often lately that your letters will soon become a nuisance. You need not fear for I would gladly get three to where I get one, but as you are so punctual about writing I can say nothing.

. . . I saw Albert Truax to meeting one day (shortly after you went to Ft. Heiman) and asked him if he had heard from any of the 3rd Regt, for I had not heard from you at the time for three weeks. He said he had not, that Mrs. Knapp was very uneasy for they had not heard from Herman in a long time and thought there

58. In 1857 Stephen Dicken was recorded as twenty years old and living in Hastings. He joined Company F, Seventh Minnesota, in August 1862. Lizzie's May 14 letter is not in the correspondence, so the details of his wife's death are unknown.

59. For community and soldiers' values differing, see Mitchell, "The Northern Soldier and His Community," 87. For Union soldiers' sexual involvement with black freedwomen, see Litwack, *Been in the Storm So Long*, 129–30; and Jordan, "Sleeping with the Enemy," 59.

was something the matter.[60] I think I have got all the letters you have sent me but some of them have been a long while on the way.

How do you get along for shirts? I think you will have to buy some. When you do, mind and get good ones, [even] if they are higher priced, and those that are large enough. I have been sorry ever since that I had not have made you two or three new ones when you were home. Well I will leave this till to-morrow.

[May 29]

I am at Hastings writing in the post office. I recd the package you sent all safe and sound. Receive my thanks for your kindness. I will do as you wished me accepting the journey to St. Anthony and that I cannot promise.[61] If you were here I would gladly go, but as it is I should not enjoy myself very much. . . . There is such a confusion here that I dont think what I am doing. I live on the hope that you will come home and make a visit this fall. You dont *know* how much I want to see you.

    Lizzie Bowler

Fort Heiman, Ky., May 28, 1863.

My Dear Libby:

Your good little letter was handed to me last night after I had gone to bed. I knew I was going to receive a letter from Libby next mail, so I was not disappointed.

I received a letter from Amon this week, in which he informed me that he was getting much better than he had been. I am very glad to hear it; for if anybody is ever deserving the sympathy of mankind it is a sick soldier away from home. . . .

Considerable excitement was created in the camp of our Regt. by the receipt of a Harper's Monthly containing a *quaisi* history of the Indian campaign in Minn. last fall, but really nothing, more than a garbled version for the benefit of Col. Marshall and a few others. The 3d Reg., we are informed, arrived at Fort Ridgely and then the sage historian leaves them while Col. Marshall, Gen. Sibley, et all deal out death and destruction to the bloody "injuns" at Wood Lake. "Such is life." Verily, the justice of history is the reward of the brave.

We are having some lively times now. Scouting parties are out continually after Guerillas. We have now here, besides many we have sent to Columbus, over 100

---

60. Mrs. Knapp was Emily Knapp, a twenty-five-year-old mother of one who lived in Nininger in 1860. Herman was probably Herman Pettibone, in the Third Minnesota. The connection between the two is unclear.

61. Lizzie intended "excepting" rather than "accepting."

prisoners. Skirmishes with them are quite frequent. Day before yesterday Capt. Baker had a skirmish with fifty of them about thirty miles up the Tennessee, killed and wounded several, and captured ten without losing a man. Sergt. Pettibone is out now to guide Major Mattson with a force of three hundred.[62] Pettibone is a great favorite on account of his energy and bravery. He is out most of the time.

I have got Dave Morgan in the Guard House, and have preferred charges against him, for disobedience of orders.

I am just called on to go on duty as officer of the day. . . .

> Ever yours
> Madison.

Fort Heiman, Ky., May 30, 1863.

Dear Libby:

. . . I enclose you a ring made out of muscle shell taken from the Tennessee river. I do not send it because it is costly or pretty, but because it is a relic of this country. You must get Mr. Macomber to work it of nice and small, and then perhaps you might wear it.[63]

The 3d Regt. received marching orders to-day to go to Vicksburg, calling at Memphis for orders. It is possible that we may go no further than Memphis. A transport has just come up for us, but four companies being out on a scout we cannot go until Monday. The 111th Ill. will go on this transport to Paducah. The 25th and 27th Wis., and the 40th Iowa go below with us.[64]

Our friends of the 111th are quite literary. I will send a *verbatim et literatum* copy of a note from their chaplain, which was sent to our Adjutant last Sunday.

---

62. Initially Company D's captain, Hans Mattson was promoted to major in May 1862. Andrews explains, "The regiment's principal duty at Fort Heiman was to break up Confederate conscription in the surrounding country, and with this object, and in part mounted with horses from the country, it made numerous enterprising scouts, which often involved long and wary marches. Three of these were under the command of Major Mattson. In the last one, he, with Companies B, D, G and H, Third Minnesota and a detachment of Companies A and D, Fifteenth Kentucky Cavalry, left Fort Heiman May 26th and marched through several counties on the west side of the Tennessee and on both sides of the Big Sandy" (see "Narrative of the Third Regiment," 163).

63. Madison probably meant that Mr. Macomber should work it "up" to fit Lizzie's finger. Mr. Macomber was a watchmaker in Hastings. See *Hastings Independent*, 15 April 1861.

64. Andrews states, "May 29th, General Hurlbut, from Memphis, telegraphed General Asboth to abandon Fort Heiman and 'send, with all possible dispatch, the Third Minnesota by steamer to Vicksburg,' with five days' rations, six wagons, one hundred rounds per man, and only shelter tents" ("Narrative of the Third Regiment," 163–64).

It is as follows: "Forte Heiman Ky May 25th/63. The musitions of the 3d Minnasota will pleas gave the signal for Devine Sirvis at 3 PM near the Arber. J. B. Wolland Chaplin 111th Ill."[65] Good, isn't it? . . .

Libby, find out if you can whether your mother thinks it best for me to be at home this fall. Do not let her know that I make the inquiry. You can tell her that I leave it with you and that you want to know what to do in the premises. *Do not forget* that I told you about going to St. Anthony, but be sure and go if you do not stay one day. Is —— to be a young Jeems, or the other thing?[66] Let me know. . . .

> Ever your
> Madison.

Steamer Izetta, Columbus, Ky., June 4, 1863.

My Dear Lizzie:

I must write you once more before we leave here. We left Fort Heiman yesterday, seven companies on the *Bon Accord,* and three companies (D, F, and H) and some 200 contrabands on the *Arizona.* Arrived at Paducah before night and were all transferred to the U.S. Transport Izetta. Our trip thus far has been quite pleasant. I was fortunate enough to secure a good stateroom, and have laid in an ample stock of the necessaries of life—crackers, cheese, ham, &c., to last me through to Vicksburg.

We brought down from the Fort Col. Dawson, Maj. Alger, and Capts. Howard and Griswold, all of whom we had captured up the Tennessee river. They had the freedom of the boat upon their parole of honor; talked freely with us, but seemed somewhat cast down. We bade adieu to Fort Heiman with regret, for we had got comfortably situated and were doing a good business in the line of catching up rebels.

While there we freed upwards of 1000 slaves—male and female, old and young. The males have nearly all enlisted in the colored regiments which are being raised here. The negro women are objects of pity indeed; yet they seem satisfied with being free at almost any cost. They, like the white women down here, practice snuff dipping—a most disgusting practice I assure you.[67]

---

65. James B. Woolard was listed as the chaplain for the 111th Illinois Regiment. See www.rootsweb.com/~ilcivilw/f&s/111-fs.htm.

66. Madison is asking whether they will have a "little Jeems" (James, a baby boy) or a baby girl.

67. For freed black men joining the Union army and freed black women's conditions, see Jones, *Labor of Love, Labor of Sorrow,* 49–50. Dipping snuff meant to put pulverized tobacco into the mouth with a stick or brush.

We arrived here to-day at 12 o'clock, and were immediately paid off for the two months ending April 30th. I have expressed $160.00 to you to-day to Hastings. Ten dollars ($10.00) of it belongs to Eugene and is to be given to his wife when you get a chance to do so. . . .

We are brigaded with the 25th and 27th Wis. and 40 Iowa Infy., 2nd Ill. Cavalry, and, I believe, an Ohio Battery, under command of Brig. Gen. Nathan Kimball. It is a crack brigade. We start for below at five o'clock to-morrow morning. It is now eleven at night. I am in the cabin writing upon a table surrounded by officers engaged in the same occupation. The cabin floor is covered with sleeping soldiers dreaming perhaps of home, and oblivious to the trials before them.

I have had a real good time among my acquaintances here to-day. I took dinner with my old boarding mistress, Mrs. Byron. . . .

Now, Dear, *dear Libby,* you must write to me very often; for, deprived of almost every other enjoyment, I shall long more than ever to hear from you. I wrote you a jesting, frollicking letter about "colored women," &c., a few weeks ago, just to see what you would say and to see whether you would think me in earnest or not. I have not heard from it yet. Upon reflection I think I ought not to have written so, and you must forgive me. I could not of course as an honest man who loves a dear virtuous wife, think of believing or acting as the tone of that letter would intimate. I hope I may never do anything to cause you [to] blush in secret for me or to doubt for one moment my adhesion to the right and my love for you.

Libby, let your first and only consideration be to *take good care of yourself.* Since I am assured that "something is so" I cannot help loving you more and more every day. . . .

> Now, Dear Libby, with many sweet kisses, Good-night!—Good-Bye!
> Madison . . .

                                                        Yazoo River, June 8, 1863.

Dear Libby:

I am going to write just a few words to let you know where we are. We passed Memphis yesterday, and arrived at Youngs point opposite the mouth of the Yazoo to-day. We are now ten or twelve miles up the Yazoo; have just landed. Our Regt will march out to the rear of Vicksburg, six miles from here, this afternoon. There will be a grand bombardment to-night, and I presume our assault to-morrow. . . .

> Ever yours
> Madison

Haines Bluff, Miss., June 12, 1863.

My Dear Libby:

. . . I did not borrow the money I sent you—it was a part of my pay. I am not at all afraid of your getting "on a spree," and as to your spending the money, that is just what money is for. I want you to go to St. Anthony if you can; my not being there will make little difference. Have nobody but Whitney to take your photographs, and get good ones. I think standing is a good position for a lady; but consult your own taste or the artists—they know best. Perhaps you had better have some of them colored. I should like two or three colored to send to my friends, and one to keep. Never mind the cost, and *do not delay* until it is too late.

I have only one of the shirts which I brought from home—the last one you made—and you would not know it, it is so dingy. I bought two woolen shirts at $3.50 a piece, and they are almost too small. It costs a great deal to live and dress decently down here. I paid $5.00 for a pair of nice shoes, and wore them out in four weeks. A new sash cost me $20.00, a sword-belt $5.00, a blouse $12.00, and a pair of shoulder straps $6.50. Good cotton stockings cost from $.50 to $1.00 per pair.[68] It is very hard to get washing done here any way decently at all. But who cares! We shall be able to make a living some way, if we do not lay up a cent; and we ought to be content.

You say that I do not know how much you wish to see me. I thought I left you in a "fix" to do without a man for some time; but it seems not. Well, I will try and go home one of these days and make a—"*visit;*" that's what you call it. But to be serious. You may be assured that nothing would give me more pleasure than to be with you again. I think of you day and night. O, just one sweet kiss would be worth a thousand dollars to me.

I have not heard a gun since sunrise. There was a terrible cannonade last night for about three hours. The light artillery seemed to play in as rapid succession as a bunch of fire crackers would burn, while the heavy seige guns and mortars chimed in at the rate of about five in a minute, with a roar which shook the earth. It is reported that Pemberton was trying to cut his way out then, and that he has now surrendered. The fact of no firing makes it seem probable. Johnson and Braggs pickets are within four miles of us to-day, and a fight is momentarily expected.[69]

68. Madison probably bought these items from the sutler, who "held a sort of commission for the job giving them sole power to deal in certain commodities with the soldiers in the camps," and thus they "could charge all the traffic would bear" (Shannon, *The Organization and Administration of the Union Army, 1861–1865,* 253–54).

69. Confederate general John B. Pemberton headed the garrison of Confederate soldiers at Vicksburg, where Grant had begun a siege after attempting to capture Vicksburg

Johnson Truax says: let it be known that he is well, and that he will not write again during the war, for he gets no answers from his letters. You are not very constant in reporting the progress of "little Jeems." I guess it is getting to be an old thing with you.... Be sure to take good care of yourself. Do not go to *walking* to Hastings or elsewhere too much; for I would not have anything happen [to] you for anything in the world....

Ever yours. Madison.

{side margin of first page} I guess you will soon get tired of my letters, I write so often.

Nininger June 18, 1863
Thursday evening

My Darling Husband

I have just returned from Nellie's pic-nic. I must now write a few lines to my absent Husband that I would give more to see this evening then attend half dozen such places. I wrote to you last Sunday so you see it has not been a week since I addressed one of my poor apologies for a letter to you, but as my mind dwells on you most of the time I will occupy [a] few moments in writing a few lines more. There was quite a number attended the pic-nic and all seemed to enjoy themselves. They had a good dinner, music, singing, swinging and all other sorts of amusement, and to finish up with a short speech from Gov. Donnelly.... Eugene wrote to his mother that he had to enlist over again three years from the time that he is promoted but that it was no worse for him then it was for you for you had to do the same. I do not understand how it is, but if it is so you need not be afraid to tell me, for I know if your health remains good you would never be easy to leave the army until this war is over, and I should never be the one that would persuade you to do so against your will. Eugene wrote that he could have got a furlough this spring but thought he would wait till fall. I think if Eugene can get a furlough you can. I do want you to come home so much if you can without it being too much of a put out. I am writing in the dark so you must excuse all mistakes.

---

on May 22, 1863. Confederate general Joseph E. Johnston had pulled together an army near Jackson, Mississippi, and Confederate general Braxton Bragg had another army near Murfreesboro, Tennessee, but neither could relieve Pemberton. See Donald et al., *The Civil War and Reconstruction*, 351–65.

Friday morning

I forgot to thank you for the ring. It is very pretty. I wish I could send you a present but any thing I could send would be of more trouble to you then it would be good so I will wait till you come home to stay. By the by, I almost forgot to tell you that you have lost your farm across the road. Mrs. Faiver & Donnelly have bought it. They gave twenty dollars an acre. Would have got it for fifteen if it had not have been for old Case. That is too bad isn't it?[70]

I want you to tell me what you want me to go to Saint Anthony so much for. Kate remains pretty much the same. Her neck looks as though it would break very soon. We had a call from Mary and Gus last evening. They send their love to you. There is no news to write, consequently my letters are rather dull but you must take the will for the deed and call them good. The people think if we don't have rain soon that the crops will all be a failure. The wheat is all turning yellow.

We have got the pump fixed belonging to the cistern. It does real well. Now dear Madison, wishing you all the happiness and every thing else that heart can wish—excepting the society of b——k l——s, I bid you Good Bye with lots [of] kisses and an arm full of hugs for my hubbie.[71] Hoping you will excuse all my nonesense.

I will again say good Bye

Yours ever
Lizzie

June 24, 1863

Dear Libby:

To-day has been very warm. Have been over to the 43d Ill., and had some good lemonade with Capt. Arasinius. Have to go on picket to-morrow for two days and nights.[72]

---

70. Following the financial panic of 1857, many people left Nininger City and township, either selling or abandoning their land. Mary Faiver, Ignatius Donnelly, and James H. Case all purchased land in the area as investments or to sell later once the economy recovered. See Guelcher, *More Than Just a Dream,* 95, 128. For Minnesota's economy and land prices, see Jarchow, *The Earth Brought Forth,* 63–64.

71. Lizzie probably means "black ladies," referring to Madison's May 24 and June 4 letters.

72. Carl Arosenius was captain, Company C, Forty-third Illinois Infantry. See www .rootsweb.com/~ilcivilw/r050/043-c-in.htm.

{copy from scrap written while on picket} Out on picket, June 25th.

Am on picket five miles from camp and two miles out from Hayne's Bluff. Lt. Col. Thrall of the 22nd Ohio is officer of the day. The 22nd Ohio is what used to be the 13th Missouri. While the Lt. Col. was showing me where to post my picket, I happened to ask him if the 13th Mo was probably down there, when to my surprise he informed me that he belonged to that Regt. which belongs to the 2nd brigade of our division, and was encamped within thirty rods of our Regt. Wm Govett is Capt. of Co. A. You may bet that I shall hunt him up when I go back to camp.[73] The heaviest firing I have ever heard has been going on since 4 o'clock this afternoon. The signal for it was given by rockets. Grant now has 500 guns bearing on the rebel works—the greatest array of cannon ever in any seige or battle on this continent.

(June 26th)

Am still out on picket. The boys have been out and gobbled a beef, and we are luxuriating on fresh beef, milk, and blackberries, green corn, &c. The firing yesterday was an assault on the main rebel work by Gen. Logan['s] division. The works were blown up by mines and one side of the fort carried and held by our men. Gen. Sherman with Smiths division of the 16th Corps and several divisions from the different corps before Vicksburg is now out toward Mechanicsburg to confront Johnson. All the troops here have to keep in readiness to march at a moments warning. The 25th Wis. has gone up to Cypress Bend, near Helena, to prevent the rebels from firing into our transports, several of which have been severely injured in that way. Charley Russell and several other of my boys witnessed the heavy fighting yesterday.[74]

. . . It seems almost an age since I heard from you, and I begin to feel worried about you. Well, it is getting dark, and I must bid Libby Good-night. *I do hope you are not sick.*

73. For a history of the Twenty-second Ohio Infantry (Thirteenth Missouri), see Larry Stevens, "Twenty-second Ohio Infantry," www.ohiocivilwar.com/cw22.html. For Lieutenant Colonel Homer Thrall and William Govette's service, see cwss, www.itd.nps .gov/cwss/soldiers.htm.

74. On June 25, Union engineers exploded a mine under the Confederate line at Vicksburg. One reason that Vicksburg was so important was that it stood on a bluff over the Mississippi, making Union river vessels easy targets for Confederate fire. Union general William Sherman went after Confederate general Johnston's army near Jackson on July 4. For General John A. Logan, see Warner, *Generals in Blue,* 282. For General Andrew Jackson Smith at Vicksburg, see www.swcivilwar.com/GrantMemoirsVicksburg38.html.

(Saturday, June 27)

Dear Libby: As I came in from picket I called and introduced myself to Capt. Govett. He knew who I was in a minute. Soon got acquainted with him. He is greatly changed from what you described him—is fleshy and browned up by the sun. He accompanied me to my quarters where we have been talking all day. He spoke very affectionately of all your folks, saying Aunt Susan and Uncle Sam were as kind folks as ever lived. Lizzie was, in his opinion, the finest looking girl any where about Nininger. Looked at your picture, and thought you must have been sick, it looked so thin. Showed me his wife's and baby's picture. She looks like a fine, sensible woman. [And?] he expects another young soldier in a few months. I did not tell him what I expected. . . . We have the news here that Port Hudson is ours. . . .[75]

> Ever your affectionate
> Madison

> Snyder's Bluff, Miss., June 28, 1863
> Sunday

Dear Libby:

Lieut. Jameson is out on picket to-night, and Capt. Govette is here to occupy his bed and keep me company. He has been out on fatigue duty to-day.[76] Have just received three letters—one from Libby. . . . You wish to know whether it is warm down here. It is *very warm*. I never experienced anything like it before now.

(Monday, 29th)

Have been "all over" with Will to-day—on the transports, visited the Gunboat DeKalb, and got our phizes taken for "Aunt Susan" as Will calls her.[77] His Regt. has been paid off to-day. I am so tired to-night that I think sleep will be relished by me. I have been down to the bayou and had a good wash this evening. Saw

75. Union general Nathaniel Banks laid siege on May 23 to Confederate-held Port Hudson. Port Hudson was not surrendered, however, until July 8, so Madison reports a rumor.

76. Andrews describes fatigue duty as "felling trees in the ravines" for wood structures to aid in defending a position and "digging riflepits." He continues: "The weather was intensely hot, and the labor of chopping down the gum, oak and other sorts of trees of primeval growth which filled some of the ravines was severe in the extreme" (see "Narrative of the Third Regiment," 165).

77. "Phizes" might have been the way either Aunt Susan or Will Govett pronounced "faces."

one man get his leg bitten by an Alligator. Quite a number have been bitten since we came here, one man killed.

In regard to that money, I want you to *use enough* to make you comfortable and to keep you dressed as a good little wife ought to be dressed if *it takes it all*; but if there is more than you can use in that way, dispose of it wherever you see a good chance to make it earn something, or procure anything we may need to keep house with. If it is to be kept idle, why, it is better off in your hands than in a bank. Gus Case writes that there is no chance for us to get that land we were trying for. If you see any chance to buy cheap in any good location let me know of it.

(Tuesday 30th)

Have had Regt inspection and muster to-day, and now have to work hard for a few days making out Muster and Pay Rolls, quarterly returns, monthly return, &c, &c. The weather is intensely warm. . . . We have pretty exciting news about Lew's being in Penn., stirring up the stay-at-home Dutchmen and Copperheads.[78] I am glad to hear it. It will do good in the end, and besides the rebels in that direction will get a whipping for once and find out that an offensive in movement is a little more risky than the defensive which they have been long practicing.

(Wednesday, July 1, 1863)

Have been hard at work all day, writing. Capt. Govette has been here this evening talking a perfect stream. He wishes to be remembered to you and all the rest of your folks. Grant blew up two rebel fortifications to-day in front of Vicksburg, gaining considerable advantage. Three darkies were blown over to our men—one of them alive. I am tired and must be brief; so, Dear Libby, sweet sleep, pleasant dreams, and a kind Good night.

(Wednesday, July 2, 1863)[79]

Heavy firing is going on to-night at Vicksburg. Wish you could hear it. We expect something to be done on the 4th to celebrate the day. The rebels are building flat boats preparatory to an attempt to cross the river and escape to Louisiana some

---

78. Lew is Lewis Govett, William Govett's brother and Lizzie's friend Minnie's estranged husband. He left Nininger in 1859. Copperhead was a label used for Democrats or those who were willing to accept peace without forcing the seceded states to return to the Union. "Dutchmen" was another name for Germans. There had been antidraft protests in the fall of 1862 by Germans. For attitudes about Germans' sentiments toward the war, see Reardon, "'We Are All in This War,'" 20.

79. This should be Thursday, July 2.

of these dark nights. The 5th Regt is among the troops they would have to meet on the other side if they attempt to cross.[80] The 22nd Ohio moved out two miles from here to-day; so Will and I cannot visit so often now. I am lying in bed and writing. Lieut Jameson lies on his bed reading a novel. The boat from Young's Point has just whistled. We expect a mail by her. Hope it will bring me a letter from Libby.

(July 3 1863)

... I wanted a letter from Libby to-day, but did not get one.

(Saturday, July 4th morning)

There has been a deathlike silence at Vicksburg since 6 PM yesterday. It may be the calm which precedes the storm. We expect to hear some heavy work before night. A National salute is just being fired at Youngs Point. It is cloudy and gives promise of a cool day. I should like to know how you are celebrating the 4th in Nininger.

(10 A.M.)

The magic words are spoken. Vicksburg is ours! Every heart is glad. Over 150,000 men are at this moment rejoicing over the event. The gordion knot which has held this great army here so long, is now cut, and this army, released from the spell which has bound it, is at liberty to do something to avert the disasters threatened elsewhere—to re-inforce Hooker and drive Lee back to Virginia; pursue Johnston; re-inforce Rosecranz; or assist Banks to take Port Hudson—any one or all of these things, we can do, as our authorities shall decide. The rebel flag was hauled down and the white flag run up at 9 o'clock this morning. The negociations were made last night, and our troops are at this moment in possession of the long-coveted rebel works.[81] Regiments are out in line hurrahing and innumerable bands are playing patriotic tunes. Our Band, within ten feet of my tent, has played Hail Columbia, Dixie, and Yankee Doodle while I have been writing this. It seems as though they never played better than now. This 4th of July will be long remembered by us.

80. The Fifth Minnesota was posted across the Mississippi River in Louisiana. Many in the regiment crossed the river to celebrate Vicksburg's surrender on July 4. See Carley, *Minnesota in the Civil War,* 123.

81. Confederate general Pemberton discussed terms for surrender with Union general Grant on July 3, and the formal surrender occurred on July 4. All together, 30,000 Confederate soldiers surrendered at Vicksburg. For another Third Minnesota soldier's view of the surrender, see a letter submitted by Peter Panchot to the *Hastings Independent,* 30 July 1863.

(Evening, 10 PM)

Twenty-two thousand rebels stacked their arms and surrendered to-day, besides the many sick and wounded. It is a glorious victory. Port Hudson must soon fall, and then the Mississippi is once more open, opened too by the strong arm of the Northwest. Sherman's Corps passed out past here this afternoon for Black river with Pontoons. About 2000 Cavalry are in the rebels rear and with this army in front Johnston will have work enough.

> Well I must bid you good-night
> Madison

Snyder's Bluff, Miss., July 5th, 1863

Dear Libby:

We have this moment received orders to march in ten minutes with 100 rounds ammunition per man and 5 days rations so if you do not hear from me in a week or two you will know that it is because I am where there will be no chance to write. Eugene wants you to tell Rose Good-bye for him. Give love to all. Good-bye

> Ever your loving
> Madison

Oak Ridge, Miss., July 5th, 1863

My Dear Libby:

We left camp at Snyder's Bluff about 9 o'clock this forenoon and marched out here in the heat of the warmest day of the season, thus far, with dust ankle deep part of the way. We are twelve miles from Snyder's Bluff, sixteen from Vicksburg, and four from Black River. The 9th Army Corps was having a skirmish with the rebels this side of the river as we arrived here. We could hear the firing, but did not get near enough to participate. As near as I can study it out, the troops here are only waiting until Sherman gains Johnston's rear by crossing the river further up and passing around his right flank. Meantime we engage the enemy's attention in front, and when the time comes, shall move forward across the river and have a fight unless the rebs get out of the way too soon for us to catch them. Ours is the only Regt. of the 3d Division out here—the rest of the division being at Snyder's Bluff yet. The object in detaching us is more than I can divine.

(Monday, July 6th)

All but our Regt. has moved up to-day, and we are left to guard the forks of the road which leads out here from Vicksburg, divides, and leads to Black river. There was considerable cannonading about 12 o'clock last night, in front feeling the enemy on the other side of the river I presume. The boys are slaying cattle, pigs, sheep, &c., and having a good time generally. Blackberries and peaches are abundant, and are fully appreciated by us. The officers of Co D, H, I & F, have taken quarters in a church. We sleep on the seats, and dine on the pulpit for a table. The Regt. is stretched out about a half a mile in a line of rifle pits with two pieces of the 11th Ohio Artillery behind an earthwork in the center. The church is on the extreme left, and a fine residence (Col. Griggs quarters) on the right. Sherman crossed on brigade yesterday, and had a skirmish. The main body of his troops will soon follow.

The mail came out to us to-day, and brought me your good letter of the 18th. You must not think I take it for nonsense—it is one of your best, and full of the overflowing of a kind heart. I should have enjoyed it if I could have been to the picnic with you. I like pic-nics. . . . I will explain that re-enlistment you referred to. When one is promoted he has to be discharged from the service in the old grade, and then be mustered in in the new grade or office. Only the commissioned officers were mustered. Many of the non-commissioned officers objected, and Lieut James, the commissary of Musters, referred the matter to the Sec'y of war. I have been discharged from the service twice since I came south this time—once as Sergt., and once as 2nd Lieut. No one is mustered in for less than three years, unless he enlists under a special call for men for six months or a year, as in the case of the recent call by the President. There is no probability, however, of our being kept longer than the terms of enlistment of the Regt. I am not afraid to tell you anything which concerns either of us in the least. I have nothing to keep from you, and do not intend to have if I can help it. I could have got a furlough for any of my company or for myself in the spring; but not during the seige of Vicksburg. When the press for troops is over I can do so again. I think it quite likely that I shall be able to get a furlough this fall. A recent law of Congress allows the furloughing [of] a certain percent of each Regt. when in the opinion of the Commdg. Genl. of a department, it can be done without injury to the service.[82]

I am sorry to hear so poor a report of the crops in Minn. this season. Hope you will have rain in season to save them. Then the cistern is in full blast at last, is it? That is the greatest event of the season for the quiet of Rose Hill. If Kate's swelling should break, I presume it would be better for her. I would give anything I possess to have her get well again. I accept those kisses and hugs in the same spirit which prompted them, and in turn send you twenty kisses for every one of yours. Suppose it would not do for me to send you too many hugs just now, so I will bid you Good-night. Madison

82. See Andrews, "Narrative of the Third Regiment," 169–70.

(Tuesday, July 7th)

... Have just been down to the creek and had a good wash, which makes me feel refreshed. Sherman's force all crossed the river to-day, and stirring times are anticipated.

(Wednesday, July 8th)

We had a severe thunderstorm last night, and a hurricane too. Large trees were broken down by the wind. A field officer of one Regt. was killed and several other men wounded by the falling trees. I never saw such a perfect torrent of rain before. The air was completely filled with it, and the wind hurled it down with great velocity. There has been fighting to-day out to the front. It is reported that we re-occupy Jackson, and have captured 7000 prisoners there.[83] I received an order from Gen. Kimball to-day, detailing me on a court martial at Division Head-qrs.; so I shall have to return to Snyder's Bluff to-morrow or next day. It is very warm and sultry this evening. Lots of sweet kisses and a kind Good-night to Libby.—Madison.

(July 9th)

Nothing new to-day. Start for Snyder's Bluff to-morrow morning 5 o'clock, to attend the General Court Martial. Maj. Mattson has been detailed too, in place of Maj. Smith, who is absent; so I shall have company from my own Regt. Have just been having a good time over a half dozen cans [of] peaches and pears, with Col. Griggs, Maj. Mattson, Capts Swan, Vanstrum, and Hodges, and Lieuts Jameson, Greenleaf, and Taylor.[84] There is talk of our division having to go to the Potomac. Well, I must bid you good-night

    Lots of sweet kisses and one good hug.
    Madison

(Friday, July 10th, Snyder's Bluff, Miss.)

Arrived here this morning about 9 oclock after a pleasant horseback ride of twelve miles. Maj. Mattson has two horses, and he has, very kindly, tendered me

83. Again, Madison reports a rumor of events that would happen in a few days. Union general Sherman's troops were on the move to surround Jackson, Mississippi, where Confederate general Johnston was located. On July 16, Johnston withdrew from the city.

84. General courts-martial comprised five to thirteen commissioned officers to hear a commissioned officer's military case. See DeHart, *Observations on Military Law*, 37. Captain Swan and Lieutenant Greenleaf were both in Company I; Captain Hodges was in Company K; Lieutenant Taylor was in Company H; Major Mattson had been in Company D, as was Lieutenant Vanstrum.

the use of one of them during our stay here. I ride on a saddle worth $125.00, which, Major Mattson captured from Col. Dawson, rebel. "Big thing," isn't it? The court of which I am a member consists of ten members—one, a Lieut Col, two majors, and seven Captains. Lieut. Col. Dwight May of the 12 Mich is President of the Court. He is from Kalamazoo. I do not think much of him—he is a kind of loose, don't care man, with no dignity becoming the President of a Genl Court Martial.[85] If we remain in session until all the cases are disposed of I shall not get back to the Regt for four or five months. There are already one hundred cases to be tried. There are charges against Capt. Govette.

(Saturday, July 11th)

I will try and close this garbled mess to-night. Have just been out taking a ride, and got caught in a shower. I think of riding out to the Regt to-night as we have no session to-morrow. In your last letter you wish me every wish of my heart "except the society of black ladies." Now, you do not think, I hope, that the society of b——k ladies is a wish of my heart. Far from it. No one has less desire for that than I do. When I see you I will explain how I came to write what I did about the b——k l——s. I have not spoken to one of them hardly since I came here, much less to associate with them. You know of course that I am not opposed to the society of ladies, yet I do not think near so much about such things as I did when I first left you. The more one indulges the more he desires. How is it with you? . . .

> Ever your loving
> Madison

Nininger July 7th 1863

My Dear Husband

I am now seated to write you a few lines but whether I accomplish it is more then I can tell for it is so warm that I cant hardly live. . . .

I am going to give you a lecture now. In one of the letters that I got from you you say that among the rest of the things strewn about your table was cigars. Did you say that to see what I would say or are you getting to be a real smoaker? If so,

---

85. For the role of the president of the general court-martial, see DeHart, *Observations on Military Law*, 45. Dwight May advanced to colonel in the Twelfth Michigan Infantry, despite Madison's low opinion of him. See cwss, www.itd.nps.gov/cwss/soldiers.htm.

when you come home again you and I will have to occupy two beds. I would rather you would visit the black ladies then learn to use tobacco. Do you hear?[86]

What kind of a time did you have the 4th? It was so warm here that [I] think those who went to celebrate it must have suffered with the heat. I was not forther than the door yard all day so you may imagine what kind of a time I had. I wish you were here to see what a pretty flock of ducks Ma has. I believe there is twenty one in all. I really dont think you can read this horrible scribble. I have written it on my knee with nothing under it. Do you see that I am getting lazy?

Mr Donnelly got a letter from you yesterday. Minnie says she wishes you would send her a few quarts of blackbarries if you have so many down there. Am has come back to Mankato. He was not able to march and carry a knapsack.

I[t] is reported here to-day that the rebels have been defeated in Pennsylvania. I do hope it is so. . . .[87] My health is pretty good. . . . Now Good Bye for two months longer. . . .

> from your Affectionate Wife
> Lizzie

{in pencil, top of first page} Wednesday 8th I heard guns firing in Hastings last evening. I hope they have recd the good news that Vicksburg is at last ours. Good-morning.

> Lizzie

Nininger July 19th 1863

My Dear Madison

. . . Ma recd the pictures you sent her. She is very thankful to bouth you and Bill for such a nice present. She knew that it was Bill as soon as she saw the picture.[88] I am glad you come across him. How do you like him? Is he steady now or does he drink? I suppose he smokes yet for he used to be the most inveterate smoker I ever saw. I hope you will not take lessons from him as long as you are learning to keep company with such habits. Well I must quit teasing you about using tobacco as I am afraid you will be getting spunky.

---

86. Antismoking reform was not as widespread as other social reforms like temperance, especially before the 1880s. There were those, however, who advocated abstinence from tobacco for health reasons, as well as those who felt a woman's duty was to raise children based on sound principles of morality and self-control. For Victorian-American moral attitudes about tobacco use, see Tate, *Cigarette Wars*, 12, 23.

87. Lizzie refers to the Union victory at the battle of Gettysburg on July 1 to 3, 1863.

88. Lizzie refers to Will Govett as Bill.

I am waiting with all patience to get a letter from you written after the surrender of Vicksburg. I think you must have witnessed some terrible scenes for the last four weeks. Last evenings dispatch brought word that Richmond is ours. I sincerely hope it is so.[89] I think Will was very confidential telling you about his young soldiers. That is just like him. He always tells everything he knows. I think they are rather a prolific concern. He is almost as bad as you are. Oh such folks for babies. . . .

I was out to Hampton last Monday, the first time I have been more than three miles from home since you left. I got Yeagers horse and Uncle Peters buggy. Ma and Kate went with me. We stayed at Mr Warsops and got dinner and left. Kate and Ma and I went to Aunt Margarets and took tea, and then came home.[90]

. . . I am pretty well excepting a very bad pain in my chest, the same pain that used to trouble me last winter. I guess it will be better some of those days. I am at Aunt Sarahs. I wish you were here to go home with me. I hope to see you before a great many months.

Lizzie

{top margin second page} Are you well? I think you[r] picture looks as though you have fallen away. Lizzie

Snyder's Bluff, Miss., July 19th, 1863
Rooms Gen. Court Martial.

My Dear Libby:

. . . If to-day's mail does not bring me a letter from you I shall think that you are sick.

My friend Hunt started for Minn. yesterday. He promised to call at your house if possible for him to do so.

I am going out to the camp of our Regt. this afternoon to see how the boys get along. Col. Griggs has resigned and gone home, which makes it seem lonely to have been so long associated with him. By his resignation the Regt loses a good officer.[91]

---

89. The Union army would not capture Richmond until the beginning of April 1865.

90. It is likely that Lizzie borrowed the horse from either Conrad or his father, Charles Yeager, both of Nininger City. Andrew Worsop lived in Vermillion Township, just above Hampton Township, in 1860.

91. Regarding Colonel Griggs's resignation, Andrews writes, "At Oak Ridge, Col. Griggs, on account of poor health, and to the regret of the regiment, tendered his resignation, which was accepted, and he was succeeded by Lieutenant Colonel Andrews, who took command July 16th" ("Narrative of the Third Regiment," 166).

There has been some fighting in this vicinity lately, but the result is not yet known here. We could hear cannonading day before yesterday. Yazoo City has been taken by our troops, but not without the loss of the gunboat DeKalb, blown up by torpedos. We captured 200 prisoners and six guns. It is reported that Grant has gained a victory at Jackson.[92]

There is considerable sickness here in the army—fevers, &c. The deaths in the 25th Wis. have been one or two a day during the last two or three weeks. Only one of our Regt. has died since we came here—Ripley of Co. "C" died a night or two ago, of Typhoid fever.[93]

Libby, you must be very careful of your health now. Do not work hard. I feel very anxious to see you, but cannot say positively when that will be....

>   Ever, your loving
>   Madison.

>   Snyder's Bluff, Miss., July 21, 1863[94]

My Dearest Lizzie:

Yours of June 30th is this moment received. I am so rejoiced to hear from you and learn that you are well, that I can hardly contain myself.... Your kind offer of kisses for my frequent letters is cheerfully accepted. I hope that I may be where I can get them soon.... Our Division is under orders to embark at once, but where we are going I do not know. To Memphis I think. Transports have just come up from Vicksburg for us. Our Regt is on its way here. It is terribly warm to-day. There have been ten funerals here to-day. I am not the least sorry that I "was naughty," but am glad, though I do not like to have you suffer on account of it.

>   Lots of kisses and a Good-bye.
>   Madison

92. For the USS *DeKalb*'s loss, see www.geocities.com/Pentagon/5106/dekalb.htm. Sherman surrounded Jackson and forced Johnston's retreat, not Grant. See McPherson, *Ordeal by Fire,* 359.

93. By war's end the Twenty-fifth Wisconsin Infantry had lost nearly 410 to disease. See www.civilwararchive.com/Unreghst/unwiinf2.htm#25thinf. John D. Ripley died at Snyder's Bluff, Arkansas, on July 14, 1863. At a camp near Memphis on August 3, 1863, William D. Hale noted, "Our sick report of this morning is 109 in the 550 present—there are none dangerously sick, and most are rapidly convalescing. We left the Yazoo in *good time* certainly. The 25th Wisconsin lost 30 men there, and has now *nine tenths* of the men on the sick report" (3 August 1863, Hale Papers).

94. This letter was written at the end of a letter from his sister Sarah, dated July 5.

Nininger July 26, 1863
(Sunday afternoon)

My Dear Madison

I should have written to you yesterday but there is no regular mail days from Nininger now, and when it is sent it has to be taken to Hastings so I send my letters to Hastings and mailed there when ever I have an opportunity. It seems to me that I never wanted to see you so much since you have been gone as I do to day. It is a beautiful cool day and everything looks so pleasant if you were only here we would have such a nice walk. I rec'd a letter from you last Monday partly written the day of the surrender. I hope to get another to-day when the folks come home from Sabbath school. I feel very anxious to hear whether you have left that place and if so where you have been sent. What do you think of war by this time? Is there any better prospect in your opinions of its closing then there has been? It seems to me that the south cannot stand it much longer at the rate things are going on now.

I wish I could tell you some news but I cannot. There is nothing going on now but making ready for and harvesting. The crops are much better then was expected they would be. It has been so dry. . . .

While I am writing my little bird is keeping time by singing one of his sweetest songs. I want you to tell Will that I dont think he appreciated the letter that Minnie and I sent him very highly as he would have answered it before this. Remember me to him and tell him I should like very much to see him [even] if he did used to call me *Miss Romp.*

. . . Tell me whether you can come home this fall. I want to see you so much. I should think you would get tired of reading my poor apologies for letters. They are written so poorly, but I know my hubby will look over all mistakes. Pa has come home and not brought me any letter from my Madison so I shall have to wait patiently till I do get one.

Again good Bye from your loving Wife Lizzie

Helena, Ark., July 30th, 1863.

My Dear Libby:

. . . I am glad to hear that you are as well as might be expected under the circumstances. You seem bound to lecture me for smoking. It is a very little smoking that I do, so you will have to lecture without a subject. I care nothing about cigars, only once in a while when I am lonely just to pass away the time.

It is cheering to me to learn that you begin to have some hope for the Union cause. For my part I am not more sanguine of success to-day than I was in the darkest hour since the commencement of this conspiracy against the gov't. I have always felt confident that the South would have to succumb sooner or later to the overwhelming forces of the North, or of the Gov't rather. Besides, Providence will never suffer a rebellion to succeed, which has for its motive the propagation of so wicked a thing as slavery. I feel as sure of that as I do that I am a living being. . . .

I have received at last the orders in relation to my court martial at Columbus. I enclose them to you. You will notice that I am *"honorably"* acquitted, which leaves me in better standing than before charges were preferred at all, for an *"honorable* acquittal" upon a charge against one's character, is the best kind of a recommendation, and is so regarded among military men.[95]

Two hundred and forty of the 3d Regt were out on a scout yesterday. We went out eleven miles, frightened a squad of guerillas, gobbled about 100 negroes and as many mules, and returned to camp all safe and sound. We are encamped on the bank of the river, and about 1½ miles below the town. It is quite a pleasant spot, covered with scattering timber.[96]

Yesterday about sundown the steamer Samuel Hill passed up and landed at the Levee with an unarmed Regt., which I at once surmised to be my brothers Regt returning home. Somebody from town came into camp and said it was the 22d Maine, so I posted off at once, and when I got there I found that it was the 21st Maine, and learned that the 22nd had passed up a day or two before. I remembered having seen his Regt. when it went up, but did not mistrust that it was his Regt. You may well believe that I was disappointed to learn that my brother had passed within twenty rods of me and I not see him at all. Well, such is life. . . .

> Ever your loving husband,
> Madison.

Helena, Ark., August 4th, 1863.

My Dear Libby:

Your frollicking letter of July 19th was received yesterday. To read your letters one would think you were a young coquettish girl of sixteen. It must be that you are in good spirits nowadays. Well, I am glad of it, and hope you will remain so until I am once more free to return to you, then I know you will be all right.

95. An honorable acquittal meant that the charges, which affected the accused's honor, had been fully disproved. See DeHart, *Observations on Military Law,* 182.

96. The Third Minnesota was part of a campaign into Arkansas and arrived in Helena on July 26. Andrews reports, "July 29th half the regiment marched eight miles to a plantation and returned with two wagon-loads of ears of green corn" ("Narrative of the Third Regiment," 166).

You need not be so fast to lay that *little matter* all off on me, for you had something to do in the premises as well as myself, and, unless I am mistaken, you would do the same thing over again without much coaxing. You are very sly, indeed! I guess you have forgotten how you used to keep me awake when I wanted to go to sleep. I have not forgot it, if you have. You talk about me being an awful fellow for babies! That sounds well! Don't you feel like blushing a little when you come to reflect. No, Mrs. Lizzie, you cannot pass yourself off for a prude where you are known. In the first place you do not *look* like one, and in the next place you do not *get acquainted* like one.[97]

You asked me a question which I wish you had left out; it was, whether Will drinks now; but I will answer it. Once in a while he does drink, and drinks too much, but generally he is all right. He drinks very rarely when with me, for he knows I do not like to see him drink. I talk to him for it sometimes, and he makes good promises, yet says he must drink some while he is in the army, but is going to be a teetotaler when he leaves the army. His drinking and his abrupt temper gets him into disrepute somewhat, but he enjoys the reputation of being one of the bravest officers in his Regt, and of having the best Company. He gave me a soldiers memorial to-day to send to you, and wished me to remember him to all of your folks. . . .

You think I must have witnessed many vivid scenes while at Vicksburg. I did, indeed, witness many, but they seem like a dream and are easier to think about than to describe. After the surrender for two or three days there was a continual stream of rebel soldiers passing our camp, paroled and homeward bound, sad and discouraged. *Well do I know how they felt;* for I have been there once— *Murfreesboro!* Our boys used to vie with each other in acts of kindness to the poor, paroled rebs as they trudged by our camp with their knapsacks on their backs, leaving their boasted giberalter in the hands of their conquerors. Most of them seemed to think the South must succumb now. Our boys used to divide their rations with them and they all chatted as kindly together as though they had always been dear friends. No taunting allusions were made by either party.

One day Adjt Morse, Sergt. Major Hale, and myself were riding out to Oak Ridge, passing them continually when at last we overtook one poor, emaciated little, old fellow with an immense pack and so tired out that he could not walk more than five steps in a minute, and then he would rest for five or ten minutes,

97. Although public expressions of sexual intimacy were avoided by middle-class Americans in the nineteenth century, "so long as private matters were kept private, men and women were allowed to practice a sexuality that was open-tempered, passionate, and playful" (Berry, *All That Makes a Man*, 115).

and then trudge on again his legs bending and writhing with pain.[98] I drew Adjt Morses flask of whisky, cherrybark and quinine from my saddlebags and gave the poor fellow a drink, and encouraged him to go on to his home, some sixty miles distant. How tremblingly he reached up for the flask, saluting us at the same time, and how piteous he looked I shall never forget. Returning the next morning I met him about a half a mile from where we had overtaken him. Such, thought I, are the "rights" which these poor fellows have secured by fighting.

An expedition will leave here in the course of a week for Little Rock. The 3d Regt is going. Another brigade has been added to our Division. Gen. Kimball started for Columbus to supercede Gen. Asboth. Col. McLaine com'ds our Division. Gen. Logan is expected to take command of our corps in place of Hurlburt [who] resigned. Maj. Gen. Steele is here, and is going to [take] command of the expedition to Little Rock.[99]

The Genl. Court Martial convened again to-day for the first time since we left Vicksburg. Well, the light is burning low, and I must close. . . .

> Ever your loving
> Madison

> Camp 3d Minn. Infy., near
> Helena, Ark., Aug. 9th, 1863.

My Dear Wife:

. . . While you were writing your letter, eating fruit, and enjoying the quiet of Rose Hill Sabbath, your soldier friends here were disembarking from the Marine boat Autocrat, marching down the Levee, pitching camp, and doing other things incident to soldier life, hardly thinking about Sabbath, or knowing perhaps that it was sabbath day.

I am rejoiced to hear that the wheat crop in Minn. turns out to be good after

98. Madison refers to William F. Morse, who was mustered in as the adjutant for the Third Minnesota in June 1863, and Sergeant Major William D. Hale. Hale did not mention this specific episode in his letters home, but he did comment on seeing the paroled rebels after Vicksburg as "tired looking just as if just up from a sickness, dirty & ragged & poorly rough shod. . . . Many command a strong desire to be exchanged & go at it again 'and if we get you in this fix we will treat you as gentlemanly as you have us,' as many wanted to go *home* and *were* going home—with a shake of the head—indicating twould be some time before they came back" (16 July 1863, Hale Papers).

99. Colonel William McLean of the Forty-third Indiana temporarily commanded the Second (Kimball's) Division. Major General Frederick Steele was instructed to leave Helena with an army and "expel the Confederate forces from Arkansas and permanently occupy the state" (Andrews, "Narrative of the Third Regiment," 166).

all the fears entertained by the farmers that they were to have poor crops. I can assure you that I should be as happy to be with you as you would be to have me. I think of you almost continually and feel more anxious than ever about you. I do hope that you will get along all right with your sickness. I shall be with you if possible this fall. Just now it is impossible for anybody to get a furlough. But as soon as this "Arkansas Expedition" terminates it will be different, then [there] will not be so much necessity for keeping men and officers so closely. Joseph Pitcher, of Co. F, went home last week on 20 days furlough, which I got for him before the recent orders of prohibition of furloughs.[100]

You wish to know my opinion about the prospect of a speedy close of the war. I cannot predict in regard to *time*. I have always felt implicitly confident that the South would be conquered ultimately. Our recent successes do not make me entirely confident of a speedy close of the war; but it seems to me that they ought to settle all doubts in the minds of weak, doubting Thomases about the North being unable to put down this rebellion. Peace *may* come soon; but it may also be long deferred. Every thing seems to be going in favor of the Union armies just now, and should our great successes continue for a few months longer we may safely predict a speedy peace; but the fortunes of war are varying as the winds, and temporary reverses may come to check the victorious progress of our armies, which may yet prolong the war months or years perhaps. Yet, on the whole, as it now stands, there is reasonable hope for peace before another August shall come with its heat and sickness to decimate the ranks of our army.

The health of our Regiment is good compared to that of others. While the men of other regt's have been dying off rapidly we have lost but very few—none since we arrived here. A few days ago the 25th Wis., which came south with 960 strong, was called on for a picket guard of twelve men *and could not furnish it,* there not being well men enough to take care of the sick.

This force has been reorganized to go on the proposed expedition to Little Rock. Our brigade is now composed as follows: 40th Iowa, 27th Wis., 126th Ill., 22d Ohio, (Wills Regt.) 3d Minn., and a battery of Missouri Artillery. It is now the 2nd Brigade, 2nd Division, Arkansas Expedition. The 25th Wis., 35th Mo. and a colored Regt. form one brigade to garrison this place while the Expedition is in progress. Col. Wood, of the 22nd Ohio, commands our Brigade. The 12th Mich., 40th Iowa, 55th Ill. and 3d Minn. are pronounced the best Regt. in the 16th corps, by the Inspector Genl. The 16th corps is honored by having Maj. Gen. Logan assigned to command it, and Gen. Grierson, of raid notoriety, assigned as chief

100. Joseph Pitcher was a twenty-four-year-old Hastings farmer; his younger brother John Pitcher was also in Company F.

of cavalry in it. Maj. Gen. Steele, who commands this Expedition, is one of the best Generals in the army.[101] We shall probably start in the course of a week.

Everything is being got in readiness. Boats are loading with supplies to go up White river to the point where we are to cross. Gen. Davidson will join us there with 10,000 cavalry. The Genl. Court Martial is in session yet. We hope to get it dissolved when the Expedition is ready to move. Commissions came this morning for Lieut. Col. Andrews to be Col., Major Mattson to be Lieut. Col., Capt. Foster to be Major, and Lieut. Devereux to be Capt. Co. "G." Capts. Baker and Webster have tendered their resignations....[102]

You need not think that your letters are at all tiresome to me. I wish I could have one every day. I think I shall keep a Diary during the continuance of the Arkansas Expedition. Do you think you can stand the infliction of another diary?

Will Govette sends his regards to "Miss Romp" and all the rest of Aunt Susans family. While he was going the rounds as officer of the day a few nights ago he came to my quarters about 12 o'clock and woke me up to help him smoke cigars and keep awake until the moon was a long way up. He kept me awake until almost daylight, so that I was glad when he had gone and left me to sleep....I cut him up the other day by giving him a lecturing for his foolish pro-slavery notions. He is opposed to Lincoln's proclamation of Freedom. I am conceited enough to believe that I shamed him if nothing more. I had listened to it until I got tired; so I "broke out...."

> Ever your loving husband
> Madison.

> Nininger Aug 10th 1863
> Monday

My Dear Hubbie

I ought to have written to you before this. It is eight days since I last wrote to you, but I have been so nearly frantic with the tooth-ache for the last three days that it was impossible for me to write or do any thing else that required any head work. I rec'd a letter from you yesterday written while on the boat on your way

---

101. For more on Benjamin Grierson, who conducted a cavalry rout from Tennessee through Mississippi and into Louisiana, see Johnson and Bill, *Horsemen Blue and Gray,* 85–87. Starting with the siege of Vicksburg, the Sixteenth Corps experienced significant changes in command and organization. Kimball's Division, of which the Third Minnesota was a part, joined the Seventh Corps in August 1863 when it undertook the Arkansas Expedition. See www.civilwararchive.com/CORPS/16thcorp.htm.

102. For the various changes in the Third Minnesota's line officers' commissions, see *Annual Report of the Adjutant General,* 116–20.

to Helena. I am glad you have got away from that sickly place for ever sinc you have been there I have been anxious and yet almost afraid to hear from you. I hope you will have to stop at Helena and not go with the Regt. I am writing with all patience to get the letter that sets the time when you can come home. You *do not know how much I want to see you.*

You want to know which will have little Jeems. I will very soon give you an answer. I think I have the best claim to him for I know I have had more trouble with him alread[y] then you have and that is not the worst of all, for it is not over with yet. And any way if you will persist in smoking, I dont think you would be a fit person to take care of him, for you would learn him bad habits such as I dont intend to allow in a son of mine.

You will see that this sheet is all daubed up. I must tell you how it happened. I heard the cats making a terrible fuss out at the door and ran out to see what the matter was. While I went out one door, old puss came in the other, and the first lounge she made was on the table right on my letter with her dirty feet, so you must please excuse it.

. . . I have never heard any thing that Bill Allison told about you. I dont think it makes any difference what he says.

Well I must say Good Bye. Next time you write to me what time you think you can get [a] furlough. They are having quite a time with the Indians some where near Beckford or Glencoe.[103] We have had three of the most horrible thunder storms this last week that I almost ever saw. The crops are much better then was expected.

> From your loving Wife
> Lizzie

> Helena, Ark., Aug. 12th, 1863.
> (Evening.)

My Dearest Libby:

I must now write you a few lines of "Good-bye," being on the eve of starting off on a long Expedition, during which my opportunities for writing will be limited.

The 1st and 3d Divisions started day before yesterday, and the 2nd starts to-morrow morning at 4 o'clock. Gen. Steele reviewed this division to-day. At

---

103. In the summer of 1863, several whites were killed by Indians in Wright and Meeker Counties. For Indian activity during this period, see Folwell, *A History of Minnesota,* 280–83, 287–89. Dakota County was visited by some "St. Paul Sioux" in the summer of 1863. The Indians stopped by several homes to obtain food and also took some additional items, but there was no violence. See *Hastings Independent,* 23 July 1863.

11 o'clock A.M. the General and staff accompanied by Col. McLean, comd'r of Div, and Col. Wood, comdr of our Brigade, rode up in front of our Regt. We presented arms in our best style, and then marched in review in common time. Gen. Steele asked Col. Andrews where his colors were, and was politely informed that we had—lost them. It is a shame that we cannot have a flag. Minnesota ought to present us with a flag for what we did in the Indian Campaign last fall. The Third Regt. stands the highest of all the regiments in the Expedition. Encomiums are showered upon it every day by almost everybody who witnesses its drill and parade exercises. The glory of the old "Third" has not yet departed.

Our first move will be upon Little Rock. From then, it is rumored, that we go to the Rio Grande. We take sixty days rations with us.[104]

The General Court Martial was dissolved yesterday, and I have been very busy ever since, getting my company ready for a long march, which is no light job. . . .

In one of your letters you ask if I am not thin in flesh, by my appearance in the picture which I sent to Mother. I look so in the picture, but am not in reality, I weigh 175 lbs. Will and I sat three times for that picture, and the first two were good except Wills, who wiggled about too much. I did not care much about my own, but wanted to get a good one of Will. I am in the best of health at present, and hope that I may remain so.

Libby, I cannot promise you that I shall be in Minn. as soon as you may wish to see me. If so disposed, it will be difficult for me to get Leave of Absence during the Expedition, and that may be longer than I at first anticipated. Yet I shall be with you before winter if it is a possible thing to do so.

I wish I could be with you to-night and have a good long talk. O, for one good sweet kiss before we leave for the hard work before us. You must not be discouraged at the prospect of not seeing me as soon as you have expected. You have indeed been remarkable for the philisophical manner in which you have borne the many anxieties which I have caused you. I cannot help loving you all the more for it. Now Libby, do not let your troubles wear you down, but keep up good spirits. . . .

> Ever your loving
> Madison . . .

104. Capturing Little Rock was viewed with great importance not only by the Union army but also by Arkansas's citizens, who, according to Hale, "generally represent that when the 'Rock' is taken and the reb armies driven from the state, Arkansas will ask decidedly to come back under the old flag." The expedition did not proceed directly to Little Rock. Its first phase included a four-day march and camping near Clarendon, Arkansas. See undated portion of 3 August and 19 August 1863 letters, Hale Papers.

Nininger Aug. 17, 1863

My Dear Madison

... You seem to think because I write all kind of nonsense in my letters to you that my spirits must be good. Sometimes if I were to write to you just as I feel you would not think so but I find the best way is to make the best of everything, and I know that it is not very pleasant for a lonely feeling soldier to receive dreary lonely letters. Therefore, when I have the blues I dont do much writing, and if I do happen to, I put nonesense in instead of sense.

I should try and be more contented if it were not for poor Kates sad situation, but that is some thing that is continually before my eyes to make me feel badly. She is able to be about most of the time but I think she is getting weaker all the time. I have my mind fully made up that she can never get well again. You may know that it is sad, sad indeed to see a loved sister fading away daily and know that you must soon look upon her for the last time. But such is the way that we all must go.

... There is singing school at Nininger every other Sabbath evening. Mr. Merrill from Hastings is this leader. Mr. Hartson has been here to attend the last two. Mr Hickman and family leave in a few days for Sauk Centre. Sarah is very much pleased with the idea of going. ... [105]

Well, I must say good bye for it is so warm and the flies trouble me so that I shall have to stop writing. ...

From your loving wife
Lizzie

Clarendon, Ark., Aug. 22nd, 1863.

My Dear Libby:

You see I am still here. The Expedition is here too; but will surely move by to-morrow. The first Brigade of the 2nd division is crossing the river this morning and the 2nd Brigade will cross this afternoon. Meantime I propose to write you a letter in answer to one I *expect* to receive *sometime*. I have rec'd no letter from you since several days before I left Helena; and as we have received two mails since then I conclude that you must be sick, or I would get letters from you. I am very, *very*, anxious to hear from you, to learn whether you are well.

105. Moses D. Merrill, a twenty-eight-year-old clerk, lived in Hastings in 1860. P. Hartshorn was the justice of the peace in Hastings. Sauk Center is approximately 120 miles north and west of Nininger.

I feel sore and lame to-day in consequence of a long ride which I took yesterday; otherwise I am quite well. I must tell you about my ride yesterday. I was woke up at 4 o'clock night before last and ordered to report at once at Brigade Head quarters for instructions, which proved to be for me to take command of a foraging party consisting of 160 men with 25 teams. So by three o'clock the next morning we were off and by half past eight we were at Lawrenceville, twenty miles from here, and where Federal soldiers had never been but once before, about a year ago. By making inquiries I learned that two miles further on was the plantation of one Redman, where I could get plenty of corn, poultry, &c.; so we pushed on until we arrived there. It took but a short time to empty his corn cribs and depopulate his poultry yard. Peaches, apples, apricots, and garden sauce suffered too, I assure you.[106] As soon as the train was ready I put a Lieutenant of the 22nd Ohio in charge with orders to return to Lawrenceville, halt and feed for one hour, by which time I would be with him again.

Then, taking five good men and a contraband guide, all mounted on good horses, I struck out to see what I could find in the country beyond. Our guide knew the country to perfection, having lived there and run away on his "Missus" horse only a few days before; so we followed bye paths and visited every body in the neighborhood. Not being very well armed and, being in small force, we had to keep on the lookout, for the country is full of guerillas. At places where we expected to find them we put on bold faces and dashed forward as though they were just what we wanted to find. At the various plantations created quite a sensation. The country was full of fruit and at almost every step through the woods we started up deer, wild turkeys, quail, &c.

No Federal soldiers had ever been there before; so we were quite a wonder. The ladies flew about almost frantically and what few men were left took their arms and horses and hid from us. At last we discovered one guerilla and gave chase, but he wheeled off into a bye path and we lost his track. At another place we found where fifteen of them had passed, and also where they had breakfasted, and afterward learned that we passed the same party who avoided us, fearing to try us on, and it was fortunate for us that they did.

After eight miles ride we turned up at the house of one Tom Winston, who is in the rebel army. His wife, a good looking, pleasant-faced young woman received us politely, invited us to take some peaches and set the servants to get dinner for

106. In a similar vein, William D. Hale commented on August 19, 1863, "All the plantations along the road are thoroughly stripped of green corn, old corn, meat, chickens & stock of all kinds. Theres no effort to repress the foraging spirit of men for it would be useless. These people are finding *war* to be a terrible thing at their own doors" (Hale Papers).

us. After an hours rest, a pleasant chat, and a good dinner (which we paid for) we started for Lawrenceville.[107] On the way we stopped at "contrabands" home. The contraband, one of the most intelligent I ever saw, got out the Banjo, and gave us a tune and a song. His "Missus" *affectionately* reproved him, for running away and asked him to leave the horse he had stolen a few days ago. He told her that he sudder run away dan hab her run him off to Texas, and as for stealing the horse, "You know, Missus, I had to get away de bess way I could and when you pay me de money I len you den I gib you de hoss."[108]

Off again we arrived at Lawrenceville to find the train gone over an hour, so we followed on, but soon had to go slowly on account of one of our number being taken so sick as to hinder him from riding faster than a walk. Six miles this side of Lawrenceville we met two mounted guerillas who fired at us and then run into the woods out of our reach. At just a little after dark we arrived in camp, much to the surprise of all hands who thought we had been "gobbled." It seems that the Lieut. sent out a squad of the 5th Kansas Cavy. when he started from Lawrenceville, to hunt us up and they heard of these fifteen guerillas which I have referred to and returned to the train with the news that we were no doubt captured.

. . . Take good care of yourself, and if you are unable to write be sure to get Dollie or someone else to write for you.

> Ever yours truly,
> Madison.

Duvall's Bluff, Ark., Aug. 26th, 1863.

My Dear Libby:

Being once more at a halt and having nothing in particular to do just now, I will write you a line, so that you may know where to find me. The Ark. Expedition left Clarendon day before yesterday as soon as the 3d Regt.—the last—had crossed, and, instead of going directly toward Little Rock, as I expected, came up the river to this place. The sick were brought up by boats, and suffered terribly during the passage. Upwards of twenty died—none from the 3d—during the trip. The weather is extremely warm, and the men have given out at a fearful rate. Several Regiments have less than 100 men for duty. The 3d has 350—the most of any regt in

107. For Arkansas women's response to Union soldiers' foraging, see Bunch, "Confederate Women of Arkansas Face 'the Fiends in Human Shape,'" 176-77.

108. Madison, like many soldiers, tries to represent dialect in his letters. The runaway slave says that he would sooner run away than have his mistress send him to Texas and that, when she paid him money he had lent her, he would return her horse. For white women and changing relations with slaves, see Faust, *Mothers of Invention*, chap. 3.

the Expedition. In many cases the strongest men drop down on the march, utterly helpless. Peter Panchot, of my company, who never gave out before, was taken down yesterday. Eugene is much better, and will be ready for duty in a few days.[109] I am well—have not ridden a step on the march since the Expedition left Helena. Gen. Steele has received orders from Gen. Hurlburt to mount the 3d Minn., but Col. Andrews does not want it mounted unless he can get an order from the Secy. of war to have it *permanently* mounted, with all the privileges of Cavalry.[110] There has been no fighting here yet, except slight skirmishes. Our company captured a rebel train of cars yesterday. There is a rail-road from here to Little Rock. This is now our base of operations instead of Clarendon which is not occupied at all by our troops now.

It is uncertain when we start for Little Rock. We have received orders to have the men furnished with clothing for sixty days. We shall probably receive reinforcements before we leave here. I am anxious to hear from you once more. . . .

Truly and affectionately your
Madison

109. William D. Hale corroborates this spread of illness: "We are enjoying our rest very much, but our men seem to be getting sick . . . and all the Regts show a bad sick report in so short a time, having started with the best men of their commands" (19 August 1863, Hale Papers). Andrews comments that during this expedition many men suffered from malaria and that the sick list was over 1,000 by August 23. See "Narrative of the Third Regiment," 167.

110. See *Hastings Independent*, 20 August 1863, for a report on Andrews's request.

Madison in uniform

Madison and Lizzie's wedding photograph, November 30, 1862

Portrait of Susan Justason Caleff,
Lizzie's mother

William D. Hale of Cannon Falls,
enlisted in Company E of the Third Minnesota,
appointed sergeant major, serving in
the quartermaster's department

Christopher C. Andrews of St. Cloud,
initially captain of Company I,
promoted to colonel of the regiment
and finally to brigadier general

Hans Mattson of Red Wing, originally from Sweden, initially captain of Company D, promoted to major and finally to colonel of the regiment

Otto Dreher of St. Paul, originally from Germany, enlisted as a sergeant in Company F, eventually promoted to captain of Company A of the Third Minnesota

Murfreesboro, Tennessee, December 1862, several months after the Third Minnesota's surrender

*Third Minnesota on dress parade in front of the Arkansas state capitol,
during their occupation from September 1863 to the end of the war*

Officers from Company F at Camp Minnesota in Nashville, Tennessee, early spring of 1862:
from left to right,
unidentified,
Sgt. James Madison Bowler,
unidentified,
Sgt. Otto Dreher,
1st Sgt. David Morgan
(the two unidentified men probably were
sergeants William E. Allison and Bernard McKenna)

I Hope You Will Soon Have the
Pleasure of Visiting Your Family

AUGUST 1863 TO FEBRUARY 1864

Late in the summer of 1863, both Lizzie and Madison anxiously awaited the arrival of their first child. As Madison sat down to write to Lizzie on September 16, worried about her imminent childbirth, Lizzie's friend Minnie Govett and her sister Kate wrote letters to Madison conveying the news about the birth of a daughter. Even as the family rejoiced in little Victoria Augusta's birth, however, Kate Caleff was wasting away. She died just a month later. As Madison settled in for a comfortable winter in Little Rock and wished Lizzie could be with him, Lizzie felt more duty bound than ever to remain with her parents and care for her infant daughter. Adjusting to motherhood took some time. Victoria suffered from colic and nursed frequently. If pregnancy had prevented Lizzie from venturing too far from home, a young infant in a Minnesota winter proved even more limiting. Although she must have had help from her mother and sister Dollie, Lizzie's letters indicate that she had primary responsibility for her "fatherless babe" and that she felt it keenly.

In the meantime, Madison enjoyed Little Rock and wished only that Lizzie and their new daughter would join him. Although he claimed to defer to Lizzie regarding child rearing, Madison still voiced his concerns about Victoria from afar, especially instructing Lizzie to have Victoria sleep in a cradle so that he could sleep with his wife when he returned home. Madison anticipated a furlough to Minnesota when his company reenlisted for an additional three years of service. His return was delayed, however, after he broke his leg when seats at a circus he attended collapsed. Lizzie's final letter in this chapter conveys her anxiety about his recovery, sounding almost as if he had been injured in battle. Fortunately, this accident was Madison's only war wound. Madison finally returned to Nininger in March 1864 for a six-week furlough and recovery.

* * *

Nininger August 30th, 1863

My Dearest Madison

... I must confess that I felt badly when I read your last letter and learned that instead of coming home, as I had partly made up my mind or at least was in hopes you would, that you were going farther and farther away. I had one real good [cry] and then concluded I would get on a good stack of patience and wait five or six months longer, for I have learned to wait for the movements of soldiers with a great deal more patience then I used to....

I received the Memorial that Will sent. Please present my thanks to him for it. To-day is a beautiful day here. I wish my Hubbie was here, then I should feel happier then I now do. I suppose by the time that this letter reaches you, or maybe before if things go on as I expect they will, you will be entitled to the name of *papa*. How I want you here now. You do not know how much I dread that time. I would give anything if it w[as] only over with. If you were here I would not care so much.

I know I shall have all done for me that can be done, but for some reason that I do not know myself I wish you were here. Kate's health remains bout the same.

There is the greatest quantity of plumbs this year I ever saw. Minnie and I went two or three days ago. We got all that we could carry home.... I guess you will know that I dont feel in any humor for writing letters to-day without my telling you. This is so scribbled up.

(5 oclock Sunday)

Do has returned [from Sunday school] but has brought no letter for me. I wish I could [kn]ow where you are and what you are doing to-day but that cannot be so I shall have to hope for your safety.

Madison, now that you have started on a long, tedious and dangerous march you must not forget to look to your Heavenly father for protection. Were it not that I can look to him sometimes I should cease to hope longer. Now dear hubbie, I must say good Bye, hoping you will return in safety. With many kisses, I remain

        Your loving wife
        Lizzie

... When I am sick if I can't write I will have Do write often. Dont you worry about me, for everything will be attended to that can be. Write as often as you can....

Nininger Sept 6th 1863

My Dear Husband

It has been two weeks since I last heard from you. You may imagine that I am beginning to feel very anxious about you. We are daily hearing of awful outrages by the guerrillas. I hope it will not be the fate of your Regt to fall in with an over-whelming number. I would as soon any one belonging to me would be left to the mercies of the savage. To read the account of the destruction of Lawrence is enough to make ones blood run cold. Lieut. Col. Adams came home a few days since. He is still suffering very much from his wounds but is able to walk about town on crutches.[1] I cannot write much to day so you will have to be content with a very few uninteresting lines.

My intellect is completely cloged so that I cannot wrote a letter if I were to try ever so hard. I ought to write to your sister Sarah but cannot now. . . .[2]

Now dear hubbie, Good Bye.

{top margin of second page} Be a good boy and come home as soon as you can.

From your loving wife Lizzie

Bayou Metaire, Ark., Sept. 9th, 1863.

My Dear Libby:

The mail goes out to-morrow morning and I must write you a word or two. I have had another sick spell since I wrote you from Brownsville, but have got all right again once more. Hope I shall not be troubled again. We left camp at Brownsville last Sunday morning and arrived here Monday afternoon. Merrill's Horse which was in advance, had a spirited skirmish with the rebels on the very spot where we are now encamped. There was some loss on both sides. There is firing between the rebel pickets and ours almost every day. The rebels are in

---

1. Kansas experienced significant guerilla activity during the war years, particularly raids led by William C. Quantrill. Quantrill's mounted guerilas attacked Lawrence, Kansas, an abolitionist stronghold, on August 21, 1863. One hundred fifty citizens were executed by Quantrill's band. See Josephy, *The Civil War in the American West*, 373. Charles P. Adams was a Hastings physician and newspaper editor in 1860. He was promoted to lieutenant colonel of the First Minnesota in May 1863 and was wounded at Gettysburg. See Moe, *The Last Full Measure*, 243, 272.

2. It is worth noting that this letter took only half of the sheet of paper. Normally, Lizzie filled the entire sheet, so it is clear that she really was not feeling well or up to writing.

force two miles from here on the other side of the Arkansas, a few miles further up the river the rebels have a fortification.[3]

A heavy force of cavalry and artillery is out to-day reconnoitering the enemy's position. We expect to attack them to-morrow and, if successfull shall be in Little Rock by to-morrow night or next day. We are ten miles from Little Rock.

We have other game besides rebels. One regt has a young bear for a pet. A few mornings ago a fine large deer dashed right through the whole length of our camp while we were at breakfast. He *did not stop long.* Sergt. Pettibone and I have been out picking grapes. We got about a peck of nice muscatine grapes which grow wild here in great abundance. They are as large as wild plums in Minn. and quite sweet.[4] I have to take my company out for inspection of arms, so I must close. . . .

> Ever Your loving
> Madison.

3. Andrews notes that the Third Minnesota "camped two and a half miles north of the Arkansas River and ten miles from Little Rock. There was here a halt of two days, partly to enable Gen. Steele to select the best place for crossing the river, during which we tested Arkansas sweet potatoes and watermelons. Commencing in the vicinity of Brownsville, the advance of the column, naturally, had met more or less resistance, resulting in several spirited skirmishes, and there had been repeated occasions when, from the firing in front, the regiment seemed liable to be called into action." On September 10, there was fighting at Bayou Forche, and Little Rock was captured. See "Narrative of the Third Regiment," 167. Merrill's Horse was the Second Missouri Cavalry, led by Captain Lewis Merrill and part of General John Wynn Davidson's Division. See "Second Missouri Cavalry," hometown.aol.com/dlharvey/merrills.htm.

4. It is interesting that Madison wrote to Lizzie about picking wild grapes while Andrews mentioned cultivated sweet potatoes and watermelons. On September 9, 1863, William D. Hale explains the camp and foraging more fully. The spot where the Third Minnesota camped was not only the site of a cavalry skirmish but also a plantation. Hale states, "The plantation is the finest I've seen in the south, of quite 1000 acres of cotton & corn land fully 600 now in the biggest corn I ever saw—*20 feet high.* Has a tollerable log House for Head Qrs and innumerable negro quarters, is really one of those cotton *Hells* so widely depicted by 'Uncle Toms Cabin.'" Hale provides a detailed description of the foraging, including soldiers digging up fifty acres of sweet potatoes, filling their pockets, handkerchiefs, and haversacks with them. He explains their actions by saying, "A small retribution has fallen upon the place for it is thoroughly devastated. The immence cornfield is feeding our animals, its fences burned, its cattle & hogs killed, its beehives robbed—the work has been *thorough,* and our mess has had its share." Such "work" occurred on a larger scale during Sherman's march through Georgia a little over a year later.

Hd.qrs. Post of Little Rock,
Little Rock, Ark., Sept. 16th, 1863.

My Dear Libby:

. . . We have received one mail since we occupied Little Rock, but it brought me nothing from you. You can hardly realize how anxious I am to hear from you now. Do have Dollie or some one else write often, if you are not able to write for yourself.

I find it impossible for me to get away to go home at present. I am very pleasantly situated, and should enjoy myself firstrate, but for my anxiety about you.

Col. Andrews is commander of the Post of Little Rock, and he has appointed me Post Adjutant on his staff. We have an elegant office with nice furniture, and lighted by gas. It was formerly occupied by Albert Pike, the Poet and lawyer, now a rebel General. I mess with Col. Andrews, Lieut. Col. Mattson, Maj Foster, and Lieut. Potthoff, (Post of M. on the Col's staff.)[5]

We have a fine private residence on one of the main streets, and plenty of furniture, good beds, &c. We also have several colored servts (both male and female) to cook and do washing for us. This I assure you is much better than bivouacking out in the woods among the wood ticks, chiggers, &c, and living on soldiers rations as we had been previous to our arrival here.[6] The health of the troops is improving since we arrived here when they can get good water and high ground to encamp upon. During the march we got very poor water to drink—most of the time nothing but Bayou water.

We now have four Regts. for Provost and Post duty—the 3d Minn. and 43d Ill. Infy. and the 3d Iowa and 7th Missouri Cavly. There are 500 rebel prisoners in the

5. An adjutant communicated orders on behalf of his commander. Albert Pike was a brigadier general in the Confederate army given command of the Department of Indian Territory by the Confederate government. He had a checkered career and, in the summer of 1862, was forced to resign his position in Indian country. See Josephy, *The Civil War in the American West,* 323-24, 360-61. Albert Potthoff was in the Forty-third Illinois Infantry. See www.rootsweb.com/~ilcivilw/reg_html/043_reg.htm. Regarding occupying Little Rock, Andrews writes, "September 12th, the colonel was by special order detailed as commander of the post of Little Rock, with a brigade composed of the Third Minnesota, Forty-third Illinois and Seventh Missouri Cavalry, for service in preserving good order in the city. . . . Post headquarters were in a bank building opposite the capitol. The private quarters or mess of the colonel and the field officers of the regiment were at a cottage, a few rods distant, and owned by Mr. Waite, a citizen" ("Narrative of the Third Regiment," 168-69).

6. William D. Hale also described the men's improved comfort; they now had easy access to water and to buildings to house administrative functions for the Union's military operations. See 15 September 1863, Hale Papers.

Penetentiary, which we have to guard. We have plenty of business on hand all the time at present, requiring the assistance of three clerks and three mounted orderlies. I hope that when we get things settled down, we can get along with less work.

O, how I wish you were not likely to be sick; I would have you come down here sure. We could get a good house and everything necessary for living in comfortable style. But, as it is, I suppose you will have to stay where you are. . . .

This place is quite pretty and very pleasant. The inhabitants, left here, are for the most part very docile and many of them really for the Union. Some are rebellious, but most of them seem truly rejoiced to be relieved from Confederate despotism.[7]

Well, I must close. Give my love to all the folks.

> Ever your loving
> Madison.

Nininger, Sept, 16th /63

Mr J M Bowler
Dear sir

I hope you will excuse the liberty I take in thus addressing you. I am now acting for Lizzie, as she cannot write you just now. But I must hasten and let you know that you are again promoted. You can now assume the dignities of *Father,* for you have a nice little daughter, not so very little either for she weights 7½ pounds. Her age a few hours, for she arrived this morning about 9 oclock. Almost every one says she looks like you, I dont know.

Lizzie is quite as well as can be expected, and if she has no drawbacks she will soon be able to write to you again, I hope. All seem very much pleased with the little stranger. I hope you will soon have the pleasure of visiting your *family.*

The family are well as usual. Perhaps Kate will write some so I will close leaving the particulars for Lizzie when she writes.

> Excuse this from a friend
> M M Govett [Minnie Russell Govett]

P.S. I wish you would remind Charlie that he is indebted to me for several letters and I should like to hear from him soon. MMG

7. In regard to the sentiments of the local population, William D. Hale comments on September 15, 1863: "The rich & violent rebels have fled. Large numbers of those remaining are Union—and are delighted at the change and nearly all are glad of the change." Colonel Andrews corroborates Madison's conclusions, especially as the Third Minnesota displayed "exemplary conduct, intelligence and friendly intercourse with the people, contribut[ing] not a little to the development of loyal feeling" ("Narrative of the Third Regiment," 169).

[Nininger, Minn. Sept. 16, 1863]

Dear Brother

I take up my pen with the intention of writing a line to you if I can, it being the first attempt I have made in many months. You cannot expect much. As Minnie has written you the particulars concerning Lizzie's illness, I will only say we all rejoiced that she was at home with us when she received the tears of sympathy and smiles of joy of her parents and sisters instead of the care of some heedless nurse if she had been far separated from her home and friend.

Dear Brother, a husband may do his best but you know a mothers hand has a balm in our hours of affliction. I thought of you a great many times last night and wished you were here.

The babe is a fine little thing, very fleshy and plump. Lizzie says she intends that Sarah Bowler and I shall name it. Have you any objections? Its Aunt Kate gave it its first present this morning because it was a girl.

I cannot write much more as I am already exhausted. My health is so poor. I have but little enjoyment in this world and do not hope that it will ever be any better. I hope you will be able to come home this fall on a visit. Do write to me sometimes. I am pleased to hear from you at any time. They all join me in love to you. Please to give my love to William Govett. Tell him I would gladly write to him if I could.

> From your affectionate sister
> Kate [Caleff]

Nininger Sep 25, 1863

My Dear Husband

While lying here this morning I thought I must try and scratch a line to you. I am in bed and beside me rests your little daughter with all the innocince of a little lamb. Dont you wish you could see her? Every one says she looks like you. She has large blue eyes and will be pretty (I think) when a few weeks old.

She was born on the 16th. I got Minnie to write to you as soon as I got better. I was very sick. Did not know as I ever should be any better for a few hours, but with the assistance of Dr Cummings and the kind hand of Providence to watch over me I was brought safely through and am now getting along as well as I can.[8] It is fur weeks since the last letter that I recd from you was written. I cannot imagine what the reason can be that I do not hear from you. I sometimes think

---

8. Daniel J. Cummings was a physician in Hastings in 1860.

perhaps you are coming home but that is too good news to think off.[9] I do hope to hear from you when the mail comes in to-night.

. . . If it is agreeable to your wishes I should like to have Sarah and Kate name this babe, as it is altogether likely it will be the only chance poor Kate will ever have, as her time here I think is but very short. . . .

Now Madison, we have got to prepare ourselves to lead the erring feet of a little one through this sinful world. You may depend that I feel my inability as a mother sensibly. We must pray to God for assistance. Though we are far sepparated, yet we have one consolation, that our prayers are heard.

The 6th and 7th Minnesota Regts have been ordered south—the 15th of Oct. Texas is where they expect to go.[10]

As soon as Hickmans folks got to Sauk Centre they had to go into a fort. The Indians are so bad. They hardly dare go out door[s].[11]

My sheet of paper is not very nice but it is all I have at present so you must excuse. Do come home as soon as you can and get a furlough for as long a time as you can get.

I would send you a lock of babies hair if she had any to spare.

> Good Bye
> From your loving wife
> Lizzie

> Head Quarters, Post of Little Rock, Arkansas. [letterhead]
> Oct. 3d, 1863.

My Dear Lizzie:

. . . I recd a letter last night from Piercy. He is at McMinnville, Tenn. Sends his regards to you and all the rest of the folks. I presume he has seen some fighting by this time, as Rosecranz has had a severe battle beyond Chattanooga.

---

9. Lizzie meant "four" weeks instead of "fur" weeks and "think of" rather than "off." These slips, while not unlike some of her other misspelling, and her use of legal-size blue ledger paper rather than standard paper, seem to indicate a rush to write Madison a letter as soon as possible after childbirth to assure him that she was well.

10. According to Carley, the Sixth Minnesota was not ordered south until June 1864 when they went to Helena, Arkansas. The Seventh Minnesota did leave on October 7, 1863, for St. Louis and then traveled to Paducah, Kentucky, in April 1864. See *Minnesota in the Civil War*, 208–9.

11. Sauk Center was located near the Dakota's Upper Agency. Minnesota regiments returning to Fort Snelling stopped at Sauk Center after an unsuccessful summer campaign against Indians on the Great Plains. See Folwell, *History of Minnesota*, 277.

It seems very unfortunate that Rosecranz was not properly reinforced, so as to enable him to hold his own against the overwhelming force which the rebels were able to concentrate against him by railroad from Richmond, Charleston, and Mobile. The only wonder is, that he was not annihilated. Almost anybody but he would have been. As it is he has met with a severe defeat, if all accounts be correct.[12]

Everything goes on well here. A few bushwhackers killed every day, more gobbled up by Yankee Cavl'y, and still more taking the oath and enlisting in the Union army. The 3d Regt. have got some 20 men already. The citizens are arming and organizing to defend themselves against guerillas, and it is almost a daily occurrence for them to bring in some of these reb bushwhackers whom they have captured. Here everything is encouraging. If these things were transpiring in the army of the Potomac Uncle Abe would have to sneeze over it and make a proclamation, and the NY papers would have big headings to magnify it to the world. But, being in the west, and especially in Ark., it is hardly noticed.[13]

I am very anxious to hear from you again. . . .

Ever your loving hubbie
Madison

Head Quarters, Post of Little Rock, Arkansas [letterhead]
October 5th, 1863.

My Dearest Lizzie:

Yours of September 13th together with letters from Kate and Minnie, dated the 16th, were received this morning.

For a month past I have felt the deepest anxiety about you; but Minnies letter gave me great relief, as well as a thrill of joy which I shall never forget. I feel very anxious still about you, for I know there is much danger yet.

It strikes me that you were a little selfish in having it a *girl* instead of a *boy* just because I was not there to attend to it. But I will not quarrel with you about that; indeed, I am glad it is a girl—it will be company for you when I am away from home. If it were a boy, it would be like me and go off and leave you as soon [as] it got large enough.

12. Madison refers to Union general Rosecrans's defeat at the battle of Chickamauga, September 19 to 20, 1863. Rosecrans retreated from that battle to Chattanooga, where his troops were nearly surrounded and received inadequate supplies.

13. The war in the West was underplayed by the immediacy of armies massed near both the Union and the Confederate capitals. See Josephy, *The Civil War in the American West*, xi–xii.

You do not know how much I love you now. O, if I could only be with you to-day, I would give all I am worth. It almost makes me condemn myself, to think how much you have had to suffer. I only wish that I could show you how much sympathy I feel for you, how grateful I feel toward you for having endured so much for my sake. I imagine now that I see you with your little babe in your arms, looking at it and thinking of "Mad." The picture makes my heart soft and tender like a child's.

Lizzie, for your love, your patience and heroism, you have my warmest love, my heartfelt gratitude, and my sincere thanks. I want to see another letter in your own hand writing, and then I shall feel assured that you are out of immediate danger.

I shall write often to you, as you request. Give my love to all the family. Give the little one a kiss for me. For yourself accept lots of kisses and a good bye for the present.

> Ever your loving husband,
> Madison.

> Nininger Oct 13 1863

My Dear Husband

Ten days has passed since I last wrote to you before, but [I] really could not, for when I felt like writting this little daughter of mine was so cross that I could not. She has the cholic terribly. I wish you were here to help me take care of her some of these long nights.

She grows very fast. I wish you could see her. She grows to look more like you every day. I think she will be pretty when she is a few weeks older. She will be four weeks old to-morrow. I have got real smart. Have been to Nininger once. Uncle Peter came up Saturday and took me down there to spend the day. Brought me back at night. But visiting with babies I found to be poor business so I think I shall not visit much this fall.

Kate is very miserable. I do not think she can live a great while longer.

The 6th, 7th, and 9th Regts went down the river last week. Am did not go. He is at Mankato with several others of his Regt who was left there to guard the fort an[d] town. He is pretty well but not so they thought him fit to go south. . . .[14] Do come home as soon as you can.

> Lizzie

14. The Seventh, Ninth, and Tenth Minnesota regiments went south in October 1863. The Sixth Minnesota did not go until 1864. See Folwell, *History of Minnesota,* 304-5.

Head Quarters, Post of Little Rock, Arkansas [letterhead]
October 21, 1863.

My Dear, Dear Lizzie:

I feel more like crying than writing to-day, but am going to write just to let you know how badly I feel, for I cannot write anything else. We have received no mail for the last twelve days. The last letter I have received from you was written before you were taken sick, and the latest news received from you, was by Minnie's and Kate's letters of Sept. 16. Just think of it! Over a month ago—five whole weeks, and not a word from my Lizzie! I worry about you night and day. O, if I could only be assured that you and your little birdie were well, it would be a great relief to me. We expect a mail every evening when the cars arrive from Duvall's Bluff, but are doomed to disappointment as often.

The Rev. Mr. Putnam, of Afton, our new chaplain, arrived yesterday just from Minnesota. He used to be a musician in our Regt., and was discharged over a year ago.[15]

I have sent a letter by Major Mitchell to be mailed at St. Louis, for you, containing a check for $250.00 on the Asst Treasr of the U.S. at St Louis. I hope you will get it all right. If you can, exchange it for Treasury notes at the Bank in Hastings. If you see any good chance to invest your surplus money in anything which will insure a living for us, you can do so. But, as I have told you before, I insist on your using enough to make yourself respectable—go well dressed, if you have enough to keep you so. You know my Libby is my all, and I want her to appear well.

. . . Lots of sweet kisses and a good hug for you. Kiss my little birdie for me.

Ever your loving hubbie,
Madison.

Head Quarters, Post of Little Rock, Arkansas. [letterhead]
October 23d, 1863.

My Dear Lizzie:

Yours of Sept. 25th—so long and so eagerly looked for—came at last by last nights mail, the first we have received since two weeks ago yesterday.

The cars came in early yesterday evening, and I felt it in my bones, that they had brought a mail, so I posted of[f] to the Post Office, where I found Dr. Ayres, P.M.[post master], sorting out the mail for the different divisions. By the time he was through I had an Ambulance on hand and took the mail for our Division up

---

15. From Afton in Washington County, Simeon Putnam enlisted in September 1863 and died in Arkansas a year later.

to Gen. Kimball's Hdqrs., where the General's staff, the Division P.M., and myself sorted it out to the regiments in double quick time. Then I took the Third's
mail to my room and culled out the letters for Col. Andrews, Lt. Col Mattson,
Major Foster, and myself, and when I came to your letter, which I knew by the
handwriting, you may be assured I felt rejoiced. It is the best letter I ever received
from you, in style and composition, and so full of womanly bearing and tender-
ness it made my heart come up in my throat and brought the tears to my eyes.

My mind was hurried back and dwelt intensely on my dear, beloved Lizzie
and her little birdie. I felt almost that I could see my house once more—the same
objects, the fences, the same house standing out on the familiar prairie, and the
plainest of all, I could see my poor, sick Lizzie, with her little birdie by her side,
lying in bed and writing those sober lines to me. As I read your letter, and as
imagination carried me back to you, I could feel my heart drawn closer than ever
to yours by the strong, silken chords of deep, pure love, almost increasing to ado-
ration. O, how I want to see you once more, and press you to my bosom—to rest
my rough cheek once more against yours, and to rest my head once more beside
yours on the pillow where I can tell you in words the love I cannot express in
writing. The only regret I have is that I am not worthy [of] the love of one so pure
and so good as you. I am too rough, too wicked for you. Yet I do not know what I
should do without you. During the last two years, amid all the trials and troubles
which are common to the soldier, I have felt happy, and one dear object alone has
made me so—the thought of my Dear one has ever soothed my heart in the severest trial.[16]

Your suggestions as to our duties are good indeed. It is truly a great responsibility we have to direct the life course of our little one. I am content to leave her
to you. To be a true woman she should inherit and receive by tuition your own
womanly, angel-like nature instead of my rough characteristics. Let her be like
her mother, and I shall truly be a loving father.[17]

I am pained to hear that you have so little hope for sister Kate's recovery. I
have cherished the hope, that since her swelling broke, she might recover. Give
her my sincere love and sympathy. . . .

The only hope I have of getting home before the Regiment's term of enlistment is expired, is that I may be sent home to bring on the drafted men for our
regiment. I think that Lieut. Col. Mattson will grant me that favor if any one is

---

16. For more on men's worthiness and women as inspiration, see Berry, *All That
Makes a Man*, 182–84.

17. For women as primary child rearers, see Ryan, *Cradle of the Middle Class*, 186; and
Cott, *The Bonds of Womanhood*, 84–85.

sent at all. The longest leave of absence allowed by law to an *officer*, is twenty days, except the War Department [can] grant a longer one in a special case. Officers on leave get only half pay and allowances for the time they are absent.[18] Besides, twenty days leave of absence would not give me time to go home, turn around, and reach my regiment, before its expiration; much less, give me time to be with you any desirable length of time. But I shall do the best I can. I want to go home as badly as anyone can want, you may be assured.

I want to see that little one, which, you say, is *going to be pretty*. I think the idea that she looks like me, must originate in over-imagination—those "large *blue* eyes" do not sound much like looking like me. Is she a good natured baby? I have not heard yet what her grandmother and Grandpa and her aunt Dollie think of her. I suppose Do thinks that it is no great shakes, and that it will be an annoyance to her when it learns to cry good. But I must not make light of this matter. It cost you a great deal of pain and sickness. You can hardly realize what anxiety it gave me, for sometimes I felt almost sure that it would be the means of taking you away, and then I used to blame myself for causing so much trouble and then going away from you to stay so long. . . .

> Ever, your loving hubbie,
> Madison.

Nininger Oct 23, 1863

My Dear Husband,

. . . I am glad to hear you are so comfortably situated after so long and tedious march, but I do think that miserable old General might give you a furlough to come.

I am getting along pretty well. Think it will not be long until I feel quite well again. When I was sick I was so very sick that the Dr was obliged to give me medicine that was so forcing that I have not entirely got over the effects of it yet. If he had not have given me something I do not think the babe could ever come into the world alive.[19]

She was five weeks old day before yesterday. You can't think how she grows. Dont you wish you could see her? When she gets a few weeks older (if you do not come home soon) I will get her picture taken and send to you.

18. The law mentioned was "An Act for enrolling and calling out the national forces, and for other purposes," approved March 3, 1863. Sections 31 and 32 address the issues of pay and duration of furloughs. See *The War of the Rebellion*, 91–93.

19. The medicine Lizzie refers to was probably chloroform or ether, both of which were used by physicians at midcentury. See Leavitt, *Brought to Bed*, 117–27.

I have not seen Gus nor Mary in eight week[s]. Mary has been sick about for two weeks. I do not know what the matter is with her but have my opinion the cause.... Mr. & Mrs Donnelly left yesterday for Philadelphia. She will remain there while he goes to Washington.[20]

Well it is now eleven oclock at night. I must quit scribbling and finish this in the morning. The babe is cross yet but not so bad as she was....

(Saturday morning 24)

I recd a letter from you this morning dated Oct 10th. You speak of me going down there. I could not give the thing the second thought while things are as they are at present. I should leave Kate with one foot in the grave and the other almost there and Ma would go almost frantic if I should attempt such a thing, beside[s] many other reasons. I would be glad enough to be with you but think I shall have to wait until you get sufficiently satisfied of soldiering. I hope that will not be a great while longer.

You seem to be enjoying yourself & I am glad you are. I cannot say that I enjoy my self very much. There is something before my eyes continually to keep me from feeling like enjoying life very much. You have no idea how Kate has changed. She is nothing but a skelaton. She does not attempt to walk any more. She is either carried or moved in a chair from room to room and every where else she wants to go. She has a bad cough. Her mind is so weakened it is like that of a child. I want you to try real hard to get a furlough before winter. What would I give if I could see you this morning? ...

    Lizzie

{back page top margin} Your daughter is very well and grows like a little pig.

Nininger Nov 6th 1863
Friday morning

My Dear Husband

I now seat myself to answer your letter which I rec'd Sunday & should have answerd it before, but I did not feel much like writing for the last week. I have pressed the last kiss & have taken a farewell look at my dear dear sister. She died

20. The Donnellys were both originally from Philadelphia before they moved to Minnesota. Ignatius Donnelly was in the House of Representatives from 1863 through 1868. See Ridge, *Ignatius Donnelly*, chaps. 5–8.

last Tuesday after two long years of severe suffering. She was only sick abed four days but her suffering was intense. She died the death of a sincere Christian, prayed for the hour to come when she should be relieved from such suffering. She said all she wanted [was] to live for she did not want to leave the rest of us. She told me to bid you good bye for her & tell you to be sure and live so that when you come to lay down on a dying bed that you will be willing to submit to whatever God sees fit to put upon you. Poor thing, we have every reason to believe that she is now reaping her reward in Heaven. Blessed thought. I hope that we shall all meet her again.[21]

The draft came all safe and sound. Our little one is real smart. I expect she will be a spoiled child. She is a real pet. Pa think[s] more of it then he would if it was his, and Do think[s] there never was a baby like it. Kate and Minnie recd their letters the day before she died. She called the little one Victoria after she got your letter. She would not name it before.

. . . I do want you to come home. Try and get a furlough if you possibly can.

> from your ever loving wife
> Lizzie

Little Rock, Ark., Nov. 14, 1863.

My Dear Lizzie:

Another letter from you at last, which somewhat relieves me from the gloom of that horrible dream. You ask if I do not wish to see your little birdie. Indeed, I do wish very much to see her, and her fond mother, too. It makes my heart ache to think of the sickness, suffering, and pain you endured to bring that little "gem" into the world. I can do nothing more than love you for it. I wish I could have endured it in your stead. You know, Libby, I would have done it cheerfully, gladly—as I love you tenderly. In imagination I see you prostrated by that awful suffering, lying, during those long days, with your innocent "copy" by our side, and wishing, perhaps, that Mad were there to help beguile those weary hours, to give assurance of his deep sympathy, to look with a father's eyes upon the little "prize" you have given him, to thank you for what you have endured in his behalf, to rest his head upon your pillow and tell anew the story of his love. O, what shame I could not be there.

21. There was not an obituary in either Hastings newspaper. For the importance of female kin at a relative's death and ideas about relationships continuing after death, see Motz, *True Sisterhood*, 39, 41.

How, Lizzie, shall I ever be able to repay you, to make amends for my absence? How can a rude ingrate like me requite one so self-denying, self-sacrificing as my Lizzie, my *dear wife* has been? Libby, you must not blame my General. He would grant me all the leave of absence allowed by law, upon my asking it; but I do not ask it. You already know my reasons for not doing so. Are they sufficient? If not I will bide your wish, and do as you decide. I am indeed well situated here, have a good position; but that does not lessen my obligations to you nor my desire to see you again. Here is a pleasant, cheerful city, surrounded by warlike camps of tired veterans and resounding with the noise and resplendent with the pomp of military. Amidst all this we have an elegant building for Hdqrs.—a fine house to live in, plenty of everything to eat and wear. I have a good room, plenty of furniture, including a fancy little bedstead with two mattresses and plenty of good warm blankets. *But here's the rub.*—I sleep on the back side and on the foreside is my unwelcome bedfellow, "Miss Painful Vacancy." I can hardly bear her.—She does not lie up so close, put her arms around my neck, and kiss me like Lizzie used to. Isn't it too bad, Libby?

By the way, Libby, you must buy a little baby bedstead for birdie, and learn her to sleep in it, for I cannot permit anything or any body to come between Libby an[d] me. If she demurs to the arrangement you tell her that the little bedstead is a present from her soldier father. Anyway, make her sleep in it. Will you? Yes, I know you will. Lizzie, you have of late written to me only once in every ten or twelve days, and, one of your letters having gone astray, leaves a space of 20 or 24 days without a word from my dear ones. Now, is this fair? Would you feel that I did my duty if I were this tardy? I know you would not—you would say I had forgot to love you. But I will not be that cruel. I know you have a good excuse—you have been sick and still have a little one to tire you and to trouble you, and therefore I will not ask more of you. I will not be cruel enough to ask a careworn, loving mother to add to her already too great toil by tasking her perplexed mind to write oftener to me. But I wish it were so that you could write more frequently to me. But as it is not I will not ask it. I know that Libby loves me and thinks of me often, and that is all I can ask.

Poor Kate! How sad I feel to think of her. No doubt she will leave us soon; but I cannot bear to think of it. Give her my sincere love and sympathy in her affliction. What about Mary Case?—What is the matter with her? Please remember [me] to Mary and Gus when you see them.

. . . Kiss little "birdie" for me.

> Ever your loving hubbie,
> Madison.

Little Rock, Ark., Nov. 20, 1863[22]

My Dear Wife:

I send you brother Joseph's letter, thinking that perhaps it may be of some inter-
est to you to read. I hope he will take it into his head to go to Minn. in the spring.
If he does, I know he will make it his home. Lizzie will receive him like a brother,
I feel assured.

How are my loved ones to-day—my little birdie and her mother! I wish I
could see them. Does it not make you feel proud to be called mother? I know it
does. But you must not grow old like a mother. I want to find my Lizzie young
and blooming as ever when I go home—she must have *good* clothes, and keep
those *"gollies"* up in good time.[23] When I go home I shall take you by surprise,
and if I find things not to my liking, O, I shall *scold*—like an offended husband.
Now you mind. Just think how afraid you would be, and how you would quake
and tremble if I should scold. Wouldn't you?

. . . I enclose a pass for my little birdie when she comes to Little Rock to see
her father.

Ever your loving
Madison

Head Quarters, Post of Little Rock, Arkansas. [letterhead]
Nov. 27, 1863.

My Dear Wife:

The sad tidings of dear sister Katie's death reached me at about 11 o'clock last
night. I was in the midst of the pleasures of a Thanksgiving party given to the
officers of Col. Andrew[s]'s command by the mess to which I belong. My pleasure was
of short duration when I caught sight of that dark striped letter. My first thought
was "Lizzie, Oh! she is dead," and my heart sank in my breast. When I opened it
and read, I thought it must surely be that the little one was gone. I did not think
of Katie until I read the sad lines, for I was so deeply moved by the thought that
at least one of my dear ones had left me, that I could think of nothing else.

22. This letter was written on the blank last page of a letter dated October 26 from
his brother Joseph Bowler in Lee, Maine, to Madison. Joseph Bowler's nine-month
enlistment in the Twenty-second Maine had expired August 4, 1863. See www.state.me.us/
sos/arc/archives/military/civilwar/22meinf.htm.

23. Madison's reference to "gollies" is probably a sexual euphemism about her
breasts. He did not want Lizzie to look like an old "mother" as she nursed their infant,
and in later letters he mentions wanting her to stop nursing Victoria.

Poor Katie! She has gone at last. We know that she is in Heaven, but that even does not, cannot, drive away our sorrow. I did not think sister was so near her death. I wanted to see her again and talk with her before she died; but it is too late now—*my dear, dear sister is gone.*

I have thought about her almost continually since I received your letter which informed me of her low condition. I wrote a letter—a farewell letter—but was afraid to send it; for I have never given up the hope that she might recover, and my letter might have injured her. It is a great pleasure to me to know that she remembered me so affectionately while on her death-bed; but her farewell words to me brought the hot tears to my eyes. How terribly must [the] father who loves her so tenderly and watched her every want, feel the blow; and our dear old mother, too, must feel sad indeed to see her first-born whom she has seen grow up from infancy to womanhood, torn ruthlessly from her by the cold hand of death. And you, Lizzie, must feel it deeply; for I know you loved her very dearly; and I often think how you used to speak to me about the sad prospect of Katie's leaving us. Your affectionate mindfulness of her, made me love you more than ever.

It is a great consolation to know that she died a sincere christian, and we have every reason to believe that she is better off than if she were with us. I am well suited with the name she left for her little niece—I could not think of having her called by any other name since "Victoria" is the deathbed legacy bequeathed to my little one by her dying Aunt.

I am pleased to hear that father and sister Dolly think so much of the little one. I had begun to think that nobody but you and I cared for her. But what does her grandma think about her? I shall not be content if she does not love her first grandchild.

. . . Be sure and have Victoria's miniature taken for me the first opportunity. I do wish you could come to Little Rock and make me a visit. It would be much more pleasant down here where it is warm and where Mad is, than in Minnesota this winter. . . .

> Ever, your loving husband,
> Madison.

> Head Quarters, Post of Little Rock, Arkansas. [letterhead]
> Dec. 4, 1863.

My Dear Lizzie:

The last letter received from you was on Thanksgiving evening. I was disappointed this morning to find no letter from you in the very large mail which arrived this morning—the only mail since Thanksgiving. I sent a letter by Lieut.

[Otto] Dreher, who started home recruiting several days ago. I also sent money by him to get you a silk dress in Chicago, and sent a package of old letters which I want you to preserve. I have never destroyed one of your letters yet. I presume several of your letters—*one*, I *know*, written about the 1st of Oct. have never been received by me. I regard their loss as very great.

Ever since the commencement of your sickness I have been extremely anxious to hear from you often and to see you. I have thought of you almost continually, and am almost crazy sometimes. I want you and the little one so much. In dreams I can see you as plain as day with your little fondling in your arms.

Is baby very troublesome? I know you must get very wearied taking care of her. What pleasure it would be to me to relieve you from your cares by holding little one for you awhile, and see you enjoy a little rest. It is not right for me to stay away from you. I feel that I am not doing my duty by you. Does little one keep you from your sleep?

O, well! Mad will be home one of these days, and then he will hold baby and do everything to make up for past delinquency. He will give Libby lots of kisses and hugs enough to make up for a whole year. I am well. . . .

> Ever your affectionate hubbie,
> Madison.

> Head Quarters, Post of Little Rock, Arkansas. [letterhead]
> Dec. 10, 1863.

My Dear Wife:

I have not heard a word from you for two weeks. Oh! if you only knew how heavy it makes my heart feel to go so long without hearing from my "dear ones at home," you would, I know, write to me daily. I think of you more by night when all is still and I have no business to engage my attention. I feel the loss of your company more than ever since I see, almost every day, others enjoying the company of their wives. Last evening I attended a party at Gen. Steeles. Generals Davison, Salomon, and Carr, and a host of colonels, majors, and captains were there; also many women, wives of officers.[24] There was dancing, eating, drinking, and talking. It was too much for me, and I went home at about 10 oclock, to lie down and think of Libby and my little one. . . .

24. Frederick Steele was in charge of the Union forces in Arkansas in 1863; John Wynn Davidson and Eugene Asa Carr were each in command of cavalry divisions; Friedrich Saloman had been in command of some Union forces near Helena even before Little Rock's occupation. See Warner, *Generals in Blue*, 474, 112, 70-71, 418, respectively.

I want you to send me some of your photographs to send to my friends. Do spunk up and get some taken. You must look natural just like the little girl who used to reach her arms up around my neck and give me a kiss....

Ever your loving hubbie,
Madison.

Head Quarters, Post of Little Rock, Arkansas. [letterhead]
Dec. 12, 1863.

My Dear Wife:

Your letter of Nov. 14 was received yesterday. I do not doubt but that you were greatly disappointed because I did not go home in the fall. I can assure you that it was as much a disappointment to me as to you. I feel, too, the pain of having been the means of your disappointment. I know it is wrong, *very wrong*, in me to stay so long away from you. I have been for the last month debating in my mind whether or not to resign. I have been almost miserable on account of my posi-tion—my duty to my country requiring me to neglect my duty toward my family; and if I had done, or should yet do, toward my family as I ought to do, it would in after years, give me the shame of having quit the service of my country at a time when it would appear dishonorable to do so. The thoughts of my dear wife waiting so lonely and patiently, make my heart feel sad; and when I read her words of kindness and affection, and her fond description of her little one—its pretty face and blue eyes, it makes me feel as though I could not stay from home any longer than just time enough to reach the side of my Lizzie where I could see the picture myself.[25]

I am pleased to hear that you think our little one pretty. Be sure and have her miniature, as well as your own, taken, and send it to me as soon as you can con-veniently do so. Look at those blue eyes and give that little mouth a kiss, all for her father....

Monday, 14

I was interrupted Saturday in writing, and have deferred closing this letter until now. You speak about how greatly you miss sister Katie. I know that I shall miss

25. Stephen Berry argues that for a Southern soldier "so long as a man could see him-self through the idealized eyes of a woman, he would continue to fight. If ever he could not, romance and patriotism, love of woman and love of country, might become disaggre-gated, and then he would be forced to choose between them" (*All That Makes a Man,* 192, 216). Although a Northerner, Madison, too, needed Lizzie's approval so that his sense of duty to her and to the Union could be one and the same and not competing obligations.

her too, when [I] return and find her place vacant. It is very hard to think that I shall not see her when I get home again. As long as I live I shall ever miss her. In Irving's beautiful words:—"Sorrow for the dead is the only sorrow from which we refuse to be divorced. Every other wound we seek to heal; every other afflic-tion to forget."[26] How very true and touching are those words to one who has ever had occasion to sorrow for the dead....

> Ever your loving husband,
> Madison.

Nininger Dec. 17th 1863

My Dear Husband

I have at last succeeded in getting the babies picture taken for you. You will see that it is a very poor one but it is the best I could do. I had five taken before I could get one that was worth keeping. She would not sit still....

You do not know how surprised I was last Tuesday morning on looking out the window. I saw two soldiers getting out of the stage. Taking the second look, I saw that one of them was Lieut. Otto. For one moment my heart was in my mouth for I knew not what reason. When he came in, we asked him how you were. He said he left you well but "pretty mad" in the most [?] dutch manner I ever heard. I told him that I thought he was real selfish to not let you come. He said there was a girl in St. Paul that wanted to see him as much as I wanted to see you. We wanted him to stay to dinner. He said he could not for he felt as though every hair in his head and every nerve in his body was drawing him to-ward St Paul, but promised to come and make a visit before he went back again.

The dress that he got was very nice. I think Otto displayed excellent taste in selecting it. Receive my most sincere thanks for such a nice present. I hope sometime to repay you for your kindness to me. I have now made up my mind that I shall not see you till the expiration of your three years, as my hopes have all been blasted so many times. I shall not hope any more but wait patiently till I see you.

... I should have had [a picture taken] and sent you, but I had not time, and another thing I am so thin of flesh that I thought I had better not. Nursing babies does not agree with me. I never was so poor in my life.

You speak of what we will call our next. I think if we have another that you

---

26. This is a quote from Washington Irving, "Rural Funerals," in *The Sketch-Book of Geoffrey Crayon, Gent. in Washington Irving: History Tales and Sketches* (Cambridge: The Library of America, 1983), 873.

will have to take the burden on your back, for I do not think I could stand another such a scrape for over six years.[27]

I have been four hours writing this letter. I write two or three lines and then
I have to nurse baby a while for she is very cross to-night.

(Friday morning)

... If I were selfish enough to consult no ones feelings but my own, I should like
to go to Little Rock. But I feel that I can do *you* no good, and it would almost kill
Ma to take the baby and go away. She feels so lonely since Kate's death. You ask
what she thinks of your little daughter. I assure you she thinks a great deal of her.
This is a horrible cold morning. Yesterday was the first snow storm. I hope Otto
will come and see us again before he goes back.... Baby was three months old
the day she had this picture taken. Be careful (please) and take care of it, for if
she lives she will prize it very highly when she grows.

> {top margin first page} I am not going to say anything about you coming home,
> for you know when you can come better than I do.

> {top margin inside page} You can see by this picture what a fat baby your
> daughter is....

Lizzie

Little Rock, Ark., Dec. 18th, 1863.

My Dear Lizzie:

Your excellent letter of Nov. 24th was received yesterday—the best letter you have
written in many weeks with the exception of one which you cannot excel—the
one you wrote just after your sickness. The kiss from Birdie came all right. I send
her one in return; and you will please give it to her for me. Of course you must
not think of discarding the name, Victoria, which sister Katie left for our little
birdie. You can add such other as you please; but you could not add one which
would please me better than the one—Augusta—which your kind regard for the
affectionate remembrance I entertain for my departed mother, has already sug-
gested. You could not have touched me on a more tender chord, than when you
propose to call your first born after my dear mother.[28] O, Lizzie, you are contin-

27. The next baby was born September 14, 1866, and lived only eleven days. See
Appendix A.
28. Madison's mother's name was Clara Augusta.

ually doing things which make me love you more and more. An Angelic nature has skilled you in the art of playing upon the hearts of those around you.

I am pleased to hear that you have subscribed for Godey's Book. Be assured that it will ever give me pleasure to have you keep yourself supplied with an abundance of the best of reading matter. I am very glad to hear that you have been able to visit our friends Gus and Mary. I hope you will do so often. They have been good and true friends to us; we have all started out on wedded life to-gether, and I desire to cherish the friendly intercourse which we have formed with them, through life. They are worthy friends. I hope to hear of Marys early recovery from sickness. Convey to them my kindest regards. . . .

Johnson Truax has been quite sick but is well again now. He is a Sergeant now. You wish to know if I am well. I am. I weigh 185 lbs. now. I was much heavier a month ago. I am anxiously waiting for that picture of yourself and little birdie. . . . I send you lots of kisses and hugs.

> Ever your loving
> Madison.

> Head Quarters, Post of Little Rock, Arkansas. [letterhead]
> Dec. 21, 1863.

My Dear Lizzie:

Yours of Nov. 30 and Dec. 1 were rec'd this morning. I hasten to reply to the business matter, and will answer the rest some other time.

You say that Mr. Dodge offers his land—house &c included—for $1100.00—$500.00 down, and the rest in one year at 7 per cent interest. Now, I am going to talk a little, and *after* I get through talking I shall *say something*. Financially speaking, it would be a fair investment. . . . If I recollect rightly, though I never took much notice—the house is cheaply got up and cannot last long—the other improvements of like nature. I may be in error. Besides, one year ago, if I am not mistaken, Mr. D. offered the place for $800.00. I think he appears rather grasping; and a good financier could make him lower those figures ($1100.) considerably, rather than lose a good trade. . . .[29]

Now I have had my say and I leave it entirely with you to do as you think best. We want a home, and I think that would make a very good one. Land, too, I presume, has advanced in value during the past year. I have no doubt but that I can

29. Madison is responding to a letter that Lizzie wrote that is not part of the correspondence. A J. A. Dodge lived in Nininger with his family in 1865.

furnish the money as required. Be assured that I shall be fully satisfied with whatever action you choose to take.

Ever your loving,
Madison.

Little Rock, Ark., Dec. 23d, 1863.

My Dear Lizzie:

How is my darling and how does her little "Birdie" this fine morning? I wish I could see both of you and give you a good, sweet kiss apiece. You still express some hope that I may visit home before many months. There is only one hope left now, aside from resignation. The 3d Reg't. has less than one year to serve, and is therefore subject to the Veteran Volunteer order, which grants $402.00 bounty to those who re-enlist for three years or during the war; and where ¾ of a company or reg't. re-enlist they may be ordered home with their officers for furlough and re-organization.[30]

Over ¾ of Co. "K" have re-enlisted, and I have no doubt but that ¾ of Co. "F" will be in by next week. Should such be the case we may all be home in the course of a month. Eugene and Charley Russell have re-enlisted. You speak of the delay of my letters in reaching you. I do not see the reason of it. Your letters come to me much more regularly now than they used to. I think you will get letters enough for a while, for I have written one nearly every day for the last week.

You must not allow yourself to feel any uneasiness about your expenses. I want you to use money to buy everything you need, if it takes the last cent. Prices are indeed high; but not so high in Minn. as they are here. I have spent $138.00 for boots alone since I left Helena. Also $50.00 for an overcoat and $30.00 for two pairs trousers. I sent to St. Louis and got a dress coat for $32.00, which would have cost $45 here. Shirts cost from $5.00 to $12.00 a pair. Drawers ditto. Eggs fifty cts, Butter from 50 to 75 cts. Just think of it. It has cost me a great deal for board and clothes since I came to Little Rock. I shall not have to buy any more clothes for a year.

30. Andrews devotes an entire section of the narrative to "Veteranizing." General Order 191 from the War Department on January 25, 1863, stipulated that those who reenlisted for another three years would "receive one month's pay in advance, and a bounty and premium, amounting in all to $402. . . . As soon after the expiration of their original term of enlistment as the exigencies of the service would permit, they were to receive a thirty days' furlough" ("Narrative of the Third Regiment," 169-70).

This morning Col. Andrews made me a present of a volume of Shakespeare. The colonel is a dear friend to me; but estimates me far above my real worth. What are you going to do for Christmas? Wish I could take dinner with you. . . .

We have pretty lively times here now. Col. Andrews Brigade has Brigade drill three times a week. They make a fine display.[31]

. . . Kiss little "Birdie" for me. Lots of sweet kisses for you.

> Ever your loving
> Madison

Nininger Dec 24, 1863

My Dear Madison

I have just got my little one out of my arms for the evening. Will now try and write a few lines to my absent husband. It is Christmas eve. Do is standing on one side of me making minced pies for Christmas. Says if you will hurry and come home you may have a piece. We have been having a great snow storm enough to make real good sleighing. I wish you were here, if we would have a good sleigh ride but that cannot be so I shall have to content myself to stay at home & take care of my little fatherless babe until next year, and then I hope we will not be so far apart.

I have not seen Otto since the day he called on his way to St. Paul. He promised to come and see us again before he returned to the regt. I hope he will, for I want to see him. I did not read the letter you sent by him till after he was gone, and consequently did not know that he was going to be married until after he was gone.

You ask me if I do not feel proud to be called mother. If I were capable of setting a right example before my little one I should be, but I know I am not. . . .

I have got the worst cold I believe I ever had. My head aches so to night I shall have to leave this till to morrow, otherways I am pretty well. So good night.

Christmas morning

Merry Christmas to you. You ask if baby is good nights. I have never been up with her but two or three nights since she was born, but she has always been very troublesome in the day time, though she is getting better now. To-day is a very dull day for Christmas. I think it will be a stormy day.

---

31. Andrews also explains: "During the autumn and winter, when the weather would admit, brigade drills were conducted by the colonel on the ground in front of St. John's College, with the Third Minnesota and 43rd Illinois divided into three battalions" ("Narrative of the Third Regiment," 169).

... I don't know about you tending parties where there is so many ladies. I am afraid I shall lose you. I believe I shall have to get some of your brother solders to look after you. ...

>from your loving wife
>Lizzie ...

>Head Quarters, Post of Little Rock, Arkansas, [letterhead]
>January 1st, 1864.

My Dear Libby:

A happy new year to you and a new years kiss for my little Birdie. O, if I could only be with you to-day, I would give all the world. But it is no use to sigh over what cannot be helped. ... I hope the fear of the draft will drive about two-thirds of those home patriots into the service, and draw in the other third.[32]

It is very interesting to me to have you write all about your little one. I shall be a stranger to her when I return, and she will be afraid of me, will she not? You must tell her all about her papa, so she will be glad to see him.

It is quite cold here to-day, the coldest ever known here, say the inhabitants. Our first snow fell yesterday, and is still on the ground.

I have been thinking about whether you cannot buy Mr. Russell's land if you do not purchase of Mr. Dodge. It is a more desirable piece of land than Mr. Dodge's, being much larger. I should be willing to pay $25.00 per acre, if I could not get it for less. At $35.00 an acre it would be, in my opinion, a better bargain than Mr. Dodge's at $1100.00. Do you not think so? But I leave it with you entirely to do as you think best. I have $100.00 to send you as soon as I get a good opportunity. If you need it at once, I will send it by mail. I hope that by the time this war is over we shall be able to have a home somewhere to enjoy. It would no doubt be much more pleasant to both of us to be by ourselves. Every day that I am away from you seems like a diamond lost. If I could only lie down by your side to-night and tell over the long story of my thoughts during our years separation, my joy would know no bounds. I lay a long while awake last night thinking of my birdies at home and wishing I were with them. ...

>Ever your loving,
>Madison.

32. On March 3, 1863, Congress passed the Enrollment Act. It "made every able-bodied male citizen (plus aliens who had filed for naturalization) aged twenty to forty-five eligible for the draft." See McPherson, *Ordeal by Fire*, 384.

Jan. 8th 1864

My Dear Husband

... We have not had a down river mail at Nininger for 8 days on account of the snow being so deep on the mail rout. But I hope to get a letter from you tomorrow, as they expect the mail in. Oh! Oh you may [be] thankful you were not in Minn. for the last week. It is said by every one that there has never been so cold a day in their remembrance as New Years day was (I know I never did). There was a great many frozen. It was reported that there was three stage drivers drove into Red Wing frozen to death. Since then it has been contradicted. They were not frozen to death but were very nearly.[33]

... I had no one but little "Vic" to sleep with me. I really thought I should freeze. You dont know how often I wished you were here to sleep with me, as I know you used to be a good warm bed fellow. Never mind. I will forget the present & look forward to next winter for that comfort.

My health is not very good, nor never has been since baby was born, but I do not expect to have much better as long as I nurse her. She is so large. I think I never saw a fatter baby then she is. I will not nurse her longer then spring for she eats well now.[34] I never saw a little child like her that liked music such as she does. Ira Hayford from Afton was over here with his fiddle. He could keep her quiet when nothing else would.

The drafting day is over and they did not draft, just as I thought, for I never did believe they would draft in this state. I have been thinking what Otto would do now. Go back without any drafted men. I have looked in my St Paul papers for his marriage but have never seen it. I hope he will come here before he returns to Little Rock. There was three weddings in Hastings New Year's day....[35]

33. On January 7, 1864, the *Hastings Independent* reported that the temperature on January 1, 1864, was thirty-five degrees below zero and had remained at least twenty below. "We have heard of no persons frozen, but few persons who have been nipped with the frost, though men have been on the road during the severest weather, though the stir has not been as lively as usual."

34. See McMillen, "Mothers' Sacred Duty," 333–56. Although McMillen's study is of Southern women, Lizzie's attitudes about the adverse effect of breast-feeding on her health are nearly identical, as is her commitment to not wean until her baby is more than six months old.

35. For more on recruiting in the state in late 1863, see Folwell, *A History of Minnesota*, 337–38. For the three marriages, see *Hastings Independent*, 7 January 1864. These were Belle Patch and Edward Waite; George Torrance and Belle Leonard, both on January 1; and Mr. Argetsinger and Sarah Knapp on December 30.

Well it is now ten o'clock. I must go to bed to dream of my absent hubbie. By the way, I must tell you what I dreamed the other night. I thought you came. When you came in, baby was lying in the cradle. You passed right by her and never looked at her. That made me sort of spunky & I would not show her to you. Then baby cried and spoiled the rest of my dream.

> Well good night from your loving wife
> Lizzie...

> Head Quarters, Post of Little Rock, Arkansas, [letterhead]
> Jany. 19th 1864[36]

My Dear Lizzie:

I must try and write you a few lines occasionally until I get started for home, so that you will not worry about me.[37]

I have got pretty well acquainted with Birdie already by looking at her miniature. It is company for me. The small-pox has broken out in the 3d Regiment—five cases having already occurred. I fear that it will detain us from going home for some weeks yet. I hope not, however. I was vaccinated about fourteen years ago, and again about a week ago. I have a great dread for small-pox.[38]

I wish you would get Birdie vaccinnated as soon as possible. It would be a good idea for you to get vaccinnated, too....

> Ever your hubbie,
> Madison

> Head Quarters, Post of Little Rock, Arkansas,
> Jan. 22 1864

Dear Madam [Lizzie]

I write at the request of your husband to inform you of the accident he met with day before yesterday evening. At my request he accompanied me to the circus that evening, also in company with Maj Foster and Capt Vanstram of our regi-

36. On the back of this letter, Madison wrote, "Written the day before I broke my leg."
37. Veteran reenlistment progressed slowly until January 5, 1864, when the regiment was called together and urged to reenlist for patriotism and state pride. By January 7 reenlistment had been accomplished; Company F left on furlough on February 7. See Andrews, "Narrative of the Third Regiment," 170.
38. On smallpox, see Tucker, Scourge, 31–32.

ment. We had barely taken our seats in the crowded audience, when the seats on the whole of one side of the circus gave way, and hundreds of people fell with the frame work to the ground. Your husband was sitting beside me, and remarked as soon as we were thrown down that his leg was broken. It indeed proved true. His right leg was broken a few inches above the ankle. Our surgeon Dr. Wedge happened to be near by. Gen. Steele's ambulance was also at hand and he was immediately by the kind aid of numerous friends who in a minute were by his side, placed in the carriage and taken to our quarters. His leg was soon set by Dr. Wedge aided by Dr. Greeley, and I am happy to say he is getting along very well. It is not a bad break, and will not confine him more than five weeks it is thought. I believe he will be able to go home with the regiment which will perhaps go in the course of a month. He could then be moved upon a steamboat undoubtedly without any trouble.

He has frequently mentioned you and has expressed a desire to be at *home*; but he has however been as cheerful as usual. Still he of course suffers considerable pain at times. You may be sure he will have every attention that can possibly be furnished,—the attention even of affectionate friends. He will have you informed frequently how he gets along. I have the honor to be very respectfully

> C. C. Andrews.
> Col &c

{side margin inside page} I expect I shall not detail any one in his place, on the theory that he is equal to any one else as he is, though of course he is not troubled with any duty.

Head Quarters, Post of Little Rock, Arkansas,
Jan 27 1864

Dear Madam:

I wrote you a few days ago about your husband having his leg broken. It affords me the greatest pleasure now to inform you that he is constantly improving, and is able to sleep pretty comfortably nights. Sergeant Truax stays with him all the time and he has two attentive volunteer watchers every night, besides the attention of his mess, and other friends, and what aid is needed of our three house servants. The best medical aid of course.

> Very respectfully
> Your obt serv't
> CC. Andrews.

Nininger Feb 1st 1864

My dear, dear husband

You cannot tell the depth of my anxiety to-night. I am as one with their hands tied to know that my dear husband is lying suffering. That I cannot do anything to eleveate his sufferings is trouble for me to live. You may depend that I was somewhat stunned at noon to-day when papa came home and told me the dreadful news of your being hurt, for I had just about made up my mind that you would be home during this week.

Sometimes I [am] wicked enough to think that I have more afflictions to encounter then any one else, but why do I murmur, for I know that it is God's will that it is for some good end. He maketh all things that are hard to endure. You know that he saith those that he loves he chasteneth & now dear husband feel it so in your case. Bear it patiently, for you know not for what good purpose it was ordered to be so. Lean upon God in your lonely hours and he will be your comforter.

Were it not for baby, I would start for Little Rock immediately. But I know that it would not be prudent for me to do so, as my health would not permit of my enduring hardship and exposure with so much care as she is. But I entreat of you not to give up and get low spirited. Keep up good courage & you will come out all right. . . . I feel so anxious to hear whether you are hurt any where beside your leg and how badly that is injured.

Our baby pet is as smart as a bee. I guess she will be able to say papa by the time he comes if he does not hurry. . . . Mind and dont you try to move too soon. Take the best of care of yourself. If there is nothing but your leg broken, you will be able to come home in the course of five or six weeks. If you were only here I should not care so much. Keep up good courage and think this affliction is all for the best. Mind and dont allow yourself to get the blues. I will write to you often. . . .

> from your anxious and loving wife
> Lizzie

Write very often if you are able. If not get some one else too.

Little Rock, Ark., Feby. 6th, 1864.

My Dear Lizzie:

. . . It is a great comfort to me to read [your letters]. You seem to think the idea of my going home almost too good to be true; but be assured that I shall start for [the] house just as soon as it is proper for me to attempt to travel. My company together with Cos "A" & "D" were relieved from duty yesterday and will start for Minn. in a day or two. It will be two or three weeks before I shall attempt to go home.

My broken leg is doing exceedingly well, though I am not yet able to leave my bed. I am entirely willing to believe that the trade you have made in buying Mr. Poors house and land, is a good one for us.[39] It is very desirable indeed that we have a home of our own. Of course you got some competent person to make the necessary papers in legal form. It is a matter in which too much care cannot well be exercised. I am glad that you did not buy of Mr. Dodge, for I dislike to humor such men by feeding their selfish desires. I do not like the tribe to which he belongs. I wrote to you long ago to get a crib for "Birdie" to sleep in. I suppose you have done so—you know I do not want her where you will be paying her a share of the attention due me. Do you hear? . . .

> Ever your loving
> Madison

39. Samuel Caleff, Lizzie's father, bought land from Albert Poor in the northeast quarter of the northeast quarter of Section 24, with the deed filed on April 15, 1864. See Dakota County, *Dakota County Abstract Book*. Samuel Caleff's land was in the northwest quarter of Section 24. See Guelcher, *More Than Just a Dream*, 105.

Do, Libby, Look on the Bright Side of Things

APRIL 1864 TO APRIL 1865

After Madison recovered from his broken leg, while on furlough in Minnesota, he returned to Little Rock, accompanied by new recruits to fill the ranks of the regiment. Still captain of Company F, Madison also began recruiting black soldiers for a colored regiment. He hoped that when the regiment was mustered in, he would gain a higher-ranking position with increased pay, prestige, and possibilities. Recruiting was difficult, however, because of the lack of forward movement of the Union army in Arkansas. The Third Minnesota and other regiments were garrisoned at Pine Bluff, Devall's Bluff, Little Rock, Helena, and Fort Smith, but these were defensive positions. While cavalry skirmishes and limited infantry engagements continued, the Third Minnesota suffered through the summer and fall from malaria, or ague, which Madison experienced recurrently. Regimental surgeon Dr. A. C. Wedge estimated that most of the new Minnesota recruits and draftees were stricken with malaria; eighty-nine recruits and thirty draftees died. Wedge commented, and Madison would have agreed, "I would much rather have been in a hard fought battle every week during the summer (in a healthy locality) than to spend such a summer in that deadly locality."[1]

Learning of Madison's sustained illness, Lizzie could not understand why he would remain in the army. Although her worries about his health contributed to her waning support for the war, she also succumbed to the general war weariness experienced by the North from April through October 1864. With a military stalemate outside of Atlanta through the summer and bloody battles and an ongoing siege at Petersburg, Virginia, through the winter, the Northern public grew tired of the war. Democratic sentiment was at its height in the late summer, and

---

1. For Wedge's report, see Andrews, "Narrative of the Third Regiment," 174–75. For Madison's desire to fight, see Joseph S. Bowler to James Madison Bowler, 1 September 1864, Bowler Papers. Joseph wrote, "You say that you wish you were in this Department to participate in the campaign around Richmond. Thank God, rather, that you have been kept out of it. Haven't you seen enough of the 'Horrors of war' yet?"

President Lincoln feared he would lose the fall election in 1864. Through all of this, most Union soldiers felt a renewed commitment to the war and chastised people at home for their lack of faith in its successful completion.[2] Madison and Lizzie's exchanges in the early fall demonstrate this strikingly.

Another of Lizzie's preoccupations concerned their farm. Although the farm was in her father's name, Lizzie and Madison were responsible for paying the mortgage and maintaining it. Madison offered advice but gave her full authority to make decisions and transactions regarding their financial matters. With Madison gone, Lizzie remained at her parents' home and rented their farm out to Nininger farmer Albert Poor, from whom they had purchased it earlier that year. Their arrangement was fraught with difficulties. Lizzie struggled to collect unpaid rent money from him. Poor stayed on the farm until October 1864, when at the last minute he moved onto a relative's farm nearby, which left Lizzie to find new tenants before the winter. She rented their property to the county as a poor house for five dollars per month to house local war widows and their families. She also hired a local farmer to plow the land. Like many other Civil War wives, both Northern and Southern, Lizzie did her best to carry out her husband's business until he returned, but with mixed success.[3]

Separated for all but three months of their nearly two-year marriage, the Bowlers agreed that they wanted to live together. By November 1, 1864, however, Lizzie and Madison had come to an impasse about where that would be. Through the winter, they engaged in a verbal tug-of-war. Madison wanted Lizzie and Victoria to join him in Little Rock, whereas Lizzie argued that Madison's primary responsibility was to return to his family in Minnesota. They each employed a variety of strategies to persuade the other to move, ranging from teasing, tempting, and innuendo to playing on guilt and notions of duty.

Nininger April 21 [1864]

My very dear husband . . .

Oh! You cannot tell how lonely I have been since you left. I wish that I could blot this week out of any remembrance, for it has been a sad, lonely one indeed. I am sorry that you have to stay in St Paul so long, as long as you have to go down river.

2. See McPherson, *For Cause and Comrades*, 142–45.
3. This is discussed much more for Southern women. For example, see Cashin, "'Since the War Broke Out'"; Faust, *Mothers of Invention*, 65–66; and Clinton, *Tara Revisited*, 109–10. For Northern women running farms themselves, see Livermore, *My Story of the War*, 135–36, 145–49; and Silber, *Daughters of the Union*, 42, 55–58. On making financial decisions, see Betts, "'Dear Husband,'" 150; and Kiper, *Dear Catharine, Dear Taylor*, 17.

How are you getting [along]? Have you felt agueist since you left? I hear that Ft Pillow has been captured. If so, how are you going to get along? . . .[4]

. . . Do write often, for I shall feel very anxious to hear from you till I know that you are safely landed at Little Rock.

> Now dear hubbie a good by & kiss f[rom your] dear loving wife
> Lizzie

Steamer "Davenport," LeClaire, Iowa, April 27 1864.

[To Lizzie]

Left St Paul Saturday night after a week of tiresome waiting for a St Louis Boat. I never spent so lonely a week before, I believe, as the week I lay in St. Paul. It was painful to be so near home and yet not able to be there. I do not believe I smiled during the week I felt so blue. We arrived here last night and have waited in vain for the wind to go down in order that the boat may pass the rapids and Rock Island Bridge in safety. It is now four oclock P.M. and no signs of the wind easing. At this rate we shall not reach Little Rock before the expiration of dog days.

Ammon gave me your letter which I was very glad to get. O! You do not know how very lonely I have been since I left you. If there is any prospect of my remaining long at Little Rock you *must* come down.

Ammon is along with me. I make him sleep with me for companys sake.

There are several babies which continue to remind me of the little one at home, which has been dancing before my imagination ever since I left home. I would walk five miles lame as I am, just for the privilege of holding her in my arms for one hour. . . .

Give my love to all the folks, and give Birdie twenty kisses for me.

> Ever your
> Madison.

St Louis, Mo.,
Hunter's House, May 1, 1864.

My Dear Wife:

I arrived here yesterday morning—but when I be able to get away is uncertain as the down river boats are so croweded with troops moving south, that I have not

---

4. When Madison returned to Arkansas, he was in charge of recruiting blacks for a new "colored regiment." Lizzie worried about Madison leading a black regiment, especially because of the Confederate government's stated policy to execute white officers in those regiments. After black soldiers surrendered at Fort Pillow, Tennessee, on April 12, 1864, some of them were executed by Confederate soldiers. See Glatthaar, *Forged in Battle*, 156–57.

as yet been able to secure passage. I got paid yesterday and sent you by express to Hastings $250.00.

If Mr. Poor wants $100.00, you may loan it to him upon proper security at 10 or 12 percent. I only offer it as a matter of accommodation to him. Had rather loan it for a year or so, but if he wants it on short time he can have it. As to the rest, you may do with it as you please—use it for your own wants or advance it on the mortgage against your farm....

Ever yours.
Madison.

P.S. I want you to have your things in readiness so that you can come to Little Rock at any time I may send for you.

Madison.

Nininger June 2 1864

[My] Ever dear Husband[5]

... You still speak as though you wished me [to] come to Little Rock. I gladly would be with you but under the present [cir]cumstances I do not [think] it best. Some times I [feel] that if I had wings I could fly to where you are f[or] five minutes in your society. Now is the time we ever are to enjoy life, that we should be enjoying it, that we should be w[here] we could share each others joys & sorrows [but] how little satisfaction to be thus separated.

[My] ambition is a great one, where day times we [would] enjoy the society of ea[ch other] & at night we [would] lie us down & emm[brace] each other in our arms.... Baby is up beside me. You have no idea how fast she has [im]proved since you left. She [ja]bbers all the time. Can say [pa] & mama most as plainly [as] any one. She can sit [up] ... can change her seat on the floor every few moments butt I hardly know how for she does not creep.

... Piercy is as big a brag as ever. [I] should think to hear [it] told that he was the com[dg] General of the Western dept.... Where is Hem Pettibone? Was his wound [of] much consequence? ... Always when you write mention Robt Poor if you know h[ow] he is, for Mrs Poor f[eels] very anxious about h[im].[6] I was down & spent the afternoon with Mary Case day before yesterday. She [has] a

---

5. The left side of the letter is torn away, so many words are missing.

6. Twenty-one-year-old Robert Poor was recruited to join Company F, Third Minnesota, in February 1864. Mrs. Poor was probably Louisa Poor, who lived in Hampton Township in 1860.

nice little babe but I [don't] think there will ever be any danger of any more for [Gus] will kill himself work[ing].[7]

We have not had any [rain] to speak of since you [left]. Every thing is drying up. [If there] is not some soon there [will] not be anything raised in [thi]s part of Minn worth mentioning. . . .

> from your ever loving wife
> Lizzie

[I] forgot to tell you what a [good] little thing baby was to [be] weaned. She has never cried [a] moment in the night [since] she was weaned.[8] LSB

Little Rock, Ark., June 3d, 1864.

My Dear Lizzie:

. . . I judge from the tenor of your letter, that you will not come to Little Rock. I have a nice place engaged for our board. . . . But I shall not look for your coming any more—though you promised that you would come when I sent for you. I should not complain, however; and I do not wish you to do an act against your own judgment and inclinations, just for my sake. I could not think of having you come here unless it should perfectly accord with your own wish and will.

But Lizzie, you must pardon me for my petulance, displayed in the foregoing. It is only the wicked overflowing of a lonely, disappointed heart. I shall try to make myself contented hereafter without adding to your troubles—already too many on my account.

Am truly pleased to hear so good an account of your and baby's health. Surely God's mercy and kindness to myself and my family should be acknowledged by more cheerful conduct and more thoughtful gratitude than I am wont to display. . . .

Poor Will. Govette is sick at the officers Gen. Hospit'l, within thirty or forty rods of my tent. He is confined to a dark room, with inflammation of the eyes, and can scarcely see at all. I was in yesterday and spent the afternoon—wrote him a letter to his wife. He is entirely free from the effects of liquor, which renders him much more agreeable in conversation and displays to the fullest extent his naturally warm free-hearted disposition. Asked me all about Nininger and its old and new people, to the minutest particular. The time passed the most agreeably of any I ever spent with him. I think he will not drink again. Will spoke very feelingly of your folks, and he cried when Katie's name was mentioned. Wanted to

7. Mary and Gus Case had a daughter, Marion Ardelia Case.
8. For weaning and who decides when it should occur, see McMillen, "Mothers' Sacred Duty," 338-40, 344-45.

know all about her death and where she was buried. Wished to be remembered to all of you. . . .[9]

> Ever your loving,
> Madison.

Little Rock, Ark., June 7th, 1864.

My Dear Lizzie:

. . . Was greatly pleased to receive your photograph, as I have had no miniature of you since I left home in April. It does not do you justice, however. I would sit and keep sitting until I got a negative to suit me. . . . I am glad to know that you have thought it best to wean baby. I hope you will enjoy better health now.

It must look very lonely since Aunt Sarah's house was moved away.[10] I supposed Aunt Sarah still stays with you. . . . I am sorry to hear that you have so little rain. It must be very discouraging to farmers. We have plenty of it here. . . .

Yesterday there was a grand review here. Maj. Genl. Daniel E. Sickles reviewed our Army Corps. It was a grand affair I assure you—the finest I have witnessed since the commencement of the war.

Day before yesterday I was down with the ague. I have had no chill to-day— thanks to quinine and cathartic pills. . . .[11]

> Ever your
> Madison . . .

{on last page lower corner} Do not forget that note, given for insurance on our house. It is in Mr. Caleff's name, and is to be paid at Thorne's Bank.

Little Rock, Ark., June 15th, 1864.

My Dear Lizzie:

. . . Have not heard a word from Maine since I returned to Little Rock. Think the folks there must have forgotten me. I was quite unwell last week with ague, but am quite smart again. Will Govette is getting some better of the inflammation in

9. John H. Case reports that Katherine Caleff was buried in the northeast corner of her father's farm. See "The Caleff Family of Bluff Landing—Nininger," *Hastings Gazette*, 30 December 1921.

10. Lizzie's letter of May 17, 1864, is not in the correspondence, so it is unclear whether Aunt Sarah's house was floated down the river to Hastings or moved by land to some other location.

11. Ague is a fever with chills. It was a common complaint by early pioneers who located near wet lowlands. Malaria was also sometimes called "ague."

his eyes; but long confinement has debilitated him somewhat. I saw him to-day, and read to him a batch of letters which he had just received from Philadelphia and St. Louis. . . .

Yesterday I attended the funeral of Col. F. H. Manter, Gen. Steele's Chief of Staff. Col. Manter was from St. Louis, and was colonel of the 32d Missouri Inf'y. He had but recently returned from an important mission to Washington. He was thrown to the ground while riding a fiery horse, his forehead striking the ground, splitting open his skull, and terminating his life in two hours. The death of Col. Manter gave me a peculiar sadness. I made his acquaintance early last fall, and our official relations called us together frequently. While confined to my room last winter, he called several times, and manifested much sympathy for me. The funeral escort was composed of the 29th Iowa Infy, and a section of Artillery. Gens Steele, Soloman, Cass, West, Bussey, and Andrews, with their staffs, and a numerous throng of officers and men followed his remains to their last resting place. How sad the thought that one so honored, so promising, should be cut off in the midst of his career, in the prime of manhood. But such is the will of God, and we should not complain; but should let such incidents admonish us to be prepared—we know not who shall be next.[12]

I presume that baby is much less trouble to you now that she is weaned and sits alone. I hardly see how you concluded to wean her, unless it was because I ceased to request it, and appeared wholly indifferent about it. I hope that you will not take to nursing her again, thinking that there must be danger in it on account of the approval of one so inexperienced as myself. You know you say that I know nothing about little children; so just the opposite of my opinions must be correct. . . .

> Truly,
> Madison.

Little Rock, Ark., June 17th, 1864.

My Dear Lizzie:

. . . You refer to our separation and you say truly that the measure of our earthly happiness cannot be full until we are together once more. I believe that no one can realize the truth of that expression more forcibly or more keenly than I do.

---

12. Colonel Manter commanded the Thirty-second Missouri Infantry after serving in an artillery unit. He had served as chief of staff for General Steele since the Vicksburg campaign. His death and funeral were announced through a general order. See U.S. Army, Dept. of Arkansas General Order No. 39. For more on generals Eugene Carr, Joseph Rodman West, Cyrus Bussey (cavalry), and Christopher Columbus Andrews, see Warner, *Generals in Blue*, 70–71, 552, 59, 8, respectively. For soldiers' use of religion to face the fear of death, see McPherson, *For Cause and Comrades*, 163–70.

It does me good to hear that you have ventured out of doors long enough to go a fishing. It gives me hope. I trust that you will get in the habit of going out oftener than heretofore, now that baby is weaned and can be left in other hands.

... Heman Pettibone is with the regiment at Pine Bluff.[13] He is 2d Lieut. of Co. "H." His wound was very slight. He behaved nobly I learn. I have not seen Robt Poor yet. I think I shall go down to Pine Bluff next week. I have not found my coat yet, and do not expect to. As to being a good boy you know I am never "naughty." You wish to know what I have to do. Well, a great deal. Have as much business as any regt'l comd'r.—making reports, drilling the regt., sending recruiting parties to different stations, providing for the sick, and getting recruits examined and mustered. I have recruiting parties at Duvalls Bluff, Pine Bluff, and Brownsville. Yesterday I sent a party to the mouth of White river.

I tent with Lieut. Gustafson. Once in awhile I ride out—sometimes call on Gen. Andrews and at other places where I have friends. There are no less than eight officers of the 3d Regt. on detached duty in this town—Capt. Hodges, Sup't Military Prison, Lieuts Greenleaf and Champion, on Gen Andrews staff, Capt DeKay, Asst Pro. marshal, Lieut Morse asst commissary of musters, Lieut. Grummons comdg convalescent camp, and Lieut. Gustafson and myself in the colored business. I forgot Dr. Greely, surgeon Mility Prison. ...[14]

Give my love to all, and give baby two hundred kisses for me.

    Truly,
    Madison.

                                 Rose Hill, June 26th, 1864

My dear Madison

... The river is very low now. The boats can scarcely get along. I was at a Caravan in Hastings yesterday. When I went in, I happened to get on the top seat—could

---

13. Madison refers to Prentice, *Prenticeana; or, Wit and Humor in Paragraphs*. Most of the Third Minnesota was at Pine Bluff, Arkansas, during the summer of 1863. They built fortifications to prevent Confederate capture and suffered from malaria. See Andrews, "Narrative of the Third Regiment," 174.

14. John G. Gustofson was first lieutenant in Company D, from Red Wing. Promoted to brigadier general in April 1864, C. C. Andrews was with most of the Third Minnesota at Pine Bluff. Madison's duty was to recruit soldiers for black regiments. See Andrews, "Narrative of the Third Regiment," 173-74. Captain Hodges was from Company K, Third Minnesota, and enlisted in Eyota, Olmsted County. Lieutenant Damon Greenleaf from Company I enlisted in St. Paul. Lieutenant Ezra T. Champlin of Company G enlisted in Wabashaw. Lieutenant William F. Morse of Company I enlisted in Morrison County. Captain Willet W. DeKay in Company E enlisted in Red Wing. Lieutenant William Grummons in Company C enlisted in Mower County. Madison had consulted Greely regarding

not help thinking about the time you went to the circus & got on the top seat. I see by the St. Paul daily that John Moulton was murdered. Awful to think of, is it not?[15]

. . . Do you hear from Joe? Is he in those terrible battles? . . . I am glad you are not on the Potomac. If you were, I should not have one moments rest.[16]

In this letter you will find a necktie. I do not send it because I think it so pretty nor because I think you have none. But I send it because Lizzie mad[e] it with her hands & it comes from your home & I think you will prize it more highly then you would if you had bought it. Get some of your lady friends to put something inside of it to stiffen it & then it will not muss so easily.

Baby is very well but this warm weather makes her very fretful daytimes & nights. The misquitoes almost eat us up. *I am sure that there will be no necessity for me to go down cellar to eat plumbs this fall.* Do you know what this means? . . .[17] This is a beautiful evening. How I wish you were here. We would have a nice walk. . . .

> Yours ever
> Lizzie

Little Rock, Ark., July 2d, 1864.

My [Dear] Libbie:

Have not heard from you since my last writing. Am getting anxious. The mails are kept back on account of the rebel blockade on White river. Shelby with a battery and 1800 men occupied Clarendon for several days, destroying one gun-boat and completely stopping navigation on White river until he was driven off by our forces under Gen. Carr. We have had no mail for several days in consequence.

Kate's health problems in the winter of 1863 and had been under his care for his broken leg in January 1864.

15. The caravan was Mabie's Grand Menagerie, which staged a performance on June 25, 1864. See the advertisement in the *Hastings Independent,* 16 June 1864. John A. Moulton's murder was reported in the *Hastings Independent,* 9 June 1864. The article states he was murdered by guerillas. He had been a sergeant in Company F, Seventh Minnesota, but was discharged February 16, 1864, for a promotion to lieutenant in the Sixty-seventh Regular U.S. Colored Infantry. Military records do not confirm his death or his discharge from the Sixty-seventh. The article suggests, however, the fear of Confederate threats to kill white officers of black regiments.

16. Lizzie refers to the bloody fighting from the Battle of the Wilderness on May 5 through Cold Harbor on June 3.

17. Lizzie's mention of not needing to eat plums in the cellar seems to be a coded way to tell Madison that she was not pregnant. She predicts, however, that his newly married sister Sarah is expecting. Her pregnancy is confirmed in the Bowlers' letters of August 7, 10, and 21 and September 11.

Marmaduke with artillery and several thousand men is now reported to be at St Charles. If this be so, we shall get no more mail until he is driven away and the river opened to navigation again.[18]

... I am trying to get the photographs of all my brother officers of the 3d Regt. Last Monday I went down to Pine Bluff when I saw the Regt once more. While there I was three days in the Hospital with the ague. Saw Robt Poor, Willie Calahan, and Ed King.[19] They are well. Eugene, Pettibone and everybody else you know are well. The Regt. has very hard work now—picketing and working on fortifications. Snakes are plenty there. Alligators too. Robt. Terrill, Co "G," came near dying from the bite of a moccasin [snake] while asleep [in] his tent.

[I] have heard from brother Joseph. He is in Co. "K,": 11th Maine Infty, 10th Army Corps, under Butler. He was at Bermuda Hundreds when he wrote. In one fight his Regt lost 100 men and one-third their officers killed and wounded....[20]

> Truly, your hubbie,
> Madison.

Rose Hill July 3rd 1864

My Ever dear husband

... It is Sunday morning & I am going to Sabbath school so I have but a few moments to write, for I want to put it in the office so it will go on to-nights mail. I rec'd yours of the 15th last Monday. I think when you wrote you felt rather sarcastic if you really think I would do as you speak of there. I think you had better try & find some of those southern girls that wouldn't be so willful. Well, I will stop writing about weaning babies & talk of something more sensible.

Tomorrow will be the 4th. I wonder what you will be doing. I expect to stay where I am as beaux are scarce. I saw a notice in the Pioneer that the 3rd Regt

18. For military activity in Arkansas in the late spring and summer of 1864, see Sutherland, "1864," 126–34. For more on Confederate generals Joseph Shelby and John S. Marmaduke, see Warner, *Generals in Gray*, 274 and 212, respectively.

19. From Nininger, William Callahan, Robert Poor, and Edward King were all mustered into Company F in February 1864 when the company was on furlough and engaged in recruiting. For disease and medical care in Arkansas in 1864, see Gillett, *The Army Medical Department*, 249.

20. Joseph Bowler joined the Eleventh Maine Infantry, Company K, after serving in the Twenty-second Maine. He wrote to Madison on June 7, 1864, explaining that he had reenlisted. From May 17 to June 14, the Eleventh Maine was at Bermuda Hundred, Virginia, as part of the Petersburg campaign. See Joseph S. Bowler to James Madison Bowler, 7 June 1864, Bowler Papers; and www.state.me.us/sos/arc/archives/military/civilwar/11meinf.htm.

would be home some time during the month. I was to Hastings a few days ago and sat again for my picture. I guess I have a good negative this time. I tried hard enough, for I stood nine times. . . .

Baby is well. She has but two teeth, yet she can kiss & pat her hand & cut up all kinds of performances. She grows prettier every day & grows to look more like you every one says. The rest of the folks are well & all send their love to you. Aunt Sarah had a letter from Am a few days ago. He was at Paducah, just going to march. He knew not where. . . .

> Ever yours
> Lizzie . . .

Little Rock, Ark., July 8th, 1864.

My Dear Lizzie:

. . . I wrote to you about a week ago, enclosing photographs of Capts. Vanstrum and Webster. . . . In this I enclose photograph of Capt. J. L. Hodges, Co. "K," 3d Minn. Be sure and get a dozen more of mine, if Mr. Beach can make good ones. The last half-dozen wre poorly taken. The Lieut. Taylor, whom you met on the boat last spring, is now Captain.[21] You have his picture. . . . Lieut. Pettibone is here on business, and I shall be able to send your note to Robt. Poor in a day or two. I saw Robt. last week at Pine Bluff. He was well. If anything is "the matter" with Rose I can find out when I see Eugene. If I do I will let you know. By the way, you have not kept me posted in regard to your-self. Send me as many of your photographs as you have to spare when you get them. Will Govette is getting better very slowly. He sends his regards to you. I was in to see him to-day. He comes over to my camp occasionally when the sun is clouded. . . .

> Truly your husband,
> Madison.

Little Rock, Ark., July 10th, 1864.
(Sunday.)

My Dear Lizzie:

. . . You ask "how I live and how I get along with my darkies." Well, my private quarters consists of a Wall Tent, in shape like a small house—nine feet square,

---

21. The *Hastings Independent* extolled the talents of photographer E. A. Beach on September 29, 1864. His family was listed in the 1865 census of Hastings. Isaac Taylor was commissioned as captain of Company H in April 1864.

four or five feet high at the eaves, and eight or nine at the ridge-pole. The frame consists of two light posts and one light cross pole over which the tent is stretched and stayed by ropes and small stakes or pins. Over the tent is stretched a "fly" conforming to the roof of the tent, only it is a little higher at the eaves. This makes the roof double—less likely to leak—cooler in the sun and a very little warmer in the shade. The entrance is through an opening at one end, extending from the bottom nearly to the top. Here the cloth overlaps and closes by tying with strings, like a strawtick somewhat. On the left side as you enter is my bed, consisting of a mattress and two wool blankets stretched on a low, pine bedstead. Along the right side is another occupied by Lieut. Gustafson, who, by the way, is suffering with fever and ague while I am writing this. Opposite the entrance stands a table with two drawers in which may be found brushes, corubs, tincture of myrrh, books, one pipe—*not mine*—and divers and sundry other traps.[22] Three chairs—strayed from some secesh habitation—make up the sum total of the furniture unless a very prongy bush, used as wardrobe, may be considered as furniture. In front of the tent is an awning of bushes, closed on the sunshiny sides, which renders it quite agreeable to those who do not like too much exposure to the hot sun. Close round also stand several friendly oaks, casting their shade over the tent. Such is my present habitation. Can you see it in imagination?

On the immediate right of my tent stands another Wall tent occupied by Lieut. Jno. E. Jenks—you saw him and his wife on the boat—and used as Hd Qrs. Lieut. Jenks is Adjutant.[23] About thirty feet in front of these is a row of wall tents occupied by the rest of the officers. Beyond these are the tents of the men about one hundred and twenty in all, and shaped just like the roof of a house; quite steep, but without walls. The walls of the Wall tent can be rolled and fastened up to the eaves making it quite cool in warm weather. I mess with Lieut. Evander Sullivan, my Quartermaster. "Uncle Alfred," a colored man, cooks for us—bacon, ham, pork, beef, potatoes, beans, hominy, rice, bread, butter, coffee, tea, dried fruit, &c., with ocasionally a pie or nice rich pudding, which Alfred manages to trade for with a colored girl who predominates in the neighboring kitchen of Mr. Hanger. This is, however, all unknown to "massa."

In regard to the darkies, I get along well with them. We have drills and dress parade every day. They take hold of music readily, and we already have a good martial Band. Abner—Ottos old servant, whom I tried at Hastings to get for

22. Tincture of myrrh is an antiseptic mixture.

23. John E. Jenks had been a private in Company A, Third Minnesota. In the 112th U.S. Colored Infantry, he was a first lieutenant and adjutant. See cwss, www.itd.nps.gov/cwss/soldiers.htm.

Mr. Caleff, is one of the drummers in the band. Recruiting now is very slow. But little can be done until the army moves again, which may not be until about the 1st of Sept. We hope, however, to fill up four companies soon, as we lack but few men, which will entitle us to have a Lieut. Col. mustered.[24]

I am rejoiced to know that your health improves, even though it be but little. You must straighten up, pluck up courage and take exercise, if you have to go as far as *twenty rods* from the house.... Kiss Birdie for me. Does she show any signs of going alone yet? ...

> Ever your
> Madison.

Rose Hill July 10th 1864

My dear Madison

Tis again Sunday & I must write to my absent husband.... I am seated by the table in the kitchen writing. Do is seated just behind me reading. Papa & Aunt Sarah are in the other rooms reading & last but not the least (in size) is up to Knapps....[25] I have never told you that our folks have got the front room plastered & the kitchen papered.

Oh! I must tell you what a beautiful rain we have had, but the thunder & wind that came with it was not very beautiful. Everything looks more as if it would live & grow....

The rastberries are very pleanty this year. Do you get any down there? If not, I wish I could send you a dish with some nice cream such as my Jenny gives. If I could enjoy the thought that I should have my husband with me this winter in a home of our own, what pride I would take in fixing things. But I suppose I shall have to wait till the time comes.

How is your leg? Does it trouble you any more?

Mr. Donnelly has been having trouble since he went to Washington, so Aldrich writes to Case. He has had two trials for some of his rogery....[26]

24. For difficulties with recruiting black soldiers, see Glatthaar, *Forged in Battle*, 61–70. For Uncle Alfred's identity and the Third Minnesota's recruiting of black soldiers, see Larson, "Private Alfred Gales," 274–83.

25. Lizzie refers to Reuben and Emily Knapp, a couple in their thirties who lived in Nininger.

26. Cyrus Aldrich was a Minneapolis Republican who had tried to secure a Senate nomination when Ignatius Donnelly was lieutenant governor. Donnelly reluctantly cast the final ballot that lost Aldrich the nomination. Aldrich must have corresponded with James R. Case, a Nininger mill owner and influential businessman. Donnelly did have trouble in Washington, D.C., as a member of the House of Representatives. He voted

You cant think what a smart little thing baby is getting to be, but she gets pretty spunky (like her dady) some times, & then I have to whip her just the way I am going to serve him when he comes home to stop, when he gets angry and throws the books about. . . .

> Yours ever
> Lizzie . . .

Little Rock, Ark., July 17th, 1864.[27]
(Sunday afternoon.)

My Dear Wife:

. . . I have been so lonely to-day, all day that I have been at a loss what to do with [myself]. I feel so lonely . . . at [last I] resort to writing for company [not] because I have anything wor[th sayi]ng. Since dinner I accidently [came] upon the June number of Harper's Magazine, and have just got through with what the titles suggest to me as worth reading. . . .

What do you read nowadays? Of course you retain your usual aversion to the *Home Journal,* and do not read that. I presume that your oldest daughter takes so much of your att[ention] that you have but little time [given] to reading. Last Monday I went to [Pine Blu]ff, saw Gen. Andrews. Tichenor, and [I] stayed three days, returned to Little [Rock,] have been sick ever since. I [am] now enjoying a huge boil on my ch[eek]. Recruiting goes on quite slowly. By order of the War Department our regt. is designated as the "112th U.S. Colored Inf'y."[28] Pretty tall figures. . . .

> Ever your loving hubbie,
> Madison . . .

July 22, 1864

My Ever Dear Madison

After waiting patiently nearly three weeks, I got a letter from you this morning. Comparing dates with your last, I found they were written sixteen days apart. Can it be that my absent husband is getting so negligent that he only writes once in two or three weeks when he knows that I am waiting so anxiously to hear, or

---

against Elihu Washburne, a powerful and well-connected Illinois Republican, as Speaker of the House. Washburne's brother in Minneapolis organized a whispering campaign in March 1864 to destroy Donnelly's reputation. He accused Donnelly of shady business dealings, treachery, and swindling. See Ridge, *Ignatius Donnelly,* 70–71, 75, 81.

27. This letter has a large hole in the left center.

28. The 112th U.S. Colored Infantry was organized in Little Rock from April through November 1864 and served on post duty there. In April 1865 it transferred to the 113th U.S. Colored Infantry. See www.civilwararchive.com/Unreghst/uncolinf4.htm.

has one of your letters gone astray? Do, do, write often for you do not know how uneasy I feel when I do not hear from you. Oh, this awful war! What would I give if it were only ended.

Baby is quite unwell. She is cutting four teeth. Has them most through. She has bad the diarrhea now for ten or twelve days, which makes [her] very fretful & she is loseing flesh very fast. I have to be very cautious about her diet. The weather is very warm as has been, [but] not warm neither for it's *hot*. I [don't] remember of seeing so warm a day as it was last Monday.

Piercy is down to Nininger on a twenty days furlough. Him & Mary Case & her daughter was here & spent the day one day this week. Tis quite a pretty baby. Piercy's health is very poor. I think it has not done him any good being in the army.

If young men only knew how it sounded they would not take up with the habit of blasphemy as most all soldiers do. When you come home we must have a photographic album for our photographs. . . . You have never told me whether you intended to come home this fall or not. Tell me in your next. How many recruits have you for your Regt? Aunt Sarah is here. She is in a great stew, for the news has just come that the 7th has just been in a battle. . . .[29]

> From your loving wife
> Mrs. J. M. Bowler

{top margin first page} P.S. *If this reaches you before the 3rd Regt comes home, send pa a little black boy. He wants one.* . . .[30]

Rose Hill July 29, 1864

My dear Madison

. . . I can scarcely hold my head off from the pillow I have the sick headache so badly. The weather is dreadful warm here this summer. To-day is enough to melt any one & yesterday was worse. Oh dear, I will be glad when cold weather comes.

Baby was real sick yesterday but is better to-day. The warm weather almost kills her, though she is not near so fleshy as she was when you left.

I keep writing to you. Do not know whether you get the letters or not. I have not rec'd any letter from you since my last, which was written nine days ago. Some times I almost think that my absent hubbie is learning to forget me. Can it be that

---

29. Aunt Sarah Caleff's adopted son, Amon McMullen, was in the Seventh Minnesota, so she would have been upset.

30. Samuel Caleff probably hoped that he could secure farm labor from a freed slave while his nephew and son-in-law were not there to help farm. For Northern and Southern whites' requests for black labor during the war, see Forbes, *African American Women during the War*, 60-61.

I displeased you so by not going to Little Rock that you cannot forget it? I cannot think of any other reason why my hubbie that used to write every week & sometimes twice that now I only get one letter in four or five weeks. Ma is very lame this summer. Her feet & hands swell very much. I do not know the cause. The rest of the folks are well. Ma wants you to write to her.

. . . The farmers are all busy harvesting. They have cut all the grain in the big field in front of our house. It looks beautiful. . . . How is your leg? Does it trouble you any now? I am afraid you will stay down there & have the ague till you ruin your health. Now do write often, for I feel very anxious about you. . . .

> from your loving wife
> Lizzie

P.S. Try & get Col Andrews photograph. I should like to see it. . . .

> Little Rock, Ark., Aug. 7th, 1864
> (Sunday)

My Dear Lizzie:

. . . There seems to be some trouble in my company, I learn. Eugene Stone and Nick Obrien have retired to the ranks and Bill Allison has been reduced. Jasper Martin is Orderly Sergt. now. . . .[31]

Libby, I have got reduced down to the two shirts which you made me while at home, and cannot get any here that suit me so well as these. Besides, prices are very exhirbitant here. Now I am going to ask you to purchase cloth and get somebody to make me two or three more. I do not want you to do it. My only object is to get good shirts at a reasonable rate. Everything is high priced here. . . .

> Ever your loving hubbie,
> Madison.

> Nininger Aug 10 1864
> Wednesday evening

My dear Madison

I have just got my little charge to bed. I will try & scribble you a few lines. . . . Piercy left for Ft Snelling last Thursday. He is very miserable. I do not think he will live long if he does not get better soon. I assure you that Piercy has not gained any thing by way of morals since he joined the army. It makes my blood run cold to listen to the [oaths] as they flow from his mouth. That is one request that I have to make, that you never allow yourself to get into the habit. I do think it an

---

31. There was a Joseph Martin, not Jasper, from Cannon Falls, Goodhue County, in Company F.

awful practice beside the wickedness that it is.[32] He was very anxious to get a letter from you. I met Mr. Donnelly yesterday. He thinks your daughter is splendid, that Maine & New Brunswick together done pretty well that time. He has got his nomination as representative for the next year after a hard struggle. He did not come to see [his sister-in-law] Mrs Favior till he had because in Minn three weeks, he has so much engaged in his political campaign. . . .

(Thursday Morning)

. . . Everything is suffering terribly from the drought again. The corn, potatoes, beans, & all other kind [of] vegetables are dying. The discription of your home was very interesting to me. Wish I could pop in sometimes & have a chat with you. How did you like your photographs? I hope [so]. They were taken to please you. . . . Give my love to Mr Will. When is the 3rd Regt coming home? . . . You ask a question in one of your letters. I will now answer you as long as you are so anxious to know. My reasons for wanting you home are numerous & some times that among the rest.[33] Now I have answered you candidly as you asked me too. Good By for the present.

Lizzie

. . . I think it a first rate story but you must find something more substantial to read sabbaths than those foolish stories. Do you know it or else I shall begin to think that you are not a good boy.

{top margin last page} Mama's lameness is not any better. Baby is very well now.

Duvalls Bluff, Ark., August 14th, 1864

My Dear Lizzie:

. . . I came over from Little Rock this morning with the 3rd Minn. Veterans, on their way home. Upon my arrival here I took a chill and my fever has just let up, so that I can improve the few moments left in writing to you.[34]

32. For attitudes about oaths and cursing, see Lowry, *The Story the Soldiers Wouldn't Tell*, chap. 4.

33. Madison's indirect question on July 8 was whether Lizzie was pregnant again. Lizzie hints here that intimacy and the possibility of a second child were some of her reasons for wanting Madison to return. The last part of this paragraph and the next were written perpendicular across the top of the first page.

34. Andrews discusses the late furlough: "When, on Sunday, August 14th, Companies B, C, E, G, H and I arrived at Devall's Bluff *en route* home on veteran furlough, their

I hope that you will not do me the injustice to believe that I would neglect to write you on account of being picqued at your decision in relation to your coming to Little Rock. I have written to you often. I do not think one-half of sixteen days have ever elapsed without my writing, except perhaps when I went to Pine Bluff, when I could not send a letter if I had been well enough to write it, as no boat returned to Little Rock for a week or so. My letters must have gone astray, or been tampered with. I am very sorry indeed to have you and baby so sick. . . . Do take care of yourself and baby in the best possible manner. . . .

> Ever your loving hubbie—
> Madison.

P.S. I send $100.00 by Lieut. Pettibone. Should he call, make my house pleasant to him. . . .

Nininger Minn. Aug 15, 1864
Tuesday evening

My dear Madison

To-night is so beautiful that I must spend some of it in doing something else besides sleep. Thinking that a letter is as aceptable as anything I can do for you, I will scratch you a few lines. . . . I do hope that you will continue to think that home is the place for you. Till you come, I do not like to say anything to persuade you about it but you can easily imagine what my wishes are. When I read the many accounts of the almost sure destiny of all officers of black Regt's. [then] I can almost know what yours will be. . . .[35]

Victoria has been quite sick for two or three days but is quite well now. Her teeth are troubl[ing] her very much. She has got quite thin & I am glad of it, for she is a great deal smarter then when she was so fat. Can creep all over the floor, has lots of funny little actions, is a great singer. I wish you could see her. I believe you are trying to pok fun at me about Mary's baby. Her baby is rather pretty. But I do think Vic is full as good looking. . . . I was a plumbing to-day. Got nearly a bucket full of nice ones. There was a splendid rain a few days ago which makes

---

situation was pathetic. Many of the poor fellows were so lean and pale that their own mothers could scarcely have recognized them." Many of the new recruits, as well as veterans like Madison, fell ill with malaria during the spring and summer of 1864. See in particular Dr. A. C. Wedge, the regiment's surgeon, in Andrews, "Narrative of the Third Regiment," 174-75.

35. For the Confederate policy toward captured white officers in command of black troops, see Donald et al., *The Civil War and Reconstruction*, 344.

everything wear a different aspect. It is very sickly here this summer. I was real sick for three or four days with the dysentary but am well now & Do is sick. Ma is not much better. Her feet are very lame. . . .

> From your loving wife
> Lizzie . . .

Nininger Minn. Aug 21, [1864]
Sabbath evening

My dear Madison

. . . I was up to Spring Lake to meeting this afternoon, listened to a splendid sermon from Mr. Humphrey.[36] How I wish you were here to go to meeting with me. I cannot nor do not enjoy any thing when you are away. Sometimes I almost envy some of the girls when I see them going about with their husbands & think that they might take a turn while you come home after spending three long years in the army. I know that I ought to be thankful that things ar[e] as well as they are while thousands have been cut down by sickness & sword, that you are still spared unharmed. But my lonely [heart] will rebel sometimes. Mr. Petibone's family got news of the death of their son who was in the 6th Regt a few days ago. Was sick but a short time, I believe.[37] Baby can creep all over the room now. Do not think she will walk when she is a year old. She's so heavy. She is well of the summer complaint now. She has had it for the last six weeks. Hers had two quite sick spells with it.[38] They are having quite exciting times here about the draft, or rather making up money to buy substitutes with (or rather recruits). Sixteen hundred dollars is the sum required, I believe. . . .[39] Prices here now are terrible, sheeting

36. Mr. W. H. Humphrey also preached at Sunday schools at the university. See *Hastings Conserver,* 26 April 1864.

37. From Red Wing, thirty-two-year-old John H. Pettibone was mustered into Company F, Sixth Minnesota, on August 15, 1862, and died not quite two years later on August 2, 1864, in Helena, Arkansas. Based on the 1860 census, he would have left a young daughter and a wife, Mary.

38. The summer complaint was a common term for diarrhea, which was often caused by the heat's promoting bacterial growth on food.

39. John H. Case states that war meetings were held in the schoolhouse in Nininger to raise money to pay for new recruits' bounties, which prevented Nininger men from being drafted. See Biographical Sketches, P–W, folder 2, Case Papers. The implementation of the draft prompted the *Hastings Independent* and the *Hastings Conserver* to track enlistments in Dakota County between January 1864 and September 1864. For the first draft call, the quotas for enlistment were 212 and 36 for Hastings and Nininger, respectively,

cotton $1.00 per yard, Calico 50, cotton batting 80 c pound. Spools that used to be five cents apiece are now cost 15 & 20, Tea $1.60, $1.75 Sugar, 3½ for a dollar & very poor at that.

I think if this war does not end pretty soon & that failure of crops that the people in Minn. will begin to feel it. The Indians are getting quite terrible. Some above Mankato again. The papers are giving it to Father Abraham for not hanging all those Indians that were convicted. By the way who are you going to vote for for president? Be sure & tell me.[40] Have you ever thought any thing about sending that cotton home that we were talking about, or would it cost more then we could get it here for? I have two quilts to quilt but cannot think of paying such a price for badding. . . .

> {*written perpendicular over the front page*} *Ed & Hannah are living there in the same old way. I do not know whether they will make a match or not. Mrs Moulton is there now. She has not heard anything from John. George is in Idaho.*[41]

Good night Ever yours
Lizzie . . .

Little Rock, Ark., August 24th, 1864.

My Dear Lizzie:

. . . I presume that the 3d Reg. Veterans are at home by this time, and enjoying their furlough. They deserve to enjoy themselves, for they have had a very hard time this summer. The balance of the Regiment, now at Pine Bluff, have been mounted and equipped as cavalry since the veterans left for home. Eugene writes

---

and then increased to 260 and 42, respectively. These were met by the end of May 1864. *Hastings Independent,* 28 January 1864 and 2 June 1864; *Hastings Conserver,* 24 May 1864. A second draft call was issued during the summer, and intense recruiting took place to meet Hastings's quota of 88 men and Nininger's quota of 13 by the end of August 1864 (*Hastings Conserver,* 30 August 1864).

40. Abraham Lincoln commuted the sentence of all but thirty-nine Dakota in 1862, a very unpopular action in Minnesota. Lincoln also ran for reelection in 1864. Lizzie seems curious about Madison's voting in the November elections, since she could not vote—passage of the Nineteenth Amendment being over fifty-five years away.

41. In her June 26 letter, Lizzie mentioned a report that John Moulton had been murdered. His mother had heard from his first lieutenant by July 10 that John had been captured, but his death had not yet been confirmed. George was another son. The January 21, 1864, *Hastings Independent* commented that Idaho gold fever had lured some men to go to Idaho. In his September 30, 1863, letter to Madison, John Moulton wrote that George was "still chaceing up gold mines being now in Idaho Territory."

me that Rob't. Poor was very sick in the Hospital, hardly expected to recover. I have not heard from there since Eugene wrote. When I hear I will write again so that Mrs. Poor may know how he gets along.

I am very anxious to get another letter from home, to learn how you and baby get along as you were both sick at the date of your last letter. I hope to hear of your recovery. Do take every pains to preserve your health. Take sufficient outdoor exercise and proper diet; and do not work hard enough or long enough to become fatigued. *Now regard my request* IN THIS RESPECT if in no other.

I have broken my ague again, but how long it will stay broken is a question for time to determine. I am feeling quite well now, though I am quite weak, and do not seem to gain much strength. I am trying to diet on vegetables, but their scarcity renders it difficult to obtain them. I bathe occasionally, too. That would be good for you.[42]

Will Govette and his company have been mustered out, and have gone home to St. Louis. Will was glad to get away. Another company of the 22d Ohio is being mustered out to-day....[43]

> Ever your loving husband,
> Madison.

Little Rock, Ark., Aug. 27th, 1864.

My Dear Lizzie:

... I am much rejoiced to learn that you and Birdie are so much improved in health. I sincerely hope that you will not get sick again. Am sorry to hear that Piercy is so weakly after his three years honorable service. I hope that he too may recover his wonted health. When I left him in Tenn., he was quite strong and healthy.

I cannot promise you in regard to going home next winter, to stay. My present intention is not to go; yet I may go out of the service before that time. "There is no telling what a day may bring forth." I do not know but that the condition of my health may compel me to resign. The ague still troubles me occasionally. Cool weather may drive it away. My leg does not trouble me much now, except when I walk too much. While fresh I can walk without limping.

I received a letter from Amon yesterday. He was in Adams Hospital at Memphis—pretty well, though not able to march with his Regt. Since the date of his

42. For health regimens, see Walters, *American Reformers,* chap. 7.
43. Having completed their original three-year enlistment, these units did not reenlist, as Madison's regiment had.

letter—Aug. 17th—Forest has been into Memphis and captured quite a number of the soldiers who were in the Hospitals.[44] The chances are that Amon was one of the captured, he not being wholly unable to march. I trust, however, that he is all right. I presume that Aunt Sarah hears from him quite often.

There are fears of an attack here—at least Gen. Steele fears it. But I do not think there is much danger. The rebels made an attack at Ft Smith, up the Ark. river, not long since, but were repulsed. They also attacked and captured some of our cavalry on the railroad between here and Duvall's Bluff, this week. There is great apathy in this Department. Nothing at all will be done until Sherman gains such a victory as will enable him to spare troops to come here, or until we have a change of commanders here. . . .[45]

> Truly your hubbie
> Madison.

Nininger Minn. Sept. 2nd 1864

My Ever dear Madison

. . . You cannot imagine how it makes me feel to know that you are down there dying by inches with the ague & ruining your constitution forever & yet say that you are going to remain in the army as long as the war lasts. You cannot know what my feelings were when I read your letter, for I thought that you would certainly come home some time during the fall or winter, & I do not see any more prospect of the war ending for the next three years then I did three years ago, nor half so much. My prayer to God is that you will never be permitted to lead that Regt of negrows into battle, for I feel well assured what your fate will be if you should. I have always said that I would never try to hinder you from doing what you think is your duty, but I will try and influence you from doing that you do not think is your duty, & I want you to really think the matter over whether it is your duty to spend all the best of your life away from those who love you best

44. For Confederate cavalry commander Nathan Bedford Forrest's attack on Memphis, see Wyeth, *The Life of Nathan Bedford Forrest*, 469–77.

45. For military activities in Arkansas in late summer and early fall 1864, see Sutherland, "1864," 134–42. Andrews comments, "During the summer the enemy occasionally showed himself near Pine Bluff." Clearly, officers in the Third Minnesota felt like Pine Bluff had been unhealthy for their men and their actions there and later at Devall's Bluff not crucial to the war effort. Andrews says relatively little about their time there. See "Narrative of the Third Regiment," 175. General Sherman had been moving toward Atlanta in the late summer of 1864. After outmaneuvering Confederate general John Bell Hood, Sherman took the city on September 3.

and sighs for your presence ever[y] moment of her life time or to come home & get a good little house & live happy as we should while others who have had the comforts of home take their turn in the battle field.[46]

Baby is better then when I last wrote but is very poorly yet. We have tried everything but find nothing to stop her dysentery, but her last tooth that she is cutting came through to day. I am in hopes she will soon get well. Now she cuts her teeth very hard I have not had a good nights sleep in nine nights. Ma's feet are a little better she thinks. The Dr gave her some medicine when he came to see baby which she thinks helped her. The rest of us are all well. I have not felt so well as I do now for a year. What do you want done with your field that you want it ploughed this fall?[47] When you write, tell me what you wish done with the whole establishment. I believe Albert talks of moving to Nininger this fall but do not know for certain yet. I will have the shirts ready to send by Herman Pettibone with your coat & gloves.

... Is Will left the army for good or is he home on a furlough? If so *how long is it?*[48] Did he get my letter I wrote to him?

What is all the boys get reduced to the ranks for & specially Eugene Stone? ...

... Well, it is now after ten oclock. I must stop. I was not in earnest about what I said about going to Little Rock, but I did feel bad at not receiving any letter.

> Believe me, ever your loving wife
> Lizzie ...

Little Rock, Ark., Sept. 7th, 1864.

My Dear Lizzie:

... Think I have not answered [your letter]; though I believe I wrote the day before I rec'd it. The ague mixes my head up so that I cannot remember anything hardly. Your account of baby's actions is very interesting. I think surely that she must take after me, since you say she is quite a singer already. No doubt she will grow more like me as she learns to sing better. I hope she will get over with the trouble with her teeth pretty soon, and flesh up again. I should think it about time for her to begin to learn to walk. Am sorry to hear of Dolly's being sick. It

---

46. For Union women's growing reluctance to support the war in 1863 and 1864, see Bell, "A Family Conflict," 151–56; and Silber, *Daughters of the Union*, 130–31. For family members questioning white soldiers' decisions to take commissions in the U.S. Colored Infantry regiments, see Glatthaar, "Duty, Country, Race, and Party," 344–45.

47. Lizzie probably meant "wanted" rather than "want it."

48. Lizzie triple-underlined "how long is it" in her letter.

seems that you are all taking turns at being sick. Am glad to hear that you had rain in season to save something in the line of crops. Did you raise any flowers this season? How did our garden produce? Did Mr. Poor leave my apple trees and currant bushes? I should like to be there to go plumming with you. The soldiers are so much plentier here than the fruit [so it] is that everything gets gobbled up in double quick time.[49] Blackberries are not so plenty here as in other parts of the south. There are few peaches and apples in the market. You must not give yourself any uneasiness on account of my being with a colored Regiment. There is, in my opinion, little danger of my Regiments being engaged for many months yet. Gen. Steele fears an attack here; but nobody else seems much concerned about it....[50]

> Truly your hubbie,
> Madison...

Little Rock, Ark., Sept. 11th, 1864.

My Dear Lizzie:

... You seem to be possessed with an increased desire for me to go home. I feel that I am not treating you fairly by staying so long away from you; but hitherto you have given your consent, and left me freely to my own choice. I wish very much to see you and be with you. I can hardly express how greatly I desire it. But, at the same time, it has been my intention all along to remain in the army until the end of this war. I cannot disregard your expressed wish in a matter of so much right and reason on your part; yet I do not wish to be compelled to leave the army until I can see fully and clearly that we have a country in which we can live in peace and security—an undivided country and a good government.[51] Without these I would not live in the country—I should leave it, *sure* I think a few months hence will give us much light. If the copperhead ticket should be successful, the country I fear would be ruined. If the Union ticket shall succeed, and Abraham Lincoln, or any other good union man shall be elected president, the rebels will then see no hope. Besides I think the two great campaigns in Georgia and in Virginia must come to some definite result before many months. At Atlanta the armies are in such position that a day may decide the result. It may take

49. For Confederate guerillas and Union troops exhausting civilian food supplies in Arkansas, see Sutherland, "1864," 141–42.

50. For lack of substantial Confederate threat, see Sutherland, "1864," 139–42.

51. For justifications to remain in the army, see McPherson, *For Cause and Comrades,* 134–38.

weeks or months longer to decide in Virginia. But should we be successful in beating these two great armies before election, there would be literally no opposition to the re-election of the Union ticket; and no doubt about the safety of the government need be feared.[52] I am surprised that you should ask me how I intend to vote. You ought to know me better than that by this time. Do you think I am in earnest in staying in the army or just in fun? I shall vote the Union ticket if I live and am permitted to vote at all. Any person—kin or former friend—who shall vote for the nominee of the Chicago convention, I shall regard with contempt, as much my enemy as an armed rebel.[53]

I was at Duvall's Bluff yesterday and day before Maj. Gen. Mower's division saw Capt Kennedy, Lt Collins and Patch, Joe Bottomley, Arthur Fish, Frank Morey, &c&c. John King, George Wheeler, and Amon are sick at Memphis. Their Division will reach Brownsville to-day. There is going to be an expedition sent out somewhere about here soon.[54] It is just a year ago to-day that we marched into Little Rock.

In five days more baby will be a year old. Am glad to hear that she is well. Does she ride any in her carriage? . . . I wish the draft would come off and take every man in Nininger who is able to fight. . . . Please make up your mind to let me stay in the army until I take a notion to go home. . . .

> Ever your loving hubbie,
> Madison.

52. Madison refers to General Sherman's troops, who had captured Atlanta in early September. Grant's troops were locked in a siege at Petersburg, Virginia. This would last until April 1865. Madison was correct about Union military success affecting voters' opinions about the presidential election.

53. The Chicago convention was the Democratic convention, which selected former Union general George B. McClellan as the Democratic Party's presidential candidate. See Waugh, *Reelecting Lincoln,* chap. 21. For soldiers' attitudes about Democratic supporters, see McPherson, *For Cause and Comrades,* 144–45; and Davis, *Lincoln's Men,* 202–3.

54. All of the men Madison mentions were from Dakota County, mostly Hastings, and in Company F, Seventh Minnesota, with one exception: John King was captain of Company G, Fifth Minnesota. Carley states, "In the late summer 1864, Confederate Gen. Sterling Price and a force of twelve thousand launched a campaign to take St. Louis and invade Illinois. The Union army gathered in Arkansas to move into Missouri and intercept him. The 5th, 7th, 9th, and 10th Minnesota Regiments were part of the Sixteenth Corps under Gen. A. J. Smith assigned to chase Price. Leaving on September 17th the army marched from central Arkansas to Cape Girardeau, Missouri, proceeded up the Mississippi to St. Louis by boat, and marched to the Kansas border, skirmishing with Price as they went." Price left Missouri at the end of October, and these regiments returned to St. Louis in November. See Carley, *Minnesota in the Civil War,* 162.

Little Rock, Ark., Sept. 16th, 1864.[55]

My Dear Lizzie:

. . . I am rejoiced to learn that your health is so much improved. You must use every precaution to preserve it. I hope that baby will recover her usual good health, now that she has done cutting teeth for the present. I did not wish you to make those shirts for me; I only wanted you to *get them made.* It will be far too much for you to do while you have baby to care for, especially when she is sick. I am truly surprised at the position you have taken lately. You seem to be wholly absorbed in the one idea of getting me out of the army and getting me home. While I feel grateful to you for your affectionate interest in my welfare, I must at the same time, chide you a little for your lack of confidence in the ultimate triumph of our cause. I am very sorry indeed that you should hear to the voice and clamor of those arround you, who would *never* lift a hand for anything but their own selfish interest. I do not claim to be very patriotic—in fact I think I have done less than I might and ought to have done—but when I come to weigh the matter with a view to leaving the army, I find it out of the question for me to do so. I did not enlist for fun or profit, and I do not stay now through any such motives. I want to see this rebellion *put down*; and I firmly believe that it will be; if not for ten years, it will in the end. I think, however, that the end is much nearer than we anticipate. Lizzie, do not permit yourself to make expressions or entertain thoughts in these trying times, which you will have occasion to regret hereafter. Do, for my sake, distinguish yourself from the doubting and the weak-kneed, by placing yourself quietly in the ranks with those who have naught to speak but words of encouragement and which will inspire confidence instead of sickening doubts.

As to Negro Regt's. you are unduly frightened. I have started to raise one and nothing but lack of ability shall deter me from it; and if I am ever offered the opportunity of leading it into battle I hope that I may be endowed with the nerve to do it without "fear and trembling."

{*written perpendicular over the first page*} *Do, Libby, look on the bright side of things. You cannot pain me more than by identifying yourself with those who are ever finding fault with the Government and who are ever expressing doubts about the issue of the contest. I do most heartily detest such incidences of human weakness. The more they doubt and grumble the more set I feel in my determination to keep from their midst until I can return and point to an emphatic*

55. Madison's September 12 letter is not included here. It was written on the back of a letter from his uncle James H. Bowler, Bangor, Maine, dated August 1864.

refutation of their doubts and fears, in the shape of a restored union. By all means,
Libby, do be a true union heroine.[56]

Madison . . .

Little Rock, Ark., Sept. 24th 1864.

My Dear Lizzie:

. . . I heard from Pine Bluff a few days ago. Robt Poor is dead. This will be hard news to his parents.[57] There is a painful rumor afloat here, that Liut. Pettibone is dead. I sincerely hope it may not prove true. It is quite sickly here now. Nearly all the men of the 3d Regt. who are on recruiting service with me, are sick. I trust to cool weather to benefit them. Liut. Otto Dreher has been promoted to Capt of Company "A." Lt. Jameson is 1st Lt. Co "F" and Orderly Sergt. Thos Hunter of Co "K," has been appointed 2d Liut. Co. "F."[58] There is much dissatisfaction in the Regt. on account of the way Col. Mattson makes promotions. He will get himself into trouble, I think.

You wish to know the length of Will Govette's furlough. Long enough, I guess, to give entire satisfaction, as it is for during the war.

Gen. Mowers division, including the 5th, 7th, 9th, & 10th Minn., is out on an expedition after the rebels under Price and Shelby. We expect to hear a good report from them soon. Quite a number of Minn. sick have arrived here, unfit to go on the search. Capt Hodges of the 3d, Supd't. of the Mil. Prison, had his wife here. She came day before yesterday.[59]

Write often. I am very anxious to hear about baby. . . . Do with our house and land just what you see fit. You know better than I do, as I am not there to see. Mr Poor owes $22.80 rent yet.

Truly your hubbie,
Madison.

56. For soldiers asking wives to be patriotic, see McPherson, *For Cause and Comrades*, 135–36.
57. Robert Poor had enlisted in February 1864. He died on August 24, 1864, at Pine Bluff, Arkansas. Robert Poor's parents were probably Martin and Louisa Poor, who had lived in Dakota County since the early 1850s. See Biographical Sketches, P–W, folder 2, Case Papers.
58. For these changes, see *Adjutant General*, 116–21.
59. For General Mowers's division's activities, see Folwell, *A History of Minnesota*, 305–7. Captain James L. Hodges's wife was Anna; they had three children under ten years old in 1860 and lived in Eyota, Olmsted County.

Little Rock, Ark., Sept. 27th 1864.

My Dear Lizzie:

... Am thankful for the photograph which [your letter] contained. Poor little Birdie, how she must have suffered. I sincerely hope that she will not be so sick again. Give her a kiss for me. I know you will give her the best kind of care. ...

You say that Mr. Poor wishes to rent the house for another year. I leave it entirely with you. I will only add, that I think it might be well to rent it until August or Sept. 1865, which would give us time to repair it a year from this time, which is, I think, as soon as we shall be able to use it. The lowest rate of rent we could take for the use of the house and land for one year would be $150.00. Or I would consent to take $125.00 for the use of both until Sept. 1, 1865. The house alone could be rented for $30.00 or $40.00 less than both. But do for the best; and I shall be satisfied.

I am in the officers Hospital. Have been here since the 23d. I had my last attack of fever and ague over three weeks ago. It was severe. Since then I have had diarrhea. About a week ago the Medical Director sent me here. I think I shall get strong again as cool weather comes on. Major Webster of the 3d, Capt. French of the 5th, Capt. Pratt, Capt Hall and Chaplain Edwards of the 7th, and Capt. E. H. Kennedy of the 10th are here sick.[60] I get good care and good treatment. My appetite is quite good—too good; for my disease requires careful diet. ...

Ever your loving husband,
Madison.

{side and top margins on first page} You ask how we feel about the election. I believe I told you my opinion in a former letter. The soldiers here will give their votes for Lincoln to one for McClellan, sure & probably a still greater majority. There are but two McClellan men among 47 officers in this Hospital. You mind what I advised you in a former letter. Do not fail to let those miserable copperheads understand which side of the fence you stand on.[61] Madison

60. For the status of medical care, see Shryock, "A Medical Perspective on the Civil War," 161–73; and Bollett, *Civil War Medicine*, 218–21. Madison lists Alpheus P. French, captain of Company I, Fifth Minnesota; Frank H. Pratt, captain of Company C, Thomas G. Hall, captain of Company E, and Elijah E. Edwards, chaplain, Seventh Minnesota; and Ebenzer H. Kennedy, captain of Company E, Tenth Minnesota. See cwss, www.itd.nps .gov/cwss/soldiers.htm.

61. For the soldiers' vote, see Waugh, *Reelecting Lincoln*, 348, 354–55.

Nininger Sep 28, 1864

My dear Madison

... Well, it seems that I have got to spend this winter without you and as many more as you think your duty to stay. If you will & must stay in the army I will give my consent for this winter, but I can never consent for you to spend another summer in such a place as you now occupy.

Madison, why do you talk to me so about my patriotism? I do not want to be any more patriotic then I now am. I have been willing to make almost any sacrifice to have the north gain her part in this awful contest. For three years you know I have waited patiently, have always tryed to look on the bright side. But "patience will cease to be a virtue" some times & how can one help it? As long as your health remains good, I did not feel as I now do. But now you are ruining your constitution by staying there, when if you were in some healthy climate you might soon regain your usual good health. You cannot expect me to love this country as you do, nor feel willing to sacrifice that that I would not be willing to sacrifice for my own country. Could I vote I would be just as anxious to vote for Lincoln as you are . . .[62]

But I will let this subject rest for the present. Time will tell how all these things will come out. You ask me if I do not shudder at the thought of my narrow escape in connection with Oliver. I do not. Had I ever been foolish enough to be Corwin's wife I bet we would have ended our day together without. He was like the husband I now have, loved his country better then he did his wife & he does not think much of either I guess.[63]

I do not know the reason that he left her, but folks say that it was her own & her peoples fault. I did not make those shirts alone. Minnie helped me. I have not had a chance to do much sewing because baby was sick. She has been so cross. She is cutting more teeth now. Thinks everything of her carriage & loves to ride in it. She does not walk alone yet but can shove a chair across the room. . . . I want you to excuse the letters that I send to you. They are all written so badly. I write altogether in the evenings & some times feel pretty sleepy and always in a hurry. I feel sleepy now but if you were here I would wake up and not go to sleep till three o'clock to-morrow morning. . . .

---

62. Lizzie was from New Brunswick, Canada. Ellipses are in the original.

63. Oliver Corwin lived in Nininger City in 1857. His wife is unidentified. For another wife frustrated with her husband's commitment to country, politics, and the military at the expense of his family, see Jabour, "'The Language of Love,'" 130-31.

{top margin of front page} Mr. Poor left a few currant bushes & a good many apple trees. Good Bye

    from your loving wife
    Lizzie

Little Rock, Ark., Oct. 2d, 1864.
(Sunday)

My Dear Lizzie:

. . . I had the pleasure of meeting Dr. Etheridge, of Hastings, this morning; also Mr. A. C. Dun from Farribault, and Allen Harmon of Minneapolis, Commissioners to receive the soldiers vote. Mr. Harmon used to be a neighbor of mine in Lee. I had a good long chat over old times. Capts Pratt and Kennedy have just left for Minn. I feel quite lonely on that account.

In a former letter to you I enclosed a silver half-dollar for Birdie. Did you get it? In this I enclose two little pieces of poetry. You can judge of their appropriateness to you and Birdie. I also enclose some leaves from a flower which grows or blossoms on a bush larger than the plum tree in Minn. The flower very much resembles the Hollyhock. The bush tree resembles the Thornbush. I do not know its name. We are getting very anxious to see a mail here once more. I feel sure that when Lieut. Pettibone returns I shall receive a letter from you, if I do not before. I expect to see him about the 10th. I presume he has had a good time at home. If it did not cost so outrageously I should be tempted to get a leave of absence. Everything is so costly here that it is about all one can do to live to say nothing of traveling. In this Hospital we have to pay $1.00 per day for poor board. I must try and raise enough to pay up for our land. How much is it? And when does it become due? There is no telling when we shall ever get any pay again here. We have but one paymaster, and he is out of money. . . .

    Ever your loving husband,
    Madison.

Little Rock, Ark.,
October 6th, 1864.

My Dear Lizzie:

Nothing to do but sit about in the Hospital and read; so I will while away an hour in writing to you. Guess you will get tired reading so many letters from me, especially as I have nothing interesting to write about. I am gaining strength every day—think I shall be able for duty soon. All the Minnesotians, but Major Webster and myself, have left the hospital, having been ordered to Memphis. It seems quite lonely since they left. Major Webster has been down with Rheumatism. I think he will resign.[64]

Capt. Hodges wife very kindly provides the sick Minnesotians here with an occasional basket of delicacies, which makes us feel that we are not entirely forgotten. They keep house in town. . . . (An ambulance has come to take us out to ride; so I will close for the present.)

(Sunday, Oct. 9)

I left off writing above, to go out riding. The next day Major Webster and myself rode on horseback two miles down to Capt Baker's, formerly of the 3d, but who is now running a cotton Plantation.[65] Mrs. Baker is with him. We had an excellent time—*and a good dinner.* Getting to be quite an epicure, am I not? . . . I also had the pleasure of voting for Abraham Lincoln, the commissioners having visited the Hospit'l. for the purpose of receiving our votes.

Lt. Pettibone has not arrived yet. I look for him sure by the 12th. The Hastings papers which you have sent by him, will be a treat to me; for I have not seen one this summer or fall. The coat, gloves, and shirts will come just in the nick of time— thanks to my faithful, loving wife. Never mind the high prices of goods. Buy whatever you need, as long as money holds out. As long as our health is spared there will be some way to provide money. If we come to want, kind Providence will provide for us in some manner, if we only do our duty.

You must not get discouraged because I do not go home. The time will come if we both live when we shall be together again. I shall not stay away from you one minute longer than I am obliged to after an honorable peace shall be declared. I do have a good desire to serve until that event shall occur. I heard from Pine Bluff yesterday. The 3d Reg. is suffering terribly. It has but fifteen or twenty men for duty. Lt. Liljegrew of Co. "D," is dead. Surgeon Smith, the Medical Director of the Department, has made application to have the Regt. ordered to some healthier locality.[66] I expect the order will be made soon. . . .

Truly, your husband,
Madison.

64. Major William Webster resigned on November 12, 1864.

65. Captain Edward L. Baker of Company E, Third Minnesota, resigned February 10, 1864. For Northerners moving to the South to run plantations, see McPherson, *Ordeal by Fire,* 429–30.

66. Madison refers to Second Lieutenant Olof Leligrew. Andrews states, "During its stay [in Pine Bluff] thirty of its original members died from disease, besides many more recruits, and nearly all suffered much sickness." Andrews includes an account of the illness

Nininger Oct. 14th 1864
Tuesday evening

My dear Madison

... Piercy has just left here. He is making his last visit at Nininger before going to New york. He intends starting next Tuesday. I never saw him looking better then he now does though his health is not very good. There is nothing to write in the way of news. Everything is so dull. ...

They are getting along finely making molasses. Some that they have made is very nice. Some days they make 25 gallons. If you will come home we will make a candy party for you. I was in hopes it would begin to get more healthy in Little Rock. I do hope you will get over the ague when the weather gets cool. ... Papa has sold his oxen & bought a horse. We are having beautiful weather now but very dry. Baby is real smart again. As getting as fat as a doe.[67] Her & Do have been writing you a letter on the bottom of this sheet. It is bed time. I shall have to stop scribbling for the present. Do write often.

      Yours ever Lizzie

I did not send the papers that I was going to but I have cut the pieces out that I wished you to see. Will send them in this as you will be more likely to get them.—Lizzie

{at the bottom in a shakier script} Dear Papa, I want you to come home Dady. I is very well. good bye

Little Rock, Ark.,
Oct. 23d, 1864.

My Dear Lizzie:

... Today is Sunday. I have read the Bible some and the papers considerably, trying to while away the time; but my heart is so full of home yearnings, that I am at a loss to know what to do with myself. If you and Birdie were only by my side I should be content—my happiness would be complete. But it is not so. The only relief for me, is in writing. I expect you sometimes feel bored by my numerous letters, all so much the same thing over. Yes, my heart does really feel lonely, very lonely, to-day. One hour of your company would provide the dearest boon to me on earth.

---

the regiment experienced at Pine Bluff from Dr. A. C. Wedge, a surgeon in the Third Minnesota. Most contracted malaria. He estimates that 80 percent of the new recruits were ill, and eighty-nine died. See "Narrative of the Third Regiment," 174–75.

    67. Lizzie's "As" should be an "Is."

But I must not brood over such thoughts—they only make me feel more keenly the loneliness of my situation. I must drive away such thoughts from my mind. I ought not to complain. Perhaps this activity of thought is another proof of restored health. I have not felt so well since last winter as I have for the past week. I am gaining strength and flesh every day.

I will give you a peep (an ink and paper one) into my present habitation. My camp is just on the opposite bank of the river from Little Rock. Have just got some new quarters built. They are 16 by 18 feet built of split logs, chinked with wood and clay, and covered with shakes, and have good cheerful fireplace. Furniture consists of three narrow beds, three chairs, a table, and a desk. The walls are hung thick with clothing, swords, sashes, and belts. Altogether, it is quite pleasant and comfortable. We have a colored woman to do our cooking and washing. By "*we*" I mean Lt Gustafson, Adjutant Jenks, and myself. Yesterday we replenished our larder with 1 bbl Flour ($11.55), 300 lbs onions ($15.00), 20 lbs Sugar ($6.00), 2 galls molases ($2.00), 20 lbs White Fish ($2.00), 10 lbs Coffee ($4.50), 50 lbs Pork $6.00—besides sundry other things too numerous to mention. You see that it costs us something to live.[68] We are now out of Potatoes and butter, and cannot get any, as there are none in market. Potatoes have been $5.00 per bush. and Butter $1.00 per pound. Well, I guess this will do for once. I did not intend to trouble you so much when I sat down to write. I wish you would write very often for I am so lonely here I hardly know how to contain myself. . . .

> Ever your husband,
> Madison.

P.S. I have just read this over and am almost ashamed to send it; but will for this once crowd down my shame and send it. . . .

Nininger Oct 25, 1864

My dear Madison

. . . I was glad indeed to hear that you were getting better if it is but slowly. Hope by this time that you are well again. I will get babies pictures as soon as is convenient. The scarlet fever is all about here. I have to keep Vickie pretty close at home. I am sorry to hear that so many of the 3rd Regt are sick. Hope the cool weather will have a tendency to improve their health. You wish to know how much is due on our place when I pay what Mr. Poor owes, which I suppose he will pay before long & what I have in my possession. There will then be two hundred

---

68. "Bbl" is an abbreviation for barrel.

& thirty dollars due and principle beside the interest. . . . I try to be as economical as possible but it takes a great deal to get along with. I paid Dr Thorne eight dollars for two visits, so you see that Dr to[o] are improving [with] the times. By the way, the first cost of babies now are fifteen dollars. Are you not glad that you have not any to buy this fall? I do not know yet what I shall do with the house but will try and do the best I can. I have got the pasture ploughed. The gofers are very troublesome in the garden. I have put every thing round those apple trees to keep them away but nothing seems to do any good. When you get back you will have to try your luck. . . . I am glad you are able to get something that is fit to eat sometimes. Gus & Mary are getting along finely. . . . Albert Poor is here. He keeps such a *talking* that I can not think what I am writing.

I do not want you to get your mind made on staying in the army longer then next spring, for I never can think of your staying there another summer. Instead of any feeling more willing for you to stay I miss you more and more every day. I often lie down at night but not to sleep for a long while. My thoughts wonders where you are. How I wish you were here to-night. How happy I should feel could I fold my arms around you, lie my head on the same pillow & feel the sweet kisses of my loved husband upon my face. I cannot help talking for those are my inmost feelings. May God grant that we may meet again, never to be separated again in this world, and above all prepare us both for the future world that we may not be separated there.

. . . I[t] looks very much like rain to-night. Hope it will come. There has not been a bit of rain fall in two months. The wells on Rose Hill are very nearly dry. . . .

Nininger Oct. 27

I put this apology for a letter away, intended to finish it yesterday but we had company all day. Did not get a chance. . . . The eighth Regt has been ordered down river.[69] Do not know where. . . .

Lizzie

Little Rock, Ark.,
Oct. 26th, 1864.

My Patriotic Wife:

Yours of Oct. 8th I received to-day.[70] You sign yourself as my "unpatriotic wife." I object to that *in toto*. I never intended to intimate that you were unpatriotic—

69. The Eighth Minnesota was ordered south in October 1864 and fought at Overall's Creek and Murfreesboro in December 1864. See Carley, *Minnesota in the Civil War*, 209.
70. Lizzie's letter of October 8 is not in the correspondence.

I never thought so, even. A heart so true as yours, could not possibly hold senti-ments other than patriotic. I only wished you to be less doubting, more encour-aged in regard to our cause. In the army, courage, confidence, and hope prevail; while at the north are found many grumblers and traitors; also many who are easily discouraged and who permit themselves to make discouraging expres-sions. Traitors exult when they witness this, and endeavor to increase it. I thought by the tone of one of your letters that you felt discouraged. I want you to be full of hope and confidence as long as we have a cause to fight for. Do not allow your-self in desponding moments to say anything which might cause a traitor to rejoice.[71] I know, however, you will not. I may have been rude and hasty in my remarks at the time I wrote that letter. If so, you must pardon me. You know, Lizzie, that I have never exhibited jealousy towards you in any respect whatever. I have never entertained a jealous feeling toward you. I have the fullest confi-dence in you. I regard your character for patriotism and every other virtue, as above reproach. I have had too many proofs of your love, to doubt that.

I am truly pleased to hear of you attending the Union mass meeting. I wish you would go out much oftener.[72]

. . . You must not work too hard—*be sure.* In regard to our house and land, you can do as you please about letting it. Am pleased with your idea of plowing the land. Maybe we can have some wheat of our own raising by another season.

I have not received any letters from Will Govette yet. I wrote to him recently. I heard that he and his company were again in the service.[73] I put on one of my new shirts this morning. It is a nice large one, and warm too.

In regard to your freezing you must not blame me; for you might be with me this winter if you chose to; but you did not. If you were here I could keep you warm, I know. Besides it is not cold here. The weather is very pleasant just now. You must not think that you are the only one who feels lonely on account of our separation. I cannot describe to you my feelings at times. I see many lonely hours, I assure you.

71. For civilians' patriotism, especially women's, see Hess, *Liberty, Virtue, and Progress,* 48–49; and Silber, *Daughters of the Union,* chaps. 4, 5.

72. A Union mass meeting was a public meeting to support the Union (Republican) Party candidates. A meeting was held on October 4, 1864. See *Hastings Independent,* 29 September, 6 October 1864.

73. The Twenty-second Ohio Regiment Infantry had been ordered to Camp Denni-son, Ohio, on October 24, 1864, and mustered out on November 18, 1864. Two companies of recruits and veterans were, however, formed and remained in service until August 18, 1865. See www.ohiocivilwar.com/cw22.html.

Capt Hodges and Surg. Greely have their wives here. Col. Mattson has sent for his. He is very sorry that he did not take her with him when he came down....[74]

Ever your
Madison.

Little Rock, Ark.,
Nov. 1st, 1864.

My Dear Lizzie:

... You promise to get up a "candy party" for me if I will go home. I would not object to the party, I assure you; but there inducements enough without that, had I nothing to keep me here. Since I have got to feeling well again I feel *additional desire* to be at home. You *know,* do you not? I am feeling as well now as I ever did—have appetite enough for four men. Am almost as fleshy as when I got hurt last winter. Think ... I might be tempted to give you cause for jealousy. Do you not feel as though you ought to be here to watch me?...

I presume you will be riding horse-back now that you have a horse. Did father get a buggy, too? ... Dolly and Victoria wrote a very interesting appendix to your letter—I read it with much pleasure. Hope to hear from them often. Tell them that I will reply as soon as I can find time.

We are beginning to have lively times in Little Rock, in the way of parties, &c. Col. Engleman gave a party last evening. I had an invitation, but did not attend. Col. Engleman commands the Brigade (2d Brig, 1st Div.) [to] which my Col. Regt is attached. I spent the evening with Capt. Otto Dreher, Co "A," 3d Minn. He is

74. Like Anna Hodges, Sarah R. Greely, Assistant Surgeon M. R. Greely's wife, had young children in 1860 when they lived in Minneapolis. Colonel Hans Mattson's wife was Cherstin Peterson Mattson. See Mattson, *The Story of an Emigrant,* 51. In regard to asking his wife to join him in Arkansas, see his October 19, 1864, letter: "Dear wife ... I am going to ask you to come at once if you think you can stand it here. Foster of Wabashaw is [?] sutler and will come right down. Louisa will come if you do and you can all go with Foster. You will have to drive. Is a small long [?] without furniture—bring sheets blankets, and two [?] with you also some butter. I will write to Foster to bring some dishes &c store the furniture some where. I have no money to send. Foster will help you. Write to him.... Bring some dresses along so that you can stay till May. You must expect to have a poor lonesome time and live poor, as the poorest folk if you are still willing to come then may God speed your journey and I will make it as pleasant as I can. We shall no doubt stay here all winter." His next letter, dated October 22, states: "I shall build a shanty for you and we shall have a sweet time." He wrote only one additional letter to her in 1864; she did join her husband at DeValls Bluff, Arkansas, and then returned to Minnesota in April 1865. See Mattson Papers.

sick, and is staying with Dr. Hartman, of the 43d Ill.[75] Lieut. Pettibone is aide de camp on Gen. Andrews staff. Lieut. Jameson told me that he gave Robt Poors money ($35.00) to Eugene, at Robt's request. Also his other effects. He thinks that Eugene did not send it to Robt's folks; but has spent it. Eugene is still at Pine Bluff so I have not seen him.

In my last letter I inclosed photographs of Col. Foster and Surg. Wedge of the 3d. Did you get them? . . . I presume it is getting to be quite cold by this time in Minn. Be careful, and not let baby freeze her toes. If you will come to Ark. I will keep yours so warm as can be. Suppose, however, you rather let them freeze. . . .

> Ever your husband,
> Madison.

> Little Rock, Ark.,
> Nov. 6th, 1864.[76]

My Dear Lizzie:

. . . My *thoughts* are with you [even] if *I* am not. I was [over] to Dr. Hartmans yesterday and stayed with Otto until this morning. I think I never told you that Otto compliments you—thinks by your looks, that you [are] a real good, true woman. . . . By the way Lu Pettibone [al]ways says: "Cap, I like y[our] wife very much, because I believe her to be sensible modest woman." I do not let them know anything to the contrary.

I was at Duvalls Bluff day before yesterday, and had a good visit with [some] friends. While there I [bo]ught me a horse for [riding]. If you will drop [by] some fine morning [you] may take a ride. . . . Mattson is comd'g a Brigade, which leaves Lt. Col. Foster in command of the Regiment.[77] The Regt. is getting along finely building winter quarters. The health is rapidly improving. Gen. Andrews is still in command at the Bluff. He [has] not got those photographs taken yet; but when he does I will send you one. In a few more days we shall know who is to be next President. I presume the election will be quite exciting. I am very anxious to know the result. I think, however, there is [little] doubt but that Abra[ham] Lincoln will be elec[ted].

Lizzie, I wish I could [come] in and spend this day [with] you. What a good long [talk] we would have all about everything and more too. I cannot tell you

---

75. Colonel Adolphus Englemann was originally in the Forty-third Illinois Infantry. Alexis K. Hartman was the first-assistant surgeon in the same regiment. See www .rootsweb.com/~ilcivilw/f&s/043-fs.htm.

76. The right side of this letter has a significant amount torn off.

77. See Andrews, "Narrative of the Third Regiment," 175.

how often I think of you and how anxious I am to be with you once more. I often think—and it makes me feel sad, too—of [the] morning I bade you [good] bye and left you cry[ing at] the levee. I think of little Birdie, too, and the last kiss I gave her little innocent cheek. Wish I could see her to-day. I expect she will be afraid of me when I return. Give her lots of good kisses for me. . . .

> Truly your husband,
> Madison.

> Nininger Nov. 11, 1864
> Thursday evening

Dear Madison

. . . I have been to Hastings to-day. Saw Dr Ethridge. Had quite a long talk with him concerning Little Rock. When I heard that Elijah Moulton was going to Little Rock, I put up a box to send to you of butter cake & other articles & waited for him to come till all those who were going to Little Rock had gone.[78] I then thought I would send it by express, but on enquiring to day when I took it there to have it marked that it would cost 4½ dollars to send fifteen lbs, that it would cost more then it would come to. Have not heard whether Elijah has gone or not. Am sorry, for I know butter would come in play if you do not have any. I am glad you have got such a comfortable place to live in. Wish I were there to keep house for you. You say that I might be there. I know I might, but had I gone last summer I am positive that baby would not have been alive now, for she has been sick mostly all summer as it is. But I pray that it may not be much longer that we are separated, for I cannot think of it. Some times I feel as though I could fly to be where you are. How glad I am that you are getting well again. I do hope you will continue to recover as you get quite well. You never tell me a word about your Regt. How many men have you got? Tell me all about it when you write again. Mrs Poor wished me to ask you to hunt up Robt's watch, & if Eugene had got it have him send it to her with the rest of his clothes, & she will settle all expenses. Says she wants it as a keepsake. If Eugene has not taken care of it, she will feel very hard at him. . . .

> (Tuesday evening)

I have been so sick all day that I did not feel like writing. I have been having a severe attack of sick head ache. You know I mostly always get sick after riding over the rough ground, but I feel pretty well tonight. The ground is covered with

---

78. Dr. Francis Ethridge lived in Hastings in 1860 and had been one of the commissioners to collect the soldiers' votes that Madison saw in Little Rock.

snow & the river is all frozen over. I tell you it begins to look like winter & I feel like it for it is very dreary & lonely. You do not know how glad I shall be to see spring. That is if I live, for I will then expect my wishes realized. You already know what they are.

I am glad you do not forget to read your Bible. Hope instead of reading newspapers a good deal & that a little that you will read that a good deal & newspapers little, especially on Sabbath. I know that I come very short of doing as I should, but I feel a great wish for my earthly companion to lead the way. Things of this life are very important, but I consider that of more consequence then any thing else. Dont forget [that] in that cozy little room beside that pleasant fireplace you & I can mingle our prayers at the throne of grace [even] if I am away here in Minn., for you know that it's our father that listens. They tried and convicted two Irish men for the murder of that soldier that I told you about who was killed. They ought to be hanged for such an awful crime.[79] Baby has got real smart again. Do burn this when you read it. I am ashamed to send it, for I was half asleep and very tired when I wrote the first part, & this evening I did not feel in writing humor. . . .

> Yours ever
> Lizzie . . .

> Head-Quarters 2d Division, 7th Army Corps,
> De Vall's Bluff, Ark., Nov. 15th, 1864.[letterhead]

My Dear Lizzie:

I wrote to you day before yesterday. Yesterday, I wrote a note, enclosing $100.00, which I sent by Wm Allison, who started up for home last night.[80]

I came over here yesterday afternoon. Am at Gen. Andrews. Am going up White River on the Steamer Ella as far as Augusta after Darkies and rebels. We have a guard consisting of part of the 3d Minn. and 12th Mich.[81] We'll be gone four days.

> Truly, Madison[82]

79. Lizzie explains the murder to Madison in her letter of December 25, 1864.
80. William Allison mustered out on November 13, 1864.
81. Andrews notes that on December 13 there was an expedition up the White River to Augusta with the Ninth Iowa Cavalry and part of the Twelfth Michigan Infantry, but this was three weeks after Madison's mention of going on a similar trip. There were scouting parties in November and December that rounded up prisoners, so Madison might be referring to one of these. See Andrews, "Narrative of the Third Regiment," 175–76.
82. Madison's brief note on November 24, 1864, written on the back of his brother Joseph's letter, is not included here.

Nininger Nov 29, 1864
Tuesday afternoon

My Dear Madison

I rec'd the money all safe that you sent by Wm Ellison. I believe I told you that the note on the place was due the first of Dec, but it is not until the 16th of Jan.

I wrote you a few days ago telling you that I had let the house. I was so sleepy when I wrote the letter that I really do not know what I did write. Albert had the house til it was so late in the season that chances for letting it were very few. Had it been empty six weeks before it was, I could have had several chances, but as it was I thought I had better rent it for five dollars a month then let it stand idle all winter. They have it till the first of May. Sprague is one of the county commissioners. He is to leave everything in good order as when he rented it. There is now one woman & her family whose husband is in the army, another woman & two little children whose husband died in the army, & two little orphan children, & two old persons. Jones of Hastings is over seer. His family are living in the house owned by Mrs MacDonald. We wrote to the ensurance office, as they have to be notified when there is any changes in any building that they ensure. Had the house been in good repair of course I should not have let them have it, but the plastering is very much broken & you can imagine how it looked after Poors young ones left it.[83] I got Mr Myers to plough the land for two dollars an acre at the same time they were asking three on the Vermillion.[84] I think I will have Sorghum planted in the garden between those trees so we can have some molasses

---

83. The letter Lizzie wrote to explain renting the farm as a poorhouse for the county is not in the correspondence. Guelcher notes that the state mandated that each county have a county poor farm, and in November 1864 Dakota County "proposed renting the Handyside House in Nininger for a home for the poor of the county. About twenty-five inmates, including several orphans, resided there in 1865 under the management of Mr. Jones, the poor-master" (*More Than Just a Dream*, 137). Lizzie's letter seems to suggest that the Bowlers' farm was the first location of the poor farm. In her March 25, 1865, letter she explains that the residents moved to the "large hall at Nininger," meaning the Handyside House. William Jones was the constable in Hastings in 1860. Mrs. MacDonald might have been M. M. MacDonald, the wife of the editor of Nininger's newspaper. A. W. MacDonald had edited the *Emigrant Aid Journal* from 1857 through May 1858. After the financial panic MacDonald went to St. Louis, and the couple did not appear on the census in 1860. See A. W. MacDonald to Ignatius Donnelly, 12 December 1858 and 7 March 1859, roll 6, Donnelly Papers. For the timing of establishing county poor farms in Minnesota, see McClure, *More Than a Roof*, 20–21; on page 25, however, McClure dates Dakota County's poorhouse to 1866 rather than Lizzie's more informal arrangement.

84. Farmer Frederick Myres lived in Nininger in 1860.

for next winter should we need it. By the way I never told you what a nice Sorghum cake I made for you. Have it yet. Wish I could send it. . . .

Baby is pretty well now. She cannot walk yet alone but can say "pretty & Beautiful" as plain as anyone. If she keeps well I will have those photographs taken soon. . . .

Lizzie

Little Rock, Ark.,
Nov. 30th, 1864.

Dear Lizzie:

I have not heard a word from you since the receipt of your letter containing the intelligence of Baby's sickness. In that letter you promised to write again in a day or two; and, as I have not received anything from you since then, I greatly fear that baby is worse again. O, you have little thought how anxious I am to hear how she is. . . .

A fleet of transports arrived here last week, up the Arkansas river—the first boats that have come up this river since last winter. It looks quite pleasant to see them at the levee. My sutler arrived with a stock of goods. If you were here we would go over to his "shebang" and get a stick of candy. Wouldn't that be an object? . . .

Truly your loving hubbie,
Madison.

Little Rock, Ark.
Dec 3d, 1864.

Dearest Lizzie:

. . . It is very, *very* strange that I do not hear from you. It fills me with fearful apprehensions and keeps me in dreadful suspense. I almost feel positive that something very serious has happened. It may be that Providence has chosen to send affliction upon my little family. If so I pray that I may be endowed with strength to meet it in a becoming manner. O, Libby, my heart feels so heavy I can hardly think or care for anything. I do hope that the next mail will bring me tidings from you. . . .

Truly your loving husband,
Madison.

Nininger Minn. Dec 8th 1864

My Dear Madison

I rec'd a few lines from you written on the eve of your going up White River. Since I recd it I have been very anxious to hear from you again. You may depend that I have watched the post office pretty closely but have not heard a word yet. I returned from Nininger last evening after a visit of three days, while there spent the night with Gus & Mary. They are very well & wish to be remembered to you. . . .

We are having very cold weather now. Last night was cold enough to freeze Indians. I am now going to tell you what kind of a bed I have. Have a little bed sted just big enough for me & baby that stands in the corner of Mamas bedroom so you see if you were here you would have to go upstairs or if you *did sleep with me you would have to be a very good boy & not be cutting up capers as you always are.* But if you were here tonight I believe I would try & make a little room for you. . . . I tell you it would have been a pleasant surprise to me to see you poping in someday unexpectadly, as it would have been if you had have happened to come home but was to[o] good to be true. I hope the time is not very far distant when you will come home to stay. . . . Baby is getting along real well. She can say a great many words & play like a kitten. . . . I am as your ever

    Lizzie S Bowler

Little Rock, Ark.,
Dec. 11th, 1864.

Dear Lizzie:

I think that I have not written to you since the receipt of yours of Nov. 24th, giving me an account of babys pranks. I am rejoiced to know that she is well again, and able to be into mischief. You must not blame me for her not sleeping more than she does. If she had been a boy you would have had no trouble. Does she begin to talk yet? I am surprised that I do not hear of her learning to talk, she being of the talking gender. I am sorry that you had so cheerless a Thanksgiving. Wish I had been at home to take you out for a ride. But never mind, Libby, there's better times a coming. I did not know of Thanksgiving until the day was almost gone, when some one remarked that it was Thanksgiving day. I am perfectly satisfied with the disposition which you have made with the house. A house filled with "war widows" would be an attractive place here, especially if they were for the union. How is it there?

I took a good long look at your photograph to-day; also Birdie's and Dolly's. Had a good long think about home, too.... In one of your letters you inquire about my colored Regt. We have four companies full, with full complement of officers, a Lieut Col., Adjutant, and quartermaster; and a fifth company nearly full. We cannot expect to fill the Regt until a forward move is made, which will be by Feby or March, sure, and then we can get plenty of Darkies. Gen. Steele has been relieved from the command of his Dept. by Maj. Gen. Reynolds. Our Division commander Gen. Salomon tried to get the Regts of his division to raise $50. a piece to purchase a sword for Gen. Steele. The officers of this Regt. held a meeting, and passed resolutions not to give a cent for such a purpose. He has not done right by us, and we are willing he should know it....[85]

> Ever yours,
> Madison.

Nininger Dec 18, 1864
Sunday afternoon

Dear Madison

... I cannot imagine the reason that you do not get my letters. I do not remember how long it was after writing the first letter giving an account of babies sickness that I wrote the next. But longer then I intended, for she was taken worse again directly after writing. Thought I would not write again till there was some change.

I had no hope of her recovery for several days. Neither had any one that saw her. But through the goodness of one who has all power she is well again & very well. Is fatting & growing like a little pig & as full of fun as can be. Today is dull & lonely. Pa & Do have gone to Sabbath school. Ma is sitting on one side of the stove a sleep. Aunt Sarah rocking the cradle & reading while baby sleeps & Lizzie is the last but not the least, is writing to her absent hubby sometimes half asleep too. We heard of Shermans sucess at Savana yesterday. If it only be true & Thomas at Nashville.[86] Oh how I wish the war would end. How does it look down there?

---

85. The Campbell brothers are unidentified. For similar dissatisfaction with General Steele from military leaders, see Thomas, *Arkansas in War and Reconstruction*, 295-97. Steele was relieved of command on November 29. On Major General Joseph J. Reynolds, see Warner, *Generals in Blue*, 398.

86. General Sherman's troops approached Savannah, Georgia, on December 10 and then captured it on December 21. Union general George H. Thomas's victory at Nashville occurred from December 15 to 16.

Any signs of peace? I attended a spelling school at Nininger one evening this week, a very good one too. The teacher is a very nice girl. I presume you already know that Willie Callahan is dead. Those poor boys have sheared a terrible fate as soldiers. . . .[87]

> From your loving wife
> Lizzie . . .

Nininger Dec 25, 1864
(Christmas afternoon)

My Dear Madison

. . . I will tell you about the soldier being killed. I presume you have heard about it before this. While the poles were open at Willoughbee's there was a soldier from the 2nd Cavalry on his way home (his child not being expected to live his wife had sent for him), called, & while there treated the crowd to liquor and soon all hands began to feel pretty full of talk. The most of them being irish. They soon fell into a political argument. When they threatened the soldiers life if he has voted for Lincoln, which he did, & they caught up fence rails pieces of boards & all sorts of weapons of war that was near & killed him on the spot. There was three engaged. They have been tried in the justices court & sent to the St Paul jail to await their trial, which will take place in Jan.[88] You ask if baby has not a good constitution. If you have she has, for she is just like you. Will get sick & fall all away in a few days and fatten up again as quick as a turkey. She is a great white soft pumpkin. How I wish you could see her. She has so many cunning actions & she has a bump of firmness on her head as large as there is any need of. She is troubled with that disease in her head at times but not near so badly as she was.

I will say nothing concerning my going to Little Rock. Will wait till you come

<hr />

87. The *Hastings Independent* did not mention the spelling school at Nininger. From Nininger, twenty-three-year-old William Callahan died in St. Louis, Missouri, on November 13, 1864. Callahan, like Robert Poor, who died six weeks earlier, had been recruited for Company F, Third Minnesota, in February 1864. Of the twenty-two men recruited for Company F between January and March 1864, eight died by mid-November 1864. Callahan's was the last of these deaths.

88. The *Hastings Independent* reported on November 11 that a number of men had murdered a man by breaking his skull. On November 17 the headline read, "The Inver Grove Murderers," and an article followed, detailing the murder of George Arnold, a soldier, by Thomas Eagan, Hugh McHugh, and Patrick Mehen. They were arraigned and put in jail until their trial in January 1865.

home, if you ever do & then I know that I can convince you that I did for the best. I do not wish you to think that I regarded your judgment of so little consequence, for I do not & you know it too. I do not want to insist on your coming home against your will, but I do not think it best for you to run the risk of your life by staying longer then spring or till the weather comes warm again. Our folks have all gone to meeting. I am left alone trying to write. Victoria keeps pulling at me so that I do not know what I am writing. Rather a dull Christmas. We are all well & all send their love to you.

> Ever yours
> Lizzie

> Little Rock, Ark.,
> Dec. 27th, 1864.

Dear Lizzie:

. . . I hope you do not think I would put up with such sleeping accommodations as you represent yourself as occupying, if I should go home. I guess you would change your mind if I were there. Presume you have lost all inclination for "naughty" conduct by this time, have you not?

How did you spend Christmas? I took an oyster stew in camp at 10 o'clock and at 2 o'clock dined out in company with the officers of the 112th, at Old Margaret's, the wife of one of our colored sergeants. Aristocratic, wasn't it? We had roast chicken, several kinds of pie and cake, and everything in the best of style.

Last Monday I was at DeValls Bluff. Bade Gen. Andrews Good-bye, took dinner with Col Mattson and Lady, and had a good time generally.[89] I expected to be able to send you some more money by this time; but cannot, as we have not been paid for some time, and there is no telling when that happy event will occur. No payments at all, are now being made. You will have to shift some way to get along meantime. I suppose you have heard of Willie Callahan's death. He died at Jefferson Barracks, Missouri. I cannot find anything which was left by Robt Poor. Lt. Jameson says that Eugene Stone took his watch and money ($39). Eugene has neither watch nor money now. I should think he would be ashamed even to go back to Minn. . . .

> Truly your hubbie,
> Madison.

89. General Andrews was relieved by General Shaler on December 28. See Andrews, "Narrative of the Third Regiment," 175.

Nininger
January 8th, 1864 [1865]

My dear Husband

... While I set here trying to write, there is such a fit of loneliness comes over me that I feel like taking wings. What would I give were you here? You say I must not be too sure that you are coming home in the spring. I cannot think any other then that you will come. Cannot bare the thought of your staying longer. In two days more you will be twenty seven years old. Just think how time is flying. it will not be long till you & I will be called old. I have just been thinking of the night that you set up with me at Uncle Roberts and the years as they have cooled on since.[90] How many changes. How many hours of sorrow and joy.

Most of the folks about here are talking of going to Pikes Peak, that is the poor part of the community. One of the Poors (Andrew, I believe his name is) has just come from there. I believe he has made a fortune there.[91] Baby is getting along finely. She can walk a few steps at a time now. . . .

ever your loving Wife
Lizzie

Little Rock, Ark.,
January 10th, 1865.

Dear Lizzie:

... I have half a mind to be offended at you, for calling baby a "great soft, white pumpkin," after having said that she is just like me. That looks very much like a sly way of calling your hubbie names. But if you will promise not to make pie of us, baby and I will consent to be "some pumpkins." I would give a years rent of our "farm" to see baby this very evening, and toss her on my knee awhile. Hope she will get rid of that disease in her head. I judge from your letter that you will not insist on my going home until I get tired and quit of my own accord. That's a nice little lady. Will give you an extra kiss for your kind indulgence. You need not fear as to my staying here if I see a prospect of passing another summer in the condition in which I passed the last. I am well now, and quite fleshy. . . . I sent that stone pipe yesterday.

90. It is not clear what Lizzie means by "cooled on." Perhaps she meant "coiled."
91. The gold rush at Pike's Peak, Colorado, had peaked in 1860, but gold seekers continued to try their luck. Pike's Peak's yield of gold was much smaller than those of other mines. See Marks, *Precious Dust,* 33–37, 170, 191. Andrew Poor lived in Nininger City in 1857 and was kin to Albert Poor. See Biographical Sketches, P–W, folder 2, Case Papers.

Must tell you a joke which occurred this morning at my expense. You know that I never liked rice in any form. Well, this morning I had occasion to compliment Nancy's hot cakes, for they were really good. You can judge of my surprise when she replied: "Dems rice cakes—tot you didn't like rice." It pleased Nancy mightily as well as my messmates. Presume you will be up to some game of the same next when you get me home again.

Today is the anniversary of my birthday. Am twenty-seven. Wouldn't you like to give my ears a pull? By the way, how old are you Lizzie? And when is your birthday? I have forgotten; besides you can tell the truth about it, now that you have me fast....

> Ever your loving
> Madison.

Nininger Minn Jan 22, 1864 [1865]

My Dear Madison

... Yesterday we had the first real good snow storm we have had this winter. There is now six or eight inches of snow on the ground, which makes pretty good sleighing if the wind does not blow it all off the roads, for the wind blows a perfect gail to day. Vickie sets at my feet on the floor playing. She has got quite well again. Was sick five or six days. Her double teeth are coming through. They make her sick, for she cuts her teeth very hard. Has twelve now. Can run all over the rooms. Weighs 33 lbs & is two feet 7½ high. Is called by everyone a very large baby.... We have just heard that *Grant* has taken Richmond.[92] I hope it is so but when will this awful war end.... Is Otto's wife in Ark? Knapps folks are very much pleased at Heman's promotion.[93] That Barney McKenna is at home [to] try to get a divorce from his wife. I suppose he has found some southern girl that suits him better. If you stay there much longer I expect you will be coming home on the same business. How does Eugene S. get along now? Does he drink? What could he have done with Robt Poor's things? I did not tell Mrs Poor that he hasnt got them, for she would feel so badly. She thinks very hard of him that he does not send them to her....

> Yours Ever
> Lizzie

92. Richmond would not fall to Grant's army until early April 1865.
93. Herman Pettibone was promoted to first lieutenant of Company B, Third Minnesota, on January 1, 1865.

Little Rock, Ark.,
January 22d, 1865.

Dear Lizzie:

Upon looking over yours of the 1st inst. again, I find that I did not answer half your questions in my last letter on account of my hurry in writing it.

I cannot tell you just what will become of this Regt. in the event of a forward move of the army. There is some probability of its being consolidated with two other fragments, in which event it would probably form a portion of the army for active operations. But if it should not be consolidated, a part of it will go with the army merely for the purpose of recruiting. I go to church occasionally, but just now it is rather inconvenient to attend, as we are encamped on the opposite side of the river from Little Rock and the pontoon bridge has been swept away, leaving us no means of crossing but a ferry-boat which runs by fits.

You wish to know what I think in relation to war matters. I thing the prospect is exceedingly hopeful just now.[94] The rebels seem to be intensely agitated; altogether showing signs of coming dissolution of the rebel power, and the restoration of Federal authority in the South. I hear that Gen. Andrews has gone to New Orleans with his command. Give my love to all the folks and kiss that mischievous little Birdie for me.

Ever your loving
Madison.

Nininger Jan 29th
Sabbath evening

[To Madison:]

Do wants me to fill her sheet so you will not get a very long letter from me this week. . . .[95] You ask me how old I am. Was twenty four the 9th day Sept. They are having a great time at Hastings. Try those criminals that killed that soldier on election day. The jury are mostly all Irishmen. They talk of sending for the 2nd Cavalry to protect the town, for tis thought if they are convicted that the Irish will rise. If they do I hope they will never let them go while theres breaths in their bodies.[96] I do not feel very well to-night. Will leave this til morning.

94. Madison meant "think" rather than "thing."
95. Lizzie wrote this on the top of the third page of Dollie's letter. There was no greeting.
96. According to the *Hastings Independent,* the grand jury had been in session since January 10 to decide whether to indict the election-day murderers. On January 19 the

Tuesday 31st

Yesterday I was not able to hold my head off the pillow & consequently could not finish this scribbled affair of a letter. Was taken night before last with a neuralgic pain in my left eye & side that was bad. I think I could not have endured it any more but by constant warm applications & mustard have got quite over it.... People this way have great hopes of the war ending soon. I do not know what I wrote in my letter that made you think that I was willing for you to stay in the army as long as you liked. I do not wish to usurp so much authority over my husband as to say that you must come, but you know what my wish is & you can do as you please. To day is a beautiful day, just enough snow to make good sleighing....

> Yours ever
> Lizzie

Little Rock, Ark.,
Feb'y. 2d, 1865.

Dear Lizzie:

... Wish I were with you to-day to drive away the lonely fit which you speak of. Must not allow yourself to get the blues; but live in hope of the time when we shall be together. The recurrence of my birth-day gave me similar reflections to yours in regard to the flight of time and my approach to old age. Time does indeed seem to fly with swift wings.... Baby seems to have been very slow in learning to go alone—on account of her being so fleshy, probably. I rec'd. a letter from Elijah Moulton. He writes that he heard that baby was nearly as large as you. They have not heard from John yet. The expedition which left here over two weeks ago, is on its way back. Six regiments have been ordered from here to New Orleans. Most of the Colored troops of this Department are now at this post, doing post duty. No one knows except the Comd'g. General, what is to be done this Spring. I sincerely hope that the army will move Texasward.[97] If it

---

paper reported that the jury was divided, "ten in favor of finding a bill for murder and six against.... We would be sorry to have confirmed what seems to be the very general opinion that the six Jurymen that are opposed to finding a bill are Irishmen and that they take this position because the prisoners are of the same nationality.... if it becomes known that men of a certain nationality have combined to shield the guilty of the same origin, as is supposed by some, we may expect a bitterness to be engendered, which will be fraught with most dangerous consequences.... PS Since the above was in type we learn that the Grand Jury have found a bill indicting Eagan and McHugh for murder."

97. See Moneyhon, "1865," 146.

does not, recruiting will be out of the question, and I shall give up trying to fill my regiment.

... Keep up good spirits for the sake of

Your loving
Madison.

Nininger Minn. Feb 5th 1865
Saturday evening

My Dear Madison

... I do not know what made me think so but I have looked out of the window a great many times to day thinking perhaps I might see you coming. I felt just so the day I heard you had broken your leg. Hope I am not going to hear bad news from you. 'Tis almost a year now since you came home last year. Oh! Oh! how the years fly around & how much better are we then we were one year ago? I am afraid we are neither of us any better then we were then. How often I wish you are where I could see you & talk about things that are useless for me to try to write. Sometimes I feel that the last five years of my life have been a blank. There is one subject that I dwell on night & day when the subject that ought to be constantly before me is forgotten. All night after retiring, before I can close my eyes to sleep, [I think of] every unpleasant word ever spoken between us (if ever there were any) and every unkind act & I drop to sleep wondering how I could do any thing unkind to one I love as I do you & dream of having you with me but wake up to find it all a dream. Thus pass the days, weeks & years.

We have been having quite a thaw for the last few days, something new in Minn. nowadays. After a trial of nearly two weeks, they let those irish men go last night nearly [at] mid-night. While the jury men were coming to a conclusion of the matter in the jury room, the judge and lawyers let them go. Gormon was their lawyer.[98] I expected you would think I ment to call you names when I called baby a pumpkin but will make it all right some of these times. ... It seems to me that you have got to be quite a s——er if you have had that great pipe ever since you left here. Wish Joe knew as much as I do. He would think you might very

98. The *Hastings Independent* reported the same fate for the men but not the same process. On February 9 it stated that the jury had acquitted Thomas Eagan. The newspaper suggests that the Irish community in the area had bribed the jury. The lawyers for the defendants were "Gen. Gorman of St. Paul, and F. M. Crosby and Seagrave Smith" of Hastings. The prosecuting attorneys for the county were T. R. Huddleston and L. Van Slycke. See *Hastings Independent*, 17 November 1864.

easly look upon his failings as a tobacco user. Do excuse this apology for a letter. Burn it when read, for I have the blues so badly that I cannot write tonight.

>Yours ever
>
>Lizzie . . .

>Little Rock, Ark.,
>Feb'y. 6th 1865.

Dear Lizzie:

. . . I received a letter from Lieut. Pettibone. He is at Kinserville, near New Orleans. Seems to be in high glee. Speaks of regaling with fresh oysters and oranges. Gen. Andrews is in command of the 3d Brigade, Reserve Corps, Division of West Mississippi. Gen. Steele commands the Corps. It is concentrating these, and is expected to move upon Mobile.[99]

>Feb'y. 10th, 1865

Will try now to finish this letter, which something hindered me from doing at the time I commenced it. I have been too busy since then to write.

On the 7th I rode ten miles out of town along with Mr. Foster, a brother of Lt. Col. Foster, of the 3d. He was looking after a cotton plantation which he is going to cultivate. We saw several deer and a nice flock of wild turkey. Had to swim a creek with our horses, which gave us a good wetting.

Day before yesterday a gang of guerillas, about 1000, came up within three miles of town, and committed all kinds of depredations. A detachment of the 112th and 113th were sent after them. We got off about nine o'clock in the evening, and followed them fifteen miles, when we turned back, the rebs being two hours ahead of us, and mounted. I rode all night, and got back to camp at nine o'clock yesterday morning.

I slept soundly last night, that my bedfellow, Mr. Campbell, remarked, that he believed a woman might have shared my bed in perfect safety. The consternation of the poor women and children (the men all left) was great wherever the guerrillas had been. In one family they took every article they could find—even taking the boots and shoes off the children's feet![100] I lost one of your letters during the trip. Presume some guerrilla will find it. . . .

99. Although Mobile Bay had been in Union hands since August 1864, the city of Mobile remained under Confederate control for the war's duration, despite Union plans to take it.

100. See Moneyhon, "1865," 151; and Ash, *When the Yankees Came*, 81.

If you do not think of renting our land next summer, I think it advisable to put in some kind of a crop which can be used if we commence housekeeping by next fall—say the garden in vegetables such as cabbage, *parsnips*, turnips, beets, *onions*, and *tomatoes*; and the other in wheat, principally, with some potatoes and corn. I only make this as a suggestion. You can hire somebody to do it.

Do you think there is any danger of Poor's failing to pay what he owes us? There is no knowing when we shall get any pay here. It is hoped, however, that it will be before many weeks. There is a proposition before Congress to raise officers pay. Hope it will be favorably considered. . . .[101]

> Truly your hubbie,
> Madison.

Little Rock, Ark.,
Feb'y. 18th, 1865.

Dear Lizzie:

. . . You must pardon me for having neglected so long to write to you. Last Saturday I went to DeVall's Bluff and Tuesday I returned with a cold in my head, so that I have not felt much like writing since then. Received a letter from Gen Andrews, containing his photograph which I will enclose in this letter. . . .[102]

Dear Libby, I understand very readily how you feel when you talk of being so lonely. I dare not write you how lonely I sometimes feel, or in other words, how much I long to be by your side once more, for fear that you will insist on my going home before I feel justified in leaving the service. It does seem at times as though my longing for home and loved ones would override every other consideration; but I try to choke it down. Now, Libby, do not get the blues, but be a little lady and let me stay until you know when. Any time you wish to come where I am, if I do not return to you as soon as you feel that I ought, you can do so, and I will try and render everything pleasantly comfortable. I shall either soon be in a better position than I now am, or I shall quit the service. Be of good cheer.

101. In February 1865 the House of Representatives Bill No. 767, "to increase the pay of certain officers of the Army, and for other purposes," was referred to the Senate and was under consideration by the Committee on Military Affairs and the Militia. See U.S. Congress, *Congressional Globe*, iv and 927.

102. After the battle of Nashville, the Fifth, Seventh, Ninth, and Tenth Minnesota regiments participated in the campaign to capture Mobile, Alabama, by a combination land and sea siege. These regiments traveled down the Mississippi River to New Orleans on their way to Alabama. See Carley, *Minnesota in the Civil War*, 166.

Remember that Madison thinks of his wife and little one and loves them. They are the light whose memory brightens his humble camp cottage by day and lingers in dreams around his lonely pillow by night. . . . Good night and pleasant dreams.

With much love,

    Your husband,
    Madison.

Rose Hill Feb'y. 19th 1865

My dear husband

. . . We are having rather exciting times here at present on account of the draft. Levi Countryman, Ostin Knapp, C. Sprague, Walter Hanna, & John Countryman all enlisted last evening. They are to be sent to Chatanooga to join the heavy artillery regt from this state that is now at that place.[103]

You wish in one of your letters that you were where you could cuddle into bed with baby & I. You could realize that pleasure if pleasure you had a mind too. I assure you it would be as much pleasure for me to have you. Is your house not made tight or what makes it so cold or do you not have bed clothes enough to keep you warm?

. . . We are having beautiful weather now, just enough snow to make sleighing. Do write often, for you do not know how lonely I am.

    Yours ever
    Lizzie

Tuesday morning

It has been storming for the last two days. I guess we will have rain enough this spring to make things grow. It still rains & the wind blows a perfect gail. . . .

103. President Lincoln issued a call for an additional 500,000 men in August 1864, with a draft starting on September 5, 1864, so the Nininger town board issued bonds to pay recruits on August 27, 1864. More than enough bonds were issued to fill Nininger's quota in March 1865. See Guelcher, *More Than Just a Dream*, 145. All of the men Lizzie lists lived in Nininger. Cassius Sprague was the youngest of the group; listed as thirteen years old in 1860, he would have been eighteen. The First Regiment Heavy Artillery was organized in April 1864 and stationed at Chattanooga, Tennessee, until September 1865, when it was mustered out. See Carley, *Minnesota in the Civil War*, 212.

Little Rock, Ark.,
Feb'y. 26th, 1865.

Dear Lizzie:

A mail was expected to-night, but upon the arrival of the evening train, we learned to our disappointment, that it was "all a mistake"; so I have just been reading over some of your old letters. Think we will surely have a mail by to-morrow, when I expect to hear from you again. The latest received from you is Feb'y. 5th. I read that letter over and over again, and have pondered over what you wrote in regard to your lonely feeling. It makes my heart ache, and I cannot help reproaching myself for staying away from you so long. I think of it very often, and it makes me feel sad.

I do wish that my absence did not cause you so much sorrow and loneliness. You have always been so very kind and good to me and your conduct has ever been so noble and womanly, that I cannot fail to regard your wishes as to my leaving the army and returning to my family. I realize that, by staying away from you, I deprive myself of that pleasure and happiness which nothing but the society of a loving, virtuous wife can give; but I realize still more keenly the wrong and the injustice which I impose upon you by so doing. I sincerely wish you could make up your mind to come here, but I would not have you do so just for my sake, though I should be a thousand times rejoiced to have your company here. As much as I do not wish to leave the service at present I feel myself in honor bound to do so if you ask it. Circumstances may change in a short time hence, which may make me perfectly willing to close my connection with the army; but just at present I desire to remain. If you can make up your mind to spare me a while longer, our happiness will be the greater when we do meet. My health has been excellent since I left the hospital last fall. If it should fail again, I have then done with the south at once.

I judge from your account of "expectations" that Nininger is as productive as ever. I did not keep that pipe for the purpose of using it. I quitted smoking last summer; but now I occasionally smoke cigars. There does not appear to be any prospect of a "move" from this point this season. Many of the white troops have been sent to New Orleans. A movement from there is expected, either on Mobile or into Texas by way of Red river. There being no move from here, recruiting is at a standstill. . . .

Ever your loving
Madison.

Little Rock, Ark.,
March 2d, 1865.

Dear Lizzie:

. . . I wrote immediately upon the receipt of your last letter, ordering the *"Waverly"* sent to your address, and sent $4.00 to pay for one years subscription and for a copy of Liut. Gen. Grant's photograph, which will also be sent to you. . . . It is raining smartly to-day. The Arkansas river is higher than ever before since we came here. Boats are plying briskly from the mouth to here and up to Fort Smith. Eugene Stone has permission to appear for examination before a Board which is convened for the purpose of selecting men for positions in Colored Regiments. He will be examined soon. Think he will pass without any trouble.[104] Tell Mother and Dolly to excuse my neglect in not answering their letters. I am very busy now a days, but hope to have leisure shortly, when I will attend to my duty in that matter. I have shamefully neglected nearly all my correspondents during the last month or two. . . .

> Truly your hubbie,
> Madison.

Little Rock, Ark.,
March 16th, 1865.

Dear Lizzie:

. . . There is very little transpires here, which is worth writing about; so I presume that my letters must be anything but interesting. If we were together we could find enough to *talk* about that is, if I did not go to sleep. You know I am an inveterate sleeper. I guess that you do not mean what you say when you talk about not giving me any of the goodies which you are going to raise in your garden. There's a little spot in your heart which never will permit you to act selfishly or vindictively towards me, though I might deserve it ever so much. You go on and raise a good crop of vegetables, and if I do not go home in time to help you devour it, you can pack up a winters supply and come down here. Wouldn't it be pleasant? We could have a comfortable little house all to ourselves, and you could enjoy the pleasure of new sights and new scenes in the genial winter climate of this latitude. I think that I shall know in a short time hence, whether I shall

---

104. Applicants for commissioned offices in colored regiments had to pass an examination administered by an examination board. See Glatthaar, *Forged in Battle*, 44–45, 48–54. Fort Smith is on the far western border of Arkansas on the White River.

desire to remain in the army until "this cruel war is over," or return home. If I do conclude to remain I *sincerely* hope that you will find it in your heart to consent, and that you will join me here.

Do as you think best about letting Mr. Poor retain that money. I hope that Mr. Poor will succeed in raising the requisite number of men to secure him a commission. Let me know how he progresses in his undertaking. . . .[105] I have received another letter from Gen. Andrews. He was at Banancas, Fla. Pettibone was well. The Gen. has command of a division, and is promised a separate column in the operations against Mobile. I heard from Capt. Miller, that Gen. A. was to be breveted Major General.[106] I hope it is true, for he deserves promotion as much as any man I know of. . . .

> Ever your loving,
> Madison.

> Little Rock, Ark.,
> March 24th, 1865.

Dear Lizzie:

. . . [I] have had my head filled up with matters connected with my regiment, so that I have not felt relieved enough to write. The 112th is to be consolidated with 11th and 113th. The officers have all been examined, several have been rejected by the board, and the rest recommended for positions in the new regiment to be formed. There were three Lieut. Colonels and myself, aspirants for Field positions. As I could not get the position of Colonel or Lieut. Colonel without crowding out two of the Lieutenant Colonels, I waived my claims to those positions, went before the board for the position of Major, passed all right, and have been

105. Albert Poor recruited for the First Minnesota Battalion, which was a reenlisted version of the First Minnesota Volunteer Infantry. He received a commission as first lieutenant. See the *Hastings Independent,* 26 February, 16 March 1865. According to John H. Case, who interviewed Albert Poor later in the century, "Mr Poor was employed as recruiting officer at St Paul Minn for the towns of Nininger, Vermillion and Hampton. . . . he told me there was never any draft in Nininger Township (which of course I was well aware of this as I used to attend the war meetings with my father in the schoolhouse to raise money to pay bounties to recruits for Nininger Township so that the town could fill the quota with out the draft)" (Biographical Sketches, P–W, folder 2, Case Papers).

106. Christopher Andrews was made brevetted major general on March 9, 1865. See Board of Commissioners, *Minnesota in the Civil and Indian Wars,* 178. There was a First Lieutenant Harvey Miller in Company E, Third Minnesota, but not a Captain Miller.

recommended for the position. The consolidation will take place in a few days. The new Regiment will be a very fine one, numbering a thousand men....[107]

I shall not consent to have you reproach your self by calling your letters "scribbled concerns." Your letters are good enough for me or anybody else.... I wish that you would send me a list of the photographs of officers, which I have sent you, so that I may know whose to get to complete the list of my friends in the Third. There is great expectation of the paymaster here soon. I hope to be able to send you some money ere long.

Eugene Stone has been before the Board of Examiners, and was rejected. But do not make this known. I made an effort to-day, to have the Board re-consider their action in his case; and think I shall succeed, for I think that his rejection was very improper, as lots of men, not near so posted or so capable as he, have passed.[108] Eugene has done well ever since he was detailed as clerk in Department Hdqrs. and I feared that his rejection might work him serious injury, whereas a promotion might help him to do better....

Ever your loving
Madison.

Nininger Minn. March 25, 1865
Saturday Night

My Dear Madison

How are you to-night and what are you engaged in? Wish you were where I could have a good chat with you. Tis a beautiful evening. Looks as though spring had surely come. The exhibition came off last evening. I tell you it was good. Had real nice time. Had all sorts of performances such as are usual at such places. Good music, both vocal & instrumental....

Our house is again unoccupied. The folks who lived in it have moved into the large hall at Nininger.

I have not rec'd my number of the Waverly yet. Am thankful to you for your kindness in sending for it. Baby is well & so mischevious that we can hardly live in the house with her. She can go upstairs alone....

(Sunday Morning)

One year ago today we were at St. Anthony. Wish [we] were there to-day. I feel more like visiting now then I did then. My health is very good now with the exceptions of a day of severe sick head ache very often....

107. See Moneyhon, "1865," 148–49, for the black regiments in Arkansas in 1865.
108. The examination board's decisions were final and could not be petitioned. See Glatthaar, *Forged in Battle*, 54.

I wrote to Piercy a few days ago. Sent for his wife's picture. Hope he will send it, for I am very anxious to see what she looks like. . . . The river will not open so early as it did last year. Tis broken but very little yet. Do write often & every thing you can think of. Its all interesting to me.

Lizzie

Little Rock, Ark.,
April 1st, 1865.

Dear Lizzie:

Received yours of March 8th, several days ago. It seems strange to read about your being blockaded with snow while we have green grass, flowers, and peach blossoms here. Wish you were here to enjoy them—everything is so fresh and pretty. I know that you would be delighted. Well, then Piercy has got married at last. Presume he is "a happy man at last. . . ." Am glad to learn that Mr. Poor was so successful in starting upon his military career. His pay will do much towards supporting his family. Hope he will not forget to pay that money. . . .

Eugene Stone was finally rejected by the board of Examiners. I could effect nothing for him. Am truly sorry for him. . . . The weather is so warm to-day that the sweat just rolls off me while I write this letter. Think it doubtful whether you can read it. . . .

Ever your loving,
Madison.

7

I Sincerely Wish You Could
Make Up Your Mind to Come Here

Lizzie's patience was sorely tried by April 1865. With Richmond now in Union hands and Confederate general Robert E. Lee and other generals surrendering, she expected Madison to return home with other soldiers. Even as the war wound down, Madison made no move to muster out, and Lizzie wrote, "I do not think by your letter that you are thinking much about coming home, since you have taken so much pains to get a black Regt organized." Madison's recruiting efforts had finally paid off, and he was appointed major in the 113th U.S. Colored Infantry in April 1865. Unlike his earlier letters, however, Madison did not explain his decision to remain in the army as one of duty to country. Now, Madison saw the army as a place where he could earn money to support his family and save money.

Lizzie's letter of June 2 opens with an explanation of a previous letter written when she had "a terrible fit of the blues." Next comes mention of the weather, and local gossip fills the remainder. Buried in this letter is Lizzie's concession to join Madison in Little Rock that fall. After six months of intense pleading and teasing on both their parts—and over three years of Lizzie's wistful comments that Madison return home—one might expect Lizzie's decision to set the tone of her letter, for her to have started with her decision, rather than embedding it within news of other people. But perhaps it does begin the letter. If Lizzie had the blues when she wrote her previous letter, it might have been about her loneliness, her worry for Victoria and her mother if she took her daughter south with her, her anxiety about summer sickness in a warmer climate, and her fear that she and Madison and Victoria might not return to Minnesota and her family. She was making a difficult decision, and this gave her the "blues."

For his part, Madison wrote the next day in a similar state of mind. Unaware of Lizzie's decision, Madison expressed his unhappiness over his lack of authority in their marriage. If Lizzie would not agree to join him in Little Rock, he had failed her as a man and as a husband. Even though he was a major in the Union army, he could not command his wife, and he saw this as a flaw in his masculinity, not as a flaw in her femininity.[1] It is in this letter that we read Madison at his most vulnerable. Once he received her letter, however, Madison resumed his composure and remarked with some impatience, "I just want you to make up your mind to come here; then we can talk." But making that decision and carrying out her plans to move to Arkansas were two different matters, and Lizzie would not be rushed.

*   *   *

April 5th, 1865.

Dear Lizzie:

...That consolidation which I referred to in a former letter, has come off. My Regiment is now the 113th U.S. Colored Infantry. The new officers have not yet received their commissions, but have been nominated by Gen. Reynolds, and assigned to duty as such. I am on duty as major. It makes the finest colored Regiment in the Department. We have an excellent Band of Martial Music. Wish you could hear it play. The Brigade to which we belong forms the Garrison of Little Rock, and belongs to the 1st Division, 7th Army Corps. Brevet Brig. Genl. J M Williams, col of the 79th, commands. Gen. Solomon commands the Division and post of Little Rock....[2]

> Ever your loving,
> Madison.

Nininger Minn
April 9th 1865

My Dear Madison

...I do not think by your letter that you are thinking much about coming home, since you have taken so much pains to get a black Regt organized. But never mind. I am in hopes it will not be many months before there will not be so many soldiers needed as there now is. The fall of Richmond was hailed with great joy

1. Stephen W. Berry II, although focusing on Southern men, captures the connection between men's conception of themselves and women's regard that Madison expresses. Berry writes, "The woman, once acquired, would sustain and bear witness to the male becoming; the male would in turn reconceive his becoming as a tribute to her love." See *All That Makes a Man*, 12.
2. For the Union garrisons in Arkansas, see Moneyhon, "1865," 148–49. Madison's commission as major was made effective July 10, 1865.

in St. Paul. Yesterday was the day appointed to celebrate. We heard the cannon roaring all day.[3] Last Thursday we had the worst snow storm I ever saw. The wind blew a perfect gail. It commenced with a very heavy rain so you see that our drougth is broken....

To-day is a dull lonely day. Wish you were here. Baby is well. It would make you laugh if you could see her when she gets out doors, which is every time the door is open. She puts up both little hands over her head & acts just as though she was going to fly. The ground is too wet for her to run out much yet.

Aunt Sarah's has not heard from Am yet. I think it very strange what has become of him. Is it getting sickly at Little Rock yet? I do hope you will not get the ague again.... Our folks all send their love to you & all want you to come home....

>Yours ever
>Lizzie[4]

Little Rock, Ark.,
April 14, 1865.

Dear Lizzie:

... We have received the glorious news of the capture of Richmond and of General Lee and his army. Also a success of the capture of Johnston and his army.[5] There has been great rejoicing here. Yesterday and day before two hundred guns were fired in honor of our success. Last night there was an illumination in Little Rock, accompanied with bonfires, rockets, noise, and bad whisky. The war is virtually to an end. Peace *must soon follow*. What a grand, glorious result of four years of strife! My joy is exceeded only by my gratitude to God who has vouchsafed our national safety and about ended our sacrifices of blood. I presume you are all rejoicing at the north.

I have been very busy during the past week. We have been getting the new Regiment together and moving camp. Our camp is situated on an elevated plateau at the base of Big Rock, about a mile or more above Little Rock and on the opposite side of the river. It is a delightful spot of about fifteen acres clearing surrounded by dense woods. Wish you were here to take a stroll with me and pick

3. Union forces pushed the Confederates out of Petersburg and Richmond, Virginia, on April 2.
4. Lizzie supplied Madison with the list of photographs he requested: "Colnl Andrews, Mattson, Lester; Major Medge, Jenks, Bruce; Captains Hodges, Webster, Vanstrum, Taylor; Lieuts Otto, Greenleaf."
5. General Robert E. Lee surrendered at Appomattox Court House, Virginia, on April 9. General Joseph E. Johnston did not surrender, however, until April 26.

flowers. If we are kept in the service after the war is over you must certainly make up your mind to come here. I know that you would not regret having done so. Now, be a good girl, and say—yes.

Let me know whether Mr. Poor has paid you yet, and how much is yet due on our land. I presume you begin to have some faith in greenbacks by this time, do you not?

. . . Kiss my little darling Birdie. You do not know how much I long to look upon her innocent face again. Wish she could realize that papa thinks of her.

> Ever your loving,
> Madison.

Nininger Minn April 15, *1865*

Dear Husband

Since I last wrote to you there has been reason for rejoicing & to-night (if to-days news is true) we all have reason to feel sad indeed. Was it not that there is a ruler that does all things right, I should give up in despair. I can hardly realize that one who has labored so hard & who is beloved as Abraham Lincoln was can be no more. I feel as though the people take too much in their own hands and do not look to *God* often enough in these hours of national affliction. Do remember that while your spirits are cast down and you with the many thousands mourn the loss of him who has been slain by some brutal hand, [God] will do all things right if we only ask in faith, believing he will hear.[6]

I rec'd yours of the 1st of April to-day. You speak of the many beauties of Ark. I can not say a word about Minn. There has been but very little grain sowed yet. The ground is so full of frost & wet. The ice is not out of the Lake yet. So you see that it is anything but pleasant looking here. . . . What was the reason that they would not grant Eugene S an office? What do you think of the war by this time? You do not seem to say anything about coming home. . . .

> Lizzie

Little Rock, Ark.,
April [18?] 1865.

Dear Lizzie:

. . . We have the sad intelligence of the death of President Lincoln; but have received no particulars. The first intimation we had of this painful event was from

---

6. On the night of April 14, Confederate sympathizer John Wilkes Booth fatally wounded President Lincoln. Lizzie's reaction to the news reflects that of most Union supporters at home.

the firing of half-hour guns, commencing at sunrise. Shortly, however, an order came from Dept. Hdqrs, announcing it was received. Everybody is to abstain from all business, except from necessity, officers and soldiers to remain in camp, and half-hour guns to be fired from Fort Steele until sunset. I can think of no event which could create greater gloom in the hearts of patriots, than the violent death of Abraham Lincoln. To think of good, honest Abraham Lincoln being struck down by an assassin, is enough to make the nation weep. All are sad indeed to-day. This fills the cup of vengeance to overflowing. I think now, that I never shall forgive the traitors who have brought about this terrible event. I can fight them with good will till I die, if necessary.[7]

Yesterday we had a grand review of the 1st Division by Brevet Major Genl Solomon, commanding. Our Brigade (the 2d) consisting of six colored Regiments had to cross the river on steamers. It was terribly hot, and the men suffered severely. During the preliminaries I was overcome and had to leave the line and seek the shade; but got better after a while and again took my place. I could scarcely sit on my horse while the column passed in review.

... Kiss Baby for me. Learn her to speak and revere the name of Abraham Lincoln, the people's friend.

> Ever your loving,
> Madison.

April 21st, 1865.

Dear Madison

... While sitting here late in the evening much interested in a story entitled "Nellie Raymond's letter," who should pop in but Minnie with a letter from my absent Madison. I read it with interest as I always do your letters & went to bed to dream of seeing you. Wish I could see you to-day. It is lonely & snowing as hard as it can snow. Were it not that Minnie is here, it would be very lonely. I wish Minn. would have some of your June weather. You do not say a word any more about coming home. What time have you set to come home or have you given up thinking anything about it? When you do come, I want you to be sure & bring your horse with you. If you can. I wish you would send that cotton that we talked about. I have to pay three drs for enough to put in one comforter. Goods are falling now. Can get calico for Twenty cts such as we have paid 40 cts for all winter. ...

> Lizzie

7. Madison's feelings of vengeance were not uncommon. For Union soldiers' varying responses to Lincoln's assassination, see Davis, *Lincoln's Men*, 242–45.

Little Rock, Ark., April 22, 1865.

Dear Lizzie:

... Baby must be a great source of pleasure to you, with all her cunning ways. Wish I could have her company, too, this summer. It is not sickly here yet. Will not be until in July and from then to September. I have had no symptoms of ague yet. Never enjoyed better health in my life than I do now. I will not ask you to come south at present; but if there should be any prospect of my spending another winter south, then I think you will consent to come by next September. Lots of officers have had their families here during the past winter. I have forgotten about you fooling me on the stop last April. What was it? I had considerable few on the 1st. Got all the cigars I could smoke, by my pranks. ...

I think Mr. Poor should have paid that rent before this time. Hope I shall be able to send you more money hereafter than I have heretofore. My pay is much more now than it has been up to the 1st of March, and I have now got a good outfit all paid for. Besides, things are getting cheaper every day. ...

Our late victories have been most complete and glorious; but the sad calamity which has befallen the nation in the death of our beloved President, turns our joy to grief, our symbols of rejoicing into the habiliments of mourning. How hard it is to make ourselves believe that this dreadful news is a reality. We are not only shocked at the deed, but are completely lost in sorrow and sympathy for the cruel death of him we all had so much reason to love and admire, and who deserved a better fate. But Abraham Lincoln is not dead as other men die; he lives, like Washington, in the hearts of his countrymen—yes, in the hearts of every man, woman, and child throughout the civilized portion of the world, except such as have besotted their hearts in sin and treason. May providence soothe the sorrow of his bereaved wife and children. ...

> Ever your loving
> Madison.

Nininger April 28, 1865

Dear Husband

... Mr and Mrs. Donnelly got home day before yesterday. He was not at Washington when Lincoln was killed but went immediately after so that he attended the funeral. It is good to learn from day to day that Seward & his son are still recovering.[8]

8. Secretary of State William Henry Seward and his son, Fred, who was the assistant secretary of state, were wounded by one of Booth's coconspirators. See Taylor, *William Henry Seward*, 243-44.

Was quite disapointed to hear the Lieut Col Gustafson had given up coming to Minn, for I wanted to see him & hear the news from Little Rock, as I have given up all hope of ever hearing any more from you, as you (I believe) have made up your mind to always remain in the army.[9]

...I tried to learn Vic to say Abraham as you requested. Would make you laugh if you could hear her.

It must be very warm where you are. We have not had a day yet that we have not kept the fire burning to make it comfortably warm.

April 29, 1865

I rec'd another letter from you this morning with 100 drs enclosed. It came all right. Will pay it to Mr. Hayes on our place immediately, as I have never rec'd anything from Mrs. Poor yet but hope to before long, for I want that paid up and then it will done with. When you come home try to get a nice little negro boy to bring with you. What do you think of Shermans performances? ...[10]

I saw a boat go up this morning, the first one I have seen this year. ...

{written perpendicular on the top of the first page} When you answer this, tell me when you think you will come home. You do not know how impatient I am getting to see you again. Is your health good now, as it had been during the winter?

Lizzie

{top margin first page} There will be one hundred dollars to pay on the place and ninety after I pay that.

Nininger Minn. May 14th, 1865

Dear Husband

...I heard yesterday that the 9th Regt was expected home in a few days & the rest of the Minn soldiers shortly.[11] Oh! how glad I am that the war is so near ended.

Hope it will not be long till we will see all the soldiers in their old homes again. I have been sitting here thinking over the last four years & the many, many

9. John Gustafson, who had been first lieutenant of Company D, Third Minnesota, was commissioned as lieutenant colonel of the 112th U.S. Colored Infantry. See Andrews, "Narrative of the Third Regiment."

10. Lizzie probably is referring to the surrender terms that General Sherman negotiated with General Johnston. They were very lenient, which angered some in the North.

11. The First Minnesota had already been discharged on May 4, 1864. Most of the other Minnesota volunteer infantry regiments were mustered out between July and September. See Carley, *Minnesota in the Civil War,* 205-11.

changes that have taken place & while thinking this was a verse of a hymn composed by Coper came into my mind. I will here write it down for you to muse upon. "God moves in a misterious way / His wonders to perform / He plants his footsteps on the sea / And rides upon the storm."[12]

There has enough passed for the last few weeks to make any one realize the truth of this verse very sensibly. We have but very little news. The weather keeps very cold. It froze ice as thick a[s] window glass for the last three nights....

Yours ever Lizzie

{in scrawled writing on last page} Papa, I want you to come home just as soon as the war is ended. Victoria

Little Rock, Ark.,
May 16th, 1865.

Dear Lizzie:

... You are in error as to my having made up my mind to always stay in the army. I have no such mind. I have been in the army quite a while, I admit; but not longer than duty required. My position in the army has been a poor sinecure thus far, on account of the depreciation of our currency, and the high cost of these things which I have been obliged to purchase. My experience in recruiting for my Regt. has taught me that it costs money to engage in such an enterprise. I have not, therefore, saved so much as I expected to. From this time on every day in the service will pay me more than I could otherwise gain. A recent act of Congress gives three months additional pay to every officer who remains in the service until the Government is ready to dispense with his services, and orders him mustered out. The Regt to which I now belong will in all probability be one of the last to be mustered out, if mustered out at all. I wish to stay until that time or until I can have saved something. If peace ensues as soon as we expect, my remaining in the service need not keep us separated, nor deprive us of every comfort; for the camp in time of peace can be made as pleasant as home.

We have a very pleasant camping ground now. I have erected a log cabin for my comfort. Will describe it. It is about 15 by 16 feet, 8 ft high; has one window of 12 lights, and a *front door*, quite an essential qualification, as saves the trouble of climbing through the window, which you know I am not in the habit of doing. Furniture consists as follows: article no 1—bed composed of reede bark, *double* mattress, three blankets, and two empty bed ticks for sheets. Article no 2—table,

12. William Cowper wrote the hymn "God Moves in a Mysterious Way." See www .cyberhymnal.org/htm/g/m/gmovesmw.htm.

with two good drawers, and surmounted at present with a desk for books, papers, & trinkets in general, pitcher, glass, cup, and the remnants of crackers, cheese, candy and nuts with which I satisfied the darkies of the brigade band who serenaded me last night. The beer and cigars were entirely consumed by my brother officers who dropped in for the occasion; so I have not a cigar left to muse over while writing this. (I know I'll get fits for telling this.)

But to continue: article no 3 stove; no four, saddle and other horse equipment; concluding with sabre, revolver, and clothing suspended by the wall and reposing in [a] valise. Yes, there is a wash-basin and piece of soap, and towel, and the chair in which I am sitting. Just back of the house is the green woods and flowers, through which shines the green field and river beyond which is the city. In front is the rest of the camp. Before the door is a nice gravel walk and an apple tree. Lt. Col. Steele has just come in [and] picked up my little volume of "British poets," out of which he reads, "Farewell, Othello's occupation's gone," and remarks that we can sing that when we are mustered out. But if this Othello should be mustered-out and deprived of his occupation, he will seek his Desdemona; and together we will cultivate our *farm* and live in peace and happiness. But I must be more serious. I do miss you very greatly, Lizzie. I feel the need of your presence more and more every day, of your company, your society. I long, too, to look again upon that little being with which our Heavenly Father has blessed our union. The dear little creature! How often I think of her, and imagine how she looks as she toddles about, into mischief, a trouble and yet a priceless joy to you. If I remain in the army I hope sincerely that you will join me by September. We could live very pleasantly if you were here now, and I have little doubt but that it would be healthy for you here as in Minn.; but I will not ask you to come before September; but leave it entirely with you. I am well, and have been so, ever since I left the Hospital [after the] last Fever.

Give love to all. Kiss my little birdie for papa.

Remember me to Mr Donnelly and family.

Truly your loving Madison . . .

Nininger May 20th 1865

Dear Madison

. . . We have no reason to complain of drouth now. There has more rain fell this last week then we have had in two years. If we had warm weather things would grow very fast, but the weather the most of the time is very cool. I have got all my garden made. Have lots of melons for you when you come home.

You still talk of staying in the army. Don't you think that four years is long enough to be a soldier? I think it is. If I should think of going to Little Rock, I am afraid that something would happen to make me wish I was at home again. You know you talk a great deal about "patriotic sons." While you remain in the Army I do not want to hear any thing more about sons or daughters. When you leave it, then I will talk to you.

    [Lizzie]

{written along the side and top margins back page} I am going to call on Mrs. Donnelly to morrow. Have not seen her since she returned. . . .

{written along top margin first page} I heard a few days since in an indirect way that John Moulton is still living but is in the hands of the rebels yet. Cannot give any particulars, as I do not know them. . . .

June 2nd 1865

Dear Madison

I wrote a letter to you last Saturday when I was having a terrible fit of the blues.[13] Hope you will not feel when you read it as I did when I wrote it. To-day is too warm to have the blues [even] if one felt like it. I do not, so there is nothing lost. Guess it is not so warm as you speak of in your last letter, which I rec'd yesterday. Am glad it is not, for I would give up trying to live. Yesterday was national fast day. As one could have no preaching, Mr. Donnelly made a speech on the death of Lincoln & national affairs.[14] The assassination of the president caused great excitement. . . .

You speak of visiting east without you could get eight or ten weeks furlough. You had better wait till you come home to stop, for when we go that far I must go to New Brunswick. I want to go as much as you do. I have about made up my mind to go to Little Rock this fall if you remain there. Do you think there is any prospect of your Regt leaving there? I cannot go till the weather will cool, for I

13. The letter Lizzie refers to is not in the correspondence.

14. On June 1, 1865, the *Hastings Independent* reported: "To-day is the day of national mourning and prayer. Public services will be held at the Methodist Church. We cannot but recognize God with us in our great struggle, in public and private sorrows and in returning peace. Let us bow before him in humiliation this day." Ignatius Donnelly might have spoken in Nininger, where "the good people of Nininger raise a liberty pole to-day. The exercises will consist of speeches and singing." See the *Hastings Independent*, 1 June 1865. See also "Death and Victory," *Harper's Weekly*, 10 June 1865, 355.

would not dare go to a warmer climate with Vic in the hot weather. When you write, tell me all your proposed plans.

... I saw Rose Stone yesterday. She was at the lecture. I cannot send you ice in the letter, my sheet of paper is so large. But will try to get a piece when I write again. Wish you had some of our nice sistern water. Its so cool. Tis most full.

Will send you some pieces of crape in the next letter....[15]

> Good Bye
> Yours ever
> Lizzie

I have found some pieces of old crape if they will do, if not tell me & I will get you some new. How much is your pay a month now? ...

Little Rock, Ark.,
June 3d, 1865.
(Saturday)

Dear Lizzie:

... You ask me if I do not think four years long enough for soldier life. I have served so far with but little pecuniary profit to myself. I do not consider myself under the least obligation to the Gov't., to remain one day longer. But the matter is now reduced with me to dollars and cents. I can provide for the wants of my family and myself much more easily by holding my present position than in any other manner. Yet I care not for money only so far as it will go to promote the comfort and happiness of those I love dearer than all the earth beside. A few years of service in the Army in time of peace, need not deprive us of any of the comforts of home or of each others society and at the end of that time, I can retire with something like enough to render us a competency through life, if rightly used.[16] My pay is now $190.00 per month.

I have long been indulging the hope that you would join me here by next fall at farthest. I have pictured to myself the pleasure of seeing you enjoy for a time, new scenes, the sight of a country new to you, and a peep at the novelty of camp life and of military [life]—to see you enjoy rest and recreation, such as drives and horseback riding, and walks, with few cares to weigh you down.

15. Crepe was used for mourning the president and was probably at the Fast Day meetings the previous day.

16. On middle-class men's salaries, job choices, and work, see Boydston, *Home and Work,* 136-37; Ryan, *Cradle of the Middle Class,* 153-54; and Rose, *Victorian America and the Civil War,* 74-76.

I trust, Lizzie, that you will acquit me of any purely selfish feeling in this matter. I hope that you will view this matter in the light in which I have long tried to place it before you. *I shall never disregard your wishes* by an abruptness; I shall try *very hard to* induce you to co-incide in my arrangements, and if I fail I shall accuse myself with a want of those qualifications which should be able to inspire the confidence of a true woman; and it will only be left to me to regret my own weakness, and yield to your wishes, for the sake of promoting your happiness, which shall ever be my aim.[17] This much I shall ever be ready to do, if necessary. I speak in sober *earnestness*; and if I leave the army on your account it must be at your plain say so. I shall not allow you to flatter yourself that you can "wheedle" me to do so, by making light of my schemes—my dream-*pictures*. I wish I could talk with you to-day. My heart feels heavy. From the tone of your last letter I judge that I am mis-understood. I hope that you will not, even in thought, ascribe wrong intentions to me, or get out of patience with me.

Ever your—Madison...

Little Rock, Ark., June 17th, 1865.
(Saturday.)

Dear Lizzie:

... I wish that you could have been here during the last ten days. Last Saturday we had a grand review, and another on Monday. It was a splendid affair each time. I have never seen better affairs of the kind. The colored Brigade, consisting of five Regiments, had to march through the city going and returning, and everybody praises their appearance. Genls Reynolds and Solomon say that our Brigade beat everything else on the ground in appearance and in marching. The field music of the 113th took the premium. We had out eight fifers, fourteen drummers, and eight buglers, with new instruments purchased at their own expense, in Chicago. We had out the largest Regt., except the 12th Mich.

Last Tuesday I was before a Board of officers appointed to examine such officers as desire to remain in the military service of the United States. Genl. Solomon is President of the Board. In behalf of the Board he informed me that they were sufficiently well acquainted with me to pass me without examination, and to recommend me to be retained in service. I feel considerably complimented, as it is very rare that officers pass without a searching examination.

My colonel is on the same Board, and the Lt. Col. is on another Board of some

17. See Roberts, *American Alchemy*, 72–73, 78–80. For the relationship between marital authority and masculinity, see Rotundo, *American Manhood*, 106–7, 135–39.

kind; so I have been in command of the Regiment for the last two weeks. There is not much news. Everything is peace here. All of the guerrillas bands have come in and given up, and lots of rebels from Lee's, Jackson's, Taylor's, and Price's armies who went from here, have returned which gives us a good sprinkling of gray uniforms about town. They are greatly surprised at the fine appearance of the colored Troops.[18]

Lots of darkies are coming in from Texas. I have now got the best kind of a servant, only about two weeks from Texas. Can send you a colored boy now the first opportunity, which I guess will not be until the 3d Minn. goes home. Give my love to all the folks.

> Truly your loving
> Madison.

> Nininger June 18 1865
> Sunday Morning

Dear Madison

. . . It is raining very hard to day & very dull & lonely. I do not feel in the humor for writing much to you. Will have to put up with a short letter. Our folks are all well. Baby is real smart. I have been down to Nininger for two or three days. Come home yesterday & then went out & picked a quart of strawberries. Don't you wish you had some?

. . . Aunt Sarah got a letter from Am. He was discharged the day he wrote. Says he is going to Uncle Henry, who is [in] Montgomery, Nevada Terr. Aunt Sarah is in a great state about his not coming home. . . .[19]

> Yours Ever
> Lizzie

> Little Rock, Ark., June 20th, 1865.

Dear Lizzie:

I received yours of June 2d, yesterday. Was rejoiced to know that you were in the possession of your good spirits once more. I can not fully express to you how

---

18. Some of the Confederate generals in the West refused to surrender after news of Lee's and Johnston's surrenders. Many of their soldiers did want to surrender, however, and many deserted and returned home. See Thomas, *Arkansas in War and Reconstruction*, 315.

19. Uncle Henry was Henry Caleff. He had lived in Nininger in the 1850s but went west after the financial panic of 1857. See Case, "The Caleff Family of Bluff Landing," *Hastings Gazette*, 30 December 1921.

pleased I feel to have you consent to come to Little Rock this coming fall, if I remain here. There is no immediate prospect of our leaving here. Eventually we may be sent to some other post; but we are as likely to be retained here as permanent garrison as any other Regiment. At all events we shall not be sent to any poor post, for our Regiment stands well with the commanders, and it will be given as good a chance as any other. I intended, if I should go East, to visit *New Brunswick* by all means, because my object in visiting the East would be as much for your sake as for anything else. I am not anxious to visit there until we can do so satisfactorily, and as you do not think it best to go next fall, we will postpone it, and I will devote my attention to preparing for your accommodation here; and if it will only be for the purpose of meeting you some where on the road or going home for you.

. . . I cannot give you my plans fully, for they will depend upon circumstances somewhat. It is likely that my Regiment will be retained in service for a year or two at least; possibly longer. I thought, if opportunity offered, I would remain in the service for one, two, or three years, as occasion offers, and I can do well, and save some money.

I also thought it would give you an opportunity to travel where you would not likely soon to have an opportunity, if I was out of the army. I think the trip will furnish you some pleasing [sig]hts and form a page of [ple]asant recollections in after [years.] But God alone knows what is for the best. With our short sight we may be mistaken. . . .

. . . I received the crape all right. Thank you for it. I have received a letter from Ammon. He was in St Louis. Was going to Nininger, and then away for California. . . .

> Ever your loving,
> Madison.

Nininger, June 24th, 1865

Dear Madison

I received yours of the 9th yesterday.[20] Was glad to get it, for I have felt sort of blue ever since I got your other letter. By the way you wrote, I knew you were terribly out of sorts or, to sum the whole matter up, "felt badly." But know you did not feel any more blue then I did when I wrote you the letter you spoke off in your last. But tis past.

I will come to Little Rock in the fall if nothing transpires before that time to hinder me. I do not wish you to think that it was any selfish motive that has or

20. Madison's letter of June 9 is not in the correspondence.

will keep me from going, nor was it timidity that kept me. But you know Ma is away from all her friends, excepting her own family & her trouble has been great in having one child taken from her. When I would speak of going away she would not say much, but I knew it grieved her terribly, for she has had an idea if I went South I would never return or that you would wish to remain in the army for years. And feeling as she did or does, I dislike very much to leave her, but it is entirely on her account, for you know she is a good mother and gladly she would be mother to you if you were here. If we had a home & were settled down she would not care if I did go away, but tis the idea of going away so unsettled a people. But we all pray *God* to direct us and do the best we can. For my part, I feel it my duty as a wife to go if you really insisted upon it, but thinking you would be home in a short time I always put it off thinking it more talk than anything else.[21]

I suppose you judge from my actions last winter when you was home that I cared for no other place but Rose Hill, but you must not, for if you had not have been here I should have spent most of my time in bed. I often used to think if you only knew how miserably I felt, you would then know my reason for being so care for nothing. My health was very miserable until last winter. Now I feel pretty well.

Albert Poor tried to get discharged but could not. They have never paid a cent on any of the bills they owed yet. I think A is real mean. More then all that, I [don't] know when they will. Mr. Hazletine is expected back in a few days. I tried to get it as he wants his money, but it is no use to ask the women again.[22] Think likely it will remain so till you come home to collect it. Our field of wheat looks splendidly. Tis beginning to leaf out. The worms have destroyed most every thing in Minn but wheat. Taken large fields of corn, 15-20 acres in some places so there wont be half dozen hills left. Papa has 8 acres that looks very well. Am come home a few days ago. He is staying here now. Do wants you to send her the "Bonnie blue flag" the next time you write. I have just been listening [to] a pretty piece of music entitled "A song of a thousand years," perhaps you have heard it.[23] If not will sing it for you when I go to Little Rock. What if you are ordered away from there some time between this & fall? Our folks all send their love to you.

> Ever yours
> Lizzie...

21. For competing obligations to female kin and husbands, see Motz, *True Sisterhood*, 35-36.

22. The women or, rather, woman was Caroline Poor, Albert's wife. See Biographical Sketches, P-W, folder 2, Case Papers.

23. "The Bonnie Blue Flag" was written by Harry McCarthy in 1861. It was widely sung in the South. See Commager, *The Civil War Archive*, 374. Henry C. Work wrote "Song of a Thousand Years" for piano and chorus in 1863; it was published in Chicago by Root

I want you to tell me what your plans are. If I do go to you, I want to live where you are living now if it is so we can or if it is a proper place for me to live. You need not think by my asking the question that I am uneasy about a place, for that is my last concern, but I just want to know so I can have some idea where I am going. I cannot go with an idea of staying longer then spring, for I would not like to endanger babys life. But that we will settle when [we] get down there. Vic grows fast. Is very well now and horribly mischevious. But you will say, how could she have the father she has and be any other way? I feel if I were by you I could talk a whole day without stoping. . . .[24]

Little Rock, Ark., June 24th, 1865.

Dear Lizzie:

. . . I am going to write to mother [Caleff] soon, and will mention the matter which you wish me to. I am not at all disposed to object to you manifesting an interest in my well being both bodily and spiritually, or to you lecturing me when I need it; but I am of the opinion that you as well as mother entertain erroneous ideas in regard to my present surroundings. The trials, hardships, and horrors of actual field service in time of war are not, I freely admit, very conducive to morality, but I can see nothing about an army in time of peace that is at all calculated to contaminate. The discipline is strict,—habits regular. The advantages of good society can be had more conveniently than when one works from morn till night behind the plow or at the bench.[25] I do not associate with the negroes of the Regiment. My chief associates, at present, are the officers of the Regiment, and they are mostly gentlemen. They have all passed examination before a Military Board, where one of the indespensible requisites was good moral character. But I know that I am, as I always have been, very far from what I ought to be. I hope and pray

---

& Cady. See the Historic American Sheet Music Collection, 1850–1920, at Duke University, memory.loc.gov/ammem/award97/ncdhtml/hasmhome.html.

24. Lizzie must have wanted to discuss her move further. After filling her letter paper, she wrote the last paragraph on a small sheet to enclose with her letter.

25. See Mitchell, *The Vacant Chair*, 30–32. Madison's defense of army life is interesting when juxtaposed with a letter he wrote to Susan Caleff, Lizzie's mother, on August 29, 1864. After complaining about stolen clothes and exorbitant prices for vegetables, he concluded: "Everything except depravity is scarce and high priced." He also commented, "Almost every person one meets seems to be debilitated from some cause or other." It is little wonder that Susan Caleff worried about Lizzie and Victoria's moving to Little Rock. For this letter, see Misc. Bowler/Caleff Letters, box 1, Bowler Papers.

that I may be better, that I may come to have a hope and trust in Heaven. I would not remain in the army one moment to diminish my chances for such a boon.

As to promising you that I will go home by next spring, I cannot do it. I cannot promise anything definitely; but I will say as I have said before, that I regard it as a solemn duty and a pleasure to me, to regard your wishes in matters affecting your own happiness. If my stay in the army makes you unhappy I will resign at once, unless you are willing to come here and join me. I can be happy enough here, if I can have you with me; but I cannot deny myself the pleasure of your society just to remain in the army. I just want you to make up your mind to come here; then we can talk. You can then see for yourself, and can *then* tell whether you think it better for me to resign. I read Sarah's letter with pleasure. Will return it to you in a few days. Anna seems to be taken with fits in her matrimonial peregrinations. Guess it's six in one, and half dozen in the other.

Am glad to know that little Vicki continues in good health. O, how I want to see her. Can hardly wait until September. We shall be paid again in the course of two or three weeks. I will then send you money enough to pay up all indebtedness. My horse took sick in the Spring and has not been fit for duty since, and I had to buy another, or I should have sent you another hundred dollars before now. If you consent to come I will try to meet you in Chicago by the 1st of September, if you think it advisable. . . .

> Ever your loving,
> Madison.

Nininger July 2nd 1865

Dear Madison

. . . The soldier boys are all coming home. C Sprague[,] P & Levi Countryman, Ben Mabee, Tom Callahan have all come. We (Do, Am, & I) were up to make Maggie a call last evening. . . .[26] I[t] has been raining most of the time for the last week, making up I guess for lost time.

Tis beautiful this morning. I am going to take Vic to Sunday school. Have taken her several times. She is real good. Want her to learn to be good in meet-

---

26. Cassius Sprague, Peter Countryman, and Levi Countryman had all enlisted in the Second Minnesota, Company D, in early 1865. Benjamin Mabee had enlisted in the First Minnesota, Company B, in the fall of 1864. Tom Callahan served as a citizen with the quartermaster's department. See Kump, *The Burkes, the Barretts and Others,* 330–31. Like several other Nininger and Hastings men, he might have gone to the South or the West in search of economic opportunities.

ing. When I go to Little Rock, I am going to take you & her to meeting with me. What are you going to do on the 4th? There is to be a great time in Hastings.[27] I expect to stay at home. Well, must say Good Bye.

> Ever your
> Lizzie

> Mouth White River, Ark.,
> July 26th, 1865.

Dear Lizzie:

I received yours of July 2d, several days ago. Press of business and the very warm weather have kept me from answering it as soon as I ought to have done. I begin almost to count the hours which separate us. Hope that the cool season will set in early this year, so that your coming may be hastened. Let me know about what time you will be able to start on your journey.

I am anxious to have you come just as soon as the sickly season is past; but think that you had better not to start from home before the 1st of September, as this is not quite so healthy a locality as Little Rock. I am well as usual. Get lots of nice vegetables and fruit—such as, new potatoes, green corn, onions, cucumbers, okera, cabbage, and beets; and fresh peaches, apples, and pears. Also melons, chickens, &c. Have never lived better since I entered the service. I like my new situation much. Peace reigns supreme. Have now and then to arrest some offender or other against law and order, and to scare some of the planters into permitting their (late) slaves to exercise and enjoy the full rights of freemen. Have had the pleasure of making several old wealthy aristocrats in Miss., opposite here, fork over colored children to their parents who had left their old masters and come here. Made one old scamp, named Perkins, send to Alabama and return a little mulatto girl of ten years, which he had run off there to get it away from the mother, who lives here.[28] She comes in to see "major" every day. There is a little fellow named Snoball, which I think you would like. Am going to have him live with me if you should want him when you have seen him. I believe that the negro population hereabouts think pretty well of us. I try to give them their rights so long withheld—and to assist them every way I can. Their old masters

27. For the Fourth of July celebration in Hastings, see *Hastings Conserver,* 11 July 1865.

28. For freedmen's rights and treatment, see Berlin et al., *Slaves No More,* 177-84. Madison's attitude, although patronizing, was more liberal than that of many in the Freedmen's Bureau in Arkansas. See Finley, "The Personnel of the Freedmen's Bureau in Arkansas," 100-104.

grant their freedom very grudgingly, and in many cases beyond the eye of the military, they are but little better than slaves yet. . . .[29]

> Ever your loving,
> Madison.

Nininger July 30th 1865

Dear Madison

. . . The money came through all save.[30] Papa went out to Hampton day before yesterday and settled with Mr. Hazletine. There was 195 drs due on the principle & $33.00 interest. Tis all settled so there will be no more of that. I was sorry to hear that you had been having such a time with that boil. Hope you will feel well now. Think boils are healthy. . . .[31] Is it a Town where you are stationed now? You complain of misquitoes but I bet you cannot beat us. . . .

> Ever yours
> Lizzie[32]

Nininger Minn Aug 20, 1865

Dear Madison

. . . I am sorry that you have made so much readiness to meet me on the 1st of Sep, for it will be impossible for me to get ready. I went and seen Albert about cutting the grain & he promised faithfully he would come the day appointed & the morning before he was to come sent word that he could not come. Then papa had to get some one else. When I found that he was so disobliging, I sent him a note requesting him to pay that money immediately but have heard nothing from it since. Consequently do not know any thing about what he intends to do. So you see what use it is for any one to think of any thing. There will be a St. Louis boat leave here on the 20th of Sept. If nothing takes place before that time to hinder me, I will start that day. I hope it will be so that you will meet me, for I cannot bear the Idea of going alone all the way. I hope to see Will Govette.

29. The attitude that Madison describes about white plantation owners is projected in Thomas's 1926 *Arkansas in War and Reconstruction*. For example, two chapters are entitled "The Nightmare of Reconstruction and Carpet-Bag Rule" and "The End of the Nightmare."
30. Lizzie means "safe" rather than "save."
31. Madison's letter of July 13 is not in the correspondence, and it is in this letter that he probably refers to the boil.
32. Another note addressed to "Dear Papa" followed, written very illegibly. Part of it states that Victoria weighed thirty-five pounds.

You may think me dilatory about coming but I do not make up my mind to any thing nowadays for there is so many changes. Tis a true saying "We propose but God disposes."

We had a terrible thunder storm last night kept me awake most of the night. Well, tis getting late & I must stop.

I have never told you what good preaching we have at Nininger now there is a [?] man stay[ing] at Mr. Robertson's. He was a Dr in the Crimean War. Has traveled through the Holy Land. Is a very interesting person & a very moral preacher.

Lizzie

{top margin front page} I will be prepared for those kisses and hugs.

Mouth White River, Ark.,
September 14th, 1865.

Dear Lizzie:

I arrived here from St Louis on the 12th inst. . . . You had better see Mr Poor, and get him to secure you the amount of his note, if you can. If not, you can leave the note with Mr. Caleff for collection. Anyway do the best you can, and let it rest at that. We can live, I guess, if we never get it. Let him have the good of his meanness. Maybe he will prosper by such conduct. I am feeling quite well once more. I sent you $100.00 by Express from St. Louis. My friends here welcomed me back heartily. I feel at home here. There is no town here—only a military station for the distribution of supplies. If you do not like here I will go to Devalls Bluff, as I can have that privilege.

Love to all.
Ever yours.
Madison.

Epilogue

After Lizzie and Victoria joined Madison in the fall of 1865, the Bowlers lived in Jacksonport, Arkansas, where Madison served as an agent of the Freedmen's Bureau until April 1866.[1] They then returned to Nininger, perhaps because Lizzie was pregnant with their second child and would have wanted to have her mother near her for childbirth. Their second daughter, Susan, was born in September 1866, but she died a few days later. In the next five years the family grew: Edward was born in January 1868 but died at eleven months; Amy was born in November 1869; and Burton was born in November 1871. In 1873 the Bowlers sold their farm in Nininger and moved west to Bird Island in Renville County, Minnesota. While there, Lizzie gave birth to five more children, including Katherine (1873), Madison (1875), Frank (1877), and Josephine (1881). The last, Edna, was born nearly twenty years after Victoria, in August 1883.[2]

The Bowlers essentially started over at Bird Island. Lizzie remembers, "In 1856 my father and mother with their three daughters left the eastern home with all its comforts and immigrated to Minnesota where we built a new home on the raw prairie. That experience was helpful when later I repeated it in Renville County where we had to endure so much inconvenience and hardship."[3] Before the family moved onto the new farm, Madison plowed the prairie grass and planted wheat and flowers seeds. Lizzie's reminiscence, written for her family in her later years, is filled with stories typical of early white pioneers, like those of

1. See "Major J. M. Bowler, Veteran, Democratic Leader, Dies," *Minneapolis Journal,* 18 May 1916. Jacksonville is at the confluence of the White River and the Black River in Jackson County, Arkansas.

2. See "Bowler-Caleff Family Genealogy and History," Bowler Papers. Madison worked at a planing mill in St. Anthony from June through August 1866. In October he was appointed school examiner for District 2 in Dakota County. In January 1867 he attended a teachers school in St. Paul. In 1870 he worked on the Northern Pacific Railroad during the summer. See box 2, Bowler Papers.

3. See "Bowler-Caleff Family Genealogy and History," Bowler Papers.

The Bowler family in 1892:
back row, left to right, *Walter Law (son-in-law), Madison (son), Kate, Burt, Frank, Amy;*
front row, *Victoria Bowler Law holding daughter Helen, Madison,*
Josephine, Lizzie, Edna, and Samuel Caleff (Lizzie's father)

Laura Ingalls Wilder: enduring difficult journeys in prairie schooners, accommodating unexpected guests by providing food and shelter, giving birth to the first white child in the township, not seeing other women for weeks at a time, and experiencing blizzards and grasshoppers. Lizzie's Civil War letters indicate that families and friends were very important to her. At Bird Island her sisters-in-law, Sarah Bowler and Georgette Bowler Hickock, and her sister Dorothy Caleff Adams lived with their families. Eventually, several other Nininger- and Hastings-area families also moved to Renville County, so it did not seem so lonely.[4]

4. On May 4, 1872, the *Hastings Gazette* reported that "a party consisting of Maj. J. M. Bowler, Capt. John King, J. S. Bowler, Marion Boyer, Calvin Boyer, John Johnson, and Miss Dora J. Caleff, all of Nininger in this county, took their departure on Monday for Renville County, where they have secured homesteads." Several former Nininger-area families moved to Bird Island, including Newton Poor and Alonzo Briggs. See Biographical Sketches, P–W, folder 2, Case Papers; and Curtiss-Wedge, *The History of Renville County Minnesota*, 324.

Habits and attitudes from the war lingered in later years. During the war Lizzie had lectured Madison about smoking and tobacco use. Perhaps not coincidentally, in 1877 Madison went to Massachusetts General Hospital for surgery to remove cancer on his lip and throat.[5] Madison had entered the war with firm political convictions and, in later years, involved himself in politics. He served in the state legislature in 1878 and as speaker's clerk in 1891. He also held elected positions in his school district and in Bird Island. By the end of the century, Madison had returned to his political roots. He had been a Democrat in Maine and a Republican during the war. In 1891, however, he was appointed state dairy commissioner as a Democrat and, in 1896 and 1898, ran for lieutenant governor as a Democrat.[6]

In 1901 the couple sold their farm at Bird Island and bought a house in Minneapolis. They then built a house in 1912 in the St. Anthony Park neighborhood of St. Paul. Madison died May 17, 1916, at the age of seventy-eight. After her husband's death Lizzie lived with their youngest daughter, Edna, and in 1920 moved to Crosby, Minnesota, until her death on January 24, 1931, at the age of ninety.[7]

5. See "Bowler-Caleff Family Genealogy and History," Bowler Papers; and letters, 7 August 1877 and 7 September 1877, box 2, Bowler Papers.

6. See "J. M. Bowler, State Pioneer, Once Political Leader, Dies," *Minneapolis Tribune,* 18 May 1916; and *Minneapolis Journal,* 18 May 1916. For his being a Democrat turned Republican, see Aunt Pamelia Bowler Whiting to Madison Bowler, 26 September [year unknown], Bowler Papers.

7. Lizzie left a handwritten will for her children and their families, dated August 3, 1928. The text of her will is contained in the family genealogy.

Appendix A
Bowler-Caleff Family Tree

Bowler-Caleff Family Tree

Robert Caleff (D)
Henrietta (wife)
Hasting, MN

Rob Caleff

Sarah Caleff
Nininger, MN

Amon McMullen (adopted)
7th MN

Margaret Hawkins
William (husband)
Hampton, MN

Dolly & John Hawkins (plus 6 siblings)

W. Henry Caleff
California

Peter Caleff
Elizabeth (wife)
Hastings, MN

2 children

Samuel Caleff
B. 8 February 1807
Nininger, MN
D. 21 June 1901

Katherine Caleff
B. ~1857
D. 3 November 1863

Dorothy Caleff
B. ~1843

Susan Justason
B. 31 May 1807
Nininger, MN
D. 1883

ELIZABETH SARAH CALEFF
B. 9 September 1840
M. 30 November 1862
Nininger, MN
D. 24 January 1931

Burton Haskell Bowler
B. 7 November 1871
D. 16 April 1952

Victoria Augusta Bowler
B. 16 September 1863
D. 29 November 1972

Susan Bowler
B. 14 September 1866
D. 25 September 1866

Edward True Bowler
B. 24 January 1868
D. 29 December 1868

Amy Georgette Bowler
B. 14 November 1869
D. 15 September 1910

Note: This chart is not comprehensive. It includes family members mentioned in the letters and the Bowlers' children. It is constructed from information in the letters and from the "Bowler-Caleff Family History and Genealogy," box 3, Bowler Papers.

Bowler-Caleff Family Tree

James H.
Bowler
Bangor, ME

Edward Bowler
B. 3 September 1811
Lee, ME

Clara Augusta Smith
B. 26 November 1817
Patten, ME

Joseph
Smith
St. Anthony, MN

Sarah
Smith Lowell
Calais, ME

[?]
Smith True
Patten, ME

JAMES MADISON
BOWLER
B. 10 January 1838
M. 30 November 1862
Nininger, MN
3rd MN & 113th U.S.C.T.
D. 17 May 1916

Joseph Smith
Bowler
B. 18 October 1841
Sarah
(wife)
Lee, ME
22nd & 11th ME

Sarah Frances
Bowler
B. 16 May 1844
George Haskell
(husband)
Lee, ME

Georgette
Bowler
B. 27 March 1846
Lee, ME

Clara
Bowler
B. 24 November 1848
Lee, ME

Katherine Clara Bowler
B. 25 September 1873
D. 9 January 1971

Madison Caleff Bowler
B. 26 September 1875
D. 8 August 1941

Frank Leslie Bowler
B. 9 August 1877
D. 31 March 1959

Josephine Adams Bowler
B. 1 November 1881
D. 25 April 1907

Edna Beatrice Bowler
B. 14 August 1883
D. 25 January 1993

Appendix B
Madison's and Lizzie's
Letter-writing Frequency

Note: These are only the letters for which there is a record. In total, there are 296 letters. Madison wrote 165, and Lizzie wrote 131.

1861

Month	Madison Days Sent	Total	Lizzie Days Sent	Total
April	27	1		
May	2	1	11	1
June		0		0
July		0		0
August		0		0
September	30	1		0
October	10, 19, 28*	3	2, 19*, 29	3
November		0	2, 30*	2
December	3*, 18, 22	3	6, 23, 30*	3
		9		9

*Asterisked letters are not in the Bowler Papers but are mentioned in their other letters.

1862

Month	Madison Days Sent	Total	Lizzie Days Sent	Total
January	2*, 10, 23*	3	12, 27	2
February	5, 13, 21, 28	4	1, 9, 16, 26*	4
March	13, 20, 26	3	2, 9, 16, 27*	4
April	4, 10, 13, 17, 24, 28	6	3*, 7*, 15, 30	4
May	5, 8, 15, 22, 29	5	6, 10*, 13, 26*	4
June	5, 22, 26	3	5*, 10	2
July	2, 19, 31	3		0
August	8, 13	2		0
September	5, 10, 15, 23, 27	5	14*, 28*	2
October	9, 14, 22	3	5, 19*, 31	3
November		0		0
December	17	1		0
		38		25

1863

Month	Madison — Days Sent	Total	Lizzie — Days Sent	Total
January	14, 22, [?]*, 29	4	21, 26	2
February	6, 10*, 15, 17, 26	5	7, 14, 21	3
March	3, 12, 17*, 31	4	7, 14, 22, 30*	4
April	7, 15, 30	3	5, 19, 23	3
May	7, 10*, 20, 24, 28, 30	6	1*, 14*, 16, 28	4
June	4, 8, 12, 24, 29	5	18, 30*	2
July	5 (2), 19, 30	4	7, 11*, 19, 26	4
August	4, 19, 12, 22, 26	5	2*, 10, 17, 30	4
September	9, 16	2	6, 13*, 25	3
October	3, 5, 10*, 21, 23	5	3*, 13, 23	3
November	14, 27	2	6, 14*, 24*, 30*	4
December	4, 10, 12, 18, 21, 23	6	10*, 17, 24	3
		51		39

1864

Month	Madison — Days Sent	Total	Lizzie — Days Sent	Total
January	1, 19	2	8, 16*	2
February	6	1	1	1
March		0		0
April	27	1	21	1
May	1	1	12*, 17*, 25*	3
June	3, 7, 15, 17	4	2, 20*, 26	3
July	2, 8, 10, 26*, 29*	5	3, 10, 22, 29	4
August	7, 14, 17*, 24, 27	5	10, 15, 21, 29*	4
September	7, 12, 16, 24, 27	5	2, 11*, 28	3
October	2, 6, 23, 26	4	8*, 14, 25	3
November	1, 6, 15, 30	4	11, 24*	2
December	3, 11, 27	3	8, 25	2
		35		28

1865

Month	Madison		Lizzie	
	Days Sent	*Total*	*Days Sent*	*Total*
January	6*, 10, 22	3	1*, 8, 15*, 22, 29	5
February	2, 6, 18, 26	4	1*, 5, 12*, 19, 28	5
March	2, 16, 24, 26*	4	4*, 8, 25	3
April	1, 5, 11, 14, 18, 22	6	1*, 9, 15, 21, 28	5
May	2*, 5*, 16	3	14, 20, [?]*	3
June	3, 9*, 17, 20, 24	5	2, 11*, 18, 24	4
July	13*, 17*, 26	3	2, 30	2
August	14, 24	2	11*, 20	2
September	11, 14	2	3*	1
		32		30

Bibliography

PRIMARY SOURCES

Andrews, General C. C. "Narrative of the Third Regiment." In Board of Commissioners, *Minnesota in the Civil and Indian Wars,* 147-77.

Annual Report of the Adjutant General, of the State of Minnesota. St. Paul: Pioneer Printing Company, 1866.

Annual Re-Union of the Third Regiment Minnesota Veteran Volunteers. Minneapolis, MN: The Association, 1886-1931.

Board of Commissioners. *Minnesota in the Civil and Indian Wars, 1861-1865.* Vol. 1. 2nd ed. St. Paul: Pioneer Press Company, 1891. Reprinted with vol. 2, St. Paul: Minnesota Historical Society Press, 2005.

Bowler, James Madison, and Family Papers, 1827-1976. Minnesota Historical Society, St. Paul.

Brookins, George W., and Family Letters, 1861-1865. Minnesota Historical Society, St. Paul.

Case, John H., Papers. Minnesota Historical Society, St. Paul.

Commager, Henry Steele, ed. *The Civil War Archive: The History of the Civil War in Documents.* New York: Black Dog and Leventhal Publishers, 2000.

Countryman, Levi N., Papers. Minnesota Historical Society, St. Paul.

Dakota County. *Dakota County Abstract Book.* T-115 R 17 and 18. Hastings Nininger #27. Dakota County Government Center, Hastings, MN.

DeHart, William C. *Observations on Military Law, and the Constitution and Practice of Courts Martial.* New York: Wiley and Halsted, 1859. Reprint, Buffalo: William S. Hein and Company, 1973.

Donnelly, Ignatius, Papers. M138. Minnesota Historical Society, St. Paul.

Hale, William D., and Family Papers, 1836-1915. Minnesota Historical Society, St. Paul.

Livermore, Mary A. *My Story of the War: A Woman's Narrative of Four Years Personal Experience.* Hartford, CT: Worthington and Company, 1890.

Lombard, C. W. *History of the Third Regiment Infantry Minnesota Volunteers with the Final Record of the Original Regiment.* Faribault, MN, 1869.

Mattson, Hans, and Family Papers. Box 1. Minnesota Historical Society, St. Paul.

Minnesota Adjutant General's Report of 1866 (Alphabetical Listing). Roseville, MN: Park Genealogical Books, 1997.

Minnesota State Government. *Minnesota State Census, 1865.* Minnesota Historical Society, St. Paul.

Minnesota Territorial Government. *Minnesota Territorial Census, 1857.* Minnesota Historical Society, St. Paul.

Mitchell, W. H. *Dakota County: Its Past and Present, Geographical, Statistical and Historical, Together with a General View of the State.* Minneapolis: Tribune Printing Company, 1868.

Prentice, George Denison. *Prenticeana; or, Wit and Humor in Paragraphs. By the Editor of the Louisville Journal.* New York: Derby and Jackson, 1860.

U.S. Army. Department of Arkansas. General Order No. 39. Little Rock. Broadside Collection (B6–972). University of Arkansas, Fayetteville.

U.S. Army. James M. Bowler Court Martial File (LL-600). National Archives and Records Administration, Washington, D.C.

U.S. Census Office. *Eighth Decennial Census of the United States, 1860.* Washington, D.C.: Robert Armstrong, 1864.

U.S. Congress. *Congressional Globe.* 38th Cong., 2nd sess. Vol. 35.

The War of the Rebellion: A Compilation of the Official Records of the Union and Confederate Armies. Ser. 3, vol. 3. Washington, D.C.: Government Printing Office, 1899.

Washburn, Jesse A. and Luman P., Papers, 1862–1864. Minnesota Historical Society, St. Paul.

Wheelock, Joseph Albert, Commissioner of Statistics. *Minnesota: Its Place among the States.* Hartford, CT: Press of Case, Lockwood and Company, 1860.

SECONDARY SOURCES

Ahlstrom, Sydney E. *A Religious History of the American People.* New Haven, CT: Yale University Press, 1972.

Anderson, Gary Clayton. *Kinsmen of Another Kind: Dakota-White Relations in the Upper Mississippi Valley, 1650–1862.* Lincoln: University of Nebraska Press, 1984. Reprint, St. Paul: Minnesota Historical Society Press, 1997.

Anderson, Gary Clayton, and Alan R. Woolworth, eds. *Through Dakota Eyes: Narrative Accounts of the Minnesota Indian War of 1862.* St. Paul: Minnesota Historical Society Press, 1988.

Ash, Stephen A. *When the Yankees Came: Conflict and Chaos in the Occupied South, 1861–1865.* Chapel Hill: University of North Carolina Press, 1995.

Attie, Jeanie. *Patriotic Toil: Northern Women and the American Civil War.* Ithaca, NY: Cornell University Press, 1998.

———. "Warwork and the Crisis of Domesticity in the North." In Clinton and Silber, *Divided Houses.*

Bell, Christine Ann. "A Family Conflict: Visual Imagery of the 'Homefront' and the War between the States, 1860–1866." PhD diss., Northwestern University, 1996.

Berlin, Ira, Barbara J. Fields, Steven F. Miller, Joseph P. Reidy, and Leslie S. Rowland. *Slaves No More: Three Essays on Emancipation and the Civil War.* New York: Cambridge University Press, 1992.

Berry, Stephen W., II. *All That Makes a Man: Love and Ambition in the Civil War South.* New York: Oxford University Press, 2003.

Betts, Vicki. "'Dear Husband': The Civil War Letters of Sophronia Joiner Chipman, Kanakee County, Illinois, 1863–1865." *Military History of the West* 29 (Fall 1999): 146–98.

Bollet, Alfred J., MD. *Civil War Medicine: Challenges and Triumphs.* Tucson, AZ: Galen Press, 2002.

Boydston, Jeanne. *Home and Work: Housework, Wages, and the Ideology of Labor in the Early Republic*. New York: Oxford University Press, 1990.

Bunch, Clea Lutz. "Confederate Women of Arkansas Face 'the Fiends in Human Shape.'" *Military History of the West* 27 (Fall 1997): 173–87.

Byatt, A. S. *Possession: A Romance*. New York: Random House, 1990. Modern Library Edition, 2001.

Carley, Kenneth. *The Dakota War of 1862: Minnesota's Other Civil War*. St. Paul: Minnesota Historical Society Press, 1976. First published as *The Sioux Uprising of 1862*, Minnesota Historical Society Press, 1961.

———. *Minnesota in the Civil War: An Illustrated History*. St. Paul: Minnesota Historical Society Press, 2000.

Cashin, Joan E. "Deserters, Civilians, and Draft Resistance in the North." In Cashin, *The War Was You and Me*.

———. "'Since the War Broke Out': The Marriage of Kate and William McLure." In Clinton and Silber, *Divided Houses*.

Cashin, Joan E., ed. *The War Was You and Me: Civillians in the American Civil War*. Princeton, NJ: Princeton University Press, 2002.

Christ, Mark K., ed. *Rugged and Sublime: The Civil War in Arkansas*. New York: Fordham University Press, 1994.

Cimbala, Paul A., and Randall M. Miller, eds. *The Freedmen's Bureau and Reconstruction: Reconsiderations*. New York: Fordham University Press, 1999.

———. *Union Soldiers and the Northern Homefront: Wartime Experiences, Postwar Adjustments*. New York: Fordham University Press, 2002.

Clinton, Catherine. "'Public Women' and Sexual Politics during the American Civil War." In Clinton and Silber, *Battle Scars*.

———. *Tara Revisited: Women, War and Plantation Legend*. New York: Abbeville Press, 1995.

Clinton, Catherine, and Nina Silber, eds. *Battle Scars: Gender and Sexuality in the Civil War*. New York: Oxford University Press, 2006.

———. *Divided Houses: Gender and the Civil War*. New York: Oxford University Press, 1992.

Cooling, B. Franklin. "A People's War: Partisan Conflict in Tennessee and Kentucky." In Sutherland, *Guerillas, Unionists, and Violence on the Confederate Homefront*.

Cott, Nancy F. *The Bonds of Womanhood: "Woman's Sphere" in New England, 1780–1835*. New Haven, CT: Yale University Press, 1977.

Curtiss-Wedge, Franklyn. *The History of Renville County Minnesota*. Chicago: H. C. Cooper Jr. and Company, 1916.

Davis, William C. *Lincoln's Men: How President Lincoln Became Father to an Army and a Nation*. New York: Free Press, 1999.

DeHart, William C. *Observations on Military Law, and the Constitution and Practice of Courts Martial*. New York: Wiley and Halsted, 1859. Reprint, Buffalo, NY: William S. Hein and Company, 1973.

Donald, David Herbert, Jean Harvey Baker, and Michael F. Holt. *The Civil War and Reconstruction*. New York: W. W. Norton and Company, 2001.

Duke, Basil Wilson. *Morgan's Cavalry*. New York: Neale Publishing Company, 1906.

Duncan, Russell, ed. *Blue-Eyed Child of Fortune: The Civil War Letters of Colonel Robert Gould Shaw*. Athens: University of Georgia Press, 1992.

Dyer, Frederick H. *A Compendium of the War of the Rebellion, Compiled and Arranged from Official Records of the Federal and Confederate Armies, Reports of the Adjutant Generals of the Several States, the Army Registers, and Other Reliable Documents and Sources.* Cedar Rapids, IA: Torch Press, 1908. Accessed at www.rootsweb.com/~ilcivilw/dyers/128inf.htm.

Elder, Donald C., III, ed. *Love amid the Turmoil: The Civil War Letters of William and Mary Vermilion.* Iowa City: University of Iowa Press, 2003.

Faust, Drew Gilpin. *Mothers of Invention: Women of the Slaveholding South in the American Civil War.* New York: Vintage Books, 1996.

———. "'Ours as Well as That of the Men': Women and Gender in the Civil War." In McPherson and Cooper, *Writing the Civil War.*

Finley, Randy. "The Personnel of the Freedmen's Bureau in Arkansas." In Cimbala and Miller, *The Freedmen's Bureau and Reconstruction.*

Fisher, Noel C. "Definitions of Victory: East Tennessee Unionists in the Civil War and Reconstruction." In Sutherland, *Guerillas, Unionists, and Violence.*

Fitzharris, Joseph C. "'Our Disgraceful Surrender': The Third Minnesota Infantry's Disintegration and Reconstruction in 1862–1863." *Military History of the West* 30 (Spring 2000): 1–20.

Folwell, William Watts. *A History of Minnesota.* Vol. 2. St. Paul: Minnesota Historical Society Press, 1924.

Forbes, Ella. *African American Women during the Civil War.* New York: Garland Publishing, 1998.

Foroughi, Andrea. "Ephemeral Town, Enduring Community: Space, Gender, and Power in Nininger, Minnesota, 1851–1870." PhD diss., University of Minnesota, 1999.

———. "Vine and Oak: Husbands and Wives Cope with the Financial Panic of 1857." *Journal of Social History* 36 (Summer 2003): 1009–32.

Gillett, Mary C. *The Army Medical Department, 1818–1865.* Washington, D.C.: Center of Military History, United States Army, 1987.

Glatthaar, Joseph T. "Duty, Country, Race, and Part: The Evans Family of Ohio." In Cashin, *The War Was You and Me.*

———. *Forged in Battle: The Civil War Alliance of Black Soldiers and White Officers.* New York: Free Press, 1990.

Gordon, Beverly. *Bazaars and Fair Ladies: The History of the American Fundraising Fair.* Knoxville: University of Tennessee Press, 1998.

Greene, John T., ed. *The Ewing Family Civil War Letters.* East Lansing: Michigan State University Press, 1990.

Griffith, Paddy. *Battle Tactics of the Civil War.* New Haven, CT: Yale University Press, 1989.

Guelcher, Leslie. *The History of Nininger . . . More Than Just a Dream.* Stillwater, MN: Croixside Press, 1982.

Hacker, James David. "The Human Cost of War: White Population in the United States, 1850–1880." PhD diss., Department of History, University of Minnesota, 1999.

Hage, George S. *Newspapers on the Minnesota Frontier, 1849–1860.* St. Paul: Minnesota Historical Society Press, 1967.

Hess, Earl J. *Liberty, Virtue, and Progress: Northerners and Their War for the Union.* 2nd ed. New York: Fordham University Press, 1997.

———. *The Union Soldier in Battle: Enduring the Ordeal of Combat.* Lawrence: University Press of Kansas, 1997.

Hicken, Victor. *Illinois in the Civil War.* Urbana: University of Illinois Press, 1966.

Hoffert, Sylvia D. "Gender and Vigilantism on the Minnesota Frontier: Jane Grey Swisshelm and the U.S.-Dakota Conflict of 1862." *Western Historical Quarterly* 29 (Autumn 1998): 342-62.

———. *Jane Grey Swisshelm: An Unconventional Life, 1815-1884.* Chapel Hill: University of North Carolina Press, 2004.

Hogeland, Ronald W. "'The Female Appendage': Feminine Life-Styles in America, 1820-1860." *Civil War History* 17 (June 1971): 101-14.

Jabour, Anya. "'The Language of Love': The Letters of Elizabeth and William Wirt, 1802-1834." In *A Shared Experience: Men, Women, and the History of Gender,* edited by Laura McCall and Donald Yacovone. New York: New York University Press, 1998.

Jarchow, Merrill E. *The Earth Brought Forth: A History of Minnesota Agriculture to 1885.* St. Paul: Minnesota Historical Society Press, 1949.

Johnson, James Ralph, and Alfred Hoyt Bill. *Horsemen Blue and Gray: A Pictorial History.* New York: Oxford University Press, 1960.

Jones, Jacqueline. *Labor of Love, Labor of Sorrow: Black Women, Work, and the Family from Slavery to the Present.* New York: Basic Books, 1985.

Jordan, Ervin L., Jr. "Sleeping with the Enemy: Sex, Black Women, and the Civil War." *Western Journal of Black Studies* 18, no. 2 (1994): 55-63.

Josephy, Alvin M., Jr. *The Civil War in the American West.* New York: Alfred A. Knopf, 1992.

Kallgren, Beverly Hayes, and James L. Crouthamel, eds. *"Dear Friend Anna": Civil War Letters of a Common Soldier from Maine.* Orono: University of Maine Press, 1992.

Kemp, Thomas. "Community and War: The Civil War Experience of Two New Hampshire Towns." In Vinovskis, *Toward a Social History of the American Civil War.*

Kennedy, Frances H., ed. *The Civil War Battlefield Guide.* Boston: Houghton Mifflin Company, 1990.

Kiper, Richard L. *Dear Catharine, Dear Taylor: The Civil War Letters of a Union Soldier and His Wife.* Lawrence: University Press of Kansas, 2002.

Kiple, Kenneth F., ed. *The Cambridge World History of Human Disease.* New York: Cambridge University Press, 1993.

Kump, Patty Burke. *The Burkes, the Barretts and Others.* Minneapolis: privately printed by author, 2000.

Laas, Virginia Jeans, ed. *Wartime Washington: The Civil War Letters of Elizabeth Blair Lee.* Urbana: University of Illinois Press, 1991.

Larson, Douglas E. "Private Alfred Gales: From Slavery to Freedom." *Minnesota History* 57.6 (Summer 2001): 274-83.

Leavitt, Judith Walzer. *Brought to Bed: Childbearing in America, 1750-1950.* New York: Oxford University Press, 1986.

Lebsock, Suzanne. *The Free Women of Petersburg: Status and Culture in a Southern Town, 1784-1860.* New York: W. W. Norton, 1985.

Leonard, Elizabeth D. *All the Daring of the Soldier: Women of the Civil War Armies.* New York: W. W. Norton, 1999.

———. *Yankee Women: Gender Battles in the Civil War.* New York: W. W. Norton, 1995.

Linderman, Gerald. *Embattled Courage: The Experience of Combat in the American Civil War.* New York: Free Press, 1987.

Litwack, Leon F. *Been in the Storm So Long: The Aftermath of Slavery.* New York: Alfred A. Knopf, 1979. Reprint, New York: Vintage Books, 1980.

Lowry, Thomas P. *The Story the Soldiers Wouldn't Tell: Sex in the Civil War.* Mechanicsburg, PA: Stackpole Books, 1994.

Lystra, Karen. *Searching the Heart: Women, Men and Romantic Love in Nineteenth-Century America.* New York: Oxford University Press, 1989.

Marks, Paula Mitchell. *Precious Dust: The True Saga of the Western Gold Rushes.* New York: HarperCollins West, 1995.

Massey, Mary Elizabeth. *Women of the Civil War.* Lincoln: University of Nebraska Press, 1966.

Mattson, Hans. *The Story of an Emigrant.* St. Paul: D. D. Merrill Company, 1892.

Maxwell, William Quentin. *Lincoln's Fifth Wheel: The Political History of the United States Sanitary Commission.* New York: Longmans, Green and Company, 1956.

McClure, Ethel. *More Than a Roof: The Development of Minnesota Poor Farms and Homes for the Aged.* St. Paul: Minnesota Historical Society Press, 1968.

McMillen, Sally. "Mothers' Sacred Duty: Breast-feeding Patterns among Middle- and Upper-class Women in the Antebellum South." *Journal of Southern History* 51 (August 1985): 333–56.

McPherson, James M. *Battle Cry of Freedom: The Civil War Era.* New York: Oxford University Press, 1988.

———. *For Cause and Comrades: Why Men Fought in the Civil War.* New York: Oxford University Press, 1997.

———. *Ordeal by Fire: The Civil War and Reconstruction.* 3rd ed. Boston: McGraw-Hill, 2001.

McPherson, James M., and William J. Cooper, Jr., eds. *Writing the Civil War: The Quest to Understand.* Columbia: University of South Carolina Press, 1998.

Mitchell, Reid. "The Northern Soldier and His Community." In Vinovskis, *Toward a Social History of the American Civil War.*

———. "'Not the General but the Soldier': The Study of Civil War Soldiers." In McPherson and Cooper, *Writing the Civil War.*

———. *The Vacant Chair: The Northern Soldier Leaves Home.* New York: Oxford University Press, 1993.

Moe, Richard. *The Last Full Measure: The Life and Death of the First Minnesota Volunteers.* New York: Henry Holt and Company, 1993. Reprint, St. Paul: Minnesota Historical Society Press, 2001.

Moneyhon, Carl. "1865: 'A State of Perfect Anarchy.'" In Christ, *Rugged and Sublime.*

Motz, Marilyn Ferris. *True Sisterhood: Michigan Women and Their Kin, 1820–1920.* Albany: State University of New York Press, 1983.

Murphy, Kevin C., ed. *The Civil War Letters of Joseph K. Taylor of the Thirty-seventh Massachusetts Volunteer Infantry.* Lewiston, NY: Edwin Mellen Press, 1998.

Naisawald, L. Van Loan. *Grape and Canister: The Story of the Field Artillery of the Army of the Potomac, 1861–1865.* New York: Oxford University Press, 1960.

Nelson, Anson, and Fanny Nelson. *Memorials of Sarah Childress Polk: Wife of the Eleventh President of the United States.* New York: A. D. F. Randolph and Company, 1892. Reprint, Newton, CT: American Political Bibliography Press, 1994.

Nelson, Michael C. "Writing during Wartime: Gender and Literacy in the American Civil War." *Journal of American Studies* 31 (1997): 43–68.

Nichols, David A. *Lincoln and the Indians: Civil War Policy and Politics.* Columbia: University of Missouri Press, 1978. Reprint, Urbana: University of Illinois Press, 2000.

Norling, Lisa. "'How Fraught with Sorrow and Heartpangs': Mariners' Wives and the

Ideology of Domesticity in New England, 1790–1880." *New England Quarterly* 65 (September 1992): 422–46.

Paludan, Phillip Shaw. *"A People's Contest": The Union and the Civil War, 1861–1865.* New York: Harper and Row, 1988.

Poole, John Randolph. *Cracker Cavaliers: The 2nd Georgia Cavalry under Wheeler and Forrest.* Macon, GA: Mercer University Press, 2000.

Reardon, Carol. "'We Are All in This War': The 148th Pennsylvania and Home Front Dissension in Centre County during the Civil War." In Cimbala and Miller, *Union Soldiers and the Northern Home Front.*

Rice, John G. "The Old-Stock Americans." In *They Chose Minnesota: A Survey of the State's Ethnic Groups,* edited by June Drenning Holmquist. St. Paul: Minnesota Historical Society Press, 1981.

Ridge, Martin. *Ignatius Donnelly: Portrait of a Politician.* Rev. ed. St. Paul: Minnesota Historical Society Press, 1991.

Riley, Glenda. *The Female Frontier: A Comparative View of Women on the Prairie and Plains.* Lawrence: University Press of Kansas, 1988.

Roberts, Brian. *American Alchemy: The California Gold Rush and Middle-class Culture.* Chapel Hill: University of North Carolina Press, 2000.

Rodgers, Thomas E. "Hoosier Women and the Civil War Home Front." *Indiana Magazine of History* 97 (June 2001): 105–28.

Rose, Anne C. *Victorian America and the Civil War.* New York: Cambridge University Press, 1992.

Rothman, Ellen K. *Hands and Hearts: A History of Courtship in America.* New York: Basic Books, 1984.

Rotundo, E. Anthony. *American Manhood: Transformations in Masculinity from the Revolution to the Modern Era.* New York: Basic Books, 1993.

Rozier, John, ed. *The Granite Farm Letters: The Civil War Correspondence of Edgeworth and Sallie Bird.* Athens: University of Georgia Press, 1988.

Ryan, Mary P. *Cradle of the Middle Class: The Family in Oneida County, New York, 1790–1865.* New York: Cambridge University Press, 1981.

Satterlee, Marion P. *Outbreak and Massacre by the Dakota Indians in Minnesota in 1862.* Minneapolis, 1925.

Schmidt, Mary Schwandt. "The Story of Mary Schwandt." *Minnesota Historical Society Collections* 6 (1894): 461–74.

Schultz, Duane. *Over the Earth I Come: The Great Sioux Uprising of 1862.* New York: St. Martin's Press, 1992.

Shannon, Fred Albert. *The Organization and Administration of the Union Army, 1861–1865.* Vol. 1. Cleveland, OH: Arthur H. Clark Company, 1928.

Shryock, Richard H. "A Medical Perspective on the Civil War." *American Quarterly* 14, no. 2, part 1 (1962): 161–73.

Silber, Nina. *Daughters of the Union: Northern Women Fight the Civil War.* Cambridge, MA: Harvard University Press, 2005.

Silber, Nina, and Mary Beth Sievens, eds. *Yankee Correspondence: Civil War Letters between New England Soldiers and the Home Front.* Charlottesville: University Press of Virginia, 1996.

Smith, Jennifer Lund. "The Reconstruction of 'Home': The Civil War and the Marriage of Lawrence and Fannie Chamberlain." In *Intimate Strategies of the Civil War: Military*

Commanders and Their Wives, edited by Carol K. Bleser and Lesley J. Gordon. New York: Oxford University Press, 2001.

Sneden, Private Robert Knox. *Eye of the Storm: A Civil War Odyssey.* Edited by Charles F. Bryan Jr. and Nelson D. Lankford. New York: Free Press, 2000.

Sutherland, Daniel E. "1864: 'A Strange, Wild Time.'" In Christ, *Rugged and Sublime.*

Sutherland, Daniel E., ed. *Guerillas, Unionists, and Violence on the Confederate Home Front.* Fayetteville: University of Arkansas Press, 1999.

Tate, Cassandra. *Cigarette Wars: The Triumph of "The Little White Slaver."* New York: Oxford University Press, 1999.

Taylor, John M. *William Henry Seward: Lincoln's Right Hand.* New York: HarperCollins, 1991.

Thomas, David V. *Arkansas in War and Reconstruction, 1861–1874.* Little Rock: Arkansas Division, United Daughters of the Confederacy, 1926.

Trenerry, Walter N. "Lester's Surrender at Murfreesboro." *Minnesota History* (Spring 1965): 191–97.

Tucker, Jonathan B. *Scourge: The Once and Future Threat of Smallpox.* New York: Atlantic Monthly Press, 2001.

Vinovskis, Maris A., ed. *Toward a Social History of the American Civil War: Exploratory Essays.* New York: Cambridge University Press, 1990.

Wakefield, Sarah F. *Six Weeks in the Sioux Tepees* in *Women's Indian Captivity Narratives,* ed. and intro. Kathryn Zabelle Derounian-Stodola. New York: Penguin Books, 1998.

Walters, Ronald G. *American Reformers, 1815–1860.* New York: Hill and Wang, 1978.

Warner, Ezra J. *Generals in Blue: Lives of the Union Commanders.* Baton Rouge: Louisiana State University Press, 1964.

———. *Generals in Gray: Lives of the Confederate Commanders.* Baton Rouge: Louisiana State University Press, 1959.

Waugh, John C. *Reelecting Lincoln: The Battle for the 1864 Presidency.* New York: Crown Publishers, 1997.

Welter, Barbara. "The Cult of True Womanhood, 1820–1860." *American Quarterly* 18, no. 2 (1966): 151–74.

Wertz, Richard W., and Dorothy C. Wertz. *Lying-In: A History of Childbirth in America.* New Haven, CT: Yale University Press, 1989.

Whites, LeeAnn. *The Civil War as a Crisis in Gender: Augusta, Georgia, 1860–1890.* Athens: University of Georgia Press, 1995.

Wilson, Angela. "Decolonizing the 1862 Death Marches." *American Indian Quarterly* 28, nos. 1 and 2 (2004): 185–215.

Wood, Ann Douglas. "'The Fashionable Diseases': Women's Complaints and Their Treatment in Nineteenth-Century America." In *Women and Health in America,* edited by Judith Walzer Leavitt. Madison: University of Wisconsin Press, 1984.

Wyeth, John A. *Life of General Nathan Bedford Forrest.* New York: Harper Brothers Publishers, 1904.

Younker, Mary Mason. "'I Was Some What Disappointed': Expectations of Love in Rural Michigan, 1862–1869." *Michigan Historical Review* 21, no. 2 (1995): 1–36.

Index

Lizzie's arrival in, 304–6; Lizzie's consent to move, 295–96, 299–300; Lizzie's move to, 11, 229, 243, 271–72, 286–87; Lizzie's thoughts on move, 218, 226, 231–32, 301; Madison's asking for move to, 202, 232, 245, 279, 281–83, 289, 291, 294, 296–97; officer's wives moving to, 263 & n74; Third Minnesota capture of, 9

loneliness: encouragement to overcome, 113, 276, 281; Lizzie in state of "blues," 37–38, 48, 51, 193, 278, 286, 295; Lizzie's expressions of, 42–43, 58, 247, 261, 273, 277; Madison in state of "blues," 101, 113, 155; Madison's expressions of, 39, 69–70, 95, 141, 259–60, 262, 279

Louisville, KY, 8

Mabee, Benjamin, 302

mail/mail service: enduring value of letters, 12; letter writing, 66; Lizzie's longing for, 42; Madison's longing for, 207; Madison's preserving of letters, 83, 87, 95, 167, 215, 281; preserving history through, 14; sending money by, 56–57; unreliability of, 43, 92, 108n72, 281

Maine, Bowler family origins in, 3

Manter, F. H., 234 & n12

marriage: David Piercy, 154, 285; Eugene Stone and Rose Colby, 127, 144n26; James Case and Mary Bottomly, 93n50, 124; Lizzie and Madison, 17, 133; Otto Dreher, 221, 223; reported in Hastings, 223; Sarah Bowler, 236n17; sexual intimacy in, 187 & n97, 227, 244n33, 269, 272, 280

martial law, 77n24

Martin, Jasper (Joseph), 243 & n31

Martin, Perry D., 61

Mattson, Hans, 161n51, 168 & n62, 180–81, 263 & n74

May, Dwight, 181 & n85

McClellan, George B., 91 & n47, 97n55, 252n53, 255

McKenna, Bernard, 82 & n33, 156, 274

McLean, William, 188n99

McMinnville, TN, 65, 103, 107–8, 110, 204

McMullen, Amon, 6, 17 & n5, 45–46, 119 & n4, 128, 153, 159, 167, 230, 242n29, 248–49, 298

McPherson, James, 14

medical care: in childbirth, 209 & n19; galvanism, 93n49, 102; increasing cost of, 261; Madison's broken leg, 224–25; at military hospitals, 54, 68, 77, 97, 248–49; small pox vaccinations, 41, 224; for soldiers, 80; Soldier's Aid Society, 76, 89–90, 93 & n50, 99; soldiers paying for, 257; treatments for women, 140n19. *See also* disease/illness; health

Memphis, TN, 248–49

Merrill, Moses D., 193 & n105

Methodist Church, 49n52, 60 & n69, 155, 157–58

military actions: Arkansas Expedition, 135, 185–96; battle of Ball's Bluff, 50n53; battle of Bull Run, 111 & n80; battle of Chancellorsville, 163n54; battle of Chickamauga, 204–5 & n12; battle of Fort Donelson, 44n41, 62n74, 67n5, 78n26; battle of Gettysburg, 182; battle of Mechanicsburg, 174; battle of Mill Springs, 47n46, 50n53, 62n74, 95n53; battle of Murfreesboro, 84–89, 100, 107–10; battle of Seven Pines, 99n59; battle of Shiloh, 70n9, 72n13, 78; battle of Somerset, 53; battle of the *Monitor* and the *Merrimac*, 90–91 & n45; Battle of the Seven Days, 97n55; Battle of the Wilderness, 236n16; capture of Atlanta, 228, 249n45, 251–52 & n52; capture of Fort Pillow, 230 & n4; capture of Richmond, 274, 287–88; capture of Savannah, 270 & n86; first battle of Bull Run, 50n53; siege of Petersburg, 228, 252n52, 288 & n3; siege of Port Hudson, 163n54, 175n75; siege of Vicksburg, 9, 134, 137 & n8, 146, 163n54, 168 & n64, 171 & n69, 176–78; surrender of New Orleans, 83 & n36; Third Minnesota, 105, 107; Union successes in, 53

military chaplains, 42, 60 & n69, 102 & n62, 128, 158, 207

U.S.–Dakota Conflict, 8–9, 116–31, 160, 167
U.S. government: Confiscation Act of 1862, 112n82; Emancipation Proclamation of 1862, 126 & n18, 140n17, 190; Enrollment Act of 1863, 222n32; Homestead Act of 1862, 115n89; Militia Act of 1862, 112n82, 119n4; officer pay and bonuses, 293; policy toward captured territory, 53
Union Army: bounties to avoid draft, 246n39; enlisting freed slaves, 112n82, 126n18, 169; enlisting pardoned soldiers, 205; Northern war weariness and, 228–29; officer leaves of absence and, 209; recruiting black soldiers, 228, 240; veteran reenlistment, 220 & n30, 224n37. *See also* military actions; military units

Valkenberg, William Van, 38 & n31
Vicksburg, MS, 9, 134, 137 & n8, 168 & n64, 171n69, 176–78

Wabashaw, MN, 136
war: destruction caused by, 81; Lizzie's concerns over, 42–43, 52, 242; Madison's critique of, 96–97, 111–12, 126–27; Madison's opinion on, 92, 185–86; Madison's prediction of peace, 288; political opposition to, 139 & n17; prospects for a speedy end, 47–48, 53, 56, 60, 72–73, 189; waning support of, 228–29, 249–50, 256; women's support of, 11, 76
Washburne, Elihu, 240n26

Washington County, 31n16
weaponry: artillery, 142; Enfield rifles, 146; "minnie rifle," 27; naval ships, 139, 142, 146; new guns for the Minnesota Regiment, 47; unreliability of, 39–40
Webster, W. W., 139n15
Wedge, A. C., 225, 228
Welch, Abraham E., 117, 121 & n9
Wells, Leander, 159 & n49
Whaley, Caleb Arthur, 114–15
Wheeler, George, 252
whisky. *See* alcohol (whisky)
Winona, MN, 136
Wolford, Frank, 84–85 & n37
women: African American, 169; as camp followers, 40, 62n74; as cooks, 156–57; as Dakota captives, 117, 123–24, 127–28 & n23; dealing with battlefield death, 109; dealing with finances, 229; as doctors, 92–93, 102; impact of war on, 81–82; kissing soldiers, 38; Madison's comments on, 71, 162, 170, 181; Madison's encounters with, 60–61, 194–95, 222; medical treatments for, 140n19; nursing sick soldiers, 54, 258; patriotism and war support, 31 & n15, 76, 89–90, 93n50, 99, 149, 249–50, 256; promiscuity, 73 & n16, 157, 160 & n50, 166; right to vote, 247n40; Union sympathizers, 68; wartime roles of, 10–11; as washerwomen, 40, 156
Woodruff, Walter, 32 & n18

Zollicoffer, Felix K., 46, 47n46, 68, 95n53